W9-BUH-557

The Restructuring of American Religion

STUDIES IN CHURCH AND STATE

JOHN F. WILSON, EDITOR

The Restructuring of American Religion:
Society and Faith Since World War II
by Robert Wuthnow

ROBERT WUTHNOW

The Restructuring of American Religion

SOCIETY AND FAITH SINCE WORLD WAR II

PRINCETON UNIVERSITY PRESS

Published by Princeton University Press, 41 William Street,
Princeton, New Jersey 08540
In the United Kingdom: Princeton University Press, Guildford, Surrey

Library of Congress Cataloging in Publication Data will be
found on the last printed page of this book

ISBN 0-691-07759-2

This book has been composed in Linotron Sabon

Clothbound editions of Princeton University Press books
are printed on acid-free paper, and binding materials are
chosen for strength and durability. Paperbacks, although satisfactory
for personal collections, are not usually suitable for library rebinding

Printed in the United States of America by Princeton University Press
Princeton, New Jersey

DESIGNED BY LAURY A. EGAN

And the Church must be forever building,
and always decaying,
and always being restored.

T. S. ELIOT
The Rock

CONTENTS

FOREWORD

RELIGION interacts with political life in America in countless ways, from obvious institutional ties to practices that express religious sensibilities though far removed from conventional religious settings. This interaction has never been free of controversy and promises to become even more contested in the immediate future. Yet over the last generation few scholars have concerned themselves with its implications, and recent publications about it often lack depth. As a result, only limited resources are available to inform contemporary discussion among specialists or general readers. Moreover, changes in both religious and political life demand new methods of inquiry. Earlier scholarship depended heavily on the study of the institutional life of religious bodies. It is now clear that to understand the active role of religion in the culture, and especially the political culture, requires the insights not only of historians of religion, law, and society but also of sociologists and anthropologists.

The major goal of the Project on Church and State at Princeton University, which is funded by the Lilly Endowment, is to sponsor scholarly publications on the interaction of religion and its political environment primarily but not exclusively in America. A secondary goal is to draw on disciplines beyond those traditionally concerned with church-state issues to investigate the interaction of religious and political culture.

The Project has already sponsored a two-volume bibliographical guide to literature on the church-state question in America as well as a casebook on church state law compiled by John T. Noonan, Jr.* *The Restructuring of American Religion* is the first of approximately a dozen studies that will explore facets of the interrelationship of church and state in American history and in India, Japan, Latin America, and Europe. The authors of these books, all well known in their fields, share the conviction that an understanding of religion and its role in society today requires insights from a broad range of disciplines and benefits from comparative perspectives.

The Restructuring of American Religion is a major interpretation of how religion has changed in America since World War II. Through judi-

* John F. Wilson, ed., *Church and State in America: A Bibliographical Guide*, Vol. 1, *The Colonial and Early National Periods*; Vol. 2, *The Civil War to the Present Day* (Westport, Conn.: Greenwood Press, 1986, 1987). John T. Noonan, Jr., *The Believer and the Powers That Are* (New York: Macmillan, 1987).

cious yet imaginative use of survey data and both archival and anecdotal evidence, Robert Wuthnow provides both an overview and a detailed guide. He reveals general forces at work in this period of U.S. history that help to explain what is happening to religion in particular. His book offers an excellent starting point for continuing discussion and further analysis.

In addition the series will include a community study of a multi-ethnic, midsized industrial city in the Northeast that exhibits in microcosm some of the changes charted in *The Restructuring of American Religion*. Three other volumes will analyze those periods of U.S. history most relevant to church-state questions: the period of the nation's birth—from the Revolution through the framing of the Constitution; the Jacksonian era, in which a distinctive Protestant hegemony emerged; and the decades at the end of the nineteenth century and beginning of the twentieth when large-scale immigration and industrial development remade American society. A summary volume will explore the church-state issue as it has developed throughout American history.

In order to place the American experience in comparative perspective, additional studies will analyze comparable topics in other cultures. The various patterns developed in the medieval and early modern West following the Emperor Constantine's revolutionary sponsorship of Christianity offer background to later developments in Europe and America. The very distinctive configuration of political and religious interaction in Indian society will offer a sharp contrast to Western and specifically U.S. experience. The history of State Shinto in Japan, including its relationship to Buddhism and its internal complexity, presents a fascinating exhibit of a modernizing nation state's patronage of a religion. In contemporary Latin America we find traditional churches caught up in—and differentially responding to—revolutionary political contexts. Another study under consideration would assess the shifting relations of churches and regimes in the major nations of nineteenth-century Europe.

The project will not publish studies on all the excellent topics that deserve serious scholarly treatment. Instead, we intend to call attention to the complex issue of religion and politics in the United States and a few other societies. By demonstrating the potential for new work on the subject, we hope to broaden current discussion and stimulate further scholarship.

In designing and executing this project we have been guided and supported by Robert Wood Lynn of the Lilly Endowment. Yoma Ullman has coordinated the project from the start, and her many skills, high standards, and great dedication have left their mark on it. In addition we are grateful to the Princeton University Press and especially Walter H. Lippincott, its director, and Gail M. Ullman, history editor, for their interest, encouragement, and support.

John F. Wilson
Robert T. Handy
Stanley N. Katz
Albert J. Raboteau

PREFACE

SEVERAL years ago, during an unusually busy semester, a colleague approached me about writing a book for a series he was editing on church-state relations. I said I knew little about the topic and had no interest in doing the book. But my colleague was patient. And over the following months we talked further about the project. As we talked, it became clearer to both of us that what we were really interested in was not church-state relations as such but the broader social environment in which so many of the controversial issues concerning church-state relations had emerged. Without trying to understand the broader ways in which American religion was being shaped—and reshaped—by the social environment, it seemed to make little sense to contribute further to the already bloated literature on church and state.

Once the project came to be redefined in this way it grew closer to my own interests, and I agreed to write the book. From the start I have benefited from the support and encouragement of my patient colleague, John F. Wilson, who edited the series and shouldered much of the administrative work involved in coordinating such a project. I have also shared the privilege of having Robert Lynn's warm encouragement and the generous support of the Lilly Endowment. With that support I was able to enlist the help of a number of co-workers who assisted with bibliographies, library work, and computer analysis. It was a privilege to work together in this capacity with Margaret Demarrais, Carl Kruse, Penny Becker, David Newcomb, Andrew Wallace, David Woolwine, Clifford Nass, William Lehrman, and Kevin Hartzell. I was the beneficiary, not only of the specific tasks they performed, but also of their training in history and theology, their background in sociological theory and methods, and the special perspectives they brought to the topic of American religion. Several other students and colleagues also contributed to the project by listening to half-baked ideas over brown-bag lunches, by reading working drafts of papers, and by keeping me abreast of things they were thinking about and reading. I would like to acknowledge special thanks to Robert Liebman, John Sutton, James Davison Hunter, Robert T. Handy, N. J. Demerath III, Kevin Christiano, Richard Rogers, Edward Freeland, Steven M. Tipton, and Susan Harding. I also owe a special debt to Cox's Deli for the coffee and bagels which got me going most mornings. It was also their fare that provided the occasion for many a breakfast discussion of work in progress with my wife Sally. I thank her for sharing the journey with me.

I decided not to dedicate the book to the construction crew who built the Delaware-Raritan canal system across New Jersey 150 years ago, even though many a walk along its banks provided luxuriant opportunities to reflect on what I was writing. Little did they foresee the strange uses to which their work would be put. And besides, living as they did in an earlier time of religious restructuring, the recent turns in American religion would have come to them as no surprise.

The Restructuring of American Religion

CHAPTER 1

The Question of Restructuring

MARCHERS filed past the reviewing stand hour after hour. The day was Thursday, June 6, 1946; the place, Prospect Park in Brooklyn, New York. Two years to the day since the Allies landed on the Normandy beaches, the nation now paused to give thanks and reflect on its collective heritage. But the marchers were not soldiers or war heroes. They were children: little girls in starched pinafores, wearing white dress gloves and carrying bouquets of spring flowers; little boys in neatly ironed white shirts with clip-on bow ties and paper hats. Together they marched, accompanied by brass bands and floats, past rows of admiring parents and grandparents. In the reviewing stand Brooklyn's mayor, the governor of New York, and a justice of the U.S. Supreme Court gave their approval. By public declaration all schools were closed for the day. In all, approximately 90,000 youngsters participated. The event was the 117th annual Sunday School Union parade.

Little more than a generation later, the world of the Brooklyn Sunday school parade seems strangely out of place. More than the differences in dress, or even the location, the idea of thousands of people turning out for a Sunday school parade taxes the imagination. That the event should enlist broad support from local officials and involve closing the public schools seems even less imaginable.

Social scientists, journalists, and more than a few members of the clergy would probably suggest that the contrast conjured up by this event reveals the extent to which American society has become secularized. The increased prominence of science and technology, rising levels of higher education, greater affluence, and a more secular system of government have all presumably made religion a less significant part of American life. The public festivals that attract great attention now consist of national holidays, rock concerts, and sports events; religion has become privatized. A borough like Brooklyn was able to make religion part of its public life because of strong neighborhoods, ethnic ties, extended families, and deep roots in tradition. Half a century later, Brooklyn has succumbed to the ravages of urban decay, the population has apparently become atomized, and churches have fled. The action has now shifted to the suburbs. And here religious observance has been consigned to the polite realms of inner piety. The Sunday School Union parade, indeed, no longer exists—in Brooklyn or anywhere else. By the late 1950s it was already a thing of the past.

While in some ways appealing, this interpretation clearly oversimplifies matters. The Sunday school parade may indeed be defunct, but large-scale religious spectacles continue in other forms. On April 29, 1980, for example, more than a quarter million evangelical Christians packed the Mall in the nation's capital to proclaim "Washington for Jesus." Incumbent presidents endorse gatherings of religious conservatives, clergy emerge as leading candidates for high political office, millions of dollars flow to the mail boxes of television preachers, vast segments of the population attend religious services on a weekly basis—all of this attests to the fact that religion simply has not beat a humiliating retreat in the face of secularization.

Even in Brooklyn the scenario of rampant secularization fails to square with the facts. Contrary to the image of decaying neighborhoods and ecclesiastical flight, the number of churches was actually 10 percent higher in the 1980s than in the 1940s, church membership had held steady as a percentage of the borough's population, and membership in the theologically most conservative churches had risen fivefold.

Mindful of these continuities, another contingent of interpreters would conclude that nothing has really changed at all. Seizing the opportunity to show up secularization theory as nothing more than the wishful thinking of naive academics, this contingent would point out how deeply rooted religion is in the groundwork of American society. So deep is the longing for spiritual values, they would argue, that we should expect no major changes to have taken place in religious expression over the past half century. Instead, we should recognize the strong similarities between present and past realities.

But this view is also an oversimplification. If the continuities between the Brooklyn Sunday school parade and the Washington for Jesus rally belie the logic of simple, linear secularization, the differences should also give pause to the view that nothing has changed. The Brooklyn parade was organized by neighborhood churches: children marched with their classmates while Sunday school superintendents competed with one another to bring out the largest numbers. The Washington rally was organized by television preachers who brought in people by busloads from different parts of the country. The Brooklyn parade was organized along denominational lines. The Washington rally transcended denominational lines and played on themes that united evangelicals from many different denominations. The Brooklyn parade was, and had been for many years, orchestrated by Protestant leaders as a deliberate show of strength against the 35 percent of their community who were Roman Catholics. The Washington rally downplayed the fact that its participants were mainly Protestants, drew in as many conservative Catholics as it could, and targeted itself against secularism and liberalism rather than Catholicism. The Brooklyn march also betokened an easy, taken-for-granted alliance between church and state, whereas the Washington march carried a sense of religion mobilizing itself against government—of concerned citizens trying to turn a wayward nation from its wicked ways.

THIS BOOK is an attempt to say what has changed, and what has not changed, about the place of religion in American society since World War II. It is my conviction that American religion has undergone a major restructuring during this period. Just as the Brooklyn Sunday school march seems strangely incongruent with American society as we presently experience it, so the character of American religion more generally has been altered sufficiently that we find ourselves faced with new realities that are sometimes difficult to understand or appreciate. On the one hand, the words and images we use to describe American religion are often carry-overs from the past. They no longer adequately describe the situations we experience. On the other hand, the situations we experience often seem so commonplace that we fail to realize just how much things have changed over the course of even a few years.

In saying that American religion has undergone a restructuring I mean to suggest that it has to some extent been remolded by the force of changes in the larger society. The period since World War II has, after all, been a time of momentous social change. New developments in technology, the changing character of international relations, shifts in the composition of the population, the tremendous expansion of higher education and in the role of government, new policies and new administrative systems all attest to the seriousness of these changes. To the extent that American religion is a social institution, embedded in and always exposed to the broader social environment, it could not help but have been affected by these changes. How much it has changed is the question we hope to answer.

The role of religious organizations and religious practices in these changes, however, has scarcely been passive. If religion has been restructured, this restructuring has been possible because religious organizations have had the resources with which to respond to the challenges set before them. Rather than simply being eroded, as the secularizationists would have it, American religion has been able to play its cards with the advantage of a tremendously strong hand. At the same time, its institutional strength has not for the most part been a dead letter that kept it from responding to change. The capacity to adapt has, in fact, been one of the impressive features of American religion. Moreover, its own resources have been used to give expression to many of the broader changes happening in American society, to urge reflection on the nature of these changes, and often to shape the ways in which people responded to change.

Much of the response to societal change has reflected the strength and vitality of American religion. Even casual observers have been haunted by the impression, however, that something is wrong—or at least new enough that we have yet to understand its dimensions. On all sides American religion seems to be embroiled in controversy. Whether it be acrimonious arguments about abortion, lawsuits over religion in the public schools, questions of who is most guilty of mixing religion and politics, or discussions of America's military presence in the world, religion seems to be in the thick of it. Scarcely a statement is uttered by one religious group on these issues without another faction of the religious community taking umbrage. The issues themselves shift almost continuously, but the underlying sense of polarization and acrimony continues. And these problems have clearly been conditioned, albeit in sometimes complex and indirect ways, by the larger changes in American society. Many, it seems, involve questions about religion's relation to the state. Many others have deep roots in political terrain.

MORE THAN a half century ago, the pioneering social observer of American religion, H. Paul Douglass, writing amidst the Great Depression, noted that government was beginning to play an increasing role in shaping the nature of American faith. Impressed with the thousands of churches that had played so prominent a role in providing services to their communities, Douglass was sufficiently foresighted to predict that "much of the work of the private institutions now in the hands of the church shall in the future pass over to the state."[1] Optimistically, he went on to argue that there would still be plenty of opportunities for the churches to serve. But in the future the churches would clearly be affected in more ways than they had ever been in the past by the growing functions of government. No longer would the issues be simply the traditional questions of constitutional separation of the two kingdoms, or even the much cherished values of freedom in worship. Increasingly the relations between church and state would become more subtle, more complex, more wide-ranging because the state itself was taking on more of the functions that had formerly been fulfilled by private institutions.

Writing a hundred years before H. Paul Douglass, another observer of American society also warned of the changing relations between church and state. Acutely aware of the role that churches and other private voluntary organizations played in affirming the community ties on which

American democracy depended, this observer warned that the growth of the state could interfere with the functioning of these organizations, sap their vitality, and cause individuals to become overly dependent on the state. "It is easy to foresee," he wrote, "that the time is drawing near when man will be less and less able to produce, by himself alone, the commonest necessaries of life." In order to cope with this growing economic interdependence, he added: "The task of the governing power will therefore perpetually increase, and its very efforts will extend it every day." In so doing, government would gradually take the place of private associations such as churches and community organizations with the following result: "The more it stands in the place of associations, the more will individuals, losing the notion of combining together, require its assistance: these are causes and effects that unceasingly create each other." The writer, of course, was Alexis de Tocqueville.[2]

When Tocqueville made his historic visit to America in the 1830s, the balance between government and religious organizations still weighed heavily in favor of the latter. Indeed, the 1830s were a time of great religious revival, of planting new churches, and of carrying the gospel message to an expanding frontier. Over the course of the nineteenth century and even during the first few decades of the twentieth century the number of churches, the range of denominations, and the proportion of the American population holding membership in religious organizations continued to grow. Government still played a minimal role in the larger society. Other than the public schools, its role as a source of social services remained narrowly confined, and even in education most of the control still resided in local communities. Only in the twentieth century, and particularly in the decades since World War II, has government begun to penetrate nearly every aspect of American life.

Many of the controversial issues in which religious organizations have become embroiled in recent decades focus directly on the increasingly problematic boundary between church and state. Does government have the right to keep prayers and other forms of religious activity out of the public schools? What should churches do if they disagree with the Supreme Court's position on the legality of abortion? Is the Internal Revenue Service justified in requiring religious groups to make full disclosure of their financial affairs? Given the enlarged position of government as a provider of social welfare services, how should religious values concerned with justice, equality, and peace be articulated to have the greatest effect?

In most cases these issues are fought out in church basements, in courtrooms, and in the press. Questions of legality, expedience, effectiveness, and accordance with the scriptures form the immediate contexts in which the arguments are presented. But these cases are often little more than flash points in the deeper relations between American religion and American society. They constitute the proverbial tip of an iceberg, important in their own right, tremendously consequential, yet only a small part of the matter that needs to be considered. For the effects of government on American society have been much more profound than any of these specific issues can possibly reveal. The effects are indirect as well as direct. They involve broad changes in the character of the American population, in interest groups, and in the ways in which we identify ourselves as a people. And these changes are never attributable entirely to the initiatives of government: the relations between changes in government and changes in social conditions are always reciprocal.

IT HAS GROWN customary in circles charged with government planning to conduct environmental impact studies. If a military base or nuclear waste disposal site is planned, studies are commissioned to determine the environmental impact of the new installation on the surrounding community. Similarly, in developing the annual federal budget, studies are conducted to determine the likely effects of a particular tax increase or cuts in a particular program or the addition of a new program on the economy more broadly. Questions are asked about the possible costs and benefits for businesses, consumers, for the supply of jobs, for minority groups, for the military, the elderly, and so on.

Many of the major programs that have been initiated by the federal government since World War II have had a decided impact on the religious environment, if not directly, then at least indirectly. Government policies as specific as changes in Federal Communications Commission (FCC) rulings or as general as federal incentives aimed at stimulating growth in higher education have scarcely been neutral with respect to American religion. Some of these effects have made it harder for particular segments of the religious community to fulfill their functions; other changes have given considerable windfalls to particular religious groups, greatly enhancing their position in the larger competitive economy of religious organizations. Yet, despite an official, constitutionally guaranteed stance of neutrality toward religious organizations, government policies have scarcely ever been considered in terms of their possible impact on the religious environment. Usually it has been up to religious groups to bring lawsuits against government if they felt some specific constitutional guarantee had been violated, and then usually long after the fact. The broader, less direct effects of government's role in the society have seldom received any attention at all.

The present volume may be thought of as a study of the environmental impact on American religion of the changing role of government in the United States since World War II, but only in a very general sense. The discussion is not concerned, except in a few instances, with the impact of specific government policies (for example, with the effects of civil rights legislation or the Supreme Court's decision on abortion). It focuses instead on the effects of the more general expansion of government in American life since World War II and on some of the social changes that have been closely related to that expansion. For example, the effects of expanding levels of higher education, which have been greatly encouraged by active government intervention, receive particular attention. The Vietnam War, changes in America's political and economic standing in the international community, the expansion of the high-technology sector, regional integration, and changing conceptions of the welfare state itself are among the other factors that receive consideration. The hand of government has clearly been visible in all these changes. But this has been only part of the story. Demographic, economic, and institutional changes have also been important characters in the plot. And the response of religious people to these changes has been at least as important as the effects of these changes on religious practices. Unraveling the story of American religion's restructuring since World War II, therefore, involves examining the interrelations among a complex set of actors and situations.

"Restructuring," like the term "structure," is an overused—and greatly misused—concept that requires some clarification at the outset if the word is to be useful at all. Many social scientists have grown accustomed to using structure to indicate everything except culture: the real nuts and bolts of social life, such as organizations, economic factors, social class, and social networks. My usage of the term is quite different. To me, structure means an identifiable pattern in the symbolic-expressive dimension of social life. Usually we are able to identify such patterns by looking for symbolic boundaries that divide up the social world and by looking at the categories created by these boundaries. This usage of the term is very much indebted to the writings of anthropologist Mary Douglas, who conceives of symbolic boundaries as the essence of social order. She writes, for example: "It is my belief that people really do think of their own social environment as consisting of other people joined or separated by lines which must be respected."[3] In her view, social interaction always takes place within a matrix of lines or boundaries that define the perimeter of a given society or group and that draw internal distinctions within the group. Much of our behavior and much of our discourse is, in fact, guided by these boundaries—these structures—and is concerned with making sure that these boundaries are affirmed. Consequently, symbolic boundaries are both powerful in their effects and are accorded power by the ways in which we act and think toward them. As another writer suggests: "Meaning is not in things but in between."[4]

I am not convinced that we need assume, as Mary Douglas does, that people really think about symbolic boundaries or recognize them consciously. But in a deeper sense, the very nature of our thinking and our behavior takes place in terms of symbolic boundaries. Otherwise, we would be unable to make sense of our worlds, not to ourselves or anyone else. So in this respect, symbolic boundaries are fundamental to all of social life. And rather than consisting merely of the nuts and bolts of social interaction, they include symbolism, ritual acts, gestures, discourse, moral obligations, commitments—all the things we usually think of as being important when we speak of religion.

To look at the restructuring of American religion, then, is to look at the ways in which its symbolic boundaries have changed. The changes of greatest interest are those that involve new modes of religious identification, new distinctions in the web of religious interaction, alterations in the lines of moral obligation that define religious communities, changes in the categories that are taken for granted in religious discourse. All of these require paying close attention to the languages used when people make statements about religion. But the present study is not primarily concerned with the languages that individuals use to describe their own religious commitments to themselves. It is concerned with the *public* dimensions of religious culture in the United States: the utterances and acts of religious leaders, the aggregate categories into which individuals define themselves religiously, and the ways in which religious bodies enter into public discourse on matters, for example, of collective value, politics, and economics. Much of this is concerned with what might be commonly recognized as the cultural dimension of American religion. But culture always exists in a social environment. It draws resources from that environment, reflects the categories and distinctions built into that environment, and is influenced by the environment in the very act of trying to influence it. The institutional resources of religious groups and the manner in which changes in the larger society have affected these resources, therefore, play a critical role in the discussion.

IN ORDER to appreciate fully the dimensions along which American religion has been restructured since World War II it is necessary to recapture a sense of the religious mood at the start of this period. As mentioned already, religious organizations were able to adapt to the challenges they faced after the war because they had amassed a powerful institutional heritage. The manner in which they adapted was, however, as much a function of their perception of the challenges set before them as it was of institutional resources. Indeed, the capacity to articulate a program for the future that was only loosely coupled with the vested institutional interests of the past was one of the most remarkable features of American religion in this period. In Chapter 2 I have used the rubric of "heritage and vision" as a way to tease out these connections and capacities.

The mood of religious leaders in the period immediately after World War II was also defined by a characteristic vision of the nature of the broader society. With the close of the war, business was able to return to a state of normalcy, and religious groups, in particular, were able to launch programs that had long been postponed, first because of the economic constraints imposed by the Depression, and then because of the national priorities that had to be observed in fighting the war. In many respects religious leaders were confronted with new opportunities. Yet their mood was scarcely one of unrestrained optimism. Having experienced war on an unprecedented international scale, and facing a future that contained many unknowns, they also had a strong sense of uncertainty and foreboding. The interplay between these two outlooks was a decisive factor in generating the enthusiasm needed to motivate an active program of religious adaptation to the postwar period. The ways in which visions of promise and peril interacted with one another to mold this response are considered in Chapter 3.

For American religion to have been molded as much by its social environment as in fact it was in the decades after the war required that it be actively engaged with the larger society. Deeply influenced by its own inner-worldly tradition, American religion actively put itself on the line, making itself vulnerable to social influences of all kinds. The very nature of this public role gradually changed, however. In the late 1940s and early 1950s it was possible for religious leaders to envision having a certain kind of social influence by means of the very manner in which they conceived of their own message, the culture more broadly, and the connections between values and behavior. These conceptions involved religious organizations in a wide variety of public pronouncements and encouraged them to become deeply involved in educational ministries. Only a decade or so later events would conspire to undermine many of the presuppositions on which these activities were based. And by the 1980s a whole new set of presuppositions was taken for granted in most quarters of the religious community. Rediscovering what some of these assumptions were in the immediately postwar period constitutes the focus of Chapter 4.

Having considered at some length the general institutional and cultural contours of American religion in the late 1940s and 1950s, the discussion then shifts to a consideration of some of the prominent organizational changes that religious bodies experienced, particularly during the 1960s and 1970s. These organizational changes constitute the focus of Chapters 5 and 6. Chapter 5 is concerned with the declining significance of denominationalism in American religion. This decline is particularly important to the larger thesis of this study because it in a sense represents a clearing of the decks so that other kinds of restructuring could emerge. Chapter 6 examines an organizational phenomenon that has risen in importance in proportion to the decline of denominationalism: the proliferation of special purpose groups. Just as in other sectors of the society, these have grown in importance at all levels of the religious hierarchy, surfacing within local churches, in neighborhoods and communities, within and between denominations, and at the national level. The growth of these kinds of organizations has been tremendously important in revitalizing American religion and in adapting it to a more complex social environment. At the same time, special purpose groups respond to and create divisions of other kinds in the religious community. Some of the evidence that will be considered, in fact, suggests that a relatively high degree of polarization exists among the adherents of different types of special purpose groups.

The nature, extent, and sources of this polarity in American religion constitute the focus of the next three chapters and in a sense comprise the main argument of the book. To a small degree, the current tensions between religious liberals and religious conservatives are reminiscent of those earlier in this century between modernists and fundamentalists. The continuities should not be overemphasized, however. In the years immediately following World War II, lasting well into the 1950s, a relatively high degree of unity was evident. Modernists and fundamentalists appeared to be burying the differences of the past and focusing on concerns about which there was greater consensus. In the 1960s, however, this consensus began to be undermined. These developments, and those contributing to the further restructuring of the major faiths in the 1970s and 1980s, are discussed in Chapter 7.

At the same time that many influential elements in the mainline denominations were moving to the left, religious conservatives were quietly marshaling their own resources. During the 1950s and 1960s an infrastructure was built that gave religious conservatives a strong set of interdenominational ties, a growing body of skilled leaders trained in evangelical colleges and seminaries, and increasing access to the media. Much of this growth was made possible by the fact that evangelical leaders repudiated the earlier separatism and sectarianism of fundamentalism and its tendencies toward militancy and anti-intellectualism. By the early 1970s, evangelicals had emerged as a distinct segment of the American religious community and had attracted an increasing number of persons who were dissatisfied with the trends at work in the more established denominations. However, this growth also subjected the evangelical community to influences from the larger culture. And it responded in ways that were to alter its public role radically by the end of the 1970s. These developments are discussed in Chapter 8.

Chapter 9 examines several additional factors that have fueled the tensions between religious liberals and religious conservatives. One of these is the highly polarized debate that has emerged since the late 1970s over the question of abortion. Together with a number of other issues that divide the public along much the same lines—pornography, homosexuality, school prayer—the question of public morality and its relation to governmental policy has provided a continuing source of tension between religious liberals and religious conservatives. A second issue has been the role of women, both in the churches and in the society more generally. From questions of ordination to the issue of an equal rights amendment, this issue has been deeply divisive, especially since women have long been more religiously active than men and yet have been largely excluded from leadership roles in the churches. The role of religious groups in politics more generally, the compromises involved in bringing religion into the public sphere, the role of the media, and the growing interest among political leaders in courting the religious vote have also helped to fuel the tensions between religious liberals and religious conservatives. This division, therefore, has emerged as one of the powerful symbolic barriers around which American religion has become restructured.

The next two chapters (Chapters 10 and 11) take up the question of how American religion, given its current divisions, has articulated pronouncements bearing on the legitimacy of the state and the larger society—the civil religion. Examining these pronouncements reveals that two distinct civil religions rather than one can be identified, one favored by religious liberals, the other by religious conservatives. While each of these expresses certain truths about the character of the American republic, the tensions between the two have rendered each less than satisfactory as unifying, legitimating belief systems. In the breach, a new set of secular legitimating myths oriented around the values of individual freedom and material success appears to have gained ascendancy. Yet these myths also contain inherent limitations. Whether some newly emerging mythology, perhaps oriented toward the wonders of technology, is now competing with traditional civil religion as a legitimating mode is also considered in these chapters.

Finally, some conclusions are drawn about the contemporary role of religious groups in American politics and about the ways in which the character of the American state influences religion as it tries to play a role in the public sphere. Again, ambiguities that have developed concerning the role of the state in conjunction with its own expansion since World War II appear to contribute to the tensions evident in American religion. Understanding these ambiguities is crucial to any attempt to revitalize the role of American religion as a witness to the collective values that will keep the nation strong and yet free.[5]

CHAPTER 2

Heritage and Vision

At the close of World War II religious leaders looked forward to a long-awaited return to business as usual, but the business to which they turned was to be confronted with challenges unlike any they had experienced before. At their service was a rich heritage of organizational, cultural, theological, and financial resources. Whether these resources would be used to create a strong foundation on which to build, or simply result in an ossification of archaic religious structures, would depend greatly on the abilities of responsible individuals to anticipate the challenges ahead. At the helm of the various denominations and faiths, clergy and laity found it imperative to articulate a vision of what religion was and should be. These visions, whether shortsighted or prophetic, would be decisive in charting the future of American religion. They would also shape much of the restructuring that was to take place over the next half century.

The interplay of heritage and vision serves as a convenient means of reconstructing the cultural milieu of American religion in the years immediately following World War II. The religious ethos in these crucial years was scarcely new. A vast inheritance of church building, revivalism, immigration, ethnic diversity, denominational politics, and personal devotion, as well as a long legacy of scriptural and doctrinal interpretation, had accumulated over the past century. Postwar religion was deeply indebted to this heritage and in many important respects demonstrated continuity with it. At the same time, something new was in the process of being created. As the war drew to a conclusion, religious leaders were quick to recognize that the coming of peace posed new opportunities for America and its several faiths. The planning needed to capitalize on these opportunities began almost immediately. The religious heritage was transformed into a religious vision—an image of the future that would guide the activities of religious organizations and contribute immensely to the longer range reshaping they were to undergo. The critical years following World War II were, in this sense, less a Golden Age than a vibrant staging ground from which religious leaders looked both to the past and toward the future.

An Inheritance of Faith

"Religion," remarked Harry Emerson Fosdick, one of the prominent Protestant leaders of the interwar period, "comes to us by inheritance." We are not "its first inspired pioneers"; it comes to us "as a heritage from our forefathers," not as something to be created, but "accepted"—from family, Bible, church, and tradition.[1] The "accepted" religion that Americans inherited after World War II was much the same as the faith of their forebears. Catholics, Jews, and Protestants were all well represented as were numerous denominations. Generations of immigrants, bringing national and ethnic traditions, had given it their imprint. Racial barriers, regional customs, and folk traditions lent further diversity. Pluralism was the watchword, and this was as much a function of local customs as it was of denominational variety. In Dolly Pond, Tennessee, members of a moderate-sized local church opened the usual Sunday morning service with hymns—and then, defying state laws, passed poisonous snakes around the room. In New York City, John D. Rockefeller, Jr., donated a million dollars to promote the ecumenical spirit he saw embodied in the World Council of Churches. At Fenway Park in Boston, more than 30,000 Catholics gathered for a two-hour service of singing and prayer. In Metter, Georgia, a group of about 500 Baptists assembled to pray for rain—and drove home in a downpour. In Dallas, Texas, a Methodist bishop called on parishioners to uphold the poll tax. And at Wheaton College, outside of Chicago, students turned a routine prayer meeting into a three-day marathon of testimony and revival.

Underneath this considerable diversity were also common assumptions of what religion was and should be. Overwhelmingly, it was biblical, codified in the tenets of Judeo-Christian belief. It was organized congregationally, but also showed deep indebtedness to individualistic values. Its leaders held high ideals, but were also committed to being morally and spiritually effective. American religion was intensely concerned with personal piety, but was also highly organized as a social institution. Always precarious, subject to whims of passion and interpretation, it nevertheless was deeply embedded in the cultural fabric of American life.

Attendance at weekly worship services was the most characteristic mode of public religious expression. Across the nation about a million such services were held every month. Gallup polls had asked questions about church attendance since the late 1930s, finding that about a third of the adult population claimed to have attended services in any given week. These figures, however, were still somewhat unreliable because of the method of sample selection.[2] A more reliable study was conducted in 1946 by the fledgling National Opinion Research Center, still located at the University of Denver. According to this poll, two persons in three attended religious services at least once a month, and 42 percent of the public attended every week.[3] In addition to worship services, a wide variety of other meetings drew people to the churches and synagogues. Family potlucks, Sunday school picnics, prayer meetings, church committees, choir practices, and youth groups rounded out the range of local activities. The buildings in which these services took place were enormously varied, some exceedingly simple and offering space for fewer than a hundred worshippers; others adorned with elaborate architecture and with room for more than a thousand members. But the God in whose name worship was offered was recognizably the same everywhere.

Religious rallies on a larger scale also played a prominent role in this period. Sponsored by interdenominational religious councils, highly publicized, and drawing thousands, these rallies turned private devotion into spectacular public events. Like the Brooklyn Sunday School Union parades, they bore public witness, for anyone who might be curious, of America's commitment to religious values. Gone for the most part were the tent meetings, river baptisms, and raw emotionalism of earlier revivals, but the revival's capacity to make religion a community-wide event lived on in these rallies with undiminished energy. Cities competed with one another to enlist the most distinguished speakers and to attract the largest crowds. Four thousand gathered in Detroit for its "Festival of Faith"; in Saint Louis, 19,000 packed into the municipal auditorium for Reformation Day services; outside of Denver some 50,000 crowded into the Red Rocks amphitheater for an Easter sunrise service.

Sometimes the pageantry of these services was rivaled only by holiday festivals and athletic contests. One spectator at a large religious gathering filed the following description:

> A large crowd . . . entered the stadium [and] presently the song leader appeared with his "trumpet extraordinary." He led the crowd in the singing of "gospel songs" which were peppered with his patter and the clever use of his trumpet. He put such boogie-woogie into "When the Roll is Called Up Yonder" that one hardly recognized it. . . . While a large section of the crowd munched peanuts and candy, guzzled pop and crunched popcorn, the master of ceremonies was introduced. [He] at once called attention to the presence of the crowd as a "testimony to the power of Jesus Christ in the world today." . . . A few testimonies were given from the platform by the business men who were footing the bill. A ricochetting number on the golden trumpet was followed by a passionate appeal from the leader who demanded that we sing out and let the whole state know that we are here.

The writer went on to describe a service of testimonies, preaching, and music diminished in splendor only by the color guard, banner carriers, pompon girls, and baton twirlers who earlier had led a parade to the stadium. "We went home," the writer concluded, "in the knowledge that religion was a jolly affair."[4]

At the personal level religious intensity was less easily observed, but scattered assessments indicate that commitment was widespread at least on basic tenets of belief and practice. Shortly after the war, Gallup polls revealed that 94 percent of the public believed in God, a substantially larger share than in England, Holland, Sweden, Denmark, or France.[5] In the same year, a representative study of the nation conducted for the *Ladies' Home Journal* found that 90 percent of the public engaged in prayer, 86 percent regarded the Bible as the divinely inspired word of God, and three-quarters believed in the reality of life after death.[6] Another early national survey further substantiated the wide extent of religious belief: 87 percent of those polled said they were "absolutely certain of God's existence," 83 percent believed the Bible was "the revealed word of God," 80 percent subscribed to the divinity of Christ, and three-quarters considered religion a "very important" part of their lives.[7]

Reflecting on the religious mood of the American people in his widely read book *Protestant-Catholic-Jew*, Will Herberg concluded that the level of commitment was actually somewhat more complex than poll results might indicate. Although religious belief was widespread, it seemed to Herberg to be somewhat superficial—more a matter of vogue than of deep conviction. As evidence, he cited other polls which showed that nearly half the adult population could not name even one of the four gospels.[8] Some of Herberg's fears might have been allayed, however, had he been able to foresee the results of subsequent investigations of biblical knowledge. These studies were to show that questions about religious knowledge were actually more closely associated with levels of education than with other measures of religious belief, practice, and experience. Indeed, biblical knowledge was to show steady increases over the coming decades as levels of education rose, even though many other measures of religious commitment were to decline.

Despite the fact that personal piety was sometimes shallower than critics would have liked, therefore, it was exceedingly widespread. More so than in any other industrialized country, Americans subscribed to a clear set of religious beliefs and practices. But religion was not a matter of hearts and minds alone: it was also a massive institution, the product of long years of sweat and struggle.

Institutional Resources

Deeply rooted in the soil of American life, religion was a dense forest of organizations, not easily supplanted, but capable of reproducing itself abundantly in the seasons to come. Some 250 Protestant denominations were represented, the 6 largest of which shared more than 25 million members; Roman Catholics made up another 25 million; and Jews, about 5 million. Each was the possessor not only of huge membership lists but also of a large aggregation of professional bureaucracies, educational institutions, social service agencies, and financial investments.

With more than 8 million members, the Methodist church was the largest single Protestant body. Holding property valued in excess of a billion dollars, it functioned with an annual budget of nearly $200 million. In addition to more than 40,000 local churches, it operated 77 colleges and universities, 10 seminaries, and 70 hospitals. Administering this sizable empire took an army of clergy and laity, coordinated by 67 bishops, 21 administrative bureaus, a national lawmaking body comprised of more than 600 elected delegates, and more than 100 regionally organized administrative units. Virtually anyone, it was said, who might have a religious yearning could find a Methodist church not far away. It was a major vehicle of both the spoken and written word. On a national scale, the Methodist church each year was the source of several million sermons, tens of millions of Sunday school lessons, and according to official figures, the producer of some 12 million books and pamphlets.[9]

Second only to the Methodists in size was the Southern Baptist Convention. With more than 6 million members in 27,000 local congregations, its many enterprises included 53 colleges and junior colleges, 4 seminaries, over 300 mission schools in 22 foreign countries, 46 hospitals and orphanages, a chain of bookstores, 63 periodical publications with a combined circulation of nearly 38 million, and a relief board with assets in excess of $18 million. Its receipts in 1946 totaled more than $130 million.

Next in size were the two branches—northern and southern—of the Presbyterian church (united in 1983) with some 2.7 million members in nearly 12,000 local congregations. These were organized into approximately 350 presbyteries which, in turn, were grouped into 57 synods. The Presbyterian church operated 71 colleges and 13 seminaries in the United States and was engaged in ministries in 30 other countries, including the work of 1,500 missionary preachers, 3,000 educational programs, and 350 hospitals and clinics. In 1946, its northern branch alone took in $65 million.

The other largest Protestant denominations were the Episcopal church, with 2.1 million members; the United Lutheran Church in America, with 1.8 million members; and the Disciples of Christ, with 1.7 million members. Three other Protestant bodies also counted memberships above one million: the Northern Baptist Convention, the Congregational Christian Churches, and the Evangelical Lutheran Synod.

Most of the other Protestant denominations, while adding diversity to

American religion, nevertheless contributed little to overall membership figures. Two hundred of the nation's 250 denominations were exceedingly small, making up only 3 percent of the country's total religious membership. Their combined membership was less than a quarter the size of the Methodist church alone; each, on the average, counted only about 10,000 members. There were, however, several denominations, all theologically conservative, that already had sizable memberships and were growing rapidly. The largest of these were the Church of Christ, with approximately 800,000 members; the Churches of God in Christ, with 340,000 members; the Assemblies of God, with 275,000 members; Freewill Baptists, with 255,000 members; and the Nazarene church, with 220,000 members.

Most of the Protestant denominations were predominately white. One estimate, published in 1946, suggested that no more than one-half of 1 percent of the black population attended church with whites. As a result, the black population was active in building and promoting its own denominations. In all, there were 34 predominately black denominations, the membership of which derived overwhelmingly from Baptist or Methodist roots. The largest were the National Baptist Convention of America, with 4.4 million members, and the National Baptist Convention of the United States, with 2.6 million members. The African Methodist Episcopal Church had 1 million members; the African Methodist Episcopal Zion Church, about 500,000; and the Colored Methodist Episcopal Church, 381,000. In addition, about 365,000 blacks belonged to the Catholic church and were served by 408 local churches, 306 elementary schools, and 30 high schools.

The Roman Catholic population of 25 million was organized into 15,000 parishes at the close of World War II. Supervision of these parishes was carried out by 4 cardinals, 15 archbishops, 99 bishops, and approximately 25,000 priests. Among the church's many organizations were more than 10,000 elementary and secondary schools with a combined enrollment of 3 million students, 225 colleges and universities, 388 seminaries, 800 hospitals, 367 schools of nursing, 254 homes for the aged, and 352 orphanages and asylums. The church was also active in foreign mission programs, ministries to minority groups, poor relief, care of dependent children, radio broadcasting, and publishing.

The Jewish community of 5 million at the end of the war was represented mainly by the three major groupings of Judaism: Reform Judaism, Orthodox Judaism, and Conservative Judaism. At the national level there were also approximately 250 organizations concerned with religion, culture, welfare, and mutual aid; 600 local community councils for Jewish affairs; over 200 periodicals; weekday and Sabbath schools for more than

250,000 children; 6 seminaries; 2 baccalaureate colleges; and charities with combined annual budgets of more than $150 million.

Finally, nearly 2 million members belonged to one or another of the various religious organizations that were popularly regarded as sects because they fell outside the main theological canons of the Judeo-Christian tradition. More than half this number were Mormons; another 300,000 were Jehovah's Witnesses; 225,000 were Christian Scientists; nearly 200,000 were Spiritualists; and 70,000 were Buddhists.

All together, the estimated value of property held in the United States by the various denominations and faiths at the close of the war amounted to some $7 billion. Collectively, the churches and synagogues took in revenues on the order of $700 to $800 million annually, an amount which was, as the British historian Harold Laski pointed out, nearly as large as the budget of the British government at its height before World War I.[10] In addition, approximately $200 million in philanthropic giving was channeled through religious organizations for other purposes and nearly $150 million was given to parochial schools.

A Gradual Accretion

The vast organizational infrastructure of American religion at the close of World War II had been built up gradually over the preceding century and a half. Denominationalism had been part of the religious heritage since the nation's founding and had steadily expanded during the nineteenth century. In 1800 there had been about three dozen major denominations; by 1900, this number had risen to more than 200. The increase had come about mainly as a result of sectarianism, sectionalism, immigration, and revivalism. Sectarianism and other schismatic tendencies had been especially prominent from the 1820s to the 1840s. These decades had given birth to the celebrated split between Congregationalists and Unitarians in 1825, to the division between Old School and New School Presbyterians in 1837, and the formation of a number of new denominations, including the Primitive Baptists (1827), Disciples of Christ (1832), Wesleyan Methodists (1843), and Exclusive Brethren (1848). Sectionalism prior to and during the Civil War had added to the number of denominations by generating separate northern and southern branches, most notably, among the Baptists, Methodists, and Presbyterians. Immigration, especially after the Civil War, contributed further diversity, especially among Lutheran, Evangelical, and Free churches. Between 1870 and 1900 separate denominations were established by Swedes, Danes, Finns, Norwegians, Germans, and Dutch, as well as a number of denominations organized along state or regional lines as a result of geographically concentrated immigration. Revivalism and the work of charismatic leaders had also been an important source of new denominations, contributing not only to the schisms of the Great Revival period earlier in the century but also to the later emergence of such denominations as the Seventh-Day Adventists (1860), Christian Scientists (1879), Salvation Army (1880), Jehovah's Witnesses (1897), and Pentecostal Holiness Church (1898).

The relative prominence of the various denominational traditions also had a long history. By 1850, Methodists and Baptists had emerged as the largest denominational families, replacing the Presbyterians, Congregationalists, and Episcopalians, who had predominated in size at the time of the War of Independence. The success of the Methodists and Baptists had been closely linked with the westward expansion of the frontier. In 1800, only 9 percent of the population had lived West of the original colonies; by the start of the Civil War, 51 percent lived in these territories. Both the Methodists and Baptists had been especially conscientious in following the frontier. Methodists used lay ministers and circuit riders to multiply the number of clergy; Baptists relied heavily on "farmer preachers" for the same purpose. Unlike the better trained clergy of the eastern seaboard denominations, these preachers earned much of their own livelihoods, preached in the simple language of the people, and minimized social divisions between clergy and laity. Both denominational families also relied on small groups to enlist the involvement of laity: Methodists advocated the "class meeting" for prayer and Bible study; Baptists, weekly prayer meetings and small, intimate congregations, generally numbering between 50 and 80 people. Above all, both denominational families actively took what resources they had to the people: Methodists, to the Midwest and West, founding churches in nearly every state even before statehood was achieved; Baptists, to the South and Midwest, expanding by working across racial lines and by giving pastors and laity a high degree of local autonomy.

After the Civil War, the rankings of the major denominational families in relative size remained much the same, even though all experienced major growth. When the Census of Religious Bodies was conducted in 1906, Methodists still ranked first, with 5.7 million members; Baptists came in second, with 5.6 million; Presbyterians ranked third, with 1.8 million; Lutherans, fourth, with 1.5 million; Disciples, fifth, with approximately 980,000; and Episcopalians, sixth, with approximately 890,000. The only change in ranking among the major denominational families was that of the Congregational church, which slipped from fourth place to seventh, numbering approximately 845,000 in 1906.[11]

This was a period of major expansion for most religious organizations, as the numbers suggest. Total population in the United States increased from 31 million in 1860 to 79 million in 1900 and religious membership rose even more rapidly: from less than 20 percent of the adult population at the end of the Civil War to more than 40 percent by the end of the century. Immigrants, including many Lutherans and Catholics from central, northern, and eastern Europe, brought strong religious loyalties with them. Methodists and Baptists continued to follow the population westward. And, as an increasing share of the population—46 percent by 1910—settled in urban areas, new ministries were begun, including urban revival campaigns, ministries such as the Young Men's Christian Association (YMCA) and Salvation Army which appealed to recent immigrants and those in need, and the so-called "institutional church," which sought to provide a wide variety of welfare, educational, and community services in the largest cities.

All of this took enormous resources. Between 1870 and the end of World War I, the number of local churches grew from little more than 70,000 to over 225,000. During the same period, the number of church buildings increased from 63,000 to 203,000, and the total value of these buildings mushroomed from $354 million to nearly $1.7 billion. The Methodist church alone was reported to have averaged building one new church *every day* during this entire period.

Expansion of this magnitude was not accomplished without major planning efforts and administrative reorganizations within the central bureaucracies of the major denominations. At the beginning of the nineteenth century, little denominational structure had existed beyond the local level. Bishops worked alone and continued to be only a step removed from the local pastorate. No national executive or staff was available to manage denominational affairs on a regular basis and elected assemblies met only infrequently. By the end of the Civil War, only modest revisions of this pattern had been made. Some agencies, such as mission boards and Bible societies had been founded, but these generally remained small, regionally oriented, and inefficient. Most of the work of evangelism and church planting remained in the hands of local clergy, laity, and the itinerant revivalists who forged links between communities and drew in new members.

Not until after the Civil War did the major denominational bureaucracies begin to function effectively on a national scale. By the mid-1870s most denominations had developed one or more centralized agencies, concerned primarily with such matters as missionary work and Christian training. They supervised these agencies with a professional staff whose work was reviewed annually at the denomination's national convention. Increasingly, the network of established local churches was utilized as a means of raising financial support for church planting and other expansion. National agencies also provided a relatively modest amount of planning expertise and coordination to workers in the field.

Between 1880 and 1900, financial prosperity in the nation at large, as well as the churches' success in enlarging membership rosters, permitted rapid growth in most of the central agencies. The Methodist Missionary Society, for example, saw its contributions double in these years, rising to $1.3 million in 1900. Over the same period, the Disciples of Christ increased their budget for mission work more than tenfold, to nearly half a million dollars, and Southern Baptist mission boards increased revenues fivefold, to $391,000. Not only did the number of mission workers multiply as a result; the central bureaucracies took on added size and complexity as well. Domestic and foreign missions were generally divided into separate operations; church extension programs were formed to provide money for the construction of new church buildings; specialized agencies were formed to minister to blacks; new agencies were created to supervise hospitals and other benevolent associations; boards were set up to administer pension plans for pastors; and other departments were established to oversee programs for youth and women. Many of these programs, however, were still subject to personal whims and fluctuating financial conditions.

After 1900, further steps were taken to resolve these difficulties. The most significant change lay in the area of raising financial support. Rather than relying on special appeals, as had been customary in the past, central agencies were now funded through an apportionment plan which simply allocated a share of all local giving directly to the denominational bureaucracy. Other reforms, many of which depended on having a more predictable source of income, included larger staffs of secretaries and auxiliary workers, permanent headquarters buildings, and greater cooperation in interdenominational programs.[12]

In comparison with the major Protestant denominations, the Catholic church was at once more fully institutionalized and yet more internally varied. When the first diocese in the United States was formed in 1789, the entire Catholic population numbered no more than 40,000 out of a total of some 4 million inhabitants. Over the next century great numbers were added through successive waves of immigration. Between 1820 and 1850 the largest share came from Ireland, bringing the total membership of the church to approximately 1.7 million—making it only somewhat larger than the Methodist church. In the decades after the Civil War, Germans came in large numbers, as did Italians, Poles, and other eastern Europeans. In all, more than 20 million immigrants arrived between 1870 and 1910, the largest waves coming in the 1880s and the decade after 1900. When the religious census of 1906 was taken, Catholics numbered 14.2 million.[13]

Like the large Protestant denominations, American Catholicism also underwent a period of major organizational reform. Until the end of the nineteenth century, local priests enjoyed a relatively high degree of autonomy. Vast differences from locality to locality as well as a plethora of crosscutting and overlapping programs were often the result. After the start of the twentieth century, a greater degree of centralized administration began to be evident. Disconnected charitable societies were organized, and national layers of bureaucracy were added to provide coordination. Finances, benevolences, schools, and hospitals were put on a more businesslike footing. Revivalistic work that had been carried out informally by voluntary men's communities was now formalized through the American Catholic Missionary Union and the Catholic Church Extension Society. Elaborate guidelines were promulgated for building programs, fund-raising, and purchasing, and bishops were vested with greater authority over local affairs. Increasingly, bishops who demonstrated skills in financial management and in "brick and mortar" policies were the ones to gain national prominence and prestige.

The Jewish community that emerged after World War II, though populated with large numbers of recent immigrants, also reflected a well-established organizational heritage. Some Jewish leaders complained about "an appalling amount of duplication and overlapping of effort," but this situation only reflected the pluralism and diversity that had developed from successive waves of Jewish immigration.[14] The Sephardic immigration, beginning in 1654, had predominated until the middle of the nineteenth century. After this, a much larger wave of Jewish immigrants from Germany, generally poorer and more assimilationist in outlook, came to the United States. By 1881, they comprised four-fifths of the entire American Jewish population. Then, between 1881 and 1920, 2 million Jews entered the country, coming mainly from eastern Europe. Each group brought distinctive cultural traditions and developed its own religious organizations.

Nevertheless, cooperative organizations representing large segments of the Jewish community nationally also developed at a rapid pace. The first of these, called the Board of Delegates of American Israelites, was organized in 1859. From almost the beginning, this organization worked actively to promote separation of church and state and successfully opposed a number of efforts to institutionalize Christianity as the officially recognized religion of the American republic. Other early organizations which provided structure to the Jewish community included the Jewish Alliance of America, founded in 1891, and the American Jewish Committee, organized in 1906. The latter especially played a prominent role in sponsoring national conferences, representative congresses, publications, and other activities in the decades that followed.

In addition to such national organizations, Jews in most cities were integrated into dozens of synagogues and religious voluntary associations at the municipal and neighborhood levels. In Chicago, for instance, the first congregation was founded in 1846 and the first day school in 1853. During the 1860s numerous youth clubs, ladies' societies, educational circles, and relief organizations were established. During the 1890s citywide organizations such as the Chicago Rabbinical Association and the Chicago Zionist Organization came into existence. And by the 1920s several major colleges and seminaries, welfare funds, and civic federations had been added.[15]

The greatest single decade of growth for the Jewish population had been that of 1907-1916, when the number of Jews living in the United States had increased from 1.8 million to 3.4 million. More than half a million Jewish immigrants came to American shores in each of the next three decades as well, bringing the total by the end of World War II to somewhere between 5.0 and 5.2 million. As the population increased, the organizational base also expanded. During the 1930s, for example, municipal federations were founded in nearly 100 new locations, and during the war these organizations spread to another 44 towns and cities. The years prior to and during World War II were also a time of major expansion in Jewish education. Between 1918 and 1944, for instance, the number of Hebrew schools in New York City grew from 40 to 238. Between 1935 and 1946 alone, the budgets of Jewish schools of all kinds in the United States grew threefold, from $4.9 million to $14.8 million.[16]

Weakness and Strength

More generally, the religious organizations that emerged from World War II were especially affected by events of the previous decades. They were in many ways weaker as a result of, first, economic conditions, and then, war, than they had been earlier in the century. The negative effects of the Great Depression had been felt to a great extent by most of the major denominations. Those with substantial investments in the stock market, often held in trust for denominational pension plans, and those whose members were heavily represented among investors and industrialists, were severely affected. The Episcopal church, for example, experienced a 35 percent decline in receipts between 1929 and 1934, from $46 million to $30 million, and was unable to regain the earlier figure until 1945. The Presbyterian church was also seriously affected, necessitating cuts in expenditures by approximately 45 percent between 1926 and 1936. Denominations with substantial constituencies in rural areas and among industrial workers were also forced to make serious cutbacks. Southern Baptists, for example, cut expenditures by 54 percent between 1926 and 1936, while Catholic expenditures fell by 32 percent. In total, religious expenditures by all faiths declined from $817 million in 1926 to $519 million in 1936, a decrease of 36 percent.[17]

It is worth noting that in comparison with the rest of the nation religion actually maintained itself much better financially than did many sectors of the economy. Between 1929 and 1934, for example, contributions to religion fell by only 13 percent, from $1 billion to $870 million. Over the same period, expenditures on total personal consumption fell by 41 percent, from $77 billion to $46 billion.[18] Nevertheless, the 1930s clearly did not provide religious organizations with the revenue necessary to take on any major programs of expansion.

In addition to keeping clergy salaries low, as well as making payments in kind (widely practiced in rural areas) and limiting the numbers of new clergy, churches managed to make ends meet during the Depression mainly by postponing expenditures for renovation and new construction. In 1929, approximately 10 cents of every dollar given to religion was spent on construction; between 1932 and 1936, this figure dropped to only 2.5 cents. Indeed, less was spent on religious construction during the five worst years of the Depression than in 1929 alone. These cutbacks in construction activity were to have consequences that lasted well into the postwar period.

When the war came to America in 1941, religious organizations, therefore, were badly in need of building materials to put into construction and renovation projects, many of which had been postponed for nearly a decade. The war brought to a halt the worst of the Depression, and as expenditures climbed, contributions to religion grew even more rapidly. Between 1941 and 1945, expenditures on personal consumption grew from $80 billion to $120 billion, or 50 percent; religious contributions grew from $1.06 billion to $1.74 billion, or 64 percent. Thus, the financial capacity to rebuild was rapidly increasing. But religious construction was a dispensable item that had to wait until the war was over. Building materials and construction workers were simply in too great demand to be expended on religious projects. Proportionately, expenditures on religious construction were actually smaller during the war than during the worst years of the Depression. Of the $7.1 billion taken in by religious organizations between 1941 and 1945, only $131 million, or 1.8 percent, went for construction.

When the war ended, then, religious organizations faced the task of initiating construction programs that had been delayed in some cases for as long as fifteen years. Many churches had fallen into disrepair, had not been able to expand facilities to meet needs, or were unable to relocate in new communities. Even if equity had been built up during the war to pay for these projects, restrictions on materials made it impossible to begin building. A Baptist laywoman probably expressed the view of many when she remarked, "War needs and priorities have called a halt to building plans, [but we] are sure that the Lord will enable [us] someday to build a larger edifice in which to worship Him."[19]

In the long run, however, the inability to build may have been a blessing in disguise for many local congregations. After the war, the population not only grew but also shifted in location—from rural to urban areas, from cities to suburbs, and from East to West. Having less of an investment in property or having badly inadequate facilities, church boards probably found it easier to consider relocating rather than simply expanding.

Nobody knows what the extent of this relocation was, but it certainly occupied the attention of many denominational boards after World War II and seems to have resulted in the founding of many more new churches than are reflected merely in aggregate growth statistics. In new communities in the South and West, the numbers of new churches built were especially large, but even in more stable areas it was often considerable. In the Decatur, Illinois, district, for example, there were 60 Methodist churches in 1945; 15 years later, 3 of these had died and 16 new ones had been organized. In San Diego, only 8 Baptist churches had been present in 1945; by 1960, 1 had died and 11 new ones had been born. One denomination that reported figures of this kind for the entire denomination showed that 450 new churches were started between 1945 and 1948, while 850 were closed.[20] More generally, the decade or so after World War II was characterized by tremendous growth in religious construction of all kinds. From a low of $68 million spent on religious construction in 1946, for example, projects totaling more than $336 million were underway by 1950. Much of this growth was made possible by the affluence that began to be experienced after the war in the economy at large. But to a considerable degree, it was also growth rooted in the pent-up demand for religious construction dating back to the beginning of the Depression. What had for many years been a deficit in the stockpile of religious resources, therefore, could become a major inspiration—both materially and psychologically—for religious expansion once the war was over.

Even where churches remained in good repair after the war, religious leaders were acutely aware that these buildings were not always located in the best places. In fact, projected population trends were running heavily against the spatial distribution of their local congregations. Ecumenists had long argued that some congregations were beating themselves to death by competing with three or four churches from similar denominations in the same town (sometimes on the same block) rather than combining forces to reach out to new areas. New studies suggested an even deeper distributional problem: three-quarters of all Protestant churches were located in rural areas or in towns of 2,500 inhabitants or less; yet the rural population was declining while that in urban areas was rapidly expanding.[21] Other estimates indicated that as many as 1,000 rural churches per year would need to be closed down in order to keep pace with the population's shift to urban areas. What appeared to be strength in the short term, therefore, would soon be a disadvantage if denominations did not adapt.

Already it was evident that the churches were failing to meet the challenge of life in the cities as well as they had in rural areas. Polls in Iowa, for example, showed that only 50 percent of the urban population attended church at least once a month, compared to 90 percent of the rural population. In urban Detroit, studies of religious attendance also showed lower rates among both Protestants and Catholics than in the nation at large.[22] A study of the farm population by the U.S. Department of Agriculture had also discovered a surprising indicator of the strength of religious commitment among rural dwellers—they favored sermons and religious music on the radio even more than news programs—which journalists from urban areas argued could never hold true in their locales. Critics also pointed out that denominations could scarcely be expected to attract an urban audience as long as their hierarchies were so dominated by the rural population that even denominational conventions had to be scheduled in the fall following cotton picking and corn harvests. If American religion had a strong institutional base, therefore, it was not an institutional base that could simply be maintained in the future without adapting to changing circumstances.

Of greater concern to most religious leaders at the moment, however, were the serious shortages of trained clergy that most denominations faced after the war. The picture was partly bright but mostly gloomy. On the one hand, census figures showed that the number of persons in clergy positions was growing at about the same rate as the labor force generally and had done so for a long time. Since at least 1910 clergy had comprised about three-tenths of 1 percent of the overall work force. Clergy were also holding their own in relation to the other classic professions with whom they were often compared. In 1910, there had been about 1.3 physicians for every member of the clergy; by the late 1940s, that ratio had actually fallen slightly to 1.17 to 1. In the earlier period the ratio of clergy to lawyers had been about even; by the later period, it had risen only to 1.07 lawyers for every 1.0 cleric.[23] On the other hand, most denominational officials were less interested in these global trends than in filling vacancies in their own parishes.

These vacancies were acute by the end of the war. Southern Baptist statistics showed that only 10,000 of its 27,000 churches were staffed by full-time pastors, leaving 63 percent in the hands of lay ministers, students, part-time clergy, and temporary replacements.[24] In the Methodist church, things were much the same: only 15,000 of the 40,000 congregations had regular full-time ministers.[25] The situation in other denominations was not markedly better: 25 percent of the Presbyterian pulpits were vacant and another 20 percent were filled with temporary "stated supply" pastors; 43 percent of the Congregational Christian churches were without full-time pastors; the United Lutheran church showed a shortage of 28 percent; and the Episcopal church, 20 percent.[26]

The recruitment of clergy was also deficient in other respects. One of the most serious was training. Although clergy were keeping pace with other professionals in numbers, they were by no means the equivalent of physicians and lawyers in levels of education. According to 1946 figures, fewer than half of all Protestant clergy had at least four years of college.[27] Salary levels were also far from equal to those of other professionals. Clergy earned less than half the salary of the average lawyer; less than a third that of the typical physician. Blacksmiths, bus drivers, and factory workers all earned more. To be sure, clergy salaries often did not reflect housing benefits, travel allowances, gifts in kind, or the fact that many clergy lived in rural areas where living costs were lower. But even with these differences taken into account, the rate of remuneration was strikingly low. Given these difficulties, it was not surprising, even apart from the war's demands on manpower supplies, that churches were having trouble recruiting qualified staff.

To the extent that religious leaders' plans for the future were influenced by their assessments of the present, therefore, not everything was decided from a position of strength. In comparison with Europe, where more than a quarter of the churches had sustained heavy material damage from the war, American leaders had much for which to be thankful. But there was also much to be done at home before thoughts of expansion could be entertained.

The Past in Religious Discourse

When religious officials reflected on their heritage, they had a good many facts and figures at their disposal. Most religious bodies collected annual statistics on such matters as membership, numbers of churches and clergy, Sunday school attendance, and financial giving. These were published in denominational yearbooks and made available to ecumenical organizations such as the Federal Council of Churches. Information on religious membership had also been collected periodically since 1870 by the U.S. Census Bureau. Delegates to annual denominational conventions were able, with these sources of information, to ponder their denomination's recent history, to discern trends, and to consider what they had accomplished. They were assisted in this task by the annual reports submitted for their approval by every major ecclesiastical board, by examining minutes of previous conventions, by reading the working papers of special committees, and probably most importantly, by comparing notes with fellow clergy. For most of the major faiths the business of religion was highly organized. And this meant an ample outpouring of written documents detailing organizational decisions and accomplishments. The institutional heritage of American religion, therefore, was more than simply an organizational sunk cost; it was amenable to rational reflection on the part of religious leaders.

Since many of the statistics mandated by national hierarchies had to be reported by local congregations, an awareness of the statistical past was also built into the activities of most churches. Congregations were generally required by their denominations or dioceses to keep accurate records of membership, receipts, and expenditures. Some did so behind the scenes, others proudly displayed such facts as Sunday school attendance and plate offerings on bulletin boards week by week.

Another significant form of collective memory at the local level consisted of the annual meetings, anniversaries, and other rites of passage held periodically in most churches. When members paused on these occasions to ponder their collective heritage, they remembered who they were and what they had been. Financial reports, attendance figures, and other statistics were available to prompt these memories. More commonly, the past was remembered in terms of personalities and programs. Time was marked by the coming and going of revered ministers, by the initiation of a new youth group or nursery school, the purchase of an organ, the construction of a new educational wing. Congregants were mindful, therefore, of their past as a religious community. They saw God's hand in the labors of their forebears and took courage from this memory as they looked to the future. This was the material of which congregational histories were comprised.

There was, however, a fairly clear demarcation between remembrances of the past and its uses in religious rhetoric. Sermons seldom referred explicitly to the history of a denomination or church. They drew applications for the present but seldom dwelled on the past. Religious periodicals provided devotional and inspirational meditations, news, and commentaries on current events, but seldom drew lessons from the past. At annual conventions, reports of the year were filled with perfunctory details of goals accomplished, but keynote speeches said little about these accomplishments or goals. The statistics collected and reported by religious bodies were put forth in a manner that suggested a record for use by historians in the future, but seldom became the materials for analysis of the recent past. Individuals could recount stories of important episodes in the history of their congregations, but knew them as the memories of family and friends rather than as a formal part of their faith. Memories of the war and of the Depression stayed largely in the background. Preachers and religious writers were reluctant to bring them to the surface. Church leaders knew what their congregations had achieved, reckoned with sunk costs and deficits when they planned new programs, let successful programs continue, and hoped to avoid the mistakes of the past; but these recollections were excluded from their public admonitions.

Rather than being simply a matter of oversight, the absence of public discourse about the past reflected genuine ambivalence about its uses. Having reminded his listeners that religion was a heritage, Harry Emerson Fosdick went on to encourage them not to dwell on the past, for to do so led only to a secondhand religion lacking in vitality, too dependent on institutional strength, too little mindful of the need for divine leavening.[28] To focus on the past, a Presbyterian pastor explained, was to be guilty of "a lack of progress in spiritual things."[29] Religion was supposed to be living, vibrant, culturally relevant, not a crystallization of the past. Traditions were important, but required constant revision.

Nels Ferré, professor at Andover-Newton Theological Seminary, likened the Christian tradition to a root that kept the plant of faith alive, but needed to be kept in its place rather than determining too much how the plant was allowed to grow. "The Christian roots have been growing for a long time," he said. "They are deep. But the plant has been badly cared for. [Old] traditions must be reinterpreted in the light and strength of the real life of Christianity." The contemporary generation, he urged, must throw off the dry rot of its theological traditions in order for religion to blossom and flourish.[30]

The religious heritage that found its way into public discourse, then, was not an account of the churches' immediate past or of its current institutional strength. The events that were expounded upon, when they were mentioned at all, were of heroic times when men and women of long ago exercised their faith. They were inspirational events, not analyses of church history; stories of faith, told for personal encouragement. The rhetorical heritage differed sharply from the organizational and ecclesiastical heritage of the church. It was a romantic past, a populist, undifferentiated, distant past.

Religious people, then as now, took heart from stories of the past that showed the deep religious foundations on which the nation rested. Rather than reflecting on dry institutional statistics, they allowed their vision of the future to be shaped by a romantic image of the nation's past. A favorite episode was the Great Awakening. Others included romanticized versions of the early colonies, the War of Independence, the great revivals of the nineteenth century, and the struggles of the pioneers. The religious past was retold largely in nondenominational terms, although Protestants and Catholics usually emphasized the contributions of their own traditions. It also emphasized the common person. The stories congregants loved to hear were of humble folks living pious lives of simple faith and of hardy preachers taking the gospel westward against great odds. These were heroes to be respected and admired, yet common enough to strike a resonant chord with even the humblest layperson. For example, W. A. Criswell, already pastor of one of the largest Baptist churches in Texas, called his flock to a renewed zeal for evangelism by reminding them of this heritage:

> It was the pioneer preacher with the flaming heart who went forth in obedience to the call of God to declare the whole counsel of the Almighty. As the population extended westward beyond the Alleghenies into the new territories of the American continent, these men of God, without organization or visible means of support, pushed boldly into the regions beyond. Their hardships were such as we of the present day can hardly imagine.

Heroic they were, but the descriptions of these hardy pioneers also had a distinctly populist ring. Criswell went on to point out that they did not read "polished essays," that they were not always "scrupulous of the king's English," that they would probably be unwelcome in a "fashionable pulpit in the cities," but had nevertheless managed to lead "multitudes to the cross."[31]

The image of the past told in sermons such as this was of a *distant* past, when times were presumably more in keeping with divine purposes. For those who saw in present events signals of spiritual decay, the distant past was prelude to a call for renewal. Reminding believers of the spiritual fervor of their forebears, preachers could offer visions of further decay unless people repented and played a more active role in advancing God's work.

The heritage that played the most prominent role in religious discourse, however, was biblical. Rather than point to organizational facts, or even to the heroic deeds of earlier Americans, clergy focused on the heritage of the Bible itself. Addressing an assembly of church leaders in Boston, one speaker challenged his audience to be reminded of their heritage. "We have roots," he said.[32] But the roots of which he spoke were not a denominational or national tradition. He went on to discuss the reality of faith in God, the value of a God-centered life, and the hope of divine redemption.

The leaders of American religion after the war were heir to a tradition in which religious authority was, in fact, ultimately biblical. Faith was inevitably personal, but its parameters were constrained by a revelation of divine will that was generally understood to have been codified in the scriptural canon. God had been revealed not only in individual lives but in a written form that was subject to inspection, argumentation, and therefore, to a process of consensus building. More than to any institutional tradition, this was the heritage to which religious discourse referred.

In emphasizing its biblical heritage to a greater extent than its institutional heritage the leaders of American religion were in a sense freed from having to defend their traditions. Rather than religious actions being commended on the basis of considerations about organizational resources and other institutional investments, they could be invoked on the basis of biblical principles and visions of the future. The fact that America's religious bodies were not principally concerned with protecting their traditions as such meant that contemporary social conditions, as well as the futures projected by religious groups for themselves, were to play a more decisive role in shaping American religion in the postwar period than was the institutional inheritance of the past. Institutional characteristics served loosely as resources and constraints on projected programs, but not as cultural models that had to be consciously acknowledged and maintained. In a sense, the religious future was sharply differentiated from its past, thereby giving religious leaders greater flexibility in adapting to new circumstances. While there was continuity with the past, this cultural separation of future and past greatly reinforced the degree to which religion could be restructured as it responded to the postwar environment.

A more problematic aspect of religion's stance toward its past derived from the fact that this past was not often subjected to close scrutiny. Allusions to the past often appeared to consist of convenient mythic reconstructions instead of being based on careful analysis of what had actually happened. Futures were projected in contradistinction to mythically reconstructed images of failed modernism and failed fundamentalism, of Protestant struggles with Catholics, of Catholic designs on the government, and so on. But realistic analyses of what had gone wrong or of what had been right—of the resources on which the future could be built, or of ways in which social conditions had influenced religion in the past and were likely to in the future—were seldom made. In consequence, plans for the future were often identified as a means of avoiding the errors made by mythic villains of the past, rather than being made on the basis of clear knowledge of how they might be constrained by existing institutional arrangements or by emerging social trends. This, too, increased the likelihood that religion would be restructured in the postwar period. Not only was it open to efforts aimed at changing it; it was subject to factors in the social and cultural environment to which little attention, at least heretofore, had been paid. In failing to take explicit account of the possibilities of such influences, religious leaders allowed their programs to be influenced without a great deal of conscious or premeditated resistance. Their own visions of the future were to be tremendously important, but these visions were to be formulated largely without benefit of systematic assessments of the historic and contemporary constraints that might affect their implementation.

CHAPTER 3

A Vision of Promise and Peril

FACED with the turbulence of later years, writers have often looked back on the immediate postwar period as a moment of unrivaled optimism in American religion, a time of peace and prosperity when people moved to the suburbs, bought Chevrolets, went to bed early, and repopulated the churches. In contrast to the cynicism of the 1960s and the narcissism of the 1970s, it was apparently a time when traditional values reigned supreme and popular piety still found expression in the familiar religious establishments of the past. With an entire world awaiting their message, religious leaders allegedly could not help regarding their time as one of unparalleled opportunity.

To some extent, the prevailing mood was indeed optimistic. Even before the war had ended, religious leaders were looking to the future to determine what role their organizations should play. Some emphasized new fields in which missionary work could take place as a result of peace, trade, and new regimes. Others, recognizing the serious devastation wrought by the war, encouraged congregations to shoulder the responsibility of providing relief. Preaching, church schools, fighting communism, guarding against totalitarianism, offering inner security in the coming atomic age were all discussed as priorities for ministry. Common to all these discussions was the conviction that postwar America would provide religious organizations with important new opportunities to be exploited. Churches that did not make use of these opportunities, one leader cautioned, would simply "be left standing on the sidelines."[1]

An Expansionary Mood

Shortly after the war, a small Brethren church in Seattle with fewer than 50 members decided to relocate in a rapidly growing suburb of the city. With $39,000 and a great deal of volunteer labor they managed to construct a modest church building and parsonage. Three years later their investment was valued at $150,000 and the church roll listed more than 300 members.[2] All across the country this story was being repeated. Wartime prosperity had generated what one editorial described as "immense funds for postwar building needs." As soon as restrictions on building materials were lifted, these funds were expended to bring long-anticipated plans for renovation and expansion to fruition.

In Bucks County, Pennsylvania, the old Bensalem Methodist Church added three new rooms to its fellowship hall, the first construction project undertaken since 1926.[3] In Danville, Kentucky, a new annex to the Presbyterian church had been added in 1938, but the main building had fallen into a state of serious disrepair; as soon as the war ended, plans were made for a major renovation project, finally brought to completion in 1949.[4] In Alexandria, Virginia, the First Baptist Church, with an annual prewar budget of $40,000, voted to expand its operations to more than $100,000 and formed a committee to raise money for a new facility that would double its capacity.[5] In Lewisburg, West Virginia, the Old Stone Presbyterian Church launched a five-year program to replace its 1910 educational building with a new structure estimated at $183,000.[6] In Nashville, 15 new churches went up in a single year; in Detroit, 38 new churches were built.

Between 1946 and 1949, the Southern Baptist Convention alone established 500 new churches at a cost of $97 million. In the same years, Methodists were spending almost as much on new buildings and improvements as their entire operating budget. And more was to come: by late 1949, it was reported that a billion dollars of new construction was underway in Protestant denominations. Nor was the building limited to Protestants; Catholics also embarked on major programs: 125 new hospitals were under construction, over 1,000 new elementary schools were being opened, and 3,000 new parishes were being added.[7]

With expansion of this magnitude taking place it was not difficult for many church officials to express optimistic views of the future. John LaFarge, editor of the Catholic weekly *America*, observed that it was "impossible not to rejoice" over the development and strength of the Catholic church.[8] Franklin Fry, president of the United Lutheran Church, remarked in his presidential address to the denomination's biennial convention: "We have risen into the atmosphere at last. It has been a tingling revelation of hidden power."[9] Looking back on the period, one parishioner remembered fondly: "These were the years of the 'baby boom'; [we saw] a bumper crop of this very special article. . . . The Sunday School was becoming as crowded as the local public school system [and] it was absolutely necessary to provide more room."[10]

Everywhere, church rolls seemed to be up and seminaries were bustling to turn out clergy fast enough to anticipate the demand. By 1950, the number of students enrolled in Protestant and Jewish seminaries was about double the prewar figure, while at Catholic seminaries it was up by 30 percent. And for a change, after a long lull of more than a decade, church statisticians could report proudly that the churches were growing. Southern Baptists added nearly 300,000 new members in the first four years after the war. Catholics were baptizing about a million infants each year. A study of the Methodist church in 1948 showed that membership had increased faster in the previous four years than at any time since 1925 and projected a need for nearly 3,000 additional clergy in the next five years.[11] The Disciples of Christ announced their largest annual gains in over 30 years.

A Time of New Beginnings

Church leaders' optimism was at least partly based on the feeling that the war, as it were, had wiped the slate clean of past mistakes. The war served as a symbolic demarcation of time, a liminal period associated with the nation's rite of passage from adolescence to maturity, a special moment in history that separated the old from the new. Theological arguments conceived in the 1920s and 1930s now seemed naive to many or at least inapplicable to the postwar era. Unconsciously, this may have been one of the reasons for the past being so little present in religious discourse. When the past was mentioned at all, it was often portrayed critically. Prominent theological positions now seemed dated; the world had somehow matured beyond them. Fundamentalism was pictured as being overly narrow, negative, and separatist, capable of attracting few to its version of the gospel. Modernism was recalled as a preoccupation with obscure intellectual debates, too rationalistic, too concerned with vague social issues, lacking in drive, vision, and power to motivate a vigorous personal faith. Both were seen as biased products of their times. From the new vantage point of the postwar period, both seemed stale and worn.

In some contexts the image of a clean slate suggested what could be accomplished. Stripping away the peripheral creeds, doctrines, and styles of worship, replacing them with a renewed emphasis on the essence of Christianity, was seen as a way of reinvigorating American religion. It was as if the stormy years of war had purged the air of traditional assumptions, allowing a fresh wind to blow across the religious mindscape. Faith had formerly been weakened by differences over nonessentials; now, if only Christ could be preached, rather than denominational distinctives or ethical programs, great strength could be realized. Streamline the faith, some suggested, do away with picayune differences; just focus, as one layman recommended, on "God as the loving Father of us all, and Christ as the way to God."[12]

In other settings, the idea of making new beginnings became a favored theme. America had always been a place of new beginnings: from the New World of the first explorers to the New Israel of the colonies, from the new republic to the new land of pioneers and immigrants. The end of military involvement in Europe and Asia, the return of soldiers to their homes, the need to rebuild a peacetime economy, the new set of international responsibilities, and most of all, the new weapon—the atomic bomb—signaled a time of new beginnings. Addressing the faculty of the Chicago Theological Seminary shortly after the war, Methodist bishop G. Bromley Oxnam argued that the present generation was witnessing a new beginning "as significant as was the passage from slavery to feudalism, and from feudalism to capitalism."[13] New beginnings were also a favorite theme of Reinhold Niebuhr. America had, he repeatedly urged audiences to realize, experienced a fundamental conversion, it had lost its innocence and entered a new stage in its development as a nation.[14]

The idea of new beginnings was also rooted deeply in America's biblical heritage. Believers had always looked to the origins of their religion as a symbol of inspiration and renewal. Likening their own era to that of the first century, religious leaders now called for fresh insights, fresh commitment, fresh beginnings. The image of New Testament Christianity was advanced as a symbol of youthful vitality. Clergy were admonished to regain the apostolic vision of what the church could become, to quit tradition, to be imaginative, and to support the great causes that needed their attention.

Some of the optimism reflected in these years was also attributable to America's new position in world politics. In a speech delivered in 1945, John Foster Dulles appealed to Americans to extend their conception of morality and spirituality to the rest of the world. "The United States ought to take a lead," he urged. "We are the only great nation whose people have not been drained, physically and spiritually. It devolves upon us to give leadership in restoring principle as a guide to conduct. If we do not do that, the world will not be worth living in."[15] Reaffirming the Atlantic Charter in the same year, President Truman observed that the United States "shall not relent in our effort to bring the Golden Rule into the international affairs of the world."[16] These were encouraging words for religious leaders. Optimistically, many rose to the challenge. Almost breathlessly, one editorial declared that the Christian American, "as a citizen of the world's richest and industrially most powerful nation, has a tremendous potential influence on world affairs."[17] "Christians hold the world together," stated a board report of the Presbyterian church.

Religious leaders, particularly in liberal Protestant circles, also took heart because social conditions more generally were changing. Society was becoming more complex, government was becoming more important, education and technology were becoming the waves of the future. At last, some thought, racial discrimination, poverty, and class hatred would be overcome. So sweeping were the changes that some felt, as

Francis Cardinal Spellman put it, a need for people of goodwill everywhere to undertake the enormous task "of reconstructing the very foundations of human society."[18] The cardinal's call, of course, was not for revolution or political reform but for a renewal of the spiritual foundations of American culture.

The Prospect of Doom

Perceptions of the period as one of promise, however, were only part of the picture. Although churches were growing, and despite the fact that there were new opportunities for religion, an underlying fear of imminent peril was also evident. Religious discourse was filled with prophecies of doom. Peace was certainly better than war, and prosperity was preferable to hardship, but no one knew how long these comforts would last. Expectations were uncertain. Even some of the developments that had brought about peace and prosperity posed new sources of danger. Religious leaders hoped for the best, but often spoke of the worst. Theologian John Bennett, addressing an audience at the University of Virginia just after the war, expressed it this way: "We live in a world that is appalled by the horrors of the war and its aftermath, with more baffling problems than our forefathers could have imagined, and we are haunted by fears of an even greater catastrophe."[19] Another religious spokesman stated his fears more bluntly: "The nations," he said, "were doomed to fall into the ditch."[20]

Expectations of impending catastrophe were greatly reinforced by the possibility, so recently illustrated at Hiroshima and Nagasaki, that the earth could be consumed by atomic warfare. "Our world," cautioned Albert Einstein in 1946, "faces a crisis as yet unperceived by those possessing the power to make decisions for good or evil. The unleashed power of the atom has changed everything save our modes of thinking, and thus we drift toward unparalleled catastrophe."[21] With warnings like this coming from eminent scientists, it was not difficult for religious people to believe the world was nearing an end. A young scientist who had worked on the Manhattan Project which had produced the atomic bomb, himself a conservative Protestant, wrote: "I am rather easily convinced that . . . humanity stands on a tiny ledge above the abyss of annihilation and the next ten or perhaps five years will bring an atomic war which will crumble this ledge and complete our present era." Many of his fellow church people, he said, had concluded that the time was short, so short that nothing could be done but rescue a few souls before the judgment came. It was their view "that the fire in our house of humanity is out of control and so, rather than dissipate our energies in pouring water on the fire or building new additions to the house to replace those that are burning, we must bend all efforts toward rescuing what furniture we can."[22]

In later years, during the Cold War and again in the 1970s when nuclear disarmament became a major issue, it was common in religious circles to view the atomic bomb as the underlying fear of Americans in the late 1940s and early 1950s—a fear that, some argued, was more responsible than anything else for people returning to religion in these years. Polls from the period, however, dispute this assumption. Atomic fears may have been popular among religious elites, and certainly provided food for thought whenever total annihilation was discussed, but to the general public, the atomic bomb was more likely to symbolize good than evil. A poll conducted in October 1947, for example, showed that 55 percent of the public felt the atomic bomb was a good thing, compared to 38 percent who thought it was a bad thing; an even larger proportion (70 percent) thought the United States should continue manufacturing the bomb.[23] Another poll, conducted in February 1949, found the public by a two-to-one margin in sympathy with the view that the atomic bomb had made another war less likely.[24]

More common as sources of misgiving in these years were economic fears. People who had reached adulthood by 1945 could well remember long years in the 1930s when millions were unemployed and families struggled to make ends meet. Only the war, according to most widely popularized arguments, had saved the country from further years of unemployment and hardship. With the war over, many expected the problems that had plagued the economy in those years to return. Asked if they expected their family income to be higher after the war, only 10 percent in a national poll in 1945 said they did. A year after the war, another poll showed that 60 percent thought there would be a "serious business depression" in the United States in the next ten years.[25] If there was optimism on some fronts, therefore, it was undoubtedly tempered by uncertainties concerning the economy.

Another recurrent worry was the fear that peace would not last. In contrast to the mood prevalent after the "Great War" of 1914-1918, the second war left many convinced that peace in the future was less likely than war. Many expressed doubt that the settlement in 1945 was more than a temporary respite from international conflict and these doubts were reinforced by tensions with Russia and troubles in the Middle East and Asia. "It is worse than folly," one pastor remarked, "to assume that the termination of hostilities will initiate a 'return to normalcy' anywhere in the world." And he added: "This particularly applies to the churches, whose prewar world is gone forever."[26] Polls taken in the years immediately following the war found that seven persons in ten believed the United States would be in another war within 25 years; and when conflict did break out in Korea, two persons in three thought World War III had already begun.[27]

Communism was another menacing source of fear. Well before Korea and the witch hunts of Senator Joseph McCarthy, religious leaders had begun denouncing godless communism. The United States, Francis Cardinal Spellman told a gathering of chaplains in 1945, "is, at this very moment, at war for its very soul [against the] brutal bludgeon of communism."[28] Not only was it an alien political force, it was also a false religion. And the nation must be ready, if necessary, to wage "holy war," as the editors of *America* suggested, to keep it at bay.[29] Ever a threat to religious people everywhere, communism was subtle, powerful, organized. It was just the kind of threat that raised the specter of peril to exceptional heights. Nobody knew quite what the Russians would do, now that the war had ended. Nor did anyone claim to know how strong a menace communism had become within the borders of the United States itself. But religious leaders everywhere expressed dismay. Episcopalians, Catholics, fundamentalists, Baptists, leaders of the Federal Council of Churches, all issued statements in the years immediately following the war counseling vigilance against this rising danger.

To these sources of uncertainty was added the fact that Americans' horizons had been greatly expanded by the war. No longer was it nearly as easy for the nation to live in quiet domestic isolation. The economic and military power of the United States had suddenly catapulted the nation to world preeminence and events in remote corners of the world now seemed more relevant to American interests than ever before. Newspapers and magazines clearly reflected the changing climate. In the six months just prior to the nation's entry into the war, less than a quarter of the editorials in leading newspapers had dealt with international affairs; during the war, these issues generally took up 40 to 50 percent of the space; and now that the war was over, the same percentage was being maintained.[30] Religious magazines, having covered events in Europe and the Pacific during the war, also continued to focus heavily on affairs abroad after the war. News about churches in Europe, relief programs, peace negotiations, the missionary effort in China, religious conflicts in India, and reports of visitors to Latin America became nearly as common as news about religion in the United States. During a single six-month period in 1946, for example, *America* ran over 200 articles on Europe and the United Nations, compared with fewer than 100 on the United States (and more than half of the latter dealt with foreign policy).

The significance of the new role of the United States in world affairs was not lost on religious planners. Not least of the implications they saw were new opportunities for world missions and evangelization. U.S. prominence, however, also added considerations of another kind. A view was rather commonly held that the nation had achieved stature in world affairs because of its strong religious heritage. It was more imperative now than ever before, therefore, to uphold this heritage. And preachers worried whether their parishioners were up to the challenge, admonishing them to avoid temptation, and reminding them of the dangers the world would face if they failed. The stakes had never been higher. "The fundamental problems of the human situation," wrote an Episcopal priest, "seem to be given a tension beyond anything we have thought or dreamed."[31] Often repeated were the words of Calvin Coolidge, who had argued that the very foundations of American society "rested so much on the teachings of the Bible, that it would be difficult to support them, if faith in these teachings should cease to be practically universal in our country."[32]

The war had undoubtedly contributed to Americans' sense of confidence in themselves. They had, as historian Henry Steele Commager observed in 1950, banked their hopes on democratic government and mass production, and they had won. American power, relative to that of the ravaged countries on whose territory the war had been fought, had never been stronger. And yet the new sense of American power was accompanied, as Commager also observed, by bewilderment and confusion: "Americans knew that theirs had become the most powerful nation on the globe, but they were, for the most part, embarrassed rather than exalted by their position and their power."[33] Or, if they were not embarrassed, their new responsibilities in a world that was increasingly interdependent economically, politically, and militarily considerably raised the stakes. American institutions, including religion, were being asked to take on responsibilities greater than ever before. "The question is," one religious writer asked, "does American culture in the second half of the twentieth century have enough integration, and do Americans have enough faith, courage and stamina to preserve what democracy they possess, to gain more, and to play a democratic role on the world stage where they now find themselves?"[34]

There were also continuing concerns about trends in morality. Although compared to the prominence they had been given in the 1930s some of these concerns were overshadowed by events on the international horizon, they still occupied the attention of many religious discussions. Church boards deliberated over alternative ways of curbing the "traffic in drink," crime rates pointed toward increasing levels of moral decay, divorce statistics suggested that the family was in trouble, reports came in from the cities that teenage gangs were terrorizing the streets, and pockets of illicit gambling and prostitution were uncovered often enough to serve as examples of immoral temptations. According to one national poll, a majority of the public felt that the human race was getting worse from the standpoint of moral conduct.[35]

The prevailing mood, then, was by no means one of untrammeled optimism. Some rays of hope had broken through at the conclusion of the war, but much of the sky remained dark. In the press, forecasts tended to emphasize the darkness more than the light. Only one editorial in seven, an analysis of newspaper opinion revealed, expressed genuine optimism about the immediate future.[36] As one religious observer ventured, "disillusionment, rather than optimism" was the keynote of the time.[37] "The crisis is at hand," asserted the bishops of the National Catholic Welfare Conference in their 1948 pastoral letter.[38] Others characterized the prevailing spirit as a mixture of opportunity and peril.

Some writers have attributed the uneasy, restless, fearful mood of the period to a guilt complex related to the war. Younger Americans who had not been able to fight and older Americans who acknowledged their luck as individuals and as a country in escaping the worst destruction of the war allegedly felt guilty and, as a result, feared that good times would not last.[39] There may be merit to this argument. A plausible case can also be made, however, that the uncertainties of the times were reinforced by elements of the Judeo-Christian tradition itself.

Anticipations of peril are deeply ingrained in the Judeo-Christian tradition. A popular anecdote in Jewish circles tells of the following telegram sent by a Jewish friend: "Start worrying. Letter follows." In the Christian tradition, images of impending doom range from Jesus' parable of the man whose soul was taken the same night that he decided to build bigger barns, to the apostle Paul's admonitions against evil principalities and powers, to the apocalyptic visions of Revelation. Believers are warned throughout the Hebrew and Christian scriptures not to become complacent, to avoid pride lest they fall, to be wary of temptation, to reckon with the transience and insecurity of life.

In the years after World War II, threats of communism, signs of moral decay, economic uncertainties, fears of war were all overlaid with religious images. In addition to the ills on which the newspapers dwelt there were perils of a spiritual nature. The spread of communism in eastern Europe and in China was described in religious discourse as a symptom of unfulfilled spiritual desires. Materialism in the West was criticized as a sign of religious malaise. So were the growing indications of moral decay. Even peace and prosperity were conditions that might tempt the righteous astray. They were blessings but should not be expected to last. Religious people were admonished not to become proud or too comfortable. As John Mackay, president of Princeton Theological Seminary, cautioned his graduating class in 1948: "Lovely things . . . will come to you, many things that you will cherish, that you will be proud to have. Remember this. Do not use them for ostentation but only for inspiration."[40]

Some of the former optimism that had been inspired by earlier millennial dreams of a godly America remained in evidence in these years. But the current vision was decidedly more restrained and in most cases openly ambivalent instead of confidently optimistic. The great hope of a millennial kingdom of justice and peace on earth had foundered on the rocks of two world wars and long years of economic hardship. Faith in a future world of unrestrained freedom had been betrayed by totalitarianism, just as had expectations of economic abundance. The new world that religious leaders envisioned was fraught with uncertainty. Even theologians in denominations that had led the battle for a social gospel were now critical of the naive optimism that had inspired their predecessors. They were forced to reckon with a time of new perils, symbolized most vividly by the destructive powers of the atomic bomb. Some predicted, rightly as it turned out, that the Protestant era as they had known it was over. Most clung to the conviction that some form of Judeo-Christian culture could be made to prevail. The most common response, however, was growing awareness of the tremendous odds against which the religious vision would have to contend.

The outlook commonly expressed was by no means entirely gloomy. It was not the dour reincarnation of earlier Puritan gloom and doom. Nor was it the mindset of the proverbial pessimist who, on waking to a beautiful day, counsels himself, "we shall have to pay for this later on." It was instead a precariously balanced vision of prosperity and adversity. Prosperity provided hope and gave cause to rejoice; adversity prevented believers from becoming too attached to earthly conditions. The proper view, therefore, was to let good times spur one on with renewed zeal while avoiding complacency. In the words of a popular hymn of the day:

> I thank Thee more that all our joy
> Is touched with pain;
> That shadows fall on brightest hours,
> That thorns remain;
> So that earth's bliss may be our guide,
> And not our chain.[41]

The prevailing mood expressed in religious discourse, then, was a mixture of optimism and pessimism. Almost as if it were a matter of deliberate rhetorical style, religious argumentation set the good alongside the bad and balanced fears of peril with promises of hope. The more extreme a prophecy of impending doom that was uttered, the more strongly was it likely to be balanced with visions of new horizons. Typical, for example, was the opening sentence of the joint resolution on faith and world order passed by the Federal Council of Churches in 1945. "We are living," it said, "in a uniquely dangerous and promising time"—dangerous, because of wars, suspicions, fears, hatreds, widespread moral disintegration, yet promising because faith could shine through as never before.[42] Another writer framed the thought more poetically: "New obstacles confront the Christian community today. Fresh opportunities beckon it."[43]

The mixture of promise and peril in religious discourse was particularly apparent whenever people stopped to think of the world facing the coming generation. Parents hoped the years of deprivation and anxiety they had experienced during the Depression and war would not be their children's fate. To the mothers and fathers who lined the sidewalks of Brooklyn each spring for the Sunday School Union parade, garlands and bouquets and starched dresses and bow ties symbolized a much-desired future of prosperity and peace. A young mother, in an article printed in *Bible Magazine* in 1946, probably spoke for many when she commented:

> We long to think of peaceful years ahead, normal days with fulness of living, and with little girls marching gaily into kindergarten and not through snowy, war-torn streets, and bigger girls marching to the platform to receive their school diplomas. We want to dream of little girls grown to womanhood and marching down the bridal aisle and from there to years of happiness and sheltered, joyous living. We do not want to think of them driven through the streets to an unknown but horrible fate. We desire for our children a normal life, peace and plenty throughout their life span, achievement and fulfillment.[44]

But such hopes were almost too much to entertain. Wars and rumors of war, poverty and devastation, even imprisonment, were the abiding threats foretold not only by newspapers but in Holy Writ. Religious people needed to be thankful but also ready to endure the worst. For the children, dressy clothes and pretty flowers might not be enough. This mother went on to query: "Are we preparing them so that whatever life brings of joy or sorrow they will be unshaken in their confidence in Him and of His love for them? It is our responsibility and privilege, and at present, our opportunity."

A Basis for Religious Activism

Living in uncertain times, in a world fraught with discussions of impending doom, has always tempted people to seek simple, short-circuited ideological escapes. The period after World War II was no exception. Some religionists proffered simple doctrinal formulas as the answer: Let people pray and ask Jesus into their hearts and all will be well. A doctrine of inner peace provided another option: Focus on your fears, your discouragement, your thinking; remold your outlook and all will be well. Nihilist existentialism, imported from Europe and increasingly influential in American intellectual circles, suggested to others a life of withdrawal or placing ultimate faith in sensual pleasure. Visions of apocalyptic collapse, often common in such contexts, were also not absent. "The hands of the clock of Bible prophecy appear to be moving onward and upward to the time when it must strike—the midnight hour," proclaimed the editor of a fundamentalist periodical.[45] Atomic warfare, as an instrument of Armageddon, was a significant element of these arguments. Progress in the Middle East toward the founding of a Jewish state and conflicts in Europe between communism and the Catholic church also led some to think the last days had arrived.

The apocalyptic vision of hyperdoomsayers was not, however, as popular as might have been expected. Relatively few cults or sects offered explicit predictions of the world's end. Even among more conservative-minded church leaders, the apocalyptic view was widely challenged. They agreed that the Day of Judgment could come at any time, but cautioned against making exact predictions or focusing on the world to come. Theologian Carl F. H. Henry, for example, admonished readers that fundamentalism had too often taken "major crises as the last chapter of world history" and become preoccupied with "rescuing the furniture." Fundamentalism, he said, had not been wrong in believing in a "final consummation of history," but had erred "in assuming that *this is it*."[46] Speaking to an assembly of Protestant pastors in Syracuse, publisher Henry Luce also brought to mind the widespread feeling, like that among the early Christians, that the world might be nearing an end. And yet, he urged, Christians "cannot be too much disturbed about the world's coming to an end"; the proper attitude—an attitude he said was evident among his listeners—was not one of despair but of confidence that the world could be saved and improved.[47]

The most frequently articulated response to present uncertainties, rather than making apocalyptic prophecies of doom, was to counsel vigilant activity. If times were in danger of turning bad, then religious people had a special responsibility to take advantage of the opportunities facing them. This, more than any of the other responses, was the vision articulated for the future. The mixture of peril and promise that characterized religious discourse was not simply a matter of ambivalence or moderation. It set the specific rhetorical context in which vigilance was prescribed. Promise and peril were *both* preconditions of this advice. Juxtaposed in relation to one another, they established the basis of arguing that something *could* be done and *should* be done.

Pleas for dedication to religious causes took on added urgency when they were combined with reminders of the great perils facing the world. In its 1946 pastoral letter, the House of Bishops of the Episcopal church warned its parishioners against complacency: the war was over, the bishops said, but "mankind is not yet saved." The forces of evil—"subtle adversaries"—were at work to undo both the victors and the vanquished. Christians everywhere needed to repent and turn their efforts to the costly labors of kingdom building and discipleship.[48] Even though the churches were beginning to expand, the dangers ahead required more than the usual energies to be expended. Religion was in constant battle with the forces of evil. In the words of a Methodist minister: "We must recognize that a desperate struggle is on for the soul of the world. That requires . . . a great godly company of men and women with no axe to grind, desiring only to save, serve, help and heal."[49] Others were more explicit. If foreign aggression led to another war, if secularism produced a totalitarian government at home, or if some divinely ordered natural catastrophe happened, the chance to build God's kingdom would be foreclosed. To one writer, such possibilities spelled "in capital letters . . . NO MORE OPPORTUNITY!" God's people, therefore, should reckon that "the night is far spent" and ask if they could be doing any more.[50]

The idea of time being "far spent" was a common image. Perhaps the world was not on the brink of Armageddon, but somehow peril was more imminent than ever before. Atomic warfare could bring sweeping destruction overnight. Regimes could fall as quickly as they had risen. The war had demonstrated that. Totalitarian leaders were especially to be feared. If the church was to champion liberty and moral virtue, it must do so quickly.

Imminent totalitarianism was, in fact, a favorite theme of religious writers. More than any other book, Paul Hutchinson's *The New Leviathan*, published in 1946, became a clarion call to the churches to be aware of the imminent perils of totalitarianism and to renew their efforts to combat it. "Always in the past," he explained, the church was able to take "comfort in a sense of its illimitable time vistas." But now it was unthinkable to spend millenniums hoping to convince people to work out the Almighty's purposes. "We no longer have the millenniums," he cautioned; "only a few brief years." The matter was urgent: "Haste may make waste, but delay will bring desolation."[51]

The danger of hammering away at the theme of imminent peril, of course, was that religious people would be led, not to action, but to despair. Signs of church growth and, more generally, of peace and plenty helped to allay such doubts. But religious people were also exhorted to find courage through the character of their own faith. When the odds seemed insuperable, the message of faith was that goodness would ultimately prevail. A Catholic homily, for example, delivered as the new year dawned in 1946, likened the present period to the Dark Ages and to the uncertain times that the church fathers had faced during the Protestant Reformation, but argued for active, hopeful commitment. Christians, it concluded, "can be saviors of our century if with His help we dedicate ourselves to fulfilling the small or great tasks that He gives us daily to do, if we holily cultivate the little acre that He gives us for our field of endeavor in His world." If Christians did but only a little—whatever was possible for them to do—God would ensure that "the fruits of our sanctity spread far beyond our own little acre, beyond our family and friends and workshop and parish."[52] In short, the perils were great, but even small tasks could help; believers should not despair, they should contribute.

Despair might have been particularly prominent in the Jewish population, given the horrible extent of its suffering in the war. But the cautious hope that characterized Protestant and Catholic communities was also evident here. Rather than allowing the awful fear that the Holocaust might happen again to generate despair, Jewish leaders resolved that it must not—and would not—ever happen again. They resolved that the world should never forget the tragedy and put their hope in the conviction that those who remembered would not allow its repetition. The events which led up to the founding of Israel were a special source of hope. Many Jewish leaders also emerged from the war convinced that they themselves must mobilize action. The issue was no longer one of separation or assimilation but survival. A rabbi who had served during the war as an advisor on Jewish affairs in Europe wrote, for example: "Over the past decade I have been reluctantly forced to the conclusion that the survival of the Jews must depend on their own efforts, and not on the Christian world which has been either unwilling or unable to save them."[53] At a deeper level, Jews also found cause for cautious optimism in their own understanding of God. Made in the image of God, humanity could only imitate the goodness toward which divine destiny was directed. In the long run, goodness rather than evil would triumph. As another rabbi put it: "Judaism repudiates . . . pessimism. It reaffirms its faith in man as a corollary of its faith in God."[54]

Religious leaders struggled to find ways of expressing the proper mixture of pessimism and optimism, of faith and action. One who found an expression that appealed to many was Peter Marshall, serving at the time as chaplain of the U.S. Senate. Likening the proper theological view of adversity to that of the oyster, he urged religious people to consider how the oyster responded. Neither rebelling at the injustice of having to put up with the irritation of a grain of sand, nor denying its presence, nor even just stoically enduring, the oyster instead transformed adversity into a thing of beauty. So the believer, Marshall urged, should turn troubles into divine blessings. Adversity should not be blindly glossed over by religious faith, nor should faith lead to desperate hopes of eradicating adversity entirely. Rather, faith should result in action that combined adversity and one's resources into something positive.[55]

Above all, the present mixture of opportunity and impending peril pressed religious leaders to emphasize a middle course of concerted action. People should repent from evil if they could, but not let grand hopes of saving the world lead them to despair. They should contribute what they could, always rejecting hysteria and fear. A useful phrase was coined by the Board of Sponsors of the journal *Christianity and Crisis* which, in a statement endorsed in 1946, called for an attitude of "sober serenity."[56] Action in the cause of goodness was urgent, but must not be envisioned as a quick fix. Conditions had become too complicated for that. Patience must be exercised; the new war in which people of faith must engage would require constancy, diligence, sustained effort.

John Bennett characterized the current stance as a doctrine of "permanent revolution." Christians, he argued, should constantly be on the lookout for manifestations of evil and should work for reconciliation and redemption. "Man and society must be changed again and again," he counseled. "The loves and purposes of men and of the institutions of society must be continuously renewed or corrected."[57] Writing from a similar perspective, Harry Emerson Fosdick suggested conceiving of God principally in terms of "purpose"; of seeing God as one calling people to the hard job of "getting something done on earth to redeem our race from its sin and misery, calling every man to some task which, in the place where he is put, no one can do in his stead."[58]

Not only was it necessary to be active; it was imperative to be persistent in action. As the editor of the Catholic periodical *Commonweal* put it in a 1947 article: "To be constructive in a world that is so thoroughly shattered physically and morally, you have to keep everlastingly at it."[59]

No matter what the specific religious tradition, there was much in this of the proverbial Protestant ethic—the spirit of this-worldly asceticism, as Weber had called it. Religious people were divinely compelled to be actively committed to works of righteousness and these acts were to be pursued unrelentingly, with persistence and discipline. But the current spirit was more than a warmed-over version of American asceticism. It was also linked rhetorically with religious visions of a world filled with promise and peril.

These visions gave urgency to the tasks at hand. They comprised a cultural model that was also to play a continuing role in inspiring religious action in the years to come. Religious individuals and organizations would be enjoined to work actively in the world for goodness and righteousness. And they would be enjoined to do so, not simply on the basis of some vague doctrinal tradition, but in the context of discourse about opportunities and threats. This discourse would be constantly renewed and redirected in conjunction with images of good and evil in the surrounding world. With the world perpetually filled with peril, religious people needed to do what they could to save it. Their faith should keep them from despair, giving them confidence that even small tasks could contribute to larger goals. These arguments provided a basis for the religious activism that was to become increasingly important in coming decades. Variations in these arguments would also point religious activism in different directions. Some would argue for great moral crusades, confronting evil head-on; others, for quiet, sustained, individual contributions; still others, for various escapes, withdrawals, or idealistic alternatives.

The Problem of Idolatry

The religious discourse of this period, however, also contained another important dimension that was to play a considerable role in the future as well, if only by virtue of becoming increasingly difficult to sustain. This was a relatively sharp, consistent tendency toward differentiating the spiritual realm from the life of active commitment that this realm itself enjoined. Confusing the two was, although not in so many words, condemned as idolatry. Active commitment to programs and organizations was clearly a way of maintaining the religious enterprise as an institution. The religious vision motivated and guided this commitment. It protected against its own institutionalization, however, by maintaining the spiritual as a cultural category over against any of its concrete manifestations.

The phrase "over against" was in fact commonly used in religious discourse to describe the relation between spirituality and religious activities. An earlier generation of theologians had stressed the idea of God *within*—both within the individual and within the society as God's "kingdom" on earth. The postwar generation saw the kingdom less as something within (although this motif remained prominent in self-help literature) than as a vision that stood over against the society and its religious institutions. This kingdom was an ideal, not possible to realize on earth, or even to understand fully. It was described, not as a static abstraction, but as a living, moving call from the divine—a call to follow God in ways that might well not be understood and in ways that would have to be worked out among religious people with differing convictions. As ideology, it was sufficiently vague to provide room for religious organizations to develop their own programs. It could easily be subverted by practical demands or the broader culture. It was, however, a vision that, by allowing religious organizations some distance from their own past and present, gave them flexibility in planning for the future.

Having abandoned simpler notions of the kingdom of God, liberal theologians in particular tried to find ways of articulating a vision for the church without reducing that vision to concrete programs. As a result, an eschatological perspective emerged that put religious organizations squarely in the midst of a never-never land, a state of liminality, in which something new was emerging but not yet seen. H. Richard Niebuhr described it as a state of being "at the edge of the new." The "new," in one sense, was described as an accomplished divine reality that could be trusted in, rejoiced in; in another sense, though, it was just over the next horizon, still invisible, not amenable to actually being realized and certainly not expressed in any existing institutions. Associated with this view was a mood of expectancy, of having distance from established ways, and of working toward something grand and wonderful. In Niebuhr's opinion, the desired mood was a "double attitude": confidence and joy in the invisible kingdom; sorrow and repentance for the partial, incomplete, unfulfilled work of the past.[60]

Fundamentalists, in contrast, were more likely to emphasize a literal kingdom of God, established on earth after the Second Coming of Christ. On the surface, this view should have been associated mainly with futuristic expectations of a glorious world to come, with passive withdrawal from present affairs. On closer inspection, however, fundamentalist eschatology was also generally put to a different rhetorical use. Expectations of the Second Coming of Christ to the earth were associated with warnings against false hopes, such as world peace, world government, military settlements, progress in settling domestic conflicts, and so on. The discursive function accomplished by this juxtaposition was to reinforce a sharp differentiation between the spiritual realm and concrete activities. The latter were, in a sense, delegitimated, but not absolutely; they were delegitimated only to the point of being desacralized. In other words, any tendency to confuse concrete activities—even those of churches—with the spiritual itself was cautioned against.

The symbolic activities that were placed alongside the Second Coming to differentiate the spiritual from the concrete were not random selections from the fundamentalists' repertoire. They were symbols that pointedly drew the sharpest possible contrasts. Concepts that pointed outside ordinary religious experience, that seemed impractical or utopian, provided the best contrasts. A favorite symbol, for example, was the idea of a single world government. Set alongside a utopian vision such as this, the idea of a heavenly reign of Christ seemed less preposterous. It also seemed a genuinely attractive alternative. Seldom did fundamentalist discourse set the heavenly kingdom in contrast to more mundane, taken-for-granted realities, such as jobs, family life, or church programs. It did, however, paint utopian versions of these: getting rich, always being happy, finding the perfect church. The believer, therefore, was able to participate actively in the world and in the work of the church, not having these activities entirely debunked, yet conscious of the fact that these were not spiritual realms themselves.

In this respect, fundamentalist discourse and liberal discourse were much alike. Both maintained the distinction between worldly realities and religious visions; both guarded jealously against idolatry by differentiating the spiritual from the concrete. Fundamentalist theology perhaps drew the distinction more sharply, but both placed religious hope in a category just beyond reach of anything yet attained.

These distinctions were most evident in theological contexts, but they also informed discourse on topics of more popular interest. One of these, of course, was communism. Described in religious discourse as an atheistic force bent on destroying America and its churches, communism was naturally the subject of much discussion. It is noteworthy, however, that religious discourse often paid little attention to atheism as such, or else dealt with it in terms other than simply the denial of God. Communism was often described as a partial view of humanity and, for this reason, a false hope. It was evil in that it was idolatrous. By addressing spiritual cravings with economic proposals, communism confounded the spiritual and the concrete. To the religious mind, totalitarianism was perhaps the most vivid evil in communism. It represented a collapse of the essential biblical distinction between ultimacy and the mundane, between creator and created; it identified ultimate authority with the state, a concrete social institution. As a worldview, it was inherently self-limiting because it denied the creative, prophetic tension in the biblical tradition between the transcendent and the immediate.

A similar critique was sometimes extended to the more individualistic outlook of American society. The problem addressed was not so much that of paying too much heed to individual rights or to individual freedom. Most often, the problem was identified as secularism and focused on the individual's quest for material pleasure. Here, the problem was that of confusing ultimate good with tangible products. The result, again, was regarded as self-defeating: sooner or later, people would realize that satisfaction was not ultimately obtainable from material sources. They would see that fulfillment depended on larger truths, on the creator, rather than possessions or pleasures.

This distinction was more difficult to sustain in the realm of religious activity itself than in discussions of communism or materialism. Religious activities were easier to confuse with the concept of a spiritual kingdom. As long as this distinction was part of the religious vision, however, it provided a self-corrective orientation for institutionalized religion. It pointed toward a reality beyond culture, placing religious people in an uneasy relation with their environment.

The ambiguity of this relation was often expressed in the traditional language of a "pilgrim community." H. Richard Niebuhr, for example, wrote that American religion was "a pilgrim community which makes strangely enduring settlements." It was, indeed, an "enduring settlement" in the scope of its organizational activities and resources, but it was also, in Niebuhr's words, comprised of members who "seek a Zion which cannot be located in any part of earth."[61] Much the same idea was expressed by John Mackay in describing the church as "a pilgrim life upon the road of God's unfolding purpose, keeping close to the rugged boundaries of His ever-expanding Kingdom." As a pilgrim community, the church was in essence more than its institutional manifestations; it was, in Mackay's words, "called to a frontier life," a people with only loose attachments to their institutional heritage, "ready to trek into the unknown."[62] The pilgrim community appealed to a higher authority than that of the government under which it lived, its strength came from powerful organizations firmly rooted in cultural tradition, and yet its allegiance was pledged not to these organizations but to an invisible ruler; its vision was conditioned by institutional limitations and cultural assumptions, but this ideal also called it to engage in impractical tasks and to hold out hope for its own redemption even when these tasks failed.

THE VISION that oriented American religion to its future, then, was a view of the world which rested on several precariously balanced discursive emphases. It held forth an optimistic view of the postwar period as a time of new beginnings filled with opportunities for religious organizations to exploit, yet it balanced this optimism with a sense of foreboding that precluded overconfidence and generated caution. It was a vision in which sufficient hope was offered to motivate engagement in the affairs of society, rather than allowing the uncertainties of life to promote passive withdrawal or fanatical shortcuts. Nevertheless, it drew a sharp distinction between the concrete activities in which religious people might engage and the spiritual conceptions which underlay those activities. Even the capacity to envision a program for the future was contingent on an effective differentiation between the institutional heritage of American religion and the rhetorical images with which its leaders mobilized commitment. These were all fracture lines that could become bases of serious cultural cleavage in the turbulent decades that lay ahead.

CHAPTER 4

Conscience and Conviction in Public Life

THE SPECIFIC directions into which religious efforts were channeled were conditioned by cultural conceptions of what it meant to be religious, of the character of religious communities, and of their role in shaping the larger society. These were the visions, the values, and the conceived programs that formed the basis of much of the public discourse about religion. Different religious organizations articulated competing visions, and their visions reflected an awareness of this competition, but there were also widely shared cultural suppositions. They by no means formed a consistent or coherent outlook and to think that they did would be missing the point. These conceptions—these modes of engaging in discourse about the mission and character of religion—were fraught with internal ambiguities, tensions, competing rhetorical scripts that were not wholly reconciled with one another. Some of these were to become important in later years, especially as events in American society put strain on inherent tension points, causing them to shift in one direction or another. Some conceptions were to shift only marginally in emphasis, but these shifts would alter the qualities of religious action. For the time being, they supplied the cultural molds into which religious energies were poured.

A Fellowship of Individuals

A vision that was common to all the major faiths conceived of religion as a fundamentally social or collective endeavor. Religious organizations' programs required the cooperation of their members. And these programs were concerned not only with individual lives but with helping and sharing, worshipping together, maintaining an ongoing organization, and larger kinds of public witness and social renewal. Religious communities were, in a clear sense, moral communities—communities of moral obligation, defined by shared expectations, and sustained by social interaction. Locally, the congregation manifested these characteristics very clearly, both in the informal relations that bound members to one another and in the more formal aspects of their existence as legal and denominational entities with budgets, bylaws, and governing committees. Beyond the local level, denominations and their constituent parts—assemblies, synods, dioceses—gave religion its collective character.

In a deeper sense, the character of the religious vision itself was generally thought to require moral interaction. The vision of faith was only partially discoverable by individuals; it required the support and inspiration of a community of believers. Religious practice was prototypically conceived in Western, Judeo-Christian terms as a commitment to a public body, not a life of mystical isolation. H. Richard Niebuhr, for example, drew out the essentially communal nature of American Christianity in these terms:

> The mystic vision is the sight of . . . the individual in his solitariness. It is a vision men have one by one and if it results in theology it can only issue in the sort of theology which undertakes to direct men to the measures they must take in order that they may have the private vision or which tries to describe how the miracle of vision takes place. When we see in companionship with others and communicate with each other that which we see, and correct each other's understanding or interpretation of the seen, and supply one another with patterns by means of which to apprehend the self-presented object, we cannot speak of mystical vision.[1]

In Niebuhr's view the contrast to a mystical vision was one in which religious people depended on companionship for interpretation, verification, and inspiration. Religious organizations were supposed to function as organisms in which the different members played out divine roles for the benefit of the entire body. This was the theoretical ideal and it was sufficiently institutionalized in the heritage of American religion to make organizational questions critical to any subsequent restructuring. Yet, in reality, this ideal had also been shaped, balanced, by another conception of the religious life.

Descriptions of the religious body often paid little or no attention to such vital aspects of its functioning as fellowship, mutual caring and sharing, the collective enactment of religious rituals, or the cultivation of moral obligations through actual experiences of bonding and reconciliation. In place of these, emphasis was placed primarily on the spiritual growth of individuals. The corporate body became subtly transposed into a service agency for the fulfillment of its individual members. This tendency was, of course, limited by the informal activities that actually cultivated communal ties among members, and it was less pronounced in Catholicism and Judaism than in Protestantism. It was, however, rooted in relatively well-established religious traditions. One was the tradition of preaching, in which churches served primarily as pulpits for the dissemination of ideas to an audience of otherwise unconnected individuals. A second was the emphasis on evangelism, which focused the church's activities on disseminating biblical truths to individuals outside of church rolls. A third was the view that once people were evangelized the main role of the church was to "make disciples," usually by exposing them to good preaching and involving them in Bible reading, study, and prayer. In one pastoral theologian's words: "As soon as one confesses Jesus Christ, he should be built up in Christ, so that he may attain unto the fullness of the stature of Jesus Christ, and then, in turn, go out as a missionary in the evangelization of the world."[2] Or as Carl Henry proclaimed, the church's primary task was "the preaching of the Gospel, in the interest of individual regeneration by the supernatural grace of God, in such a way that divine redemption can be recognized as the best solution of our problems, individual and social."[3] The strong emphasis on individuals and the use of personal pronouns in this kind of discourse, as well as the near absence of collective referents, reinforced the individualistic focus.

The ideal of fellowship, and related values such as love and sacrificial caring, did not drop entirely from view, but these values became difficult concepts with which to struggle. Fellowship, perhaps much more so then than now, was seldom imbued with strong positive content. It tended to be defined in the breach as an absence of selfishness. It was dependent, moreover, on individual initiative and the individual's commitment to God. How to empower the individual to be morally committed was more the issue than how to construct moral community itself. One scholar, for example, concluded a rather tortuous discussion of fellowship by remarking: "What the world today needs is Christian individuals with real depth and power. Such individuals will become the centers of this creative and redeeming fellowship wherever they are."[4] What the fellowship was like, what it would do, what would hold it together were matters left unaddressed. Fellowship was seen mainly as a byproduct of individual devotion. And its role was also mainly derivative of individual needs: to guard individuals' freedom and to imbue them with inner conviction.

One of the appeals that seemed to strike an especially resonant chord in these years was that religion champion the needs of the individual as opposed to the rising specter of vast impersonal institutions. This theme was often stressed in contrasting religion with totalitarianism. It was also evident in the manner in which evil was characterized. Not content to portray impersonality in merely abstract terms, preachers spoke of "the dead weight of ceremonialism," the "dry rot" of large institutions (including some churches), and "cold formalism and indifference." There was, they argued, a tendency out there to focus on society rather than the individual. In contrast, the message of faith focused, as one preacher put it, on "an awakened sense of the infinite worth of the individual."

> The great thing Jesus did for us was to set forth the worth of the individual, the priceless gift of personality. He worked upon the principle that society derives its life from the individuals who compose it. The individual man remains forever separate. He is incapable of fusion.[5]

Against cold intellectualism, popular sermons advocated a religion capable of expressing deep inner emotions; against an outmoded social gospel, a message of personal redemption; against ineffective concern for social ills, the need to care for individual souls.

The emphasis on individual piety was consistent with broader individualistic orientations in American culture, as religious leaders themselves were quick to point out. It was also evident to many that faith was both individual and collective, and that the precarious balance between these two emphases was one of the tipping points which led different organizations to take different paths. Less obvious at the time was the fact that religious individualism was a mode of cultural adaptation that would greatly influence the character of American religion in the coming decades. Had religious organizations been tightly organized moral communities with intensive internal ties, the effects of broader changes in their environment would likely have become manifest in distinct ways: in elevating whole organizations to greater prominence, reducing others to less significance, or creating internal divisions resulting in schisms and the creation of new organizations. All of these were to come about, reflecting the fact that religion was to a degree communally organized. A more common result of broader social changes, however, would be the indirect ways in which changes in individuals would affect religious organizations. Changes in resources, social positions, and outlooks were mediated by individuals. Religious organizations became restructured less by direct threats or opportunities at the organizational level than by the shifting sands of individual loyalties.

A Culture of Values

Whether collective or individualistic, religion's role in the broader society was also shaped by popular conceptions of culture. These mainly tended to portray culture as a set of values. In one author's words, culture could be conceived of as "that total composite of values which predominantly influence what individuals strive for in living."[6] Culture focused on the ends toward which people oriented their behavior. It guided behavior, was internalized, and reflected the character of a people. Anthropologists Clyde and Florence Kluckhohn, for example, described American culture primarily in terms of its "values," "value orientations," and "life goals," suggesting that the distinctive features of American culture could be summarized in terms such as morality, reason, pleasure, generosity, and striving for success.[7]

This view of culture was also evident in sociological discussions. Sociologists tended to conceive of values as sources of social cohesion and stability. Especially in theories that stressed the functional requisites of social behavior, values were identified as sources of societal integration and ultimately of societal survival. In his widely read *Human Society*, for example, Kingsley Davis wrote of "common-ultimate ends" as the key to societal integration. "Such ends," he argued, "stand at the top of the hierarchy of ends and hence control and regulate the rest."[8] These were, in his view, values that generally gained ultimacy and became objects of faith. Another widely read treatise which articulated a similar perspective was *American Society*, by Robin M. Williams, Jr. Social institutions, in Williams's view, were inherently dependent on values, the essence of which was strong internalized commitment by individuals. For values to be effective, he wrote, they needed to be "invested with affect and meaning."[9] Theorist Talcott Parsons had also elaborated this idea. Social action was, in his view, oriented toward the attainment of objectives. These ends were specified by cultural values and provided the basis for selecting particular courses of action. Proximate, tangible values were, in turn, organized by ultimate values that imposed a uniform society-wide rank ordering among values.[10]

If values were the cornerstone of culture, they were also thought to be the pivotal connection between personal faith and the larger society. The reasoning went somewhat as follows: the good society depends on individuals acting responsibly to uphold moral and democratic values; but a sense of personal responsibility is best supported by conceptions of individual accountability to the sacred; and this sense of accountability requires acknowledging the higher authority of the divine, guilt and punishment whenever responsibility to the divine is not maintained, and the possibility of divine forgiveness, redemption, and even ennoblement. A pastoral letter of the National Catholic Welfare Conference in 1947 clearly articulated the main components of this argument:

> Without a deep-felt conviction of what sin is, human law and human conventions can never lead man to virtue. If in the privacy of his personal life the individual does not acknowledge accountability to God for his thought and his action, he lacks the only foundation for stable moral values. . . . The moral regeneration which is recognized

> as absolutely necessary for the building of a better world must begin by bringing the individual back to God and to an awareness of his responsibility to God.[11]

An alternative formulation of the argument held that, as Parsons and others suggested, social cohesion was contingent on a clear hierarchy of values. Religion provided the capstone of this hierarchy, putting into perspective all lower-order values. An influential treatise of the period suggested that this function was clearly evident in individual lives. Religion, it suggested, enabled the individual "to form a true hierarchy of values" which, once in place, would assist the individual in selecting lesser values and would clothe the higher values with sufficient authority that they would be observed even at great personal cost. For the larger society, then, religion undergirded the law by legitimating the hierarchy of values on which law was based, by providing "effective sanctions for the observance of law and the fulfillment of duty," and by promoting cohesion through the teaching "that we are all the children of God and therefore are all brothers."[12]

Public figures who spoke about the role of religion in culture were likely, in one way or another, to portray religious faith as an essential ingredient of American civilization. For example, writing just before America's entry into World War II, the student of cultural change Lewis Mumford had likened the relation between religion and society to that between Greenwich time and local time: religion provided an absolute standard against which to measure social policies and correct the course of state.[13] Philadelphia's Bishop Hugh Lamb, addressing the National Catholic Educational Association shortly after the war, put it in these words: "Democracy without God is an empty word and morality without religion is an idle dream."[14] Pittsburgh's colorful Presbyterian preacher, Clarence E. Macartney, stated the same idea more bluntly: "The nations that forget God shall be cast into hell."[15]

From this perspective, what religious organizations did best—preaching and teaching—clearly had relevance for the larger culture. Religion's impact on cultural values was the mainstay of good morals, democracy, and social order. Some critics pointed out that scant evidence was available to prove this contention. Sociologist Louis Wirth, for example, cautioned an audience of religious leaders that: "Despite the firm and widespread belief in their efficacy to affect knowledge, belief, and conduct, we have but little reliable evidence concerning the actual effect of teaching and preaching upon attitudes and character."[16] During the war, however, the public had often been told that the strength of a nation lay in the moral character of its people. Democracy was not to be thought of simply as a cultural ideal, but also as an effective instrument of government, though only insofar as individuals committed themselves energetically to its defense. So it was with religion and values. Without the energizing effects of spiritual commitment, American values would be little more than hollow ideals. The recent war experience was sufficient testimony to the need for religious values. For, as Jesuit scholar John Courtney Murray pointed out, "when religious principles cease to govern society, society loses its moral purpose, nations pursue solely material aims, and the result is war."[17]

The traditional emphasis on revivalism in American religion was a prominent feature in these discussions. Religious values could grow stale and ineffective. "We must understand," a missions director explained, "that a formal religion kept alive by the power of tradition . . . will not suffice to save a nation from destruction."[18] Values had to be animated by moral commitment, by the kind of commitment that only genuine spiritual conviction could supply. Religion, therefore, needed continuously to be revitalized.

The pathway to a strong society had to begin with a personal revival. Only through an inward renewal could ossification in cultural values be avoided. This view was especially prominent in conservative circles in which evangelism and conversion were emphasized. As a Christian layman, writing in the popular fundamentalist magazine *Moody Monthly*, explained: "Real progress begins not with the outward, but with the inward. Only when the soul is regenerated can there be lasting and effective outward changes."[19] It was a view, however, that was widely shared in more liberal circles as well. "A revival of religion," counseled Bishop Bromley Oxnam, for instance, "in which the regenerating power of God's love and forgiveness, righteousness and justice, is let loose on the world, and by which the individual heart is changed . . . is the most certain way to . . . preserve freedom."[20] If values were the key to a healthy society, and if personal renewal were the key to healthy values, then there was really no conflict between an emphasis on individual faith and a concern for the common good.

Revival was also the key to power. Especially in the postwar setting, confronted with challenges that to many seemed greater than any America had ever faced, the values on which the American system rested needed to be given an extra boost by religious revival. Shallow humanist idealism was not enough. The world needed spiritual power. Through revival, the old would be stripped away, false hopes would be unmasked, and divine power would rise almost automatically. It would be a refiner's fire that would cleanse the culture of pretensions, humble it, so that strength could come again. Revival, W. A. Criswell intoned, "says to the people nothing of power such as they have learned to love, or ease or success." Only by telling people that they are dead, by causing them to be "bowed down before God in conscious dejection of unworthiness," could true power be born.[21]

Implicit in arguments like those of Criswell was a feeling that the churches needed to be doing more than they had to reinvigorate the culture. Fundamentalists accused liberals of not doing enough and liberals accused fundamentalists. Both, however, reflected the underlying view that religion could be an effective force in shaping values. Protestants' views of Catholics, and Catholics' views of Protestants, also reflected this underlying conviction. In accusing Catholics of attempting to manipulate the culture through government and bureaucracy, Protestants were affirming the view that religion's proper role in the public sphere was that of influencing individual values. Catholics, in turn, argued that their system of worship and education was effective precisely on the same grounds, i.e., that moral values were being strengthened through preaching and teaching.

Common to all sides was also the conviction that religious values were universally valid. Rather than being a relativized set of symbols, or simply the point of view of an embattled remnant, religious values were confidently described as universal principles, applicable to the entire society. The truths expressed in biblical values were thought to be part of the unity of all truth, part of a system that was compatible at heart with physics, with poetry, even with secular philosophy. It was simply inconceivable, given this view, that religious truths would not be regarded as applicable to the entire culture. They would ultimately prevail. Religious people, therefore, could advance their values in the confidence that they were not having to oppose an alien culture but that the truth underlying culture itself was on their side.

Subsequent cultural developments would do much to undermine these confident assumptions. Culture would come increasingly to be portrayed as a relativistic product of its particular social environment. The unity of different types of truth would be questioned on grounds of the social construction of knowledge. Conflicts between secular versions of knowledge and religious ideals would become more prominent. And the relevance of ultimate truth itself to the functioning of society would come increasingly into doubt. But for the time being, it was reassuring to think that religious values were simply a reflection of general truths recognizable by religious and nonreligious people alike.

Points of Ambiguity

There were, however, even in the major conceptions of religion and culture that pervaded intellectual discussions immediately after the war, points of ambiguity that would become increasingly problematic in future years. One of the most serious focused on the relation between values and behavior. On the one hand, values were supposed to guide behavior, channeling it in certain directions thought to be instrumental to the attainment of particular goals. In short, behavior was supposed to reflect values. On the other hand, values were supposed to be deeper, subjective, more general, more durable over the long run than behavior, while behavior could be superficial, engaged in without reflection, and situationally variable. In short, behavior might not reflect values very closely. Those who thought about values and behavior were already becoming caught up in these problems. If behavior merely reflected values, then what were values? Or if behavior did not reflect values, what did it reflect?

The problem could be resolved in two ways. One was to focus on internal states presumed to underlie behavior, rather than behavior itself. Since a single act could be engaged in for a variety of reasons, what counted must be not the act itself but an underlying state—the motives or internalized values from which the act resulted. The other mode of resolution focused more on behavior, arguing that values could be held but not acted upon, so the true measure of conviction was whether or not a value resulted in actual behavior. The former emphasized proper motivation as the basis of a good society; the latter, good behavior, even if it stemmed from any number of different motivations. While the former implicitly assumed the reality of an absolute hierarchy of values, as well as a sharp distinction between good values and bad values, the latter was more relativistic. As yet, the two alternatives were not clearly articulated. The connection between behavior and values, while tenuous, was sufficiently taken for granted that neither alternative was genuinely necessary to solve the problem. In later years, however, as the connection between values and behavior became less readily taken for granted, both alternatives would take on greater importance. The differences between the two, moreover, would become more pronounced, as religious conservatives sided increasingly with the former, while religious liberals came increasingly to favor the latter.

Another problem inherent in the connection drawn between religion and morality and morality and values revolved around the question of freedom. For it to be assumed that behavior would manifest values, freedom of choice had to be assumed. And indeed it was. Perceptions of religion's role in strengthening culture were rooted uniformly in assumptions about the distinctiveness of democracy in upholding personal freedom. The exercise of values presupposed democratic guarantees of freedom and, in turn, values were assumed to strengthen freedom in the process of being exercised. Totalitarianism was the ultimate threat since even high values could not operate freely under a system of constraint.

The Judeo-Christian tradition, however, had never placed complete emphasis on individual freedom. Always there was constraint. The balance between constraint and freedom again figured importantly in conceptions of values and behavior. On the one hand, constraint could be understood as a product of evil forces in the world, forces limiting people with good values from always doing what was right. On the other hand, constraint could be conceptualized as social arrangements, vested interests, power distributions, and so forth. In the former, emphasis naturally came to be placed more on the values that good people held internally; in the latter, on the actions taken by good people to roll back the social conditions inhibiting free individuals. These again would in future years become matters of relative emphasis in conservatives' and liberals' approaches to religion.

Yet another tension point in the current conception of values concerned the relative roles of external and internal sanctions. Values were conceived of in social terms, on the one hand, functioning for the preservation of the society; on the other hand, they were thought to require internalization to be effective and were considered important chiefly as guides for individual behavior. In the former view, values were expected to result in institutionalized sanctions; in the latter, in internalized commitments wrought through effective socialization techniques. Always the two had to be seen in relation to one another. If socialization worked effectively, sanctions were not as important. But without sanctions, socialization was not likely to be effective.

In the immediate postwar period religious discourse (as will be seen shortly) widely assumed that socialization was the most effective means of reinforcing values. Religious organizations had a heavy investment in socialization programs and focused doctrinally on arguments about evil and salvation that emphasized internal sanctions more than external constraints. They did not, with few exceptions, have the resources to impose external sanctions on the entire society through laws or government. Already, though, doubts were beginning to be voiced about the effectiveness of socialization alone. The society was becoming more complex, education was changing rapidly, the forces governing behavior were somehow becoming more powerful even as they became less understood. Over time, this would also be a problem to which conservatives and liberals would respond differently.

Religion had become a differentiated institution—"a repository of values inherently of the highest good," in Robin Williams's words—but also an institution with distinct limitations. It could conceivably exercise an important influence for good in the society as long as culture was thought of as a set of values which influenced behavior. Once that definition of culture began to be questioned, the social role of American religion would also fall into doubt. As yet, however, the extent of this questioning was minor. Religious organizations pursued their role in the public sphere energetically and confidently.

Ministries and Programs

The various faiths naturally sponsored a wide range of programs and activities, but these programs also spoke volumes about the place that religion had come to occupy in the wider society and gave hints of some of the changes that were to come. Along with building programs and membership drives, religious bodies were rapidly expanding into a whole range of new activities. One writer has characterized the time as "singularly one of contrived appeals, of catch phrases, of canvasses, quotas, and pledges."[22] It was also a time when congregations tried to encourage greater interaction among their members by providing more activities devoted to special interests. Looking back over the past decade from the vantage of the mid-1950s, the historian Oscar Handlin was to observe that the churches' "most powerful magnet was the round of practices and the social connections capable of giving order to life in American society." It was a place, Handlin observed, "where children came to learn who they were, where the right boys met the right girls, where men and women in their groups found satisfying diversion."[23] From the traditional one-room meeting house where a lonely parson offered fiery sermons on Sunday mornings, the modern religious organization had become a holding company for activities and programs for "men and women of all ages," as some advertisements in fact stated.

Changes in definitions of the pastor's role had made it easier for congregations to offer this expanded array of programs. Fewer and fewer churches continued to offer the once universal Sunday evening service, at least partly because of the growing popularity of radio, thereby greatly reducing the amount of time a pastor had to spend preparing sermons. The practice of regular pastoral calls to the homes of parish members also gradually receded, giving pastors more time to organize activities intended to bring parishioners to the church itself or to engage in more specialized ministries. Outreach programs, formerly the work almost entirely of the pastor, increasingly took the form of lay-orchestrated, door-to-door canvassing. Studies of churches also revealed a growing tendency for regular weekly business hours to be kept by church offices, a development, of course, that depended greatly on the availability of better finances for paying clergy full-time salaries and in larger churches for hiring secretarial assistance.[24]

The churches' larger role in the society was, however, conceived of primarily as influencing the society by influencing individuals. The best way for the church to make the world a better place, wrote John Bennett, was "through the work of its members in their various vocations and as citizens."[25] Another spokesman asked rhetorically: "Should we establish a lobby in Washington and put on pressure for certain kinds of political action which would, in some measure, seem to arrest the downward trend of the morals of our people?" His answer: "I am absolutely persuaded that there is something far deeper, something far better that must be done first." It would be better, he argued, for Christians to cultivate lives of personal piety, to pray, and to support the work of missionaries and evangelists attempting to spread the word of God.[26] Surveying thousands of Protestant churches just prior to the war, H. Paul Douglass had found little evidence of any kind of direct social action or political involvement. The churches saw their main mission, he wrote, as one of "interpreting and teaching Christian social relationships."[27]

There were some signs of growing involvement in direct social ministries. The anthropologist W. Lloyd Warner, studying churches in the Midwest in the late 1940s, for example, found local congregations and their ministers involved in a full round of community activities that extended into areas of moral advocacy on issues such as theater attendance, local drinking establishments, and subjects taught in local schools. In Connecticut a group of local religious leaders, including prominent names such as Liston Pope and Kenneth Underwood, organized a Citizens Political Action Committee to bring pressure on local officials. At the denominational level, interest was also evident in various social issues. In 1946, for example, the Southern Presbyterian General Assembly reorganized its Committee on Social and Moral Welfare, upgraded its budget from a mere $300 annually to more than $20,000, supplied it with a full-time staff member, and charged it with preparing educational materials on social matters. A year later the Southern Baptist Convention followed suit, increasing its Social Service Commission appropriation from $1,800 to $10,000.[28] Churches were also instrumental in organizing the Christian Rural Overseas Program (CROP) in 1947, enlisting the participation of more than 75,000 local churches in purchasing and distributing more than 75 million pounds of farm commodities valued at some $6.5 million. For the most part, however, the involvement of churches in social activities of this kind was limited to issues of morality at the local level and definitely placed political action second to social influences of a more indirect kind. As Warner noted in his research, the prevalent notion to which lip service was given was that "for the church to lobby for political measures weakens its spiritual position."[29]

Influencing the Public Sphere

The dominant conception of religious organizations' role in the public sphere reflected their emphasis on influencing cultural values. The main role of the church was, in the words of a Lutheran pastor, "to declare moral and spiritual principles" and "to inspire and instruct individual Christians to apply Christian principles in all their relationships."[30] This, of course, was a role that could be fulfilled primarily through preaching to and teaching local congregations. But even when larger religious bodies issued public statements on social issues, they tended to focus on principles more than anything else. A statement released in 1946 over the signature of 122 Catholics, Protestants, and Jews, and endorsed by the Social Action Department of the National Catholic Welfare Conference, the Federal Council of Churches, and the Synagogue Council of America, was titled "Basic Principles of Economic Justice." Its title was indicative of its content. Although the resolution contained some general guidelines for the labor movement and the state, its focus was primarily on ethical values—values such as human service and social justice.

Religious leaders widely assumed that influencing society primarily through individuals rather than some form of direct action made sense because it was effective. "It is a commonplace," said one, "that religious opinion is carefully weighed in many legislative bodies."[31] Other statements by religious leaders sometimes described government as alien, even hostile, toward religion. But the prevailing opinion among religious leaders was that government's role toward religion was at least benign. The fact that public officials took oaths before God, that prayers were routinely offered in public gatherings, and that military chaplains had played a visible role in the recent war all attested to a mutually accommodative role between religion and the state.

Public officials also reinforced the belief that religion not only should influence society by shaping individual consciences but also that this influence was effective. Speaking in 1946 at a meeting of the Federal Council of Churches in Columbus, Ohio, President Truman averred that "no problem on this earth" was tough enough to withstand "the flame of a genuine renewal of religious faith." Without a religious revival, he insisted, "we are lost."[32] In the same year, Senator Wayne Morse, addressing his fellow congressmen on labor legislation, appealed to the principles of the Lord's Prayer as the guide that should inform such decisions. In Minnesota a young mayor named Hubert Humphrey was being acclaimed by local clergy for his involvement in church work and his interest in moral values. Another outspoken advocate of religion as an influence on public morality was Dwight Eisenhower. Perhaps more than any other leader, Eisenhower repeatedly assured Americans of the relevance of religion to public life. First as a public speaker and then as a candidate for president, Eisenhower reminded audiences that the strength of a nation lay in the spiritual realm. Religion, he said in a 1946 address, "nurtures men of faith [who are] needed in the building of a new world reflecting the glory of God." The concept of freedom, he reminded listeners, was of Judeo-Christian origin. In his rhetoric, America was "God's footstool" and had been guarded by people who had "faith in a Provident God." Religion was the link to the nation's highest values—freedom, spiritual greatness, justice, unity; indeed, religion was the basis of the American Way. "Without God there could be no American form of government, nor an American way of life. Recognition of the Supreme Being is the first—and most basic—expression of Americanism."[33] To some, Eisenhower not only advocated, but embodied the spiritual in public life. As correspondent Eric Sevareid once remarked, Eisenhower believed that a great society was always "a matter of faith" and himself embodied this view as "a faithful believer who spoke of belief and faith."[34]

It was the conviction that public life could be influenced chiefly by the religiously informed consciences of individuals that in part accounts for the churches' tremendous interest in these years in membership drives. Not forgotten was the belief that religion was invalid without spiritual renewal, but membership alone had symbolic value in the public sphere. More than 700,000 members had been added to its rolls, the Methodist church proudly announced. "We will set aside $2 million next year for evangelism," answered the Episcopal church. In community after community "visitation evangelism" campaigns were launched to find the unchurched and add their names to membership rolls. In addition, the public rallies, Easter services, and religious gatherings that major and minor denominations alike sponsored—and widely publicized—let it be known that religion was a cultural force.

Some of this public display was prompted by religious divisions, especially between Protestants and Catholics. Protestants realized, not merely as an afterthought, that the massive numbers they were turning out annually for "Reformation Day" services might be an effective way of showing off their political muscles. As one prominent churchman asserted: "Some of our legislators, who hasten to do the bidding of the Roman church because of their fear of reprisal at the polls, are reminded of the fact that there are considerable numbers of Protestants who can vote too."[35] Protestants also exploited anti-Catholic fears to defend their own view of the proper manner of influencing the public sphere. No formal support of religious organizations should be allowed, they said, but fair play involving above board statements of individual conscience was perfectly acceptable. And Catholics echoed agreement. "The Church," proclaimed an editorial in *America* "is in politics as man's conscience is in them."[36]

The Role of Education

Whatever the internal divisions, the most tangible result of this conception of religion in America was an overwhelming emphasis on religious education. Leaders of all the major faiths expressed concern about the need to better educate the society in spiritual and moral values. Secular leaders, from President Truman to the presidents of many of the major colleges and universities, readily endorsed these concerns. In many communities, teachers and boards of education still practiced daily prayers and Bible reading as part of classroom rituals. In a growing number of communities released time programs were tried, often involving cooperation between Christians and Jews, as ways of giving children religious instruction. Protestants stressed the need for better programs of moral values in the public schools and called for more serious attention to religion in their own colleges and in secular universities. Jews focused especially on major expansion efforts in higher education: Yeshiva University, the Jewish Institute of Religion, the Jewish Theological Seminary, and Hebrew Union College all undertook major new programs. And Catholics made plans for an expansion in their church's parochial school system estimated at a cost of $250 million over a five-year period.

In part, the thrust toward education was initiated in response to projected demographic increases and to keep up with the growing role of education in the culture at large. Now that the atomic age had arrived, science and higher education would become increasingly valued commodities. If religion did not expand its efforts in the educational sphere, the culture would soon become entirely secular. Casual surveys by some of the larger denominations revealed that students on secular campuses were already virtually illiterate as far as biblical knowledge was concerned. At denominational colleges, the level of biblical knowledge was generally much higher, but the need for new housing, new equipment, and better faculty was more urgent.

In addition to the more general emphasis on education, religious leaders found it an area for major efforts for a reason more intrinsic to their own theological perspectives. Increasingly prominent in these years was the idea that the method by which one arrived at religious convictions was perhaps as important as the convictions themselves. Two strands of thought that often came from quite different quarters were reflected in this idea. One was that religious belief could easily be little more than lip service to a doctrine or creed unless the believer had truly arrived at his or her belief by systematic study and reflection. Often this thought was articulated most forcefully in conservative quarters. It was conditioned by the sense that believers needed to be more fully equipped than in the past to resist the challenges of secularism. They could do so, it was assumed, by carefully following a prescribed method of Bible study, memorization, cross-referencing, and prayerful meditation. The other strand of thinking was more likely to be articulated by liberal leaders whose ideas were increasingly conditioned by the growing diversity of religious views. Having themselves been unable to find an authoritative basis for espousing a particular biblical interpretation, they relied increasingly on the argument that the important thing was less what one believed than how one had arrived at these beliefs. A Baptist minister recounted a discussion among five of his fellow pastors in a hotel room in Michigan during his denomination's annual convention. The discussion had revealed a rather unsettling variety of theological opinions among the ministers present. Its result, the minister reporting claimed, was that each of the pastors came away convinced that unanimity was impossible but was, in any case, less important than method. Speaking as a defender of liberal views, he asserted: "The test . . . is not what he believes, but how he has arrived at his beliefs." Someone who has carefully studied and reflected on his beliefs, the pastor argued, stands best in the Christian tradition.[37]

This clergyman, like others of his generation, was subtly shifting the mode of religious authority from doctrinal validation to procedural validation. Sincere believers might be expected to differ in their beliefs, but those who disagreed could still respect one another as believers if they had gone through a sufficient period of searching, study, and carefully weighing the available evidence. For the churches, this emphasis of course coincided well with the growing interest in educational programs. Across the country efforts were being devoted to staffing better Sunday school programs, to getting people to read and study their Bibles, and to training pastors better in seminary to be effective teachers and Bible study leaders.

Perhaps most importantly, religious education was motivated by the desire to inculcate moral values. Individuals were the active, effective agents capable of furthering the cause of good or contributing to the stock of evil in the world. In their unregenerate condition, without proper religious instruction, individuals tended naturally toward evil. The result was social chaos and intellectual confusion. The goal of religious instruction was to halt this corrosive tendency; it was to link individuals with divine power capable of overcoming evil. The regenerate person, having received proper religious instruction, was expected to exhibit moral character and contribute to the moral quality of the culture. "The good society," said one writer, "grows from the good in men."[38]

As in the case of the more general conception of culture, there were, however, signs of change in this view of the role of religious education. Particularly in the larger denominations, those who sought to articulate programs for moral betterment were beginning to speak of the malaise in morality as if it were somehow lodged in the culture at large rather than in individuals. The power to wage war with atomic weapons and the accompanying fear and uncertainty about using that power seemed to evoke images of moral problems larger than the individual. An inability to find inner peace at the individual level, on the other hand, was often associated with the growth of technology and its tendency to lure people into reliance on material possessions. Sensuality, especially the hedonistic pursuit of sex, remained a favorite theme, but the problem was now beginning to be seen as attributable to the advertising industry or the movies or television. In area after area it was as if the war had shaken religious leaders from their previous ways of thinking and forced on them a larger consciousness of the world which left them in awe of the forces shaping modern culture. Their call to repentance remained clear, but increasingly it seemed to echo from the stratosphere rather than focusing on individual hearts.

As yet, this was only a tendency. It was beginning to be evident in diagnoses of moral problems facing American culture and it was perhaps implicit in the growing emphasis that seemed to be placed on large programs—even if these were large membership drives and large revival meetings rather than large social programs. Faced with a world of new perils and unimagined promise for the future, bigger programs somehow seemed essential if anything was to be accomplished. In the meantime, cultural constructions emphasizing values and individual spirituality remained strong. They were constructions fraught with as yet nearly invisible fissures that would begin to open up under the strains of realignment that were to develop in subsequent decades. Education was an issue of major interest to most religious bodies and would become one of the areas in which the effects of larger social processes would be felt most severely. As religious organizations invested their rich inherited resources in the future, it was one of the programs that would most inform their vision of the world to come. Theirs was also a vision shaped greatly by the different religious traditions' conceptions of one another. American religion remained an institution deeply divided along denominational lines. And these divisions would be among the institutional patterns most strongly to register the effects of the social developments that were only just beginning to take place.

CHAPTER 5

The Declining Significance of Denominationalism

REFLECTING on the character of American religion in the 1950s, Will Herberg articulated a thesis that summed up why Americans could be so secular and yet take such an interest in religion. In a word, Herberg argued that religion gave Americans a sense of identity. People identified themselves, not simply as Americans, but as Protestants, Catholics, or Jews. These three communities, in turn, imposed cultural divisions on American religion, giving it what Herberg called a "tripartite" character. Much of the tension in American religion, along with the more ordinary activities of religious organizations, he felt, flowed along the lines of this threefold division.[1]

Students of American religion were quick to agree with Herberg's analysis. Before long, empirical studies began to confirm his sense of major cultural identities revolving around the distinctions that separated Protestants, Catholics, and Jews. Gerhard Lenski's influential book, *The Religious Factor*, based on a 1958 survey of metropolitan Detroit, for example, revealed wide differences in the religious practices, social positions, and attitudes of these three groups. Not only were the three divided by differences in ethnic background, tradition, and socioeconomic standing; they were also separated from one another by suspicion, prejudice, and a lack of social contact. So severe were these divisions, in fact, that Lenski concluded the study by offering predictions of "heightened tensions" between Protestants and Catholics and between Christians and Jews that would increasingly turn America into a "compartmentalized society" not unlike the Netherlands or Lebanon.[2]

Other observers, however, soon pointed out that American religion was not only divided among the three major faiths but that Protestantism was also deeply divided internally. Denominations, they suggested, constituted an additional source of religious identity. Shortly after Lenski's volume was published, a survey study was conducted in the San Francisco area that showed major differences in the views of the various Protestant denominations represented. Episcopalians differed from Methodists,

Methodists differed from Lutherans, Lutherans differed from Baptists, and so on. Denominationalism, the study concluded, was "a major fact in American religious life."[3]

Over the years, students of American religion have continued to identify denominationalism and interfaith divisions as one of the more distinctive and consequential features of American religion. Writing in the early 1970s Andrew M. Greeley, for example, chose to title a book on religion in America *The Denominational Society*.[4] So important was denominationalism to American religion, Greeley argued, that any weakening of denominational competition could radically weaken the entire religious enterprise. Later in the same decade, denominationalism did in fact begin to fade from the forefront of discussions of American religion. New religious cults, television preachers, secularism, and ecumenism all seemed more interesting at the time. But few suggested that denominationalism was actually any less significant because of these developments. And studies still continued to speak of denominationalism as one of the essential features of American religion.

Even among the most recent assessments of the religious landscape, denominationalism has continued to be stressed. For example, a 1985 issue of the *Annals of the American Academy of Political and Social Science* suggests that denominationalism is still very much a part of American culture generally, perhaps even more so than in the period which Herberg described. Indeed, say the editors of this issue, denominational attachments "are as strong and maybe stronger today than they were three decades ago."[5]

To suggest that denominationalism has declined in significance, therefore, runs against the grain of most scholarship on American religion. Still, it is a possibility that must be considered. If denominationalism was indeed as fundamental to the structure of American religion in the period immediately following World War II as most writers thought, then any consideration of the ways in which religion has been restructured since then must address it. Has denominationalism remained constant? Or has it somehow receded in significance? Have new developments in American religion simply been superimposed on top of its groundwork? Or have these developments been accompanied by changes in that groundwork itself?

Satanic Ideologies

One does not have to search far to find evidence showing the enormous importance of tensions between Protestants and Catholics, Christians and Jews, and among members of different denominations in the years immediately following World War II. Despite the underlying agreement on many of the suppositions that we have considered in the previous two chapters, the institutional heritage of American religion was clearly fractured along lines of doctrinal and ecclesiastical tradition. And these divisions provided the cultural boundaries which gave American religion much of its internal structure. Religious leaders, in retrospect, spoke with unwitting candor about their misgivings toward the beliefs and practices of other faiths. Lawsuits, court decisions, voting, and political affairs frequently found Protestants and Catholics on different sides of the fence, while antagonisms between Christians and Jews simmered just barely beneath the surface. Early studies of attitudes and behavior in the general public also revealed high levels of interfaith separation.

Most in evidence were the conflicts between Protestants and Catholics. In 1947, following a closely contested New Jersey Supreme Court case over state aid to parochial schools, the editor of the Protestant periodical *Christian Century*, for example, declared in strident tones that Protestants everywhere should see the Catholic threat for what it was and unite to disable it: "Though still a minority as compared to the whole of Protestantism," he charged, "Catholicism has become a strong and formidable minority. It is now asserting its claim, long held in abeyance, for a privileged recognition. It will not long be content with the half-loaf. . . . Influential voices are already asking for the whole loaf."[6]

In this writer's view, Catholicism was a threat because it was strong. Others were no less negative in their assessments, but curiously saw Catholicism as a threat because it was weak. Kenneth Scott Latourette, a prominent historian at the Yale Divinity School, for example, was prompted to remark in a series of lectures at Auburn Theological Seminary that "if the future of Christianity rested with that [Roman Catholic] church, the outlook would be grim."[7] In his view, Catholicism was so steeped in tradition—more specifically, so rooted in Latin culture—that it could not help but decline. The cultural superiority of Protestantism to Catholicism was, indeed, a favorite refrain among Protestant leaders. A Presbyterian pastor, for example, wrote in an article warning Protestant youth against marrying Catholics that: "It is Protestant theology, not Roman Catholic, which has provoked men to demand free government and the overthrow of tyrants." He went on to argue: "It is Protestant church polity, and not Roman Catholic, which schools men in the actual practice of democracy."[8]

Nor were these kinds of statements simply the private views of individual pastors. Mainline Protestant denominations in these years were also prone to distance themselves from Catholics in more official capacities. At its triennial convention in 1949 the Episcopal church passed a strong resolution warning its members against contracting marriages with Roman Catholics. A few years later the Presbyterian Church, U.S.A. adopted a statement at its annual convention that condemned the "cultic worship of Mary" among Catholics. Evangelical and fundamentalist Protestants were even more pointed in denouncing Catholicism. At its annual convention in 1950 the National Association of Evangelicals passed a resolution stating that the association "views with grave concern the militant and aggressive tactics of the Roman Catholic hierarchy within and upon our government."[9] Several years later the association's president took an even more strident position toward Catholics in his presidential address to the convention, denouncing Catholicism as one of the main "satanic ideologies" opposing true Christianity.[10] In much the same spirit fundamentalist writer Ernest Gordon stated in an editorial in the widely distributed *Sunday School Times* that: "In many cities, Roman churches are nests of bingo gambling and, in the Whiskey Trust, Vatican investments are very large indeed. Back of the corrupt city machines are the Roman hierarchies."[11]

Nowhere, though, was the sense of impending peril that Protestant leaders saw in Catholicism given fuller expression than in the pages of Paul Blanshard's widely circulated book *American Freedom and Catholic Power*. Published in 1949, Blanshard's book put into print what many Protestants apparently felt in their bones: that the Catholic church was bent on taking over the country. Everywhere, it seemed, Catholics were making inroads: in government, in education, in medicine, in labor unions, even in foreign policy. The time had come, Blanshard warned, for Americans to wake up to the grave dangers lurking in their midst. And not only should they wake up, he concluded, but strong action needed to be taken, not unlike that taken during the American War of Independence, in order to overthrow the present system of alien rule.[12]

If these were the partisan views of Protestant leaders, others with presumably more neutral orientations also displayed a keen awareness of the degree of animosity that prevailed. A faculty member at the University of Chicago, writing in 1948, stated it this way: "The difference between Protestantism and Roman Catholicism is so profound that it seems almost impossible to recognize them as two forms of one Christianity."[13] Six years later the tensions between the two forms of Christianity were still so intense that *Look* magazine devoted a feature article to the subject. Among the issues identified as being most hotly contested by leaders of the two faiths were questions about state aid to parochial schools, Catholics' alleged subservience to the ecclesiastical hierarchy, and the church's political views. In addition, the article noted, Catholics and Protestants were separated by vast social differences: the former were mostly urban, represented by urban political machines, and closely attached to labor unions; the latter were still predominately rural and tended (outside of the South) to vote Republican.[14]

The specific terms on which Protestants differentiated themselves from Catholics in these years, while rooted in centuries of conflict, tended to reflect the recent experience of World War II and gained intensity by virtue of the Cold War and the rising threat seen in Soviet communism. Popular Protestant discussions of Catholics characterized them as blind followers of a totalitarian system, apparently not unlike the Nazi or Soviet regimes. The distinguishing feature of Catholicism, in these portrayals, was its subjection to papal authority. In Protestant eyes the Catholic laity had no voice in running their church. They were taught to believe in papal infallibility, had to accept without questioning everything their church taught, and rejected all churches but their own as false religions.

In contrast, Protestants saw themselves as the champions of democracy. Protestants were not the willing subjects of totalitarian rule, but were thoughtful, conscientious practitioners of democratic government. As the author of a respected study of American religion put it, the Protestant contribution to democracy was "a very distinguished one." In his view, even the most hierarchical Protestant traditions in America had been transmuted to the point that nearly all Protestant institutions were governed "in a fashion similar to the way Americans run their governments, and tend to be democratic in the same degree that Americans generally are democratic."[15]

Protestant writers generally did not deny that Catholics were correct in some of their basic teachings. But the fact that they lived under totalitarian rule was seen as a devastating flaw. It meant that individual Catholics probably adhered to a superficial faith about which they had thought little. It also meant that Catholics could not be trusted to play by democratic rules in dealing with Protestants, in advancing their own religion, or in relating to the state. These misgivings were especially likely to flare into open denunciations whenever it seemed to Protestants that Catholics were attempting to gain an unfair advantage for their institutions by manipulating tax laws or the legislative process.

On their side, Catholics were just as vehement in defending themselves and in denouncing Protestants. In the heat of debate over public transportation to parochial schools in the late 1940s Francis Cardinal Spellman, for example, told an audience in Syracuse, New York, that Protestants who opposed this proposal were nothing more than "unhooded Klansmen." These bigots, he said, "have not yet insisted that it is a violation of the American tradition of the separation of church and state for members of a fire department to extinguish a blaze in a parochial school and to save children from burning to death, and we do hope they will content themselves and satisfy their discriminatory thirsts at seeing little children left standing in the snow as publicly paid-for buses transport other American children to and from school."[16] Other Catholic leaders countered the Protestants' allegations of totalitarianism by proclaiming the Catholic church the greatest democracy on earth. Still others denounced Protestants for having a fallacious understanding of Catholic theology, described Protestantism as a shallow faith, pointed out that most Protestants were probably dissatisfied with their beliefs, and cited examples of prominent figures who were converting to Catholicism as a way of finding a more satisfactory faith.

Curiously perhaps, the tensions between Christians and Jews often surfaced less prominently in these years than did those between Protestants and Catholics. The sheer differences in numbers made Catholicism seem more threatening in many communities than Judaism. To the leadership of some of the more liberal Protestant denominations, Jews also seemed important allies to cultivate in the drive against Catholic hegemony. Especially on questions involving separation of church and state, Protestant and Jewish interests often coincided. Accordingly, Protestant leaders characterized Jews as being committed to the same freedom of religion that Protestants championed, emphasized their high levels of education and cultural awareness, and pointed out that Jews had earned their laurels as opponents of totalitarianism in the recent war. In one scholar's words, Jews were "aware of current social trends," "sensitive to current mores," "proud of American achievements," and "anxious to help in maintaining and vitalizing democratic institutions."[17]

Yet, at the popular level, misgivings about Jews and instances of overt anti-Semitism were never far from the surface. At an otherwise friendly high school basketball game in suburban Chicago, anti-Jewish songs were sung and several Jewish youths were attacked so severely that hospital treatment was required. Commenting on the incident, the editors of *Christian Century* decried the violence, but argued that Jews were reluctant to assimilate and mainly wanted to be left alone. The editorial also pointed out that Jews had an irritating fault of advocating such a high degree of religious tolerance that Christians' efforts to Christianize the society were made more difficult.[18]

The statements of religious leaders in these years also tended to take for granted that anti-Semitism was part of American culture and was likely to persist until Jews themselves became more like non-Jews. The more liberally minded saw a need for Jews to end their clannish ways, to quit thinking of themselves as God's chosen people, and to make greater efforts to interact with Christians. Those with more conservative views argued that Christians should try to love their Jewish neighbors and witness to them, but felt it was only to be expected that hatred and persecution would persist until Jews became Christians or until biblical prophecies were fulfilled. As one editor of a fundamentalist periodical put it, anti-Semitism "will not cease until prophecy and persecution are fulfilled and our Lord Jesus Christ, the true Messiah of Israel, comes to destroy His enemies and to reign in righteousness."[19] Like Catholicism, Judaism was also denigrated for being old-fashioned and unable to keep up with progressive times. Another fundamentalist writer noted: "Judaism is out of step with God. It lags behind God's revelation. In history it belongs to B.C. not to A.D. It is Old Testament religion, and the Old Testament religion was, in a sense, an interim religion. . . . Judaism in the Christian era is an anachronism, a throwback to an interim stage in revealed religion."[20]

The degree to which negative attitudes toward Jews were shared in the society at large was clearly evident in public opinion polls. On fourteen occasions between 1938 and 1946 national surveys asked the American public "Do you think Jews have too much power in the United States?" On the average, 47 percent of the respondents in these surveys said yes. Other polls conducted during the war years showed that one person in five actually thought of Jews as a menace to America. In other ways, the public also demonstrated a strong propensity to discriminate against Jews. For example, about a third of the public said they would not vote for a congressional candidate who was Jewish. A slightly higher proportion (43 percent) said "it would make a difference if a prospective employee were Jewish." And a majority (57 percent) said they would definitely not marry a Jew.[21]

While much of this prejudice was rooted in folk beliefs and other implicit assumptions in the popular culture, there was also a distinctly religious component. The study mentioned earlier of the San Francisco area, for example, showed that Protestant and Catholic church members were prone to think of Jews as "Christ-killers" who were still experiencing the wrath of God for not believing in Christ. Those who felt this way about Jews, the study suggested, were also more likely to harbor anti-Semitic sentiments of other kinds.[22]

Not surprisingly, the tensions between members of different Protestant denominations were muted in comparison with those separating Protestants and Catholics and Christians and Jews. Presbyterians and Methodists were seldom caught in the act of actually calling one another names. Yet there appears to have been a widespread perception that, for good or ill, denominational loyalties were deeply rooted and sharply defined. In part, this perception was rooted in the fact (as seen in Chapter 2) that denominational bureaucracies had grown considerably during the first half of the twentieth century, giving all the major denominations more of a national identity. Writing shortly before World War II, H. Paul Douglass had observed: "Like it or not, denominations have come to mean more than they used to. They exercise wider functions and their functioning is more necessary to the well-being of the local churches than ever before."[23] Expertise, planning, financial assistance, missionary work, and coordination were among the functions that Douglass saw as giving the denominations a more powerful hand.

In addition, lingering perceptions of theological, ecclesiastical, ethnic, and subcultural differences between denominations continued to function as sturdy social barriers. A professor of theology, looking back on the experience of growing up during this period, has recently written: "Catholics were pagans. Episcopalianism was a social club. Lutherans had departed from the faith. Presbyterians were formalistic. And Pentecostals were off-center. Now I may not have been taught these overly simplistic convictions explicitly. But I must have picked them up somewhere in my youth, because for a long time this is what I believed with all my heart."[24]

Despite these kinds of perceptions, local churches sometimes did in fact find ways in which to cooperate with one another. The idea of holding "union services," for example, had a long history, as did the practice of cooperating with one another in sponsoring holiday programs, and of periodically canceling services so that members could participate in special events being held at other churches. The denominational divisions, nevertheless, operated as significant social demarcations at the local level.

In the 1920s, when Robert and Helen Lynd conducted their first study of Middletown, they observed that denominational rivalries were apparently becoming deeper than had been the case a few decades before. And this tendency seemed to be rooted in the growth of national bureaucracies at the denominational level. Local churches still seemed willing to cooperate among themselves, but members were often critical of the national policies of one another's denominations. The Lynds also observed that most of the residents of Middletown had been reared in a single denomination, seldom switched to another, and knew little about the beliefs and practices of other churches. Church members' views of one another, therefore, were often rooted in ignorance and suspicion.[25]

By the 1950s, some of these patterns had begun to change. But ignorance of other churches and suspicions of the national policies of different denominations still seemed to be much in evidence. Frustrated by the inability to get local churches to cooperate, one leader remarked that the only thing local churches were interested in was building up the size of their individual congregations. Indifference toward interdenominational meetings was prevalent, he said, while "competition is on the increase in many if not in most communities."[26]

At the popular level, some studies showed that a fairly sizable minority of Protestants believed there was something distinctive, if not unique, about belonging to their particular denomination. Among the Protestants studied in the San Francisco area in the early 1960s, for example, about one in nine thought that "being a member of your particular faith" was "absolutely essential for salvation." And another 30 percent thought this "probably would help in gaining salvation." Baptists and Lutherans were the most likely to say that membership in their faith was absolutely essential, but in every denomination at least a third of the respondents thought that membership in that faith would probably help.[27]

In addition to actually believing in the uniqueness of their own denomination, Protestants in this period seem to have actually oriented their social contacts to a great extent around their own churches, thus by default limiting their awareness of other denominations. About a third of the Protestants in the San Francisco study, for example, said that a majority of their closest friends were from their own congregation. Among Disciples of Christ, the proportion was 42 percent; among Southern Baptists, 49 percent; and among Protestant sects, 67 percent.[28]

Much of this isolation from other churches may have resulted simply from the fact that people made friends with those with whom they associated. Some additional evidence, however, suggested that religious leaders may have been reluctant to initiate more formalized contacts with other denominations. A couple of studies, for example, probed the tolerance of clergy toward joint worship services, pulpit exchanges, and other kinds of cross-denominational interaction. The results pointed toward a relatively high degree of denominational parochialism. A study of Southern Baptist clergy in 1956, for instance, showed that 90 percent were against sharing in sacraments with other churches. An equally high percentage thought members from other churches should not be accepted without being rebaptized.[29] Nor were these feelings unique to the more theologically conservative clergy of a denomination like the Southern Baptists. At the opposite end of the theological spectrum, a 1953 study of Episcopalians also found a relatively high degree of denominational parochialism. Only 20 percent of the clergy thought it was all right to hold joint worship services with other Protestant churches in which Holy Communion was offered as part of the service. And only about half the clergy thought it was acceptable to invite ministers from other denominations to preach at their church.[30]

In the first decade or so following World War II, therefore, it appears that religious culture in America was to a significant extent informed by the divisions between Protestants and Catholics, Christians and Jews, and members of different denominations. Suspicions of other faiths lurked very near the surface and sometimes erupted in vitriolic denouncements. Clergy thought it important to maintain some of the physical boundaries separating the different faiths. And parishioners tended to act in ways that created distance between themselves and persons who clearly held religious convictions different from their own. Whether Herberg's claim that people actually derived a strong sense of their own personal identity from being Protestants or Catholics or Jews has validity is more difficult to substantiate. But the evidence does suggest that religious identities were probably shaped by these divisions insofar as public discourse was concerned.

Mergers and Memberships

The problem with sustaining these divisions and the symbolic rivalries that went with them was that they were only partially legitimate in terms of the various religious traditions' own teachings. For many years religious leaders had lamented these very divisions and had worked to transcend them. Denominational rifts ran counter to the spirit of unity that was commended in scripture. Internal divisions, critics said, weakened the strength of Christianity and sullied its witness to the world. Particularly now, at a time when the churches seemed to be faced with perils of unprecedented proportions, cooperation rather than petty denominational squabbles was urgent. Just as the nation had drawn together to win the war in Europe, so religious bodies must join ranks against the growing scourge of communism, or as Protestants saw it, the threat of Catholic totalitarianism. Thus they sang in their favorite hymn "Onward Christian Soldiers":

> We are not divided, all one body we,
> One in hope and doctrine, one in charity.[31]

Disagreements about fine points of doctrine and church polity, in this view, seemed trivial alongside the more fundamental aspects of American religion: its common faith in God, its ethical commitment to goodness and love, and its pragmatic orientation toward contributing to the common good. Addressing an ecumenical audience in New York City just before the end of World War II, John D. Rockefeller, Jr., appeared to express a prevailing sentiment when he envisioned a truly universal church that would "see all denominational emphasis set aside." Such a church, he said, would "pronounce ordinance, ritual, creed, all nonessential for admission into the kingdom of God" and would make "life, not a creed, the essential test of faith."[32]

Ten years earlier Rockefeller himself had announced that he would no longer support his own denomination but would devote his considerable financial resources to projects of an interdenominational and nondenominational nature. A supporter of the Interchurch World Movement, Rockefeller would also play an increasingly instrumental role in providing material encouragement for the work of ecumenical agencies.[33] The Federal Council of Churches, founded in 1908, had already developed an infrastructure at both the national and metropolitan levels to push for greater cooperation among religious bodies. And among Protestants at least, the concern to combat advances from Rome had given strong impetus to the idea of strength in unity.

The support found among some segments of the religious elite for greater unity was also not lacking at the grass roots. A representative survey of more than 7,000 respondents from 17 denominations in 1932 had found majority support, despite their more personal misgivings about the beliefs and practices of other denominations, for some kind of church union or cooperation in all but three denominations. Methodists and Presbyterians were opposed to maintaining present denominational divisions by a ratio of four to one; Northern Baptists and Episcopalians were marginally against maintaining the present order; and Lutherans, Southern Presbyterians, and Southern Baptists leaned moderately toward continuing the current divisions. Those who favored greater interdenominational cooperation, moreover, were about as likely to favor uniting the various bodies into a single church as they were to support the idea of merely creating a federation of denominations.[34]

By the 1950s, some of these sentiments appear to have grown stronger. Gallup polls conducted in 1937 and again in 1950, for example, showed that the proportion who favored a single Protestant church in the United States rose from 40 percent to 50 percent. Over the same period, the proportion who disapproved of such a venture decreased from 51 percent to 39 percent.[35] As yet, greater cooperation between Protestants and Catholics was apparently beyond consideration. But members of Protestant denominations, faced with the growing specter of Catholic power, clearly saw possibilities for greater unity among their own organizations even as they maintained loyalty to those to which they belonged.

The shape of things to come was augured, or so its founders hoped, by a new organization that came into being on November 28, 1950. A blinding snowstorm had raged all day in Cleveland where the meeting was to be held, and organizers were afraid that delegates might not be able to come (critics said God sent the snow to deter the anti-Christ from rearing its ugly head). But come they did, representatives from 25 Protestant and 4 Eastern Orthodox bodies, bringing to fruition an idea that had been born a decade earlier at a convocation in Atlantic City (held the same day Pearl Harbor was bombed). Over the platform that evening in Cleveland letters ten feet high spelled out the words "This Nation Under God." On the altar lay an open Bible and flanking it were the flags of every nation of the world. In the audience delegates sat on chairs painted red, white, and blue for the occasion, and had it not been for the snow, would have listened to speeches by Secretary of State Dean Acheson and President

Harry S. Truman. Such were the beginnings of the National Council of Churches.

Its goal was to promote greater unity among its 29 constituent bodies. A response to the great sense of promise and peril that religious leaders felt in the postwar period, it was an attempt to do for religion what it was hoped the United Nations would do for the world. It would represent the United States in the World Council of Churches, train leaders, engage in foreign missions, keep religious ideals before the American people, and serve as a way in which churches could influence government agencies. Organized like the United Nations itself into a hierarchy of divisions, departments, and subbureaus, it was expected to employ between 800 and 1,000 men and women from the outset. Its goal was not to replace denominations. But clearly it was an effort to provide a higher level of religious organization that could respond to the great national and international challenges of the day.

In the decades that followed other ecumenical organizations also became increasingly active. One of the most auspicious was the Consultation on Church Union, brought into being in 1962 by the United Presbyterian Church in the U.S.A., the Episcopal church, the Methodist church, and the United Church of Christ, to explore possibilities for greater cooperation and eventual union among these denominations. Through the work of this and other ecumenical movements several mergers among Protestant denominations were actually effected. In 1968, for example, the Methodist church and the Evangelical United Brethren Church merged to form one body. Six years earlier the Lutheran Church in America had been formed as a merger among five formerly independent Lutheran denominations. Several mergers among smaller denominations also took place about the same time.

The changing character of American denominationalism cannot be seen in the sheer number of mergers or in the distribution of memberships, however. Comparisons of membership statistics, in fact, point more to the continuing significance of denominationalism rather than to its decline.[36] For example, there were 54 denominations in the United States at the close of World War II with memberships of 50,000 or more; by 1985, that number had climbed to 89. Of course, the nation's population grew during this period as well, but the growth in population could have resulted in only a few of the largest denominations becoming larger. Instead, it appears to have resulted in many denominations gaining in size.

The same conclusion emerges from looking at religious membership data in several different ways. First, if denominationalism was becoming less significant in terms of sheer membership distributions, we might expect the bulk of total church membership in the United States to be concentrated among a smaller number of bodies than in the past. That is, through mergers, or through people joining the largest bodies, more and more members would be concentrated in a smaller number of large organizations. Thus the chances of any two people chosen at random belonging to the same organization would be greater. This, however, seems not to have happened. For one thing, it took 20 denominations in 1946 to comprise 90 percent of all Protestant members; by 1985, it took 25 denominations to comprise the same proportion. In other words, the bulk of Protestants were actually concentrated in a smaller number of denominations in 1946 than in 1985. Or, looked at in a different way, the 10 largest denominations comprised 74 percent of all Protestants in 1946, but only 64 percent in 1985. By this criterion, more people were scattered among a larger number of denominations in 1985 than in 1946. Still another way of looking at the evidence is to concentrate only on the three largest denominations. In 1946, 57.8 percent of all Protestants were members of these three largest organizations. In 1985, almost exactly the same proportion—57.6 percent—was still concentrated in the big three.[37]

With respect to mergers, there seems to be little evidence that mergers alone have significantly reduced the number of different denominations. If we look at the number of denominations within each major Protestant family, for example, we find that the numbers have not changed substantially since World War II, despite the fact that most mergers would have been expected to take place *within* these families. Thus, there were 46 separate Baptist denominations in 1980, compared to 38 in 1950; in each period there were 19 different Lutheran bodies; the number of Methodist bodies declined only from 25 to 24 during the thirty-year interval; and the number of Presbyterian and Reformed denominations held steady at 22 in each period.

If denominationalism has in some way declined in significance, therefore, it must be in ways other than those evident from membership statistics alone.[38] The important consideration, it appears, is not so much the numbers of members who belong to the various denominations, but whether these denominations are significantly different from one another in social composition and whether the boundaries separating them are strong or weak.

The Shifting Sources of Denominationalism

In his classic study *The Social Sources of Denominationalism*, published in 1929, H. Richard Niebuhr argued that the distinctive denominational character of American religion was rooted primarily in social divisions—in differences of social class, race, and region. The lines that divided denominations from one another, he believed, corresponded rather closely with these basic cleavages in the social structure. What kept Baptists and Methodists apart, for example, were differences in social status. And what aggravated the tensions between Protestants and Catholics were differences in immigration history and region of settlement.[39] Whether or not these differences continue to separate denominations, therefore, is one of the ways in which the changing nature of denominationalism can be assessed.

In many respects the relations between denominations and social factors have not changed greatly since World War II. Race, for example, continues to separate blacks and whites into different denominations, despite the fact that white denominations formally repudiated segregation in the 1950s and 1960s. Region also continues to separate denominations with only modestly diminishing significance. Northern and southern Methodists officially reunited in 1939, the northern and southern branches of Presbyterianism finally came together again in 1983, and the largest Lutheran bodies, which had long been concentrated respectively in the Midwest and Northeast, voted a merger to take effect in 1988. Still, denominational maps of the United States continue to display heavy concentrations of Baptists in the South, Methodists in the Midwest, Congregationalists (United Church of Christ) in New England, Mormons in the Far West, and so on.[40]

Some of the differences in social class that Niebuhr observed in the 1920s persist as well. For example, studies suggest that Episcopalians have largely retained their position as the wealthiest of all Protestant denominations.[41] Data collected by the Census Bureau in 1956 revealed that Episcopalians were twice as likely on average to hold professional or managerial positions as the remainder of the population and that their family incomes were 1.4 times the national average. Comparable studies in more recent years have found many of the same differences still in evidence.[42] Data from these studies also reveal that Presbyterians continue to have incomes above the national average in about the same ratio they used to, while Baptists continue to have incomes lower than the national average.

Other facets of these social sources of denominationalism, however, demonstrate significant changes over the past several decades. Despite the regional continuities evident among Protestant denominations, the regional distribution of Jews and Catholics has changed considerably. Particularly important to the issue of religious boundaries are regional changes that have made it more likely for Protestants and Catholics and Christians and Jews to be able to interact with one another. In 1952, for example, 61 percent of all Jews were concentrated in New York, New Jersey, and Pennsylvania. By 1980, only 36 percent were concentrated in these three states. Thus it was simply more likely that Christians in other parts of the country would come into contact with Jews.[43] The regional distribution of Catholics also made it more likely that Protestants in areas that had formerly been exclusively Protestant (or almost so) would have greater opportunities to mix with Catholics. For example, Atlanta had only one Catholic church in 1952, but by 1980 had 44. Fort Lauderdale had 4 Catholic churches in 1952, but 37 in 1980. Or to take a different example, in North Carolina the ratio of Catholics to Protestants doubled between 1952 and 1980. In Virginia, the change was nearly as great.[44]

Interregional migration is also making the country more religiously homogeneous in another way. Traditionally, the South and Midwest were characterized by higher levels of religious observance than the national average, while the West and Northeast had lower than average levels of religious observance. This was true among both Protestants and Catholics. In some ways it may have reflected denominational differences (e.g. more Baptists in the South), but it was a product of regional subcultures as well. While these differences persist, they are gradually being eroded by migration between regions. These effects can be seen by comparing natives in the various regions with newcomers to each region from other regions. Among Protestants, for example, natives of the Northeast are 6 percentage points less likely than the national average to attend church regularly, but newcomers to the Northeast from other regions are no less likely than the national average to attend church regularly. In the West, natives are 8 points less likely than the national average to attend church regularly; newcomers, only 5 points below average. Conversely, natives in the South are 6 points *more* likely to attend church than the national average; newcomers to the South are only 1 point above the national average. Overall, then, habits of church attendance are much more even across the various regions for Protestants who have migrated than for Protestants who grew up in the different regions.[45]

Still another tendency associated with changing regional patterns is for some of the Protestant denominations that were formerly identified with a particular part of the country to have become somewhat more widely dispersed throughout the nation. For instance, in 1952 only 3 percent of the Mormon population lived outside the Western region. By 1980, this proportion had risen to 19 percent. Or to take another case, only 8 percent of all Southern Baptist churches were outside the South in 1936; the figure was 12 percent in 1952, and 18 percent by 1980. Like the shifts among Catholics and Jews, these changes make it somewhat more likely that a broader variety of cultural influences will affect the members of these denominations. As a result, each denomination may embody greater internal diversity and, on the whole, resemble more closely the cultural diversity in the society at large.[46]

Several other comparisons also point to trends away from some of the social differences that separated denominations in the period immediately following World War II. For example, as recently as 1960, white male heads of households who were Catholics were still only 80 percent as likely as other white male heads of households to be employed in professional or managerial occupations. By 1976, this difference had been wiped out entirely. In the earlier period, Lutherans were only 60 percent as likely as the nation as a whole to be employed in these occupations, but by 1976 this proportion had grown to 90 percent. And among members of fundamentalist sects, the proportion in professions and management jobs was only 20 percent as great as the national average in 1960, but this percentage grew to 60 percent by 1976.

The greatest differences between the earlier and more recent periods, however, were reflected in changing levels of education. Denominations that had formerly been above average in levels of education generally converged toward the national average, while denominations that had been below average generally gained in educational attainment at a sufficiently rapid pace to put themselves closer to the national average. In 1956 Episcopalians, for example, had been 2.8 times more likely to have attained some college education than was true in the nation as a whole. By 1980, this factor had been reduced to 1.7 times. Presbyterians had been 1.9 times above the national average in 1956; by 1980, they were only 1.6 times the national average. On the other hand, Catholics had been only .7 times as likely as the national average to have been to college in 1956, but this proportion increased to 1.1 by 1980. Lutherans increased from .7 to .9 in comparison with the national average. And Baptists increased from .6 to .8.[47] While there were still some differences in overall levels of education among the various denominations, therefore, these differences were smaller in 1980 than they had been in the mid-1950s. Given the other ramifications of changes in the level of education for American religion, which will be examined in Chapter 7, these patterns of convergence become especially important.

An additional dimension along which the social differences separating denominations can be compared is the degree to which their members differ attitudinally. These differences, while sometimes rooted in other factors such as social status and region of the country, often become the operative basis for conflict between religious groups. Whether there had ever been strong differences between the major denominations and faiths on social opinions is difficult to say. Certainly social observers in the 1950s and early 1960s *thought* that denominations differed widely in their degree of social conservatism and on other contemporary attitudes. By the 1970s, however, there seemed to be little evidence that denominationalism made much of a difference on most social issues. If one looks at an extremely controversial issue such as abortion, for example, one finds that about the same proportions in all of the major denominations expressed approval or disapproval by the late 1970s. Depending on how these questions are worded, approval sometimes ran higher or lower, but the differences between denominations remained small. For instance, on a question which asked persons whether they approved of abortion for someone who simply did not want more children, the percentages answering yes ranged only between 44 percent among Lutherans, Catholics, and members of Protestant sects, and 50 percent among Episcopalians. Baptists, Methodists, Presbyterians, and Jews all scored about midway between these two figures. Other issues that have proven divisive along different lines also appear to differ little from one denomination to the next. For example, the proportions who think premarital sex is wrong vary only between 43 percent and 50 percent among these denominations. The proportions who believe pornography may in some way erode the moral fabric of society range from a low of 59 percent to a high of 63 percent. Those who think the nation should be spending more on defense vary between 16 percent and 20 percent. And those who identify themselves as political liberals range from a low of 24 percent to a high of 34 percent.[48]

The picture that begins to emerge, then, is one of greater social and cultural similarity among the major denominations and faiths than appears to have been the case in the 1940s and 1950s. While the memberships of the various religious bodies have by no means become indistinguishable from one another socially and culturally, considerable convergence has taken place. No longer are the various bodies as isolated from one another geographically as they once were. Some convergence has taken place on measures of social status. Educational levels, in particular, are now more similar across the various denominations and faiths than they were several decades ago. And the various groups do not differ substantially from one another on attitudes toward a number of salient social issues. To the extent that social and cultural differences produce barriers that are difficult to transcend or lines of demarcation that result in conflict, the reduction of these differences suggests that denominational divisions may be declining in social significance.

There is, of course, another possibility: as the memberships of different denominations become more similar to one another, acrimony could actually increase as a way of maintaining symbolic boundaries. We see this, for example, among athletic teams. Quite similar in talent and orientation, they play by the same rules and hold the same values. Yet they typically develop strong symbolic boundaries as a way of affirming in-group loyalties. Mascots, team colors, insignia, charismatic leaders, and unusual plays all serve this function. The difference, of course, is that religious groups are not engaged in direct, overt competition with one another.

And yet, there is inevitably some competition between religious groups since a gain in membership by one denomination often results in a loss in membership by another. Despite declining social differences, therefore, denominational boundaries of other kinds could still be strong.

Denominational Switching

If denominational boundaries are conceived of in Herberg's terms as identities that people adopt for life, then the strength of denominationalism is clearly on the wane. No longer are the barriers separating different denominations strong enough to keep people from crossing over them. An increasingly large number of people feel comfortable in switching from one denomination to another. Large proportions of the population also report having attended services at churches other than their own. And the type of person who is most likely to switch denominations or attend services at other churches suggests that these trends are likely to accelerate.

In 1955 a Gallup poll showed that only 4 percent of the adult population—1 person in 25—no longer adhered to the faith of their childhood.[49] Some 30 years later, another Gallup poll showed that 1 person in 3 had switched from the faith in which they had been raised.[50] In the intervening period the population had not only become more mobile religiously but denominations had also made it easier for people to switch. They had adopted policies encouraging people to join worship services with members of other denominations and had consciously downplayed many of the distinctives that had presented barriers to cross-attendance and changing memberships. As a result, the barriers that had formerly protected denominational loyalties became visibly more permeable.

Some denominations were affected to a very high degree by interdenominational switching. Data collected in the 1970s and early 1980s, for example, showed that 45 percent of all Americans who had been raised as Presbyterians now belonged to some other denomination or to no denomination at all. The same data showed that 40 percent of all persons raised as Methodists had switched to some other religious affiliation. Almost as many of those who had been raised as Episcopalians now belonged to some other denomination (38 percent). Even among Jews and Catholics, for whom the barriers against interfaith switching have generally been much higher, a striking 15 percent and 17 percent respectively had turned to another faith. And in between were groups like Baptists and Lutherans who had seen approximately a quarter of those reared in their denominations switch to something else.[51]

If actual switching from one denomination or faith to another has become this common, it should not be surprising that attending services across denominational boundaries is even more common. Unfortunately, no questions about this kind of attendance were asked over the years in order to provide a firm basis for assessing trends. But in 1984 a national study for the first time explored the extent of cross-denominational attendance. The results showed that four out of every five Americans have at some time or another attended religious services at a denomination other than their own. The results also revealed that three in five adults have attended religious services in at least three different denominations or faiths. Moreover, half of all Americans have attended services at four or more different denominations or faiths. And a third of the population has worshipped in five or more different denominations or faiths.[52] If, as sometimes is argued, denominationalism is rooted simply in isolation from other groups, then these results suggest that the barriers separating different denominations are relatively weak. Most people have clearly taken occasion to see what goes on in religious organizations other than their own.[53]

The results of this study also demonstrated that education plays a significant role in determining the likelihood that someone will have attended churches of different denominations. Persons with even some college education were more than three times as likely to have attended religious services in six or more denominations than persons who had only been to grade school. And those who had only been to high school resembled those with grade school educations more than those with college educations.[54]

Educational differences also play a significant role in influencing the likelihood of people actually switching denominations. With only one exception, persons who grew up in a particular denomination are more likely to switch to a different denomination if they have been to college than if they have not been to college. The single exception is that no differences along educational lines obtain among Jews: 15 percent have switched in both the better and less well educated categories.[55]

Most studies of denominational switching have assumed that persons only switch once in their lifetimes. In fact, about one person in five switches at least twice in his or her lifetime. And one person in ten switches three times or more. Education, again, influences the likelihood of engaging in multiple switching, just as it does the likelihood of switching at all. In a recent national study, 34 percent of the respondents who had received at least some college training said they had switched denominations twice or more, compared with 26 percent of the high school educated respondents, and only 22 percent of the grade school educated persons.[56] Insofar as educational levels have been rising sharply in the general population (as will be discussed in Chapter 7), one of the effects of this trend, then, appears to be a greater amount of movement across denominational boundaries. Or put differently, as the population becomes more educated, denominational boundaries seem to be less effective in keeping people loyal to only a single denomination.

In addition to increasing levels of education, another factor that has signaled a decline in the strength of denominational boundaries is the high degree of intermarriage that takes place across these boundaries. Studies of American Jews, for example, have shown that the proportion who were intermarried with non-Jews rose from only 3 percent in 1965, to 14 percent in 1975, and to 17 percent in 1983.[57] Trend data with which to establish the direction of changes among other religious groups have not been collected. But changes in attitudes about intermarriage (as seen in the next section) suggest that there has probably been a trend toward increasing intermarriage among different Christian groups as well. Studies in which marriage patterns among younger and older cohorts have been compared also suggest that there is probably a trend. For example, a comparison of cohorts married between 1961 and 1975 and between 1931 and 1945 showed that the younger cohort was less likely to have married endogamously with respect to their denomination. This was especially so among persons raised in the more theologically liberal or moderate Protestant denominations.[58]

The fact that people marry outside of their own denomination does not mean necessarily that they and their spouses remain members of different denominations. Indeed, much of the denominational switching that has been observed in studies of American religion appears to be rooted in intermarriage. According to one study, more than two-thirds of those who married a spouse of a different religion eventually achieved religious unity—in about 30 percent of the cases both spouses switched to a different religion, and in about 40 percent of the cases one spouse adopted the other's religion.[59] This being the case, it might appear that people do value denominational boundaries sufficiently to feel the need to belong to the same denomination as their spouse. Nevertheless, trend data suggest that even this tendency may be undergoing change. For every major denomination, a smaller proportion of married people are currently wedded to a spouse who has the same religion as theirs than was the case a few decades ago.[60]

Again, college education appears to be a factor in these patterns. Generally speaking, the college educated are less likely than the non-college educated to marry someone of their own religion in the first place or eventually to establish a marriage in which they and their spouse belong to the same religion. Among Baptists who have been to college, for example, only 46 percent say their spouse was raised in the same denomination as they were; in comparison, 67 percent of Baptists who have no college education say this. Much the same is true among Lutherans, Presbyterians, and Catholics. Jews are again an exception: those who have been to college are as likely to have married endogamously as those who have not been to college. Episcopalians are also an exception: more of the college educated have married endogamously than of the less well educated (this pattern is probably a reflection of the fact that Episcopalians on the whole tend to be relatively well educated). The same data also reveal that college educated persons in most denominations are less likely than noncollege educated persons to have a spouse whose current religion is the same as theirs. This is the case among Baptists, Methodists, Lutherans, and Catholics. The exceptions are among groups that have relatively high levels of education overall: Episcopalians, Presbyterians, and Jews.[61]

Attitudes about Denominations

If patterns of denominational switching and cross-attendance at religious services suggest a weakening of denominational barriers, attitudes toward religious boundaries suggest even more clearly that Americans do not see these barriers as immutable or even in many cases as especially important. In the first decade or so after World War II (as seen earlier), there was already substantial support for greater cooperation among the major Protestant denominations. A sizable minority, however, held parochial views about their denominations, thought their own tradition was most true to the faith, and displayed a high degree of attitudinal distance toward members of other faiths. It is not possible to adduce evidence which reveals directly that these sentiments have declined. The data that have been gathered, nevertheless, reveal exceedingly low levels of negative feeling across denominational lines and strong levels of support for interdenominational cooperation.

At present, the vast majority of members in most denominations and faiths hold positive views of one another. Data collected by a Gallup poll in the mid-1970s, for example, showed that positive feelings toward Southern Baptists in the public at large (omitting Southern Baptists themselves) outstripped negative feelings by a ratio of better than 7 to 1. And this was the *lowest* of any of the ratios reported. Attitudes toward Episcopalians ran positive by a ratio of 11 to 1. Toward other kinds of Baptists, the ratio was 13 to 1. Presbyterians were regarded positively by a ratio of 18 to 1; Lutherans, also by a ratio of 18 to 1; and Methodists, by a ratio of 27 to 1.[62] Further data collected by the Gallup poll in 1984 showed that the ratios of positive to negative feelings were still at about these levels. Negative feelings toward any of the major denominations were harbored by no more than approximately 1 person in 15 and extremely negative responses were too few to measure reliably in sample surveys of this size. The only groups for whom a sizable degree of negative sentiment was registered were the traditional sects, such as Mormons and Seventh-Day Adventists, toward whom about a fifth of the population held negative views, and fundamentalists, evangelicals, and charismatics, also disliked by about a fifth of the population.[63]

Other evidence indicates a strong willingness on the part of most church members to engage in cooperative projects with other denominations. A study of Lutherans, for example, showed that four in five were interested in having cooperative worship services with Presbyterians and that three in four favored common services with Baptists and Catholics.[64] Gallup data, which included information from persons of all faiths as well as persons who were only nominally members of particular faiths, show that better than 90 percent of the public favors more attempts by local churches to reach out to other churches. Among the kinds of cooperation mentioned most often were cooperative involvement in community projects, sponsoring interdenominational youth groups and campus ministries, joint projects to promote racial understanding, and sharing of facilities.[65]

Changes in attitudes toward interdenominational cooperation are also reflected in the official policies of the various denominations and in the experiences of clergy. Many denominations have revoked earlier restrictions which limited participation in Holy Communion or appointment to offices in local churches to persons actually holding membership in the denomination, thereby making it easier for persons to switch or to visit for extended periods in churches of other denominations. For example, by a 1968 decree the Episcopal church stated that members were "free to attend the Eucharist in other Churches holding the apostolic faith as contained in the Scriptures and summarized in the Apostles' and Nicene Creeds."[66] A decade later the Episcopal church also rescinded a policy more than four centuries old that had required persons receiving the Eucharist in Anglican churches to be members, thereby opening the way for any persons who had been baptized to participate whether they were members or not. Similarly, the Presbyterian Church in the U.S.A. in its 1967 Confession denied that belief in any particular confession could be held as a standard of membership or a criterion of belief. In addition, denominations such as these have made it easier for clergy trained in seminaries outside the denomination to be ordained. An estimated half of all Presbyterian clergy, for example, no longer receive training in the denomination's seminaries. Furthermore, affirmation of doctrinal distinctives in some denominations appears to be receding, in practice if not yet in policy, as a prerequisite for ordination or as a condition of employment as faculty in denominational seminaries.

It is little wonder, therefore, that clergy and church officials, when asked, often deny the importance of denominational distinctives and express doubt that their parishioners have much interest in them. One church official, for example, described as "totally unrealistic" and "just peculiar" the assumption that people in the pew would have much awareness of differences in denominational governing structures. A seminary professor in Texas echoed the same sentiments about distinctive denominational creeds. Not only were parishioners, in his view, unconcerned about differences in belief, but in fact these differences were inconsequential: "The central beliefs of the Methodists are the same as the Episcopalians and Presbyterians." A clergyman in New Jersey was even more adamant: "Creedal distinctions? Are there any today? We all believe in Jesus Christ. We all use the Apostolic Creed."[67]

More serious attitudinal barriers, as suggested earlier, have existed between Protestants and Catholics than among members of different Protestant denominations, but evidence also points toward great reductions in the strength of these barriers. A national poll conducted just prior to World War II, for example, showed that about a third of the public would not vote for a presidential candidate who was a Catholic. By 1960, this sentiment had changed sufficiently for John F. Kennedy to be elected as the nation's first Catholic president. A decade later, polls showed that fewer than one person in ten objected to voting for a Catholic presidential candidate.[68]

Other shifts in public opinion were equally dramatic. For instance, 41 percent of the public polled in a national survey in 1952 said they thought Catholics were trying to get too much power in the United States. By 1965 this proportion had dropped 11 points to 30 percent. And by 1979 it had dropped a dramatic 30 points to only 11 percent. The same surveys showed that in 1952 about 1 Protestant in 10 reported having had an experience that made him or her dislike Catholics. By 1979 only 1 Protestant in 50 reported having had such an experience.[69] Tolerance of intermarriage between Protestants and Catholics has also increased. As recently as 1968, only 63 percent of the public said they approved of interfaith marriages between Protestants and Catholics. Fifteen years later, this proportion had risen to 79 percent.[70] Comparisons of younger and older persons also suggested that these trends were likely to continue. For instance, in 1972 a national poll showed that only 66 percent of Americans over the age of 50 approved of marriages between Protestants and Catholics, whereas 80 percent of Americans between the ages of 18 and 30 approved.[71] Studies comparing the attitudes of teenagers and their parents also suggested that the feelings of Protestants toward Catholics were becoming more positive.[72]

Part of the reason why Protestant and Catholic attitudes were becoming more favorable toward one another was that more interaction between the two was being sponsored by their respective churches at both the grass-roots and more elite levels. As early as the mid-1960s, for example, Protestants and Catholics in South Dakota were reportedly sponsoring joint community services during an annual week of prayer; in Delaware, they were cooperating in the state council of churches; the two were promoting interracial services cooperatively in Minnesota; they were conducting a series of interfaith dialogues on television in Detroit; and were engaged in interfaith youth gatherings in Wyoming. By the mid-1970s Protestants and Catholics had produced a common catechism, Lutherans and Catholics had succeeded in settling many of their theological differences, and even Southern Baptists were reporting growing numbers of cooperative projects with Catholic parishes at the local level.

In part, the reduction of tensions between Protestants and Catholics was also grounded in considerable changes taking place in the social characteristics of American Catholics. As seen earlier, Catholics made significant strides in educational and occupational attainment during the 1960s, so that by the mid-1970s they were indistinguishable from the rest of the population on these measures of social status and were considerably ahead of some Protestant denominations.[73] In other ways, Catholics and Protestants were also becoming virtually indistinguishable. For example, studies of family size, fertility patterns, and contraceptive practices showed that, despite church traditions, few differences remained between Catholics and Protestants by the early 1970s.[74] Evidence comparing younger Catholics and older Catholics also attested to the considerable changes at work. Among Catholics who were 40 years or older during the 1970s, for example, half had been reared by a father who was foreign-born. In comparison, only 20 percent of the Catholics under age 40 in this period had been reared by a foreign-born father. The same data showed that younger Catholics were themselves less likely than older Catholics to have been foreign-born, were better educated, came from a broader variety of ethnic stock, were less regionally concentrated, were less likely to associate themselves with the traditional Catholic preference for the Democratic party, and did not identify as strongly with their own faith.[75]

Probably the most significant source of lowered barriers between Catholics and Protestants, though, was the Second Vatican Council, which took place from 1962 to 1965. Skeptical at first of the council's purposes, Protestant leaders by the end of the decade were hailing it as a major achievement. Some complained that it had not gone far enough, especially with regard to questions of birth control, but the majority saw it as a significant step toward easing interfaith tensions. A layperson from West Nyack, New York, for example, wrote that the council was "a source of joy to all Christians," particularly because it appeared to open the door for greater lay participation and democracy in decision making.[76] An editorial printed in *Christian Century* suggested that the council demonstrated a new sense of "collegiality" which held "exciting prospects" for the ecumenical movement. Even the papacy, it averred, might become an ecumenical institution.[77] Looking back on the council from a longer vantage point, an evangelical writer was able to suggest that it "threw the church's doors wide open to discourse with other Christians," including conservative Protestants who had begun to find common cause with charismatic Catholics and Catholics concerned with issues of public morality.[78]

The attitudinal barriers between Christians and Jews had been even stronger than those between Protestants and Catholics, and for this reason the changes that began to take form in the 1950s and 1960s appear even more profound. In contrast to the 47 percent during the 1940s who felt Jews had too much power, only 17 percent felt this way by 1962. The proportion who saw Jews as a menace to the United States dropped by 18 percentage points over the same period; a drop of 28 points occurred in the proportion who felt Jewish businessmen were dishonest; and a decline of 41 points occurred in the number who thought Jews had objectionable qualities. During the same period, the proportion who said they would be willing to vote for a Jewish presidential candidate climbed from 49 percent to 72 percent, while the number who said it would make a difference to them if a prospective employee were Jewish dropped from 43 percent to 6 percent.[79]

At the start of the 1960s there was, however, still a considerable legacy of tension between Christians and Jews. One study conducted during the 1960s suggested that approximately a third of the population harbored distinctly negative stereotypes of Jews, while as many as another third was tainted by mild evidences of anti-Semitism.[80] The next decade saw an increase of unrest in the Middle East, including greater controversy in U.S. foreign policy toward Israel and the Arab world over the Palestinian question and the most effective ways in which to secure U.S. access to Middle Eastern sources of oil. These controversies aggravated some indicators of negative sentiment toward Jews. But on the whole levels of anti-Semitism continued to diminish. When the study done in the 1960s was replicated in 1981, a significant decrease in anti-Semitic stereotyping was evident on most questions. The proportion of Americans agreeing that "Jews have a lot of irritating faults" dropped from 40 percent to 19 percent; the proportion who thought "Jews stick together too much" declined from 52 percent to 40 percent; and the proportion who believed "Jews use shady practices in business" diminished from 42 percent to 23 percent. Whereas earlier research had implicated Christian convictions as significant contributors to anti-Semitism, the 1981 study also found virtually no effect of strong Christian sentiments on anti-Semitism.[81]

As with Protestants and Catholics, interfaith boundaries between Jews and non-Jews also eroded with respect to views on marriage. In 1968 only a bare majority in national polls said they approved of intermarriage between Jews and non-Jews. By 1983 this figure had risen to 77 percent—nearly the same proportion that approved of Protestant-Catholic intermarriage.[82] Again, younger people and teenagers were more likely to favor marriages between Jews and non-Jews than were older people. And evidence suggested that young people were in fact acting on these impulses. In addition to the evidence already cited, a study reported in the *New York Times* in 1979, for instance, suggested that the rate of current intermarrying between Jews and non-Jews had jumped from only 10 percent in 1960 to 31 percent in the late 1970s.[83]

While much of the reason for these changes undoubtedly lay in broader social trends (some of which will be considered in Chapter 7), conscious efforts on the part of religious leaders themselves were responsible for some of the reductions in interfaith barriers. Organizations such as the National Conference of Christians and Jews and the National Council of Churches played an ongoing role in promoting dialogue across religious lines. Among Catholics, the Second Vatican Council must again be credited with initiating measures that led to improved relations, particularly in challenging some of the traditional stereotypes of Jews' historic role in the crucifixion of Christ. As the editors of *Christian Century* put it at the time, the council had "opened the way to cordial and respectful relations between representatives of Judaism and Christianity."[84] And at the local level, rabbis, priests, and ministers appear to have worked more closely together than ever before. A study of clergy in New Jersey in 1976, for example, found that seven in ten Protestant ministers felt they had learned valuable things from Jewish acquaintances in the past several years; six in ten Catholic priests felt the same way; and two-thirds of the rabbis felt they had also learned from their Protestant and Catholic counterparts. Nearly three-quarters in each group felt that understanding between Christians and Jews had improved significantly over the past five years.[85]

Meeting with a Jewish delegation at the Vatican on February 15, 1985, Pope John Paul II asserted that "relationships between Jews and Christians have radically improved."[86] And a year later he became the first pope to speak in a Jewish synagogue. It was, he declared, a fitting way in which to commemorate the twenty good years that had been initiated by the Second Vatican Council.

Denominations as Organizational Realities

In comparison with the religious climate that prevailed in the 1950s when Will Herberg made his observations, a greater degree of social and cultural homogeneity now seems to characterize the various denominations and faiths. A larger number of people move across religious boundaries to visit or join or even marry someone from another faith. And attitudes toward other faiths show a considerably higher degree of acceptance. In these ways, denominationalism has become less significant as a basis for social and cultural tensions and divisions. Some of the historic differences in regional location and social status still differentiate members of the various denominations. Marriages, social interaction, and attitudes also still reflect some of these historic lines of demarcation. But the period since World War II has witnessed a clear reduction of these symbolic cleavages. Most Americans now accept the idea that an increasing number of young people will marry persons of different religious backgrounds. An exceedingly small proportion of the population finds in denominational boundaries a basis for negative attitudes. The deep misgivings and outright hostility that separated Protestants and Catholics in the years immediately after World War II have largely receded from public view. The prejudices that promoted even deeper antagonisms between Christians and Jews, while by no means gone, have been greatly reduced during the past three or four decades. Efforts by religious leaders to promote active cooperation across religious lines have begun to bear fruit, even if the harvest has not been as abundant as some would have liked. Greater levels of regional migration, together with forces in the economy that have promoted similarities in social standing among persons of different religious heritages, appear to have contributed to the easing of religious tensions. And, perhaps more than anything else, rising levels of education have worked as a social solvent. As the population has become better educated, denominational barriers have ceased to function as hermetic categories of religious identification.

Yet it would clearly be overstating the case to suggest that denominationalism no longer carries any weight at all. The vast majority of Americans who claim some religious identity still use denominational labels to characterize themselves. Most of the new churches that are built each year still affiliate with one denomination or another. And despite the apparent growth of independent churches that carry no denominational affiliations, the number of people who are members of these churches, in comparison with the number who hold membership in denominational churches, is extremely small. According to a 1984 Gallup survey, for example, only 3 percent of the public has ever been a member of an independent, nondenominational church. As organizational realities, denominations also continue to serve as the arenas in which most of the business of American religion is conducted. Bureaus, agencies, representative assemblies, budgets, and seminaries still fall mainly into denominational categories.

The fact that religion in the United States remains organizationally structured into several dozen major and several hundred smaller denominations will be important to bear in mind in subsequent chapters that focus on some of the newer divisions that have become prominent in American religion. Were there only a single hierarchy to which all local churches were beholden, things would be quite different. Or even if there were a single hierarchy representing all Protestants, the dynamics of contemporary religious conflicts would likely be very different. In recognizing the continuing organizational significance of denominationalism, however, two caveats must also be kept in mind.

The first is that the sheer bureaucratic role of the denominational hierarchies, while enormously significant, should not be overemphasized. For a time, especially during the turmoil of the late 1960s, it seemed to many observers of American religion that the national hierarchies of the major denominations, for good or bad, were becoming increasingly powerful entities unto themselves. There was, in fact, some evidence that people were becoming alienated from the powerbrokers who operated these bureaucracies, and that the bureaucrats were set on taking their denominations on courses quite different from the ones favored at the grass roots. As the authors of a national study conducted among the members of 15 major denominations in 1972 put it:

> Out of the inherited citizenry-versus-the-colossus mentality has grown a kind of schizoid image of the church, split between the intimate local congregation on the one side and the remote, impersonal denomination on the other. Sometimes, the implication almost has seemed to be that they are pitted against each other. [There was] a tendency to concentrate resources on the community level and downgrade the denomination. It also was registered in the catchphrases of the times, the "anti-institution" and "anti-establishment" temper among youths.[87]

Some of these problems were aggravated by differences in education, outlook, and social background between the bureaucrats and the grass roots and by the fear that central hierarchies were seizing power from the local churches. Fears were also expressed that the central bureaucrats were, in the words of the authors of the same study, putting the local churches in a "financial squeeze."

How much these fears may have been well founded is difficult to establish with any precision. Some evidence, however, suggests that there has *not* been a demonstrable trend toward central agencies expanding their power relative to the local churches in the period since World War II. At the start of this period (as seen in Chapter 2), denominations had already become major business enterprises. Much of the growth had occurred gradually over a period of at least a half century. And the expansion that was initiated soon after the war led to even further growth. By 1953, for example, the central agencies of the Southern Baptist Convention were operating with a budget in excess of $45 million; those of the Presbyterian Church, U.S.A., with an annual budget of $21 million; and those of the Episcopal church, with a budget of more than $15 million. Over the years, growth in memberships, generalized affluence in the economy at large, and inflation rates have combined to greatly increase these budgets in absolute terms. And in absolute terms, denominational hierarchies have been able to sustain a larger variety of functions fulfilled by a larger number of professional staff workers. In relative terms, though, the central budgets have not expanded.

Looking again at the Southern Baptist Convention, for example, its Executive Committee utilized only 5.6 percent of the denomination's total receipts in 1946. By 1968, at the height of much of the concern about growing centralized power, this percentage had risen only to 5.9 percent. And by 1977, it stood again at 5.6 percent. The story in the Episcopal church was much the same (although the years for which comparable data are available differ). In 1945 the total budget for the work of central agencies amounted to 5.4 percent of the denomination's receipts. In 1960 the comparable proportion was 5.9 percent. And in 1967 this proportion was back to 5.4 percent. Finally, the picture in the Presbyterian Church, U.S.A., provides even more dramatic disconfirmation of the idea that central bureaucracies have expanded their expenditures relative to funds left over for other activities. In 1946 the money that went to central boards and agencies amounted to 11 percent of all denominational giving. By 1969, again amidst much concern about central bureaucratic growth, this proportion had actually declined slightly to 10 percent of total giving. And by 1982, it was down to only 5 percent.[88] By these financial criteria, which constitute one of the surer ways in which to make such comparisons, then, little support is evident for the idea that the relative importance of denominations as centralized organizations has been increasing.

The other caveat to bear in mind is that denominations by no means constitute the only organizational forms in which the business of American religion is conducted. Since World War II an increasing role has been played by other kinds of organizations that function in ways different from those comprising the official hierarchies of denominations. The growth of these alternative organizational forms is the subject of the next chapter.

CHAPTER 6

The Growth of Special Purpose Groups

AMONG the numerous curiosities that have characterized American religion since World War II, one of the more curious was an organization that emerged toward the end of a long cycle of cult and anticult activity that had begun in the 1970s. Early in 1984, a few weeks after the Reverend Sun Myung Moon (leader of the Unification Church) was sentenced to jail for tax fraud, an organization came into being under the auspices of an unlikely coalition of religious activists. Calling themselves the Coalition for Religious Freedom, the organization's leaders were inspired to action by the threat to religious pluralism in the nation at large they saw in Moon's sentencing. Seemingly persuaded that George Orwell's vision of a totalitarian society was becoming a reality in the very year for which it had been predicted, they called for religious people everywhere to join hands against further intrusion by the state into matters of the sacred. These were not "Moonies" themselves, fired by a desire to free their imprisoned leader. They were in fact staunch doctrinal enemies of the Unification Church, including Protestant fundamentalist leaders Tim LaHaye, a founding board member of Moral Majority, and Robert Grant, founder of Christian Voice. But Moon's cause was theirs, for at stake was the right to advance minority religious views without fear of state interference.

The Coalition for Religious Freedom is important in the present context not so much because of the specific issue to which it responded nor the spectacle of Moonies and fundamentalists joining forces at protest demonstrations (although both made headlines). It is interesting because literally scores of such organizations have emerged in American religion since World War II. The most publicized have generally been associated with the "New Christian Right": organizations such as Moral Majority, Christian Voice, Religious Roundtable, the National Federation for Decency, and the National Christian Action Coalition, to name a few. These, however, have been only the visible tip of a much larger iceberg. Other such groups, with vastly different political views, goals, and organizational styles, have been at least as numerous. Their causes range from nuclear arms control to liturgical renewal, from gender equality to cult surveillance, from healing ministries to evangelism. They address issues both specific to the churches and of more general concern to the broader society. Yet they are clearly rooted in the religious realm. They take their legitimating slogans from religious creeds. And they draw their organizational resources, leadership, and personnel largely from churches and ecclesiastical agencies.

Most of these organizations, however, defy typical portraits of religious groups. They do not lead to the creation of religious sects which grow into established churches. Nor do they produce new or distinct denominations. The Coalition for Religious Freedom, for example, shows no signs of drawing people away from churches, of constituting itself as a separate religious sect, or of creating a new denomination. Its very survival, depending as it does on resources from churches with radically different doctrines, requires it to avoid these tendencies. Much the same can be said for Moral Majority, the National Christian Action Coalition, and any number of other groups. Their orientation is toward a specific objective and their tactics involve mobilizing resources toward attaining this objective. When the objective has been achieved, they dissolve or (more often) find a new, but still delimited, objective to pursue. They are not for the most part oriented toward becoming membership organizations that take the place of existing churches or sects. And, while many are closely allied with established denominations, more and more of these organizations seem to be interdenominational or nondenominational.

At the same time that the significance of denominationalism appears in many ways to be declining, then, these kinds of special purpose groups seem to be gaining importance in American religion. Students of American religion have generally paid little attention to these kinds of organizations, relative to the extraordinary interest that has been devoted to churches and denominations. But if these organizations are in fact on the rise, their character, numbers, memberships, social sources, and implications for American religion all warrant consideration. As a style of organization, the growth of special purpose groups constitutes a significant form of social restructuring in American religion.

An American Tradition

Special purpose groups in religion do not signal a new invention, nor can they be considered unique to the United States. They have, in fact, enjoyed a long history, alongside churches and denominations, as ways of advancing and renewing Western religion.

With the fracturing of Christendom that accompanied the Reformation in the sixteenth century, denominationalism emerged as a potentially prominent mode of religious organization. The religious settlements that were forged in the wake of the Reformation, however, delayed the growth of separate denominations within societies by imposing state churches or territorial creeds in most of the Protestant areas of Europe, including England, Scandinavia, and major German principalities such as Saxony, Hesse, and Brandenburg. These settlements were to have an important effect on the subsequent history of denominationalism, but for the first century and a half after the Reformation they succeeded in limiting the growth of distinct religious bodies organized along denominational lines. By the middle of the eighteenth century a number of so-called "free," "dissenting," and "nonconformist" sects had managed to become established alongside the official churches—a fact that has received considerable emphasis in subsequent treatises contributing to the development of church-sect theory within the social sciences. Nevertheless, the predominance of state churches meant that many of the influential developments shaping European Protestantism came about through the workings of internal reform movements, organized as special purpose groups, not from splinter groups or separatist sects.

The Oxford movement in England was one of the most prominent examples of these special purpose groups. Originating at Oxford in 1833, this movement (also known as the Tractarian movement) promoted a revival of interest in liturgy and worship within the Anglican church, as well as a renewal of emphasis on conservative doctrine and greater cooperation between Anglicans and Roman Catholics. Not unlike some of the special purpose organizations that have developed in the United States in recent years, the Oxford movement also championed greater separation of church and state. Indeed, one interpretation of its founding suggests that it owed much to a wave of ill-feeling toward Parliament for interfering in the church's affairs.

Missionary societies provide another prominent example of special purpose groups in European religious history. During the period of mercantilism and colonial trade in the seventeenth century, for example, extensive missionary activity was carried out in the region later known as Indochina. Most of this work was carried on by members of Catholic religious orders, particularly Jesuits, Dominicans, and Franciscans. However, one of the Jesuits who had participated became convinced that there was a special need for secular priests who could train native clergy. To meet this need, he and a group of like-minded clergy in Paris formed the Society of Foreign Missions, formally founded in 1663. Through the work of this organization, native churches were eventually planted throughout much of Southeast and East Asia.[1] Over the years, many other missionary organizations came into being as special purpose groups: the Society for the Propagation of the Gospel in Foreign Parts, begun in the British colonies in 1701; the London Missionary Society, in

1795; the Society of the Missionaries of France, founded in 1815; the Pious Society of Missions, founded in 1835; and the Leopold Association, begun in 1838.

Special purpose groups founded by members of larger religious organizations for the task of administering charity, helping the poor, or reforming social conditions also have a long history. For instance, a group of wealthy evangelicals who lived near one another in a suburb of London formed an organization in the 1780s, later known as the Clapham sect, which sponsored a number of philanthropic projects. Among these were efforts to resettle blacks in Sierra Leone and eventually the formation of a protolegislative interest group which pushed for the abolition of slavery in British domains (accomplished in 1833). Another such organization was the Society of Saint Vincent DePaul, organized in Paris in the 1830s. Notable for its efforts to enlist the voluntary labor of lay church people, it spread widely as an agency for administering care to the sick and poor.

In the United States, the dynamics of competing sects and denominational pluralism played a much stronger role in reforming, renewing, and promoting the work of religious organizations than was the case anywhere in Europe. Separation of church and state, ethnic diversity, recurrent waves of immigration, and great geographic opportunities for expansion all combined with one another to ensure that sects, churches, and denominations would overshadow the work of special purpose groups. Yet the very diversity that promoted denominationalism also contributed to an early and significant rise of special purpose groups in American religion. Since at least the beginning of the nineteenth century, American religion has been characterized by a rich tradition of such groups both within denominations and across denominational lines.

Among the first special purpose groups devoted to religious causes in the United States were those organized to promote the evangelization of native Americans, immigrants, and peoples of other countries, including Europe and Asia. One of these was the American Board of Commissioners for Foreign Missions, founded in 1810. Modeled after a similar organization that had been founded six years earlier in England, the board drew its leadership principally from among students at Andover Theological Seminary in Massachusetts, which had been founded a few years earlier by conservative Congregationalists to counter the Unitarian tendencies at Harvard. During the first 50 years of the board's existence nearly 1,000 missionaries were sent out, primarily to the Orient and the Pacific islands. The board also provided a model for the founding of many other missionary societies, one of the first of which was the Baptist Missionary Society (founded in 1814). By 1860, 3 more missionary ventures had been organized and by the turn of the century this number had grown to 94.

The early decades of the nineteenth century were also characterized by the formation of a number of special purpose groups that spanned denominational boundaries. Concerned by the rising denominational strife between Congregationalists and Unitarians, New and Old School Presbyterians, and Baptists and Methodists, religious reformers created organizations that conscientiously avoided denominational labels in order to carry ministries into new areas. The American Bible Society, founded in 1816, provided a model which many other organizations were to emulate. From the beginning, it focused narrowly on the task of distributing Bibles rather than developing a broader variety of functions comparable to the ones served by local churches. Its origins, in fact, lay in the work of a number of local and regional Bible societies, mostly founded during the first decade of the nineteenth century, which came to realize the need for greater centralization and coordination. Other organizations that exemplified early attempts to coordinate specialized religious activities on a national scale across denominational lines included the American Tract Society, founded in 1823; the American Sunday School Union, 1824; the American Education Society, 1826; and the American Temperance Union, 1836. Most of these organizations followed a pattern of development that has continued to be evident among special purpose religious organizations right up to the present: leaders involved in other organizations (here, primarily the missionary societies) became aware of common interests in new causes; through the infrastructure provided by local churches, chapters of the new organization began to spread; some coordination was provided by a single office at the state or regional level; and as several of these regional operations came into being the need for coordination at a higher level resulted in the formation of a national umbrella organization.

While most of these organizations developed into formally coordinated agencies, other special purpose groups had a significant impact on the formation of American religion in the nineteenth century without ever becoming formal organizations. Fed largely by popular zeal, they contributed greatly to the vitality of local churches, often by mobilizing parishioners with special interests or by generating enthusiasm that spilled over into the more general life of local congregations. One example was the prayer meeting movement which developed in New York City in the 1850s. Begun by a group of lay people in a single church who desired special opportunities to pray together, the movement spread quickly throughout the city. By the end of six months it was estimated to have drawn more than 10,000 participants. Remaining genuinely interdenominational rather than forming new sects or churches, it was eventually credited with having added some 500,000 new members to the city's churches.

Another special purpose organization that grew largely out of the churches was the movement that became known as abolitionism, which appeared during the middle decades of the nineteenth century. Though less centrally organized than some of its predecessors, it manifested a relatively high degree of coordination and directed its efforts toward the attainment of a single goal. Advanced from pulpits, popularized through religious periodicals, and assisted by clergy and laity from numerous denominations, it linked theological and moral arguments to the question of slavery. Like the temperance movement, it also exhibited a cultural style that was to continue as a feature of many special purpose groups. Rather than being directed strictly toward serving the churches themselves, it became a vehicle for articulating religious themes in relation to issues of broader social significance. While it did result indirectly in an increase in denominationalism, particularly in the splits that developed between northern and southern Presbyterians, Methodists, and Baptists, it was not oriented primarily toward denominationalism. Indeed, its effectiveness lay in its ability to cut across denominational lines and mobilize action among the members of many different kinds of churches.

During the last half of the nineteenth century, special purpose groups in religion focused increasingly on the rising social problems associated with industrialization and urbanization. Among these were numerous temperance societies, such as the Women's Christian Temperance Union (1874) and the Anti-Saloon League (1895), which were organized to fight the growing ills of alcoholism, desertion, vagrancy, and child abuse that reformers saw ravaging the cities. At first limited mainly to local communities, the work of these societies grew to the point of eventually playing an important role in the ratification of the Eighteenth Amendment in 1919.

A whole variety of special purpose groups also came into being as efforts to carry out the churches' tasks more effectively in the new urban environment. The Salvation Army, for example, quadrupled in size between 1890 and 1915, enlisting the services of more than 35,000 volunteers by the time the United States entered World War I. Although it came closer to evolving into a distinct sect than most other special purpose groups of the time, its goals focused primarily on the specific task of ministering to the urban poor. It depended on unpaid and largely uneducated volunteers rather than trained clergy. It sponsored youth groups and open-air rallies, using its uniforms and brass bands to attract attention, rather than holding conventional worship services. And it devoted most of its financial resources, meager as they were, to the construction of orphanages and lodging facilities for immigrants rather than building churches. The strategy adopted by the YMCA followed along similar lines. Starting during the Civil War with fewer than 10,000 volunteers, the YMCA grew to 263,000 volunteers by 1895, and then mushroomed to

720,000 volunteers by the outbreak of World War I. Like the Salvation Army, it utilized the services of lay volunteers rather than enlisting professional clergy; it aimed more at mobilizing its volunteers than at cultivating members; and it organized special interest groups such as reading clubs and chapters on college campuses rather than competing head-on with the established churches.

Special purpose groups also worked closely with local churches and through denominational hierarchies to extend the reaches of American religion into untapped avenues of urban society. The Gideons International (founded in 1899), for example, used local churches to recruit business and professional men who were interested in distributing Bibles. It also drew on the contributions of church members to fund operations. Groups that broadened the churches' reach in other ways included the Catholic Church Extension Society, founded in 1905; the Pocket Testament League, 1908; the Knights of the Immaculata Movement, 1917; and the Association of Baptists for World Evangelism, 1927. Many of these organizations used up-to-date managerial techniques and had publishing equipment which was the envy of many denominational bureaucrats. And like their predecessors in the nineteenth century, they devoted a great deal of their effort to coordinating the efforts of successful local operations. By centralizing the thrust of these operations, they were also in a position to amass funds needed for larger projects, such as publishing, conference organizing, and employing professional staff members.

In short, then, American religion has been characterized by a long history of special purpose groups. Alongside its numerous sects, churches, and denominations has functioned an impressive array of organizations devoted to the attainment of more focused objectives. Many of these organizations have outlived their initial purposes and have become defunct. Others have grown steadily over the years to the point that they now operate on an impressive scale. The American Bible Society, for example, currently distributes nearly 10 million Bibles and New Testaments annually plus more than 200 million portions of scripture. Some 60,000 volunteers carry out the various activities of the society, which operates on an annual budget of approximately $42 million. More than 100 denominations cooperate in supporting this work, which includes not only scripture distribution but also translation projects, cassette ministries for the blind, hunger and disaster relief, ministries to tourists, athletic programs for inner-city youth, and services in hospitals and prisons. The society also coordinates work among approximately two dozen internationally based Bible societies which together distribute more than 25 million Bibles and New Testaments and some 450 million scripture selections each year worldwide.[2]

Numbers and Varieties

Over the course of the twentieth century the numbers and varieties of special purpose groups in American religion have grown dramatically. Though still modeled on some of the groups that began more than a century and a half ago, their objectives have expanded enormously. And with this expansion a great deal more variety in tactics, strategies, and organizational structures has also become evident. Particularly in the years since World War II, these organizations have grown to such large proportions that they now appear to cast their imprint heavily on the character of American religion more generally.

Estimates of the precise numbers of these organizations are difficult to come by because of their exceptionally diverse range of styles, administrative forms, locations, sizes, and levels of organization. Consider an organization called FISH, for example. Taking its title from the symbol chosen by the early Christian community and using this title as an acronym for "Friends In Service Here," FISH operates in more than 800 locations, mostly through the volunteer work of local church members. Its goal is to provide physical and emotional care to needy persons in the wider community without regard to religious affiliation: transportation for the elderly and handicapped, companionship for shut-ins, lawn care, home repair, meals. The organization provides materials that tell interested church groups how to initiate services of this kind (e.g., advice on setting up a telephone hotline, enlisting volunteers, dealing with crisis situations). It also gives new programs an established label with which to legitimate themselves when approaching potential volunteers, social workers, newspapers, and coordinators of community services. Yet the organization actually has no reality as an organization per se. It has no headquarters, no central staff, and no budget. Local chapters exhaust its presence. And these vary widely from one community to another.

Enumerating organizations such as FISH is nearly an impossibility. They have no legal status, no central location, and in many instances, virtually no public identity beyond the relatively few who are served by them or who donate time to keep them going. Chances are, thousands of such organizations exist. They operate largely without formal structure and yet serve as an important link between churches and the broader society.

If special purpose groups within particular congregations are considered, the problem of enumeration becomes even more complex. Anyone who has scanned the announced activities printed in a church's weekly leaflet knows their tremendous number and range. Bible study groups, choir, men's breakfast clubs, ladies auxiliaries, and youth activities scarcely begin to tap their versatility. Now there are peace fellowships, support groups for the unemployed, parents-without-partners clubs, committees on door-to-door evangelism, study groups, tea circles, long-range planning commissions, food cooperatives, exercise groups, and book clubs. All of these qualify as special purpose groups. They focus on limited objectives, attract participants with special interests, and generally do not constitute the main arenas in which the worship and instruction of the church as a corporate body take place. Sometimes they are local chapters of larger organizations within the denomination. But often they have no connection at all with the activities of other churches. Some indication of the extent to which the public is involved in these kinds of groups can be obtained from surveys (as will be seen later). Clearly, though, no reliable estimates exist as to the overall numbers of such groups.

Only by limiting attention to nationally organized special purpose groups is it possible to observe with some accuracy the overall numbers of these groups. Currently there are approximately 800 nationally incorporated nonprofit voluntary associations that meet the Internal Revenue Service's qualifications for religious organizations, but which are not themselves churches or denominations. Since there are approximately 16,000 national nonprofit associations of all kinds, these religious associations comprise about 5 percent of the total.[3]

To give some perspective on this number, the 800 nationally incorporated special purpose groups in American religion compare with some 1,200 denominations, if the very broadest definition of denomination is used; or with some 200 denominations, if a more standard figure is used; or with fewer than 100 denominations, if only those having substantial memberships are counted. By these comparisons, the number of special purpose groups is hardly insignificant.

Of course, special purpose organizations and denominations are not exactly comparable. Whereas denominations consist of local congregations that generally have distinct memberships and hold regular services, special purpose organizations encompass a much broader variety of structures. Some of their memberships overlap with the memberships of denominations, some have memberships that cut across denominations, and some operate more as clearing houses or depend on the work of a few professional staff persons rather than cultivating memberships at all. On the average, special purpose groups in no way rival the major denominations either in memberships or budgets. Yet some of the nationally incorporated special purpose groups are quite substantial. The American Bible Society, with its budget of some $42 million, is one such organization that rivals the operations of many denominations. Or to cite some other examples, the Bible Memory Association boasts a membership of 395,000 members. The Fellowship of Christian Athletes, an evangelistic association limited to professional and collegiate athletes, claims a membership of 30,000. And the Full Gospel Business Men's Fellowship, an organization founded in 1953 to promote the charismatic gifts of glossolalia and faith healing among members of established denominations, counts some 50,000 members among its 2,700 local chapters.

As these examples suggest, special purpose organizations come in nearly as many varieties as there are special purposes around which to organize. A number of them reflect the interests of constituencies with specialized talents, skills, or occupations. Unlike churches, which generally attempt to draw members from a wide cross-section of age and interest groups, these organizations take a more selective cut of the population. Like the Fellowship of Christian Athletes, they require that members not only have religious inclinations of a certain kind but that they also be qualified in other ways. The Christian Business Men's Committee, for example, was founded in 1930 to encourage business and professional men to become involved in evangelistic activities. With a membership of close to 10,000 currently in 500 local groups, it continues to appeal primarily to this particular segment of the population. Another example is the Christian Legal Society. Founded in 1961, its goal is to help lawyers, judges, and law students serve Christ in their professional lives. It also promotes discussions of legal justice and ethical practice, provides resources for studies in the relation between law and theology, and like many other special purpose organizations sponsors conferences and retreats and publishes several journals and newsletters. Other examples of special purpose groups organized around the interests of persons in particular professions include the Christian Chiropractors Association, an organization of approximately 800 members, founded in 1953; the Fellowship of Christian Magicians, also founded in 1953, with a current membership of 1,300; and the Fellowship of Christian Peace Officers, founded in 1971, with a current membership of 2,500.

In addition, a number of special purpose groups have been founded by persons whose common interests focus on hobbies or avocations that can in some way be combined with religion. For example, one organization focuses on drag racers and their pit crews. It combines an interest in trying to promote drag racing as a wholesome family sport with an attempt to encourage closer bonds among drag racers who happen to be Christians and efforts to evangelize other drag racers. Another national organization has tried to carry out similar activities among persons whose religious interests intersect with poetry. Amateur pilots, musicians, pyramidologists, free-lance writers, and former alcoholics also have their own religious associations. Most of these organizations have only diffuse goals. Their purpose is mainly to put people with similar interests into contact with one another. They facilitate communication, uphold rather distinctive sets of values, and encourage people with religious convictions to intermingle in the course of other kinds of activities.

A different set of special purpose groups focuses much more instrumentally on the accomplishment of specific objectives. The Bible Creation Association, for example, was founded in 1964 with the specific goal of promoting creationism in the public schools. Its 20,000 members engage in lobbying, attend local school board meetings, visit classrooms, and distribute materials developed by the association for classroom use in all grades from kindergarten through high school. An organization with nearly the opposite goal is the National League for Separation of Church and State. Its objectives include saving the public schools from the influence of religious groups, repealing laws based upon religious beliefs, and maintaining the civil rights of nonbelievers. A similar organization, called the Freedom from Religion Foundation, opposes the use of public funds for any religious purpose, combats prayer in public schools, and provides watchdog services against potentially illegal activities on the part of religious charities.

Many of the special purpose groups that have been founded over the past several decades function much like professional associations in other sectors of the society. Indeed, their memberships are comprised less of laity or volunteers than of clergy and auxiliary religious workers. Their existence is predicated on the fact that American religion is itself a vast industry. Thus, one finds, for example, a special purpose group called the National Association of Church Business Administrators. Its 700 members consist entirely of professional administrators employed by local churches. The organization provides job placement information, conducts research, compiles statistics, maintains a library of materials on church management, and holds annual conferences. It also gives awards to outstanding members of its profession and maintains a national hall of fame. Even more specialized is the National Association of Church Personnel Administrators. Its membership of more than 400 is restricted to church managers concerned with personnel practices. Again, the organization serves as a clearing house for technical information, runs workshops, and provides informal occasions for its members to exchange ideas. Other associations provide similar services to professional and semiprofessional religious workers of different kinds: church secretaries, who founded their own association in 1983; religious broadcasters, represented by several associations, the largest of which was founded in 1944; chaplains, who have 9 different associations; pastoral counselors, represented by 4 separate organizations; Christian educators; staff members of ecumenical bodies; Bible translators; campus ministers; and, of course, missionaries of all kinds.

In size of membership, though, the largest special purpose organizations continue to be ones that represent special segments of the broader churchgoing population. Organized both within single denominations and across denominational lines, these bodies generally target their activities toward gender-differentiated groups or age-graded populations. Many have long histories and continue to function along well-established lines of organization, but a number of others have come into being only in recent years. Women's missionary societies constitute some of the earliest of these organizations. The Women's Missionary Union, for example, was founded among Southern Baptist women in 1888. Currently numbering approximately 1.5 million members, it continues to serve as a support base for missionaries working in foreign fields. Among its activities are prayer meetings, fund-raising, care for the children of missionaries, and recruitment. Youth organizations also have a fairly long history as special purpose groups. In 1919, for example, members of the Christian Reformed Church founded the Young Calvinist Federation as a way of furthering the activities of youth groups in local churches. Today, the organization counts 15,000 members in 700 local groups in 49 states. Much of its work continues to be carried out within these local chapters. However, the national organization facilitates this work by providing training for leaders, by supplying a model constitution and other organizational advice to new groups, and by publishing a number of study guides and newsletters. The federation also maintains a network aimed at encouraging greater communication among members of local chapters, provides opportunities for youth to become involved in volunteer service projects, maintains several summer camps, publishes a hospitality directory for military personnel, and supplies speakers and youth teams skilled in music and drama for local conferences.

Groups organized by age or by gender that have been founded in more recent years include several associations devoted to the interests of the elderly, a growing number of organizations targeted to the college-age population, and groups oriented toward the changing gender roles of men and women. A group called Catholic Golden Age, for example, was organized in 1974 to minister to the special needs and interests of Catholics past the age of 50. Presently numbering some 700,000 members, it sponsors charitable work, holds worship services, and offers counseling programs on death and bereavement. This organization also functions like many secular associations of senior citizens in providing discounts on hotels and rental cars, organizing tours, and supplying insurance at group rates. Among the many special purpose groups that have been founded for college-age people are Nurses' Christian Fellowship, organized primarily for nursing students, and Campus Ministries of America, designed to promote evangelical religion among both students and faculty. Groups concerned with changing gender roles, organized primarily by women, include numerous causes and coalitions, such as the Evangelical Women's Caucus, founded in San Francisco in 1974, and the Coalition on Women and Religion, organized in Seattle in 1973.

Sources of Growth

The most striking feature of these special purpose groups is the tremendous number that have been founded within the past two decades. Since 1960, approximately 300 new organizations have been founded. And since World War II the number of new organizations totals nearly 500. This means, of course, that the majority of special purpose groups in American religion are relatively young and that the number presently in operation is far larger than at any time in American history. At the close of the Civil War, for example, no more than several dozen such groups were known to have been in existence. At the turn of the century, fewer than 150 were in operation. And at the end of World War II the number totaled only about 400. Over roughly the past four decades, therefore, more groups have been founded than during the entire previous century.

Has this growth been exceptional? Certainly not in comparison with other types of voluntary associations. In 1880, for example, special purpose groups devoted to religious concerns comprised about 5 percent of all voluntary associations, just as they do in the 1980s. And some categories of voluntary associations have grown much more rapidly over the past quarter century or so than religious associations. Nonprofit associations concerned with governmental activities and with public affairs, for example, have grown considerably more rapidly. More than half of all nonprofit associations presently concerned with governmental, legal, and military affairs have come into existence since 1960. In comparison, only about a third of the associations presently concerned with religion have been founded since 1960. And among associations currently involved with so-called "public affairs" activities, 4 in 5 have origins more recent than 1960. In absolute numbers, the 300 or so religious associations that have been founded in the past quarter century are greatly overshadowed by the more than 1,500 associations founded in this period to pursue governmental activities and public affairs.

In comparison with the trends for religious denominations, however, the growth in special purpose religious associations has been considerably more spectacular. Taking one of the more inclusive estimates for denominations as a baseline, but deleting countercultural communes, spiritualist groups, and the like, reveals that denominations outnumbered special purpose religious groups at the start of this century by a ratio of about 2 to 1. By the end of World War II, the margin had been reduced dramatically: denominations of all kinds outnumbered special purpose religious groups by a ratio of only about 1.2 to 1. And by the mid-1970s, special purpose groups outnumbered denominations—even by this inclusive standard. During the 1960s and early 1970s, special purpose groups grew at a pace at least a third faster than denominations.[4] As a proportion of the total population, moreover, membership in denominations has been relatively stagnant overall during the past quarter century, whereas membership in special purpose groups appears to have risen dramatically.

At the same time that the significance of denominationalism has been declining, then, the significance of special purpose groups in American religion appears to be decidedly on the increase. The decline in denominationalism is, in fact, further evidenced by a tendency for fewer and fewer of these special purpose groups to be associated with denominations. Forty-seven percent of the special purpose groups that were founded prior to 1960 had clear denominational sponsorship of one kind or another. In comparison, only 32 percent of the groups founded since 1960 have had denominational sponsorship. Comparing the two time periods also shows that the proportion of special purpose groups that were clearly nondenominational increased from 28 percent to 39 percent of the total. Organizations sponsored by intradenominational groups—that is, by members of one denomination but not representing the entire denomination or having official denominational sponsorship—grew from 2 percent of the total to 9 percent. And those representing cooperative ventures among two or more denominations decreased from 11 percent to 7 percent (the remainder could not be classified). In short, special purpose groups have not only increased in prominence relative to denominations but have also become more distinctly separate from denominations in origins and sponsorship.

Several factors appear to have contributed to the overall rate of growth in special purpose religious groups since the 1960s. One that has already been mentioned is the heightened degree of professionalization among religious workers. Tendencies toward professionalization have been prominent in the society at large and religious workers appear to have been no exception. Thus, the fact that new associations concerned with the interests of church administrators, counselors, and so on, have come into being reflects broader tendencies toward the founding of such associations as well as a greater degree of specialization among clergy.

Imitation of secular associations appears to be responsible for a variety of other religious groups as well. For example, many of the caucuses, coalitions, and associations that emerged to promote racial equality during the civil rights movement developed counterpart organizations within religious bodies. Formed in 1968, for instance, the American Baptist Black Caucus came into being as a way of consolidating the gains that had been achieved by the civil rights movement more generally. Its aim was to promote racial equality in hiring and employment practices within the American Baptist denomination and to further the denomination's work among inner-city youth and in black colleges. The National Black Catholic Clergy Caucus was formed the same year, as was the National Black Sisters' Conference. Other religious associations that responded to larger movements in the society included organizations concerned with gender equality, homosexuality, and cults.

Other factors that have probably contributed to the growth of special purpose groups in American religion include generalized levels of affluence, giving people time and money to devote to voluntary activities, and higher levels of public awareness through the expansion of television, other sources of mass communication, and education. New technologies, such as direct-mail capabilities and computers, have undoubtedly contributed to the development of some of these organizations. The American Baptist Black Caucus, for example, maintains a vast computerized information service for its members. Or to take a different example, the National Catholic Development Conference, which was also founded in 1968, came into existence primarily to disseminate opportunities for fund-raising made possible by direct-mail techniques and computers. And the simple fact cannot be overlooked that the founding of one organization aimed at achieving a specific goal often leads to the founding of a counterorganization aimed at preventing the first organization from achieving its goal—or at least sharing in the action if the goal is achieved. Several of the organizations that were mentioned earlier with concerns about the role of religion in public schools provide clear examples.

If there is any single factor responsible for the growth of special purpose groups in American religion, however, it is the state. The state's role in stimulating this growth has been both direct and indirect. As the state has expanded its functions, particularly in areas of welfare, education, equal rights legislation and other kinds of regulation that affect the day-to-day activities of citizens, special interest groups have arisen for the express purpose of combating, restraining, or promoting certain types of government action. Just as the early temperance societies focused on obtaining favorable legislation for their cause, so the contemporary organizations in American religion are in many cases oriented toward mobilizing political influence. And the number of groups so oriented has grown considerably in recent decades.

At the close of World War II, only a handful of religious organizations had political influence as their primary goal. Operating largely on behalf of specific denominations, these groups often represented interests clearly outside those of the religious mainstream. One of the few religious organizations specifically concerned with legislative action, for example, was the Bible Sabbath Association. Comprised primarily of Seventh-Day Adventists, who held worship services on Saturday, this organization focused its efforts mainly on trying to overthrow Sunday closing laws. Another such group was the National Reform Association, sponsored by the 5,000-member Reformed Presbyterian Church in North America for the purpose of promoting an amendment to the Constitution requiring elected officials to uphold Christian principles and for the nation as a whole to recognize the sovereignty of Christ in constitutional affairs.

Several other groups also came into being in the 1940s with political concerns as their chief objective. Two that grew out of the controversies surrounding public transportation of children to parochial schools, for example, were the National League for Separation of Church and State (founded in 1946) and Americans United for Separation of Church and State (founded in 1947). The latter has remained strong, currently drawing support from approximately 55,000 members in 115 locations and employing a professional staff of 25. It engages in First Amendment lobbying, participates in legal suits, and publishes a variety of materials. Most of the special purpose religious organizations that are concerned with the state, however, date only from the 1960s.

The organizations that were founded in the 1960s, as well as some that were not formed until the 1970s, came into being mainly as responses to government rulings concerning prayer in public schools or as reactions against these groups, often drawing inspiration from the courts for more general campaigns aimed at restricting the influence of religious groups. Americans for God, to take one example, was founded in 1968 for the specific purpose of combating the government's ban on prayer and Bible reading in the public schools. A similar organization was founded by a Texas businessman a few years later. Its goal was to promote Christian values more generally by enacting into law a Christian legal system. Also concerned with legal issues, the Christian Law Association was formed to provide legal services to conservative Christians and more broadly to advocate a conservative Christian interpretation of the First Amendment. On the other side, groups like the Society of Separationists (founded in 1963), the Tolerants (founded in 1968), and several that have already been mentioned gained life by opposing these efforts to bring Christian values to bear on the state.

The state's role in stimulating special purpose groups during the 1960s and 1970s was also evident in a wider variety of arenas. The effect of the civil rights legislation in the early 1960s, as already mentioned, was to prompt religious organizations to form caucuses and coalitions oriented toward the promotion of racial equality. Organizations such as the National Office for Black Catholics, the Union of Black Episcopalians, and the National Black Evangelical Association all drew their inspiration from this legislation and the efforts from which it emerged. As the government's involvement in Southeast Asia degenerated into massive military action, religious groups were also founded to promote peace, both with respect to the specific conflict in Vietnam and in relation to the arms race more generally. One such organization that began in this period was the Brethren Peace Fellowship. Another, aimed specifically at the question of disarmament, was the World Conference on Religion and Peace, an ecumenical organization headquartered across the street from the United Nations and devoted to bringing pressure on that body from religious groups around the world. Even in areas such as religious broadcasting and publishing, special purpose groups were established during this period to promote greater activity in areas of legislation and regulation.

The state's hand was also increasingly evident through its work in entitlement legislation. Issues of poverty, aging, and child care that had formerly been regarded as private matters now became public issues. As Harvard sociologist Daniel Bell has observed, decisions that once were made in the marketplace or by private individuals were transformed through the incantations of government officials into questions of "group rights."[5] Rather than handling these concerns through local churches or charitable agencies, religious groups found themselves increasingly in the position of setting up special purpose organizations in order to deal with new issues that were now defined as matters of public entitlement. Care for the elderly became a matter of senior citizens' rights. Family life became a question of family policy. Women's groups were faced with orienting themselves appropriately toward the equal rights amendment campaign. Handicapped persons, homosexuals, divorced persons, parents faced with child custody issues, and even children themselves increasingly became the subject of group rights on the one hand and of religious agencies oriented toward entitlement policies on the other. As homosexuality came to be redefined as an issue of equal rights, for example, numerous organizations came on the religious scene as partisans to the struggle. Not only were there gay organizations for the religious community in general, but specific organizations emerged for gay Mormons, gay Brethren, gay Lutherans, gay Presbyterians, gay Catholics, gay evangelicals, and gay atheists. As the handicapped became redefined as a political interest group, new organizations sprang up to advance their cause within churches and denominations. Even denominations that had run special programs for the handicapped for many decades found new organizations in their midst aimed at redirecting the focus of these ministries. And in the area of children's rights, new initiatives by state and federal agencies to bring schools, orphanages, foster homes, and detention centers under stricter regulative practices resulted in numerous hearings and suits involving religious organizations. Suddenly, groups like the Christian

Law Association found themselves inundated with appeals for assistance.[6]

In a considerably less direct way, the expanding role of the state also influenced the growth of special purpose groups in American religion by creating, as many have observed, a greater sense of national identity. Through public education policies, taxation, an expanded national defense budget, a federal system of social security benefits, greater standardization of federal laws and regulations, and even an expanded presence of federal government officials in the national news media—in all of these ways—a greater sense of national identity has been imposed on individuals and on the culture more generally. Private interest groups have learned that national organizations are required in order to bring pressure to bear on the political system at the national level. Corporations increasingly respond to the opportunities provided by this heightened sense of national identity by carving out national markets, engaging in national franchise arrangements, and initiating national advertising campaigns. Religious organizations have responded in a manner not dissimilar. Organizations like the National Council of Churches have given Protestants a national identity as well as a centralized agency capable of dealing with government agencies on their own terms. Even the council's internal structure, as noted in the last chapter, borrowed heavily from the manner in which government agencies were organized. And certainly this organization has drawn heavily on the symbolism of nationhood and Americanism. More generally, special purpose groups in American religion have also been deeply influenced by the growing sense of national identity. More than a third of the 800 such groups currently in operation, for example, operate from addresses in Washington, D.C., or New York City. Even though their constituents may be concentrated most heavily in the South or Midwest it is expedient for them to locate in these two cities in order to be near the centers of national and international power. And, apart from expedience, these locations give a symbolic connection between religious groups and the larger national identity. Washington and New York connote cosmopolitanism and broad national interests in ways that Duluth, or even Dallas, do not. Moreover, the very names by which special purpose groups choose to identify themselves reveal this quest for an association with the nation at large. Altogether, more than 225 special purpose groups currently function with either "American" or "national" in their titles—considerably more than the number that identify themselves, for example, as "Christian" or "religious."[7]

Despite a formal wall of separation between church and state, therefore, a growing mass of religious organizations has come into being with the state very much a part of their specific objectives. Like the secular world, where a growing number of nonprofit organizations have been founded to deal with governmental issues, the world of the sacred appears to have responded to the expanding character of the American state, either directly, or in ways as indirect as the titles by which special purpose groups choose to be known.

The Public's Involvement

Difficult as it is to determine how many special purpose organizations currently exist, it is even harder to estimate the extent of the public's involvement in these organizations. Since membership is not their main objective, at least in many cases, membership figures either do not exist or are grossly distorted. Some, for example, report memberships in the millions—obviously in reference to some segment of the broader population they intend to serve. Some base membership statistics on numbers of financial contributors rather than actual volunteers; others report only paid staff. The fact that many special purpose groups operate only in local areas also compounds the problem of estimating involvement from membership lists.

The best estimates of the public's involvement in special purpose religious organizations, therefore, come from national surveys instead of actual membership lists. These surveys, of course, cannot possibly ask about every kind of special purpose organization. But information has been obtained about some of the more general classes into which most of these organizations fall. Information exists not only on actual involvement but also on contact with different kinds of organizations and on the proportion of the population that has heard of these organizations. The kinds of special purpose groups about which this information is available include:

- Religious coalitions against nuclear warfare
- Prison ministries
- Ministries dealing with world hunger
- Holistic health activities
- Positive thinking seminars
- Group therapy sessions
- Home Bible study or fellowship groups
- The charismatic movement
- Social protest or activism
- Healing ministries

The persons surveyed were asked to respond to these kinds of groups as "current activities that cut across denominational lines" and were given the questions in the context of other questions concerned with religious belief and participation. Therefore, even though some of the activities listed are not limited to religious contexts, the responses were likely to have reflected this framework. The survey, of course, was not designed to correspond with the kinds of organizations that have been discussed thus far and therefore overlaps more with the more general idea of special purpose groups and activities than with some of the specific examples that have been given. The reason for asking about some specific activities and not others in the survey was primarily to encompass a fairly broad range of organizations that might be of interest to different segments of the population.[8]

The results of the study showed that a fairly large proportion of the public had heard of these kinds of special purpose activities. Nearly two-thirds of the respondents, for example, said they had heard about ministries dealing with world hunger—not surprising, given the attention that has been paid to this issue in the national media. About half of the public claimed some familiarity with several of the other activities on the list: home Bible study or fellowship groups (58 percent), religious coalitions against nuclear warfare (51 percent), and prison ministries (50 percent). These, of course, differ considerably in level of organization: familiarity with Bible study groups would be more likely to come from local churches and neighborhood networks; religious coalitions against nuclear warfare, from television or national organizations. About a third of the public in the study had heard about group therapy sessions and social protest activities (39 percent and 35 percent, respectively). These percentages, again, would be quite different depending on the kinds of circles in which respondents obtained their information. One person in three also claimed some familiarity with positive thinking seminars and the charismatic movement. And one person in four had heard of holistic health activities. Even though none of these activities was identified with a specific religious denomination, then (or perhaps because of this fact), they were familiar to large segments of the general public. All in all, nine out of every ten people had heard of at least one of them.

Vast numbers in the general public had also had some contact with these kinds of activities. Approximately one person in four had had some contact with home Bible study groups—a total of some 40 million people. About one person in six had been in contact with ministries dealing with world hunger. And about one person in ten had been in contact with healing ministries, the charismatic movement, or positive thinking seminars. Roughly 5 to 8 percent of the public had made contact with the other activities on the list. Again, even though the list actually asked about represents a small proportion of all the special purpose groups in operation, a fairly large segment of the public appears to have had some degree of direct exposure to these kinds of groups. In all, 45 percent of the respondents in the study said they had been contacted by at least one of these groups.

Actual participation is inevitably limited to a much smaller proportion of the public because of time, geographic location, and other constraints. But overall, one person in three said they had been personally involved with at least one of the activities on the list. Home Bible study groups were the most common: about one person in five had participated. Four of the other groups on the list claimed participants in the range of between 4 and 7 percent of the total sample: world hunger ministries, healing ministries, group therapy, and positive thinking seminars. And the remaining groups had involved 2 or 3 percent of those in the study.

How do these figures compare with other kinds of public participation? A comparison with denominational membership is particularly interesting. Certainly the third of the population that has participated in one of these activities does not stack up favorably against the two-thirds who hold membership in one of the established denominations or the even larger proportion that state their religious preference as Protestant, Catholic, or Jew. On the other hand, membership figures for many of the nation's largest denominations encompass only about the same proportion of the general public as the number involved in some of these groups. For example, the 7 percent that claims involvement in world hunger ministries is comparable to the 7 percent of the general public that lists membership in the nation's largest Protestant denomination (the Southern Baptist Convention). And the 5 percent that claims involvement in positive thinking seminars equals the proportion of the general public that holds membership in the nation's second largest Protestant denomination (Methodists). Even the 2 or 3 percent involved in antinuclear coalitions, holistic health activities, or the charismatic movement is larger in absolute size than the membership of many denominations. Indeed, 106 of the 108 denominations for which national data were collected in 1980 had memberships that constituted less than 1.3 percent of the general population apiece. No one would argue that sending a check once in a while to a world hunger ministry is quite the same as being a Southern Baptist, of course. Yet when fewer than a third of the population attend religious services on a regular weekly basis and as many as a third of the population switch denominations at least once during their adult lives, the degree of involvement in special purpose groups compared with that in denominations should not be underestimated.

These comparisons cannot be interpreted as evidence that participation in special purpose groups is taking the place of membership in denominations. Clearly it is possible to express one's religious convictions in both ways. If organizational forms supply an important clue to understanding American religion, however, the fact that denominationalism comprises only one of these forms must be given due consideration. Besides holding memberships in denominations and attending worship services at local churches on Sunday mornings, people now have the option of participating in many other kinds of groups: specialized ministries, coalitions, home fellowship groups, quasi-religious seminars, and so on. Some of these activities may be held in the same local churches in which people worship on Sunday mornings; others may be held in someone else's church; still others, outside church buildings entirely. At any particular moment, fewer of the population may be involved in any of these special purpose groups than in more established kinds of religious organizations. Almost by definition, these groups appeal to narrower segments of the population. At the appropriate stage in one's life, one may participate in a religious organization advancing nuclear disarmament; at another stage, in a group concerned with senior citizens' spiritual needs. But as far as the society as a whole is concerned, these organizations may be the ones that increasingly define the public role of American religion. Rather than religion's weight being felt through the pressure of denominations, it may be exercised through the more focused efforts of the hundreds of special purpose groups now in operation. And insofar as these groups inevitably must deal with individuals, local churches, and denominations at large, they may have an increasingly influential effect. The nature of these effects, as they have already begun to manifest themselves during the past several decades, requires some additional consideration.

Implications for the Character of American Religion

To begin on a positive note, the presence of special purpose groups in American religion clearly constitutes one of the ways in which the faith is continuously revitalized. Indeed, many of these groups grew out of movements whose aim was specifically to effect some form of renewal in established religious bodies. The charismatic movement supplies a clear example. Oriented toward a more intimate experience of the Holy Spirit, participants in the many groups that have grown out of the charismatic movement attempt to bring about spiritual renewal in established bodies as different as the Catholic church, the Presbyterian church, and smaller denominations such as the Brethren and Assemblies of God. Organizations like the Christian Renewal Ministry (founded in 1968) and the Presbyterian Charismatic Communion (founded in 1966) work to promote spiritual revitalization by sponsoring conferences, holding retreats and workshops, providing information to local churches, and giving interested newcomers an opportunity to discover people with similar orientations. Other organizations have focused on different kinds of renewal: evangelism, scripture, doctrine, liturgy, social action. Often these organizations have emerged within single denominations and in some cases have had a notable impact on the practices of these denominations. As will be discussed more fully in Chapter 9, feminist organizations, for example, have deeply affected the policies of a number of denominations. Black caucuses and task forces on homosexuality have also promoted change in many denominations. Peace groups have succeeded in getting resolutions passed by larger denominational assemblies. Biblically oriented groups, similarly, have provided the means of mobilizing campaigns to control the elective offices of major denominations (discussed more fully in the following chapter). And ecumenical groups, missions organizations, prayer fellowships, and avocational interest groups have, as already seen, supplied ways in which local churches could extend their ministries into new areas.

In addition to effecting redirections of official denominational policy, special purpose groups appear to have emerged as one of the important ways in which local churches evoke commitment from their members. Having a variety of special purpose groups as part of their overall activities provides churches with a number of different hooks capable of catching the interests of various members. Studies of church members, in fact, document that the reasons why people become involved in religious organizations can be quite diverse. When asked directly what they most like about their religious organizations, most people mention the worship service, the sermon, the preacher, or simply the chance to feel close to God. But people also mention more specific kinds of gratifications—ones that point toward the importance of special purpose groups. Some, for example, especially like activities that involve them in social issues; some prefer activities that focus on self-betterment; others like groups in which there is a sense of close-knit fellowship. Asked about specific programs that make the church appealing, some people mention activities for youth, others focus on ways to engage in charitable work, still others like groups aimed at strengthening the family. People also differ in their views of what the main focus of religious organizations should be: preaching itself, evangelistic programs, missionary outreach, community service, social action.[9]

Since religious organizations have to compete with one another for members, both at the local and at the denominational levels, it has behooved churches and denominations to provide a wide variety of special purpose groups in order to maintain the commitment of their members. Contrary to the image of religious commitment advanced by many social scientists, that commitment is not entirely a function of personal values and beliefs. Although it clearly does depend on values and beliefs, it is also a function of the vast infrastructure of special purpose groups that makes available the activities to which people become committed. These groups disseminate information about activities, draw people with common interests together, provide leadership, create opportunities in which people can become involved, and in turn thrive on the involvement they generate.

At the local level, special purpose groups are constantly coming into being and taking on new directions as leadership, information, and other kinds of resources become available. At one local church, for example, three special purpose groups emerged within the space of about 18 months: one was concerned with promoting greater equality for women in the church, another with providing care for needy people in the community, the third with revitalizing the church's worship services. All three came about when small informal groups of parishioners started to communicate with one another, discovered common concerns, and decided to agitate for changes in church policy. In each case, the church's leadership structure was sufficiently flexible to accommodate the inclusion of new members with new interests, to oversee the creation of new programs, and to form new committees so that the special purpose groups could be incorporated into the official activities of the church. As a result, people who were previously dissatisfied, and who might otherwise have left the church in search of greener pastures, stayed on and became active participants in the church. Indeed, the new special purpose groups that were established ran largely on this additional energy rather than draining resources from existing programs.

The fact that special purpose groups have been able to emerge in large numbers, both at the national level and in local churches, attests again to the adaptability of American religion that was described in Chapter 2. Certainly the groups that have emerged in recent decades can hark back for legitimacy to the long tradition of special purpose groups that began in America in the nineteenth century and in Europe before that. But many of these groups also represent genuine innovations, or at least imitate organizations in the secular world more than they do the established bureaucratic patterns of denominations, churches, or sects. The ability to innovate so successfully appears to be linked, as seen in Chapter 2, to a fairly sharp division between heritage and vision—between the institutional structure that religious groups inherit and their vision of what should be possible. The division between institutional knowledge and theological knowledge, as it were, also plays an important role in giving special purpose groups an adaptive edge. Ideas about what works as activities and organizational techniques seem in most cases to be disconnected from the deeper spiritual goals toward which these groups orient themselves. Thus it is possible to find professional associations with organizational structures obviously copied from secular associations but oriented toward high religious values. And it is possible to find pressure groups within nearly all the major denominations that are pushing for much the same kinds of reforms and that rely on organizational structures that reflect only in the smallest ways the vast differences in denominational traditions and styles of leadership. As students of American religion have so often observed in the past, a keen pragmatic orientation pervades religious activities, even when these activities focus on lofty ideals.

The vitality that special purpose groups have brought to American religion is, therefore, in some measure testimony to the adaptability of the religious institution itself. In addition, the enormous growth of these groups in the period since World War II has also been driven by changes in the broader social environment. In comparison with the two principal modes of religious organization on which social scientists have typically focused in the past—churches and sects—special purpose groups have a decided adaptive advantage in the contemporary context. Churches in the classic sense have generally tried to offer a limited range of services to a relatively large segment of the population. Worship services, baptismal rites, marriages, and funerals have been their primary stock in trade. And in many European societies where a single ecclesiastical organization holds a virtual monopoly over these services, these remain the drawing cards that are used to attract participation—often with disappointing results, of course. Sects, in contrast, have generally tried to supply a much richer, more inclusive set of services: totally involving friendship groups, an encompassing set of moral standards, leisure activities, even schools and activities in which dating and marriage selection can take place. But sects have typically been able to function only within relatively narrow niches in the larger population. After a certain point, larger numbers begin to work against the advantages of close interaction and homogeneous life styles. Special purpose groups in some ways combine the best of both worlds. Like churches they delimit the services they try to provide. And like sects they are for the most part relatively small groups of like-minded people who share the same concerns. But unlike churches they do not all try to provide the same set of services. Instead, some focus on one thing, some on another. Consequently, when viewed collectively, they embody a great deal more diversity. And for this reason, they are better able to attract the interests of a highly diverse population. Unlike sects they require relatively limited commitment. Peace coalitions certainly can become a totally encompassing way of life. But generally people expect to participate in special purpose groups for only a limited period, rather than becoming lifetime members. And their participation is restricted mainly to the specialized goals with which the group is concerned, although there may well be secondary incentives for participation as well.

In a complex, highly diverse, highly specialized society such as the

United States, therefore, special purpose groups constitute a valuable way of sustaining religious commitment. People can participate in these organizations for limited periods of time. When their interests change, or when a more pressing issue emerges, they can switch to a different organization. It is understandable, then, why these groups have grown to such an extent over the past several decades. The same kind of adaptation has occurred in almost all sectors of social life. In the marketplace occupations and products have become more specialized, and new products or variations on old ones are constantly being created to sustain consumer interest. In politics the bureaucratic state has developed more specialized functions, and political interest groups have learned the value of organizing around single issues. Even in romantic relationships, some argue, commitments have become more specialized and more delimited, with the result that marriage has become a matter of "serial monogamy" rather than a lifetime contract.

As special purpose groups have risen in prominence in American religion, they have revitalized the churches in much the same way that these changes have helped other segments of the society to adapt. Denominations have not ceased to exist but have become to a greater extent diverse federations of special purpose groups rather than monolithic, homogeneous structures. They provide some continuing degree of identity and coordination, but much of the concrete action in which religious people are engaged takes place in more specialized groups that may fall either within or across denominational lines. And at the local level, churches may still pack large numbers of people into an auditorium to participate in a single service of worship and celebration of the sacraments. But this audience is likely to be comprised of considerable diversity as far as deeper interests are concerned—diversity that gains expression in the many special purpose groups that gain shelter under the congregation's organizational umbrella. To this degree, then, the growth of special purpose groups in American religion since World War II has undoubtedly contributed positively to the survival of religious commitment.

On the negative side, special purpose groups have in many instances added further layers of bureaucracy to the already highly bureaucratized structure of American religion. In his book *Political Parties*, published in 1915, Robert Michels stressed the general trend in modern societies toward increasing layers of bureaucracy—an "iron law," he called it.[10] His conclusions came mainly from observing the socialist movement in Germany from its origins in the 1870s as an informal reform movement to a highly regimented political party in the years just prior to World War I. He probably would have drawn the same conclusions had he been able to observe the special purpose groups that have arisen in American religion during the past half century.

It is in some ways ironic to think of American religion as being subject to an iron law of bureaucratization. Usually American religion is portrayed as being fluid, voluntaristic, organized around small informal fellowship groups and local congregations jealous of their autonomy. The picture is one of little churches sustained by the deeply private religious convictions of individuals who are generally skeptical of hierarchy, structure, and authority. The contrast that casts American religion into sharp relief is the rigid, stale, ecclesiastically centralized system of state churches in Europe. Regimented formality, heavy-handed state supervision, and layer upon layer of dusty ecclesiastical bureaucracy is the image conjured up of the religious systems of France, England, or the Scandinavian countries in comparison with the American system. Yet a more realistic look at the current organizational structure of American religion reveals that the nostalgic images carried over from the nineteenth century—of the little brown church in the valley—no longer apply. Indeed, the European rector or priest carrying out timeworn duties of the state church in places like Cornwall, Bavaria, and Picardy probably comes closer to this image of pastoral simplicity than does the modern American "megachurch" with its vast network of committees, classes, community services, choirs, schools, youth programs, and interest groups.

To the huge denominational bureaucracies that were erected earlier in the century have now been added dozens and dozens of highly institutionalized organizations oriented to special interest groups within denominations, to coordinating the complex relations among denominations, and to filling in crevices with religious activities that denominations have not provided. While some of these organizations operate with a minimum of bureaucracy (an example is FISH, cited earlier), most of them have a formal structure and employ professional staff members. Taken collectively, these organizations add tremendously to the total stock of administrative decisions, reports, budgets, and supervisory tasks that comprise the infrastructure of American religion. Many of these organizations grew out of small, informal, grass-roots movements, some of which were even opposed to the growth of bureaucracy in denominations or in the state. But most of these grass-roots movements evolved into formalized bureaucratic organizations.

While the overall size of most central agencies in denominations has apparently not increased relative to the overall scope of these denominations (as seen in the last chapter), the growth of special purpose groups has added new levels of organization to most denominations. These groups often have some representation on central boards but exist mostly as intermediate levels of organization between the local church and the top administrators. They serve, in a sense, as administrative units alongside the older legislative apparatus by which local churches participate in the electoral politics of their denominations. Whereas it was once up to elected officials, clergy, or small ad hoc committees to mediate between the grass roots and the upper echelons of church bureaucracy, it is now possible to work through established special purpose organizations. Many of the black caucuses that were mentioned earlier, for example, provide formal channels for promoting the interests of black members. Groups oriented toward the practice of charismatic gifts give official organizational expression to their constituents' interests, as do the many organizations concerned with the interests of children, youth, women, the handicapped, and the aged. Since the numbers of constituents served by these organizations is often large, sometimes numbering in the hundreds of thousands, sizable numbers of professional administrators, clerical workers, publishing experts, writers, speakers, and assistants are utilized to provide the services required. The Forum for Scriptural Christianity, a pressure group organized within the Methodist church in 1966 to promote a return to biblical literalism, for example, maintains a staff of 14. A service committee devoted to promoting social action concerns among Unitarians employs 35 full-time paid staff members. And an organization of Jewish women aimed at promoting Zionism employs 50 professional staff workers.

The thrust toward bureaucratization, as seen earlier, is also especially evident in the special purpose groups that have emerged to represent more specialized professional roles among clergy and other religious workers. In addition to the general practitioners of the soul who occupy clergy roles in most local churches, the religious establishment provides opportunities for an increasing number of religious specialists: counselors, educators, educational consultants, news writers, researchers, church architects, campus clergy, church growth specialists, missions planners, staff development specialists, and so on. Not only do the professional associations that represent these specialists constitute minor bureaucracies in their own right, but the fact that such specialists can find employment at all means that an increasing number of local churches, denominations, and special purpose groups are hiring professionals other than pulpit preachers.

To the average person in the pew, much of this bureaucratic infrastructure may be invisible, tucked away as it is in New York and Washington office buildings. However, the growth of special purpose groups has also added new layers of bureaucracy to the local church. In serving as holding companies for an increasing number of special interest groups, local churches have found it necessary to provide some degree of coordination among them. If only to keep head pastors apprised of what their organizations are doing, let alone allocating funds to increasingly complex budgetary operations, it has proven imperative to form larger and more specialized levels of committee supervision. On a small scale, this kind of development can be seen in the experience of the local church cited previously. One unanticipated consequence of the nearly simultaneous appearance of three new special purpose groups in this congregation was a sudden overload on the existing administrative structure, which consisted of pastors, elders, and trustees. Incumbents of these positions found themselves not only having to monitor existing programs but also having to rework basic policy statements, hear proposals, consider ways of integrating new programs with existing activities, and listen to complaints from disgruntled parishioners who felt the pace of change was too fast or too slow. As a result, a crisis of leadership developed that was only resolved, first by creating an interim administrative system which engaged in planning, and then by creating an entirely new administrative structure. The new structure exceeded the previous structure considerably in size. Its operations were also more precisely formalized, involved a clearer division of labor around specialized functions, centralized the degree of coordination among special purpose groups, added an intermediate layer of administration, and ultimately placed a greater share of power in the hands of a centralized executive committee.

To accommodate an increasing range of special purpose groups at the local level, other churches have found it necessary to create innovative administrative structures that retain the appearance of traditional structures mandated by their denominations or thought to be in keeping with biblical guidelines but that in practice permit more complex operations to be coordinated. An evangelical church in New England, for example, struggling to retain some semblance of a traditional pastor-elder-trustee form of administration, managed to resolve its need for a more elaborate bureaucratic structure by carefully differentiating each of the three traditional roles into several functional specializations. Pastors became redefined as "pastoral staff" in order to accommodate roles such as youth pastor, minister of music, minister of visitation, and church administrator. Elders evolved into three distinct offices, called "overseeing elders," "shepherding elders," and "teaching elders," each with different qualifications and duties. And trustees came to be more narrowly defined as custodians of church property and equipment in order to make room for an administrative church council and a financial directorate. Much the same results, but via a different route, were achieved by a denominational church in the Midwest. Lacking the constraints of a strong concern for biblical administrative patterns, it became guided increasingly by practical management considerations, particularly issues concerned with promoting church growth. To this end, special purpose groups (both formal and informal) were actively promoted. And as the congregation grew, needs for coordination, planning, and leadership resulted in increasingly complex bureaucratic problems. Paid professional staff members were hired to head up some of the larger special purpose groups, such as youth groups, outreach programs, and education. Additional personnel were hired to supply support services, such as secretarial assistance, clerical work, program planning, financial administration, and long-range development. And a small army of lay volunteers was enlisted to draw up job descriptions, rethink the rationales for existing programs, coordinate special purpose groups, and provide the actual leadership for these groups.

These kinds of bureaucratic realignments in local churches give testimony, again, to the adaptability of American religion. In the New England case it was particularly apparent that even doctrinal traditions could be differentiated from the pragmatic needs of managing a growing organization. Increasingly, scriptural justifications were cited only for pastoral duties and for general statements of belief, while job descriptions for other personnel were justified simply on the basis of organizational charts and the work of committees which had in general ways sought divine guidance. In responding to increasingly heterogeneous interests among their memberships, local congregations have built up complex bureaucratic structures but yet have managed to build in flexibility by making planning and periodic evaluation a part of their brief.

The cost of ever-increasing layers of bureaucracy is that a sizable share of the spontaneity, energy, and enthusiasm that generates special purpose groups in the first place may be drawn off. Leaders who would otherwise be involved in these groups at the grass roots find themselves increasingly preoccupied with committee meetings concerned with broader questions of coordination and planning. In other cases, grass-roots enthusiasm becomes institutionalized in professional staff roles, which inevitably come to be constrained by considerations of career advancement, salaries, budgets, and organizational preservation.

An additional cost of increasing bureaucracy, especially in local congregations, is that greater and greater shares of the operative knowledge on which decisions are made becomes concealed from the larger membership or potential membership that the organization hopes to serve. For instance, in each of the congregations cited previously the growth of administrative operations was accompanied by more complex budgets which, with the aid of computers, were able to record upwards of several hundred separate line items. However, in each case, the budgets that were presented for congregational approval actually became increasingly simplified, revealing less and less information by lumping items into larger and larger categories. Similarly, the formalization of operating procedures, the development of specialized job descriptions, and the multiplication of behind-the-scenes committee work in bureaucracies of this kind make it increasingly difficult for the uninitiated to understand, appreciate, or feel part of the essential decisions that are made.

In addition to the costs and benefits associated with revitalization and bureaucratization, however, a more general consequence of the growth of special purpose groups needs to be understood. This is the heightened potential for religious communities to become fractionated along the lines of larger cleavages in the society. Denominations have actually served fairly well to prevent this from happening. Certainly they have reflected some important social divisions, as H. Richard Niebuhr recognized. But they have managed to contain many other kinds of diversity within their ranks. Special purpose groups are a different matter. In combining people who share only a rather focused objective, they run the danger of appealing to quite homogeneous groups. And these groups, instead of simply being aggregations of people who come together to worship, are likely to reflect other divisions in the wider society. As the examples already given suggest, one group is likely to consist of blacks, another of homosexuals, another of church secretaries, and still another of Christian drag racers.

In the extreme case, people in special purpose groups may never interact with people in other groups: drag racers and church secretaries may never see one another. In denominations and local churches they would have been more likely to meet. The extreme case, of course, is probably not the one that really exists. Since drag racers and church secretaries may attend the same church, they may still have occasion to interact. It is also conceivable that some drag racers may themselves be church secretaries. So their special purpose groups could have overlapping memberships. And it is certainly possible that memberships in such groups could be short-lived, resulting in more mixing over time: drag racing this year, church secretaries club next year. Should the extreme case exist, though, special purpose groups could begin to divide along broader social lines, aggravating these fractures, rather than helping to heal them. If the kinds of special purpose groups that church secretaries joined always catered to an entirely different class of people than the kinds drag racers belonged to, then the two groups might never gain much of an understanding of one another. In theory, then, the growth of special purpose groups has implications for understanding the broader cleavages that have developed in American religion.

In addition to these more obvious kinds of fractionalization, the growth of special purpose groups in American religion may have also contributed to the development of cultural cleavages along some of the fissure lines that were described in Chapters 3 and 4. Like weeds in the sidewalk, the growth of these groups may have widened the cracks that only a few decades ago consisted of nothing more than hairline seams. Some of these groups, for example, focus exclusively on individual salvation and evangelism, while others target their energies entirely toward social and political concerns. To the extent that these groups have distinct, specialized identities and distinct constituencies, they drive a potential wedge between the two emphases that have been precariously welded together in most denominational bodies and local churches. Insofar as many of these organizations are devoted to concrete, pragmatically oriented activities, leaving the more traditional teaching and preaching functions to the churches, they may also widen the gap between traditional conceptions of values and conceptions of behavior. As some examples in the next two chapters will indicate, many of these special purpose groups have also played a role in altering earlier conceptions of the proper method of infusing religious values into the political arena. The sheer growth in numbers of such organizations has made it possible for religious people to mobilize themselves much more effectively for attaining political objectives. At the same time, taking direct action in the political sphere has subjected the religious community at large to the divisiveness that invariably characterizes the pursuit of political objectives.

We can only hint at the possible role of special purpose groups in these cleavages here, leaving a fuller discussion of their nature and sources for the next three chapters. However, the data we have been examining on group memberships do contain one suggestive clue. The kinds of people who become involved in these groups, it turns out, take part in one of two relatively distinct clusters of activities. In one cluster are the following: healing ministries, prison ministries, Bible study groups, charismatic groups, and groups concerned about world hunger. In the other fall protest activities, antinuclear coalitions, holistic health groups, positive thinking seminars, and therapy groups. The memberships of the first five groups overlap sufficiently to define these groups as a cluster. And the memberships of the second five groups are both distinct from those of the first cluster and sufficiently overlapping with one another to constitute a second cluster.[11] Again, we cannot make too much of these results since the groups asked about in no way exhaust the kinds of special purpose groups to which people can belong. But the fact that the groups divide so sharply into two distinct categories suggests that this division may have other ramifications for understanding the character of American religion. We will come back to this possibility after considering other evidence on the cleavage that currently represents the most serious division in American religion.

CHAPTER 7

The Great Divide: Toward Religious Realignment

TOWARD the close of a conference among religious leaders in Chicago in 1984 a liberal clergyman confessed that the gathering had been unique in his experience. It was, he said, one of those rare instances in which liberal Christians and conservative Christians actually talked with one another. That remark became the inspiration for a major national study aimed at determining what the relations actually were between people with liberal religious views and people with conservative religious views. The results were striking, although not entirely unexpected.

A majority of the people surveyed believed there were, in fact, serious divisions between religious liberals and religious conservatives. These differences, they said, were rooted in people's backgrounds and in basic disagreements over religious beliefs themselves. In addition, the flames of controversy were thought to be fueled by conflicting views on social issues, by differences in styles of worship, by historic differences, and by differences in personality and self-image.[1]

By their own responses, people in the survey also demonstrated some of the dimensions of tension between religious liberals and religious conservatives. People who identified themselves as religious liberals were prone to stereotype their conservative brethren as intolerant, morally rigid, fanatical, unsophisticated, closed-minded, and simplistic. The animosity recorded from the other side was equally blatant. Self-identified religious conservatives thought religious liberals were morally loose, were too hung up on social concerns rather than truly knowing what Christianity was all about, had only a shallow knowledge of the Bible, and were deeply compromised by secular humanism.

Contrary to the Chicago clergyman's belief, the study found that religious liberals and religious conservatives did interact with one another on a fairly regular basis. A majority of religious conservatives said they had been in personal contact with religious liberals at least "a fair amount." And a similar proportion of religious liberals said the same thing about being in contact with religious conservatives. In fact, each side listed friends, neighbors, relatives, and fellow church members among the persons on the other side of the theological fence with whom they had had frequent contact. Yet, the nature of these contacts was described in ways that left much to be desired. Only a third of the religious liberals said their contacts with religious conservatives had been mostly pleasant. The remainder said their contacts had been mixed or unpleasant. Similarly, about six of every ten religious conservatives responded that their contacts with religious liberals had been unpleasant or at best mixed.

In short, the study confirmed what many had already suspected was a deep division in American religion: a division between self-styled religious "conservatives" and self-styled religious "liberals," both of whom acknowledged a considerable degree of tension with the other side. Added to the misgivings, stereotypes, and unpleasant contacts characterizing each side's relations with the other were deep differences in theological, moral, social, and political orientations. True to their labels, religious conservatives were committed to doctrinally orthodox views of the Bible and of God, to tough positions on abortion and pornography, and to politically conservative views on government spending and defense. Religious liberals took quite different stands on all of these issues. Furthermore, the study showed that the public was almost evenly divided between these two camps: 43 percent of those surveyed identified themselves as religious liberals (19 percent as very liberal); 41 percent identified themselves as religious conservatives (18 percent as very conservative); and only 16 percent found it impossible to identify with one or the other of these labels. The study also probed a variety of other potential religious cleavages in the American public, but none was nearly as pronounced as the cleavage between liberals and conservatives.

The results of surveys such as this must, of course, be viewed with caution. Pollsters can influence the results they obtain by the kinds of presuppositions that go into the questions they ask. But there has been enough evidence of animosity between religious conservatives and religious liberals from other sources to make these results more than believable. One church official, for example, noted much the same kind of cleavage as that suggested by the survey:

> Liberals abhor the smugness, the self-righteousness, the absolute certainty, the judgmentalism, the lovelessness of a narrow, dogmatic faith. [Conservatives] scorn the fuzziness, the marshmallow convictions, the inclusiveness that makes membership meaningless—the "anything goes" attitude that views even Scripture as relative. Both often caricature the worst in one another and fail to perceive the best.[2]

Religious leaders on both sides have lambasted the other side. Both sides have their special purpose groups that are trying to achieve results for their own constituencies and defeat the efforts of those on the opposing side. And the news media have relished the sensationalism of pious believers slugging it out with one another.

We have traced the erosion of some of the more pronounced cleavages that have traditionally given structure to American religion—the cleavages between Protestants and Catholics, Christians and Jews, and between members of different Protestant denominations. We have also examined the growth of special purpose groups as an emerging form of organizational structure in American religion and have seen briefly that members of these groups tend to divide roughly into two broad categories—categories, as we shall see, that coincide with the division between religious liberals and religious conservatives. We turn now to closer consideration of the division between liberals and conservatives that has emerged on the religious horizon. How new it actually is, what forces within American religion and in the broader society have contributed to its emergence, and what current issues are adding fuel to the fire constitute the focus of this and the following two chapters.

The Fundamentalist / Modernist Legacy

For anyone with even a casual knowledge of American religious history, the present divide between religious conservatives and religious liberals may sound much like the controversy between fundamentalism and modernism that brewed into a major cultural conflict around the beginning of the present century. Indeed, one interpretation of the current divide that appears to be fairly widely subscribed to holds that the present controversy grows directly out of the earlier conflict. Liberalism descends directly from modernist forebears; conservatism, from fundamentalism; and all that is new is the fact that both sides have somehow awakened from a period of dormancy and are again testing out their spiritual muscles on each other. The essentials of this interpretation were summarized well not long ago in a popular magazine:

> Beaten back in the Scopes trial in 1925 . . . fundamentalists retreated to rural and small-town America—especially the southern Bible Belt. While mainstream Protestantism became increasingly secular in outlook—and spiritually undemanding—fundamentalists withdrew into a rigidly patriarchal and puritanical subculture of their own. But the '60s politicized fundamentalist leaders . . . who emerged in the '70s determined to enter the mainstream culture and combat the "satanic forces" represented by feminism, gay liberation, and atheism. By the mid-'70s fundamentalist leaders . . . had joined with more secular political right-wing leaders . . . to build a powerful network of

> fundraising and lobbying organizations, political action committees, and publications.[3]

To many, the present conflict between religious conservatives and religious liberals can be summarized as simply as that.

Like other caricatures, there is some truth to this one. Some leaders on the religious right have in fact identified themselves as "fundamentalists" and espouse doctrinal views that can be traced directly to the "fundamentals" that were articulated toward the beginning of the century. Some liberals take pride in their modernist heritage and see their mission as an updated version of the earlier social gospel. But there is as much discontinuity between the present divide and the fundamentalist/modernist controversy as there is continuity. Like the delicate balancing act between "heritage" and "vision" that was examined in Chapter 2, the heritage of fundamentalism and modernism has provided only a starting point for the present division—an institutional and rhetorical legacy that has been greatly modified by the vision of religious leaders and the social circumstances with which they have had to contend.

The famous trial of John T. Scopes, a Tennessee high school teacher accused of teaching evolution, in which Clarence Darrow and William Jennings Bryan waged mortal combat, succeeded in bringing the fundamentalist/modernist controversy to national attention and implanted it forever in the minds of American historians. With flamboyant national personalities involved, political careers on the line, issues of church-state relations at stake, and extensive press coverage by the national media, it has been easy for the Scopes trial to be regarded as the natural parent of the religious controversies that have reappeared in recent years. Yet the trial itself, taken in historical context, stands more as a symbol of the demise of the earlier conflict than it does as a precursor of the present divide.

By the 1930s, much of the tension that had animated the larger controversy between fundamentalists and modernists, to which the Scopes trial had added only a symbolic gloss, was beginning to recede. This was so, in part, because the broader controversy had never been an issue of truly national proportions. Instead, it had emerged primarily within two denominations—the northern branches of the Baptist and Presbyterian churches—and had been contained largely within their organizational confines. Among Presbyterians, the conflict was particularly intense because it involved a host of doctrinal and ecclesiastical issues that divided along almost exactly the same lines: qualifications of missionaries in order to receive denominational support, views of the Bible, doctrines about the Virgin Birth and the Second Coming of Christ, different perspectives on the historic role of Calvinism, and conflict between premillennialists and postmillennialists. In the Baptist church, questions of Biblical inerrancy, literal belief in core theological doctrines, and organizational questions involving seminary instruction and missionary support also fueled the conflict. Symptomatic of the strength of denominationalism during this period, however, virtually all the issues that came to occupy the center of attention focused on questions that specifically concerned denominational policy: whether each denomination would officially endorse the rigorous doctrinal code drawn up by fundamentalists; whether a single journal or several journals would be subsidized by the denomination; who would control the purse for foreign missions; and whether local churches could deviate from the conventional Baptist practice of baptism by immersion.

For one reason or another, most other denominations failed to become partisans to these conflicts. The Disciples of Christ and Congregationalists remained largely unaffected by the dispute. Episcopalians did have liberal and conservative factions within their ranks, but the conservatives never felt comfortable making common cause with fundamentalists because of differences in liturgical tradition, styles of church government, and marked gaps in social standing and education. Missouri Synod Lutherans were the most conservative of all the large Lutheran bodies, but also failed to identify themselves with the fundamentalist movement, in part because they could not affirm premillennialist views. Methodists in the North shared the fundamentalists' emphasis on personal salvation and still adhered to a strict set of moral standards, but they too failed to subscribe to premillennial views, and were reluctant to add doctrinal tests beyond that of faith as the only requirement for personal salvation. No fundamentalist leaders of national prominence emerged from their ranks. In the South, Methodists and Baptists alike were overwhelmingly conservative—so much so that in the absence of any notable liberal leaders the fundamentalist/modernist split failed to become an issue. And in the Catholic church, Pope Pius X had largely succeeded in eradicating the fledgling modernist movement by an encyclical promulgated in 1907. Beyond that of the conservative northern Baptists and Presbyterians, therefore, the only organized support for the fundamentalist movement came from the smaller independent sects, such as the Nazarenes and various pentecostal and holiness groups.[4]

The Depression itself, though sometimes regarded as a contributor to right-wing religious movements, actually worked against the continuation of the fundamentalist movement in the 1930s. The main vehicle that had been used by the fundamentalists to maintain unity within their ranks and to popularize their message was the large annual gatherings sponsored by the World Christian Fundamentals Association. The economic hardships of the Depression, however, made travel to these conferences prohibitively expensive. After 1930, attendance at these gatherings dropped precipitously.

Another factor that ultimately contributed to the demise of the fundamentalist movement was that the majority of its leaders in the two denominations most seriously affected chose to lead splinter groups out of their denominations rather than stay and fight within their broader ranks. Although many of the rank and file (perhaps even a majority) held beliefs that came closer to those of the fundamentalists than of the modernists, this strategy effectively cut off the largest share of grass-roots supporters from the most vocal fundamentalist leaders. Only a small percentage of the members of these denominations chose to make the transition and follow their leaders into separatist organizations. For example, the fundamentalist General Association of Regular Baptists, which split away from the Northern Baptists in protest at the denomination's policies, numbered only 22,000 members by 1936, compared with approximately 1.3 million members in the larger denomination.[5] The Orthodox Presbyterian Church, organized in the same year, had fewer than 12,000 members, compared with a parent body of between 2 and 3 million members.

By the time World War II ended, therefore, fundamentalism had largely ceased to exist as an organized movement. Certainly there were many who subscribed firmly to such doctrinal tenets as the divinity of Jesus, the literal historical reality of miracles, and the verbal inerrancy of scripture—some contemporaries estimated there might be as many as 10 million "fundamentalists" by these criteria. But the organizational and cultural identity of fundamentalism had become largely that of an isolated fringe group comprised of separatist eccentrics. Religious leaders still resorted to attacks on fundamentalism occasionally as a way of demeaning their opponents. But for the most part fundamentalists were pictured as members of small isolated sects, entirely outside of the mainstream denominations, so separatist that their broader influence need not be feared, and so emotional that their views need not be regarded with much seriousness.[6] Even the most conservative religious leaders (as will be seen in the next chapter) were beginning to repudiate the fundamentalist label and opt for a new terminology that linked them with the future more than the past.

If fundamentalism and modernism no longer constituted the principal axes of controversy in American religion by the end of World War II, the legacy of this controversy did, however, contribute to the manner in which the later conflict between religious conservatives and liberals was to take shape in at least three significant ways. First, the withdrawal of the hardcore fundamentalists into small separatist sects greatly weakened their capacity to influence the subsequent development of American religion in the decades after World War II, and thereby facilitated the emergence of a new, more dynamic leadership network among religious conservatives. Second, the decision by most conservatives at the time, as well as most liberals, to retain membership in their denominations rather than forming separate splinter groups had the effect of upholding the principle of diversity within the major denominations. This principle was to be upheld throughout most of the turmoil that was to develop in subsequent decades as well. It was to have the unforeseen consequence, however, of locating much of the tension that was later to emerge between religious liberals and conservatives within denominations rather than between them. As will become clearer by the end of the next several chapters, the great divide between religious liberals and conservatives cuts directly through the middle of many of the established denominations. Finally, the fundamentalist/modernist legacy left a cultural residue that has been easily appropriated by contemporary conservatives and liberals in their symbolic warfare with one another. "Modernist" has largely been replaced by "liberal" or "secular humanist," but many of the same stereotypes are applied. And "fundamentalist," with its connotations of backwoods eccentricity, has remained a favorite pejorative term with which to label conservatives.

Hewing to the Middle

When the United States emerged from World War II, much of the present conflict between liberals and conservatives was still several decades in the future. If some tensions still remained between modernists and fundamentalists from an earlier era, these were largely overshadowed by the deeper conflicts (seen in Chapter 5) between Protestants and Catholics, Christians and Jews, and members of different denominations. A potential was there, especially in Protestantism, for those with conservative leanings and those with liberal leanings to move off in different directions. But for the time being an uncannily high degree of consensus appeared to exist within most denominations. Pressures from the outside as well as conscious efforts to hew to the middle ground forged an unusually strong coalition that largely avoided the divisive tendencies of extreme liberal or extreme conservative orientations.

At the same time that conservatives were beginning to distance themselves from the earlier fundamentalist tradition, religious leaders of more moderate or liberal persuasions were also beginning to move beyond the modernist legacy. In part, this transition was made possible by the emergence of a new generation of leaders, more moderate in their own outlooks, and less closely identified with the earlier disputes. As one writer put it, the voice of modernism was fast becoming "the tired voice of retired men."[7] But "modernism," and even "liberalism," were more generally becoming labels with which clergy began increasingly to dissociate themselves. Whereas the earlier traditions had identified concrete social programs with the task of building the kingdom of God, current theological discussions drew a sharper distinction between the kingdom of God as a spiritual ideal and social programs concerned with the betterment of society (as discussed in Chapter 4). The old views were criticized as being overly optimistic. Rather than expecting the kingdom of God actually to materialize on American soil, religious leaders now spoke with caution about the future. To a very real extent, the promise of a better future was (as seen in Chapter 3) laced with visions of peril, confusion, and impending doom. Leaders who had in their youth predicted inevitable progress now argued for a more realistic assessment of the times. The kingdom of God became a vision of hope, rather than a plan for society.

In distancing themselves from the old views, religious leaders often articulated curiously mixed perspectives that repudiated the earlier arguments even while drawing heavily on them. But in repudiating their forebears, they were again able to segment heritage from vision—to confess the sins of the fathers while calling for responsible action in the future. A more dynamic model of the relation between faith and action increasingly came to the forefront. Action was not diminished in importance. Indeed, its importance actually increased, since the balance between peril and promise was now seen to rest more on concerted effort than on inevitable progress. And faith came increasingly to be regarded as an adaptable response—a vision that could not be rooted permanently in the theological notions of the past but needed to be constantly upgraded and revised. In criticizing the earlier modernist and liberal theologies, the new generation of religious leaders seemed to be saying that their tradition was now stronger, that it had moved closer to the center, and was more closely allied with the mainstream of Christianity itself.

As they searched for a more consensual basis of theological understanding, religious leaders also paid special attention to the assumptions about the future that had been prominent in earlier fundamentalist and modernist formulations. Biblical literalists continued to promote the idea of a future in which Christ would literally return in the clouds to establish a heavenly kingdom on earth and would physically resurrect the bodies of dead believers. But the new generation of conservative leaders now added to these ideas a layer of questions about meaning: What was the relevance to this life of such ideas about the end times? How should believers conduct their lives in the period prior to the second advent? Increasingly, the emphasis shifted from thoughts about a New Jerusalem to programs of evangelism, to the work of building churches and running Sunday schools, and to the life of piety and Christian discipline. Modernists, for their part, had taken the Christian vision of the future in a rationalistic direction, stripping it of supernatural significance, and interpreting it in a way that emphasized little more than political order and material progress. But theologians were becoming increasingly critical of this interpretation. As Cyril Richardson, professor at the Union Theological Seminary, put it: "The Christian story is thus confused with an expectation of continuous progress, and it is anticipated that the time will come when we shall have advanced so far that men will dwell in peace, plenty, and brotherhood." This view, he argued, failed to take adequate account of the depth of the Christian message, particularly of sin, the resurrection, the character of divine redemption, and the full nature of eternal life.[8] For theologians like Richardson, the shift then taking place toward a more centrist theological orientation involved taking more seriously the miracle of Christ's resurrection, recapturing the idea of forgiveness, and affirming the reality of hell, as well as the Christian's hope for eternal communion with God—all doctrines to which more conservative theologians could also readily give assent.

The issue on which religious leaders of all perspectives seemed to be most in agreement was evangelism. Whether associated with the more liberal denominations or with the offshoots of fundamentalism, leaders seemed united in the conviction that the church's main business was winning souls. Fundamentalists had long preached the importance of personal salvation and of evangelism; clergy in the major denominations now increasingly joined them with their own programs of evangelism and with appeals for cooperative evangelistic efforts. "By general agreement," wrote a Protestant official in his 1946 report to the Federal Council of Churches, "evangelism is of the essence of the Christian task as Protestants conceive it." Evangelism is concerned above all, he explained, with the individual's need to make a "personal decision" for Christ.[9] The same year, the leading magazine of the most "liberal" Presbyterian body in the country adopted a new editorial policy, declaring that it would strive to be "a crusading organ for evangelical religion."[10] A year later, at its annual convention in Seattle, the Federal Council of Churches announced that its uppermost priority for the coming year was "to win the people of this nation to Christ." And by May of that year at least thirty major denominations had launched plans for evangelistic crusades and other outreach programs. Commenting on the program and a similar one organized the following year, the voice of "liberal" religion, *Christian Century*, hailed the new wave of evangelism as a major contribution to "the character and influence of the American people and all their institutions."[11]

Besides agreeing on the importance of evangelism, leaders with widely differing orientations also called explicitly for efforts to promote greater cooperation, rather than perpetuating the earlier conflicts between fundamentalists and modernists. Presbyterian leader John Mackay, decrying the earlier "horseplay" of labeling people as fundamentalists and modernists, called for emphasis in all churches to be placed on the biblical ideal of "evangelicalism," for them to preach the divine gospel and show its relevance to "the manifold ills of the human mind and spirit."[12] Writing in the conservative periodical *Christianity Today* a few years later, theologian Carl F. H. Henry adopted the same line of reasoning. "Dare we revive the modernist-fundamentalist conflict?" he asked. The answer was no. The old conflict was in his view largely dead. Both traditions had been proven untenable. And to reopen the debate would only detract from accomplishing the church's mission.[13] Elsewhere he wrote: "Let us be done with signposts on the winding road of American theology which point to the left or to the right, and let us point upward where the risen God-man is ready to save repentant souls."[14] Henry's sentiments, it appeared, were in fact shared by a large number of clergy and laity at the grass roots. As the author of one firsthand study of local congregations across the country concluded: "Those on the extremes on both sides [are] gradually moving toward the evangelical center." Those once to the left of center, he went on to observe, "stress more than they once did the importance of biblical and theological teaching and preaching, [while] 'conservative' churches are slowly yielding to the influence of ecumenical doctrine."[15] Or in the words of another writer: "The warfare which raged between 'fundamentalists' and 'modernists' is forgotten by the mass of American Christians . . . and the attempt to identify true religion with a specific theological pattern may be regarded as having failed."[16]

Even ardent defenders of the liberal tradition seemed to display a new attitude of willingness to move closer to the center. Chastened by the criticisms that their own successors were making of the liberal tradition, they seemed willing to admit the value of the evangelical perspective and were cautiously enthusiastic about finding a greater basis of cooperation with the conservative tradition. For example, Henry Sloane Coffin, president emeritus of Union Theological Seminary, remarked that liberalism and evangelicalism were both vital to American religion and needed to balance one another: "Evangelicalism without liberalism's open mind and constant search for truth," he wrote, "becomes obscurantist." By the same token: "Liberalism without evangelicalism leaves the Church impotent and her members chill in heart."[17]

It was, of course, easier to argue for burying old differences than it was to achieve an actual spirit of unity. Nevertheless, the period was, in contrast with the acrimony between liberals and conservatives that was to surface a few decades later, characterized by some remarkable demonstrations of activity and argumentation that transcended distinctions between liberals and conservatives. Not only were the officials of major Protestant denominations and bodies such as the Federal Council of

Churches that had formerly been associated with modernism turning their energies toward evangelism, the very term "evangelical" was widely adopted without any of the divisive connotations with which it would later become associated. A study guide used widely in the Methodist church, for example, declared unabashedly that Methodists shared the conviction "that every man must be won to discipleship to Jesus" and acknowledged an "overpowering concern to reach and to win all men to the Christian fellowship." A Methodist, it declared, "is an evangelical Christian."[18] Nor were these kinds of pronouncements limited to the Methodist church, which at the time did in fact remain strongly identified with a relatively conservative strand of the Protestant tradition. Describing a recent Billy Graham crusade in San Francisco, a liberal pastor from Berkeley praised the popular evangelist for his forthrightness in preaching the gospel and concluded that "thousands were encouraged to keep the family altar and to go to church; hundreds faced Jesus Christ as a challenging presence in their lives." "I hope he comes back," the pastor concluded.[19] Across the bay, at a church that was later to become a bastion of radical social and political ideas, the pastor of Glide Memorial Church held a series of seminars on methods of evangelism. In the same year, Congregationalists, Presbyterians, Methodists, and Disciples of Christ all launched major programs of preaching, evangelism, and visitation of their own to reach the unchurched. An organization called Youth for Christ, now a decade old, continued to receive broad support from fundamentalists and mainline churches alike in its efforts to evangelize high school students. It was also in these years that a young bride named Elizabeth Elliot, who thirty years later was to be counted as one of the most controversial pro-life activists on the religious New Right, won national admiration across the entire religious spectrum as the widow of one of the five evangelical missionaries killed by Auca tribesmen in the Equadorian jungle.

Years of Upheaval

The lack of acrimony between liberals and conservatives that was evident in the years immediately after World War II continued to prevail until the end of the 1950s. To be sure, fundamentalists rankled at the modernism they saw creeping into the larger Protestant denominations. And many within the moderate mainstream recognized that a perspective still existed farther to the left. But if liberalism was an identifiable religious category in the 1950s, it tended to be associated with a narrow set of denominations, particularly Congregationalists and Unitarians, just as fundamentalism was associated with the smaller Protestant sects. And like fundamentalism in the South, liberalism also conjured up an identity that was largely regional. As one scholar asserted in 1952: "Boston is the liberal capital; and it is more or less true that the farther one gets from Boston the less religious liberalism he finds."[20]

In part, it was the experience of World War II that had drawn conservatives and liberals closer to a common center, if only by showing up the limitations of their earlier formulations and by providing a symbolic break—a disjuncture in the seamless web of history—to which the newer generations of theologians could point. The continuing war against Catholicism also provided a common ground for most Protestants. Conservatives and liberals alike could join forces when it came to issues of church and state, for it was Catholicism that symbolized the aggressor. All varieties of Protestants, from fundamentalists to Boston liberals, could rally around the banner of clear separation between church and state. No matter what their conviction, they could also see the need for an active program of evangelization and visitation if the advance of Catholicism was to be stopped at the local level. The Cold War provided additional reason for Christians of different persuasions to find common ground. In the relatively intangible ways that have already been described in Chapter 3, communist totalitarianism came increasingly to symbolize the enormous peril against which Christians needed to mobilize. More directly, the Cold War also succeeded in silencing an important segment of the religious left, thereby giving it a considerably more moderate image in relation to religious conservatives. This segment of the religious left was the small, but highly visible, group of leaders who had gathered around the theologian Reinhold Niebuhr in the 1930s to advocate a "third way" between capitalism and communism—something resembling democratic socialism but legitimated by Christian theology. As the Cold War began to take hold of the public's imagination in the 1950s, anything that was not decidedly in favor of capitalism became suspect as a brand of communism. Gradually, the "third way" ceased to be an identifiable plank in the platform of the religious left.

Perhaps more than any of these factors, however, the absence of religious conflict between liberals and conservatives during the 1950s was contingent on the peculiarly pragmatic character of American religion itself. The beliefs that fundamentalists had championed earlier in the century continued to be shared widely in the population at large. Some segments of the population held more strongly to these beliefs than did others. But the differences revolved mostly around degrees of certainty, rather than around genuine alternatives to the traditional creeds. So there was, in fact, a fairly strong consensus around common tenets of the faith. Liberalism and fundamentalism continued to be labels that theologians debated. But neither represented a very clear, let alone organized, segment of the broader population. These were formal theological categories, but as perceptive observers of the religious mindscape realized, terms such as fundamentalism, liberalism, or even neo-orthodoxy failed to resonate very deeply with the sentiments of people in the pews. To the typical worshipper, religion was less a matter of theology than of simple experience. As one observer noted, the religious person "is usually trinitarian, believes in the unique inspiration of the Bible, takes great comfort in his belief in a future life, and sadly confesses that men are more prone to do evil than to do good. He believes in petitionary prayer and tends in his personal devotions to think of Jesus more as a personal friend and guide than as the metaphysical Second Person of the Trinity."[21]

Throughout the 1950s, the major tensions that gave identity to religious experience—besides those separating faiths and denominations—were the symbolic battles set in motion by the growth of various sects and cults on the fringes of religious respectability. The largest of these was the Mormons, with a membership already in excess of one million by the start of the decade. Other fringe groups with sizable memberships included the Christ Unity Science Church with almost 700,000 members, the Seventh-Day Adventist Church with approximately 250,000 members, and the Spiritualists with more than 160,000 members. Though considerably smaller in membership, several other groups on the religious fringe also had a fairly high degree of visibility: Baha'i, Vedanta, Theosophy, and the American Ethical Union, to name a few. For most members of respectable Protestant churches and Catholic parishes, these were the "deviant" religions that defined the outer limits of acceptability. Books and study guides written to warn teenagers about the dangers of false religions were likely to mention all of these groups. But even false religions during this period were relatively tame in comparison with some of the ones that were to gain national prominence in the decade to come.

The 1950s did witness the rise of several new sects and cults on the spiritual frontier, but it was not till later that the significance of these groups was to be fully realized. The Church of Scientology, for example, came into existence in 1952. An amalgam of popular psychology, folk wisdom, and spiritualism, it was to become a much-discussed fringe group by the end of the 1960s. In 1955 an inauspicious event took place, the importance of which was not to become evident until the late 1970s: a charismatic pastor named Jim Jones started an inner-city mission church in Indianapolis. Before the decade was over, two other movements had been founded that were also to become part of the religious turmoil of the following decade: one was the founding of the San Francisco Zen Center in 1959; the other was the commencement of work in the United States the same year by leaders of what was to become known as the Unification Church. These were not the only religious movements to be founded in the 1950s with views that departed significantly from the established Judeo-Christian tradition. Others, for example, included the Ananda Marga Yoga Society, founded in 1955; the Society of Pragmatic Mysticism, founded in 1954; and the Church of Divine Immanence, founded in 1952. But in comparison with the 1960s and 1970s, the 1950s were relatively quiet as far as new religions were concerned.

Most of the religious growth that occurred in the 1950s took place within the confines of the established denominations. Capitalizing on the "baby boom" of the immediate postwar period, making use of the slack that had built up in building programs during the Depression and World War II, and benefiting from the economic prosperity of the period, most churches were able to expand their facilities and enlarge their memberships. For the time being, it appeared that the main divisions giving American religion its ideological structure would remain those separating the various faith traditions and organized denominations. As yet, there was little indication of the deep division that would emerge between liberals and conservatives.

These years of relative consensus and growth were dramatically altered by the larger social unrest that emerged in the 1960s. As questions of justice, equality, war and peace, rights and responsibilities burst onto the stage of national attention, religious leaders found it impossible to sit quietly on the sidelines. Having vast institutional resources at their disposal and oriented toward active engagement with issues of conscience, they became deeply involved in the most controversial developments of the period. And in the process, a whole new set of alignments in religious outlooks began to appear.

The civil rights movement turned out to be one of the more consequential developments for the churches in the 1960s. For several decades, organizations like the Federal Council of Churches, the National Council of Churches, and many of their affiliated denominations had actively championed racial equality. Before World War II, church groups had routinely expressed their abhorrence of lynching and other acts of racial violence. And after the war, many of the large denominations, along with agencies of the Catholic church, had worked to promote governmental policies aimed at ensuring greater racial equality. Through nearly the first decade of the civil rights movement itself, the churches' support consisted mainly of resolutions and pronouncements issued as part of the official policies of denominational governing bodies. This practice, deeply rooted in the churches' more general view of influencing society by addressing itself to public values (as discussed in Chapter 4), was soon to change, however. The turning point coincided roughly with the massive march on Washington, led by the Reverend Martin Luther King, Jr., in 1963. After this date, white church leaders found it increasingly difficult to stand by while their black counterparts were staging demonstrations, engaging in active civil disobedience, and increasingly becoming the targets of racial violence. Rather than resting content with public pronouncements and official resolutions, white church leaders gradually started to become involved in these kinds of social activism themselves.

At first, clergy activism in civil rights demonstrations was limited to a small elite, often officials of denominational bureaucracies who were shielded from the pressures of grass-roots congregational politics and who enjoyed high visibility as representatives of their denominations. In a civil rights march held in Baltimore a month before the 1963 demonstration in Washington, D.C., for example, prominent church leaders who took part, and were subsequently arrested, included Eugene Carson Blake, the highest permanent official of the United Presbyterian Church; Bishop Daniel Corrigan of the National Council of the Episcopal Church; Monsignor Healy of the Roman Catholic Archdiocese of Baltimore; and Rabbi Morris Lieberman of Baltimore. As these kinds of demonstrations continued, religious officials not only marched on their own behalf but also received official endorsement from their organizations as well. Groups such as the National Council of Churches, the National Conference of Catholics for Interracial Justice, and the American Jewish Congress were among the first to give broad ecumenical endorsement to civil rights demonstrations. Over time, these endorsements also resulted in an increasing number of parish clergy, campus ministers, and young people from student religious federations taking active roles in civil rights protests. One study of Protestant clergy conducted in California in 1968, for example, showed that nearly a quarter had taken part in some kind of civil rights demonstration.[22]

The growing engagement of clergy in civil rights activism generated loud cries of "foul play" from other segments of the clergy and from many in the pews. In part, the origins of this dissent lay in lingering ambivalences toward racial equality itself. Among southerners and among people with lower levels of education or living in isolated rural areas, support for racial equality was considerably weaker across the board than it was among better educated segments of the population living in urban centers in the Northeast and on the West Coast. But the controversy that developed was as much over proper methods of engaging the public conscience as it was over racial equality. Becoming involved in direct action represented a clear departure from the widely accepted view that the church's role in public life was best fulfilled by addressing itself to the individual's conscience. No sooner had denominational officials begun taking part in direct action than resolutions began to be submitted in most of their denominations. These resolutions seldom opposed the civil rights movement in principle, but questioned the tactics of direct activism. Some opposed direct activism of all kinds, arguing on highly familiar grounds that such activism constituted a violation of the church's separation from the political arena. These arguments suggested that the churches would be more effective on questions of civil rights by staying with the tried-and-true method of applying religious values to individual consciences through preaching and teaching. Other proposals sought to differentiate individual action from denominational policy. The view expressed in these proposals was that individuals should be allowed to engage in direct action as individuals, since religious values were assumed to shape individuals' behavior. Consequently, one could not object to churchmen taking part in civil rights demonstrations if they did so as individuals. But they should not do so in the name of denominations and other religious bodies. To do so, again, was to violate the accepted practice of relating religious organizations to the public sphere. Moreover, to act on behalf of entire denominations was to violate the consciences of the thousands of individuals who comprised the memberships of these denominations.

The argument that religion best served the society by shaping individual values was predicated, as shown in Chapter 4, on the assumption that values did in fact shape behavior. As long as it could be assumed that social behavior somehow reflected broader cultural values, this definition of religion's public role made sense. This assumption, however, was always somewhat precarious. The symbolic connection between values and behavior was itself a fissure line, a seam in the cultural mosaic that could easily become unglued. And race relations was perhaps the one area in which this connection was most precarious. For it was clear that racial equality was part of the value system of American culture. And yet it was also clear—increasingly so as the civil rights movement unfolded—that this value system did not correspond closely with the ways in which people actually behaved. As Gunnar Myrdal had eloquently pointed out in his book *An American Dilemma*, a fundamental contradiction was present in American culture between the high democratic values to which it gave lip service and the practical realities of racial discrimination.[23] If it could not be assumed that values alone led to appropriate behavior in the sphere of race relations, then the traditional view of how best to relate religion to social concerns could be questioned. And clergy who engaged in civil rights activism increasingly did just that. Rather than assuming that racial practices would effectively be changed by preachments about religious values, they argued that religious people must themselves put their values on the line—that the connection between conviction and action must be dramatized by taking part in civil rights activism.

The civil rights movement, therefore, opened up a fundamental issue that was increasingly to become defined as a division between liberals and conservatives. Those who favored taking direct action came to be regarded as liberals because their stance seemed to support a speedy resolution to the problem of civil rights. Indeed, the popular term that became associated with clergy activism in the civil rights movement was "new breed." Scarcely reminiscent of the earlier controversies between modernists and fundamentalists, the new breed of liberalism was defined not so much by theological orientations as by support for direct action in the broader turmoil raised by the civil rights movement. And conservatism came increasingly to be associated with the view, not that race relations should never change, but that direct action was too conflictual, too divisive, pushing too rapidly for short-term gains at the expense of religion's longer-term place in the social order.

Before the decade had ended, another controversial issue added sharply to the intensity of this emerging division. That was the controversy around the United States' growing involvement in the war in Southeast Asia. Although the issue was different, as were the constituencies, the lines of debate were drawn much in the same way as they were in the civil rights movement. Liberalism came to mean not only opposition to the war but also support for engaging in direct action to protest the war. New-breed clergy and their supporters favored taking part in antiwar demonstrations just as they did participating in civil rights marches. And conservatism came to be associated, not simply with hawkish attitudes toward the war, but with the view that churches should try to affect society by changing the individual's conscience, and therefore his or her behavior, rather than engaging directly in social activism. Again, the war seemed to represent an issue on which the relation between values and behavior was genuinely problematic. Those who opposed the war saw it as a fundamental contradiction between the nation's commitment to values of peace and democracy and the nation's practice of engaging in military aggression. To speak as religious people only to the nation's values, therefore, seemed pointless. If behavior really did not reflect values—if society was somehow ordered by interests rather than high values—then direct action aimed at changing the social structure itself was the only effective means of bringing religion to bear on the public sphere.

The question of whether to engage in direct action or to try to influence individual consciences was inevitably associated with differences in theological orientation—and here it did parallel to some extent the earlier division between modernists and fundamentalists. Those who held firmly to the view that religion best serves society by shaping the individual's convictions continued to stress the importance of personal salvation, personal piety and morality, and therefore, evangelism, Bible study, and missionary efforts. Those who began questioning the connection between values and behavior, who saw direct action as being more effective than good intentions, increasingly focused their attention away from personal salvation and evangelism toward engaging religious people directly in acts of love or in acts committed to bringing about social justice. These two orientations—evangelism and social justice—in fact became the polar positions around which religious conservatives and religious liberals increasingly identified themselves. As a study conducted among Presbyterian clergy and laity revealed in the early 1970s, those who emphasized personal evangelism were deeply divided from those who emphasized social action. Not only did the two factions have widely differing views of what the church should be doing, but they differed fundamentally from one another on theological issues and in social backgrounds as well.[24]

Compounding the controversies surrounding the civil rights and antiwar movements in the 1960s were an increasing number of proposals for denominational mergers and for modifications of denominational positions on matters of theology and church government. Whereas the questions raised about social activism often resulted in little more than arousing the private ire of some parishioners, proposals concerning theology and church government provided occasions for collective responses reflecting group interests. Many of these proposals were motivated by ecumenical ideals, which again pitted the values to which lip service had been given against the divisions that actually separated denominations in practice. Within the Lutheran family, for example, efforts to transcend ethnic and regional divisions had made some headway earlier in the century, but had largely been placed on the back burner since 1930. These efforts were now renewed, resulting in mergers leading to the formation of the American Lutheran Church in 1960, the Lutheran Church in America in 1962, and an expansion of the Lutheran Church-Missouri Synod in 1963. Within the Presbyterian family, a merger had united the Presbyterian Church, U.S.A. and the United Presbyterian Church in 1958. Three years later a merger was effected between the Congregational Christian Churches and the Evangelical and Reformed Church. In the same year, the Unitarian and Universalist Churches merged. And in 1968, the United Methodist Church came into being, absorbing some smaller denominations, after nearly three decades of deliberation and negotiation. Other developments during this period included the formation of the Consultation on Church Union in 1962 (discussed in Chapter 5) and the adoption of a new confession stressing social concerns and liberal theology by the United Presbyterian Church in the U.S.A. in 1967.

Many of these changes, and even the proposals initiating them, generated strong reactions. Denominational mergers caused dissidents to form splinter groups in sufficient numbers that the overall number of denominations was not discernibly reduced (as seen in Chapter 5). For example, the mergers that took place in the Lutheran family resulted not only in the formation of larger national churches but also in the creation of several smaller denominations comprised of parishioners opposed to the principles according to which the larger denominations were constituted. Two of these were the Association of Free Lutheran Congregations and the Concordia Lutheran Conference. Similarly, the merger involving the Congregational and Christian Churches left two smaller denominations in its wake: the Midwest Congregational Christian Church and the National Association of Congregational Christian Churches.

Special purpose groups within denominations also became an increasingly prominent means by which dissent was expressed to proposed mergers, social activism, and other changes in church policy. In anticipation of the Presbyterians' confessional revision in 1967, for example, two special purpose groups were formed by leaders opposed to this revision, and these movements soon gained national followings. One was the Presbyterian Lay Committee, which also played a prominent role in opposing the denomination's protest activities during the Vietnam War; the other was called Presbyterians United for Biblical Concerns. Both disseminated literature, organized petition campaigns, and lobbied at meetings of the denomination's General Assembly to uphold conservative views of the Bible, doctrines rooted in the Reformation tradition, and strict concepts of moral and spiritual discipline.

During the 1960s, virtually all of the major Protestant denominations, as well as the Roman Catholic church, were affected either by the formation of special purpose groups or by schismatic movements that resulted in separate denominations. Talks of merger between the Lutheran Church-Missouri Synod and the American Lutheran Church resulted in the formation of two separatist denominations, one called Lutheran Churches of the Reformation, the other called the Federation for Authentic Lutheranism. In protest against the southern Presbyterians' support of the National Council of Churches, its involvement in social activism, and talks of merger with the northern Presbyterians, a sizable splinter group left the Presbyterian Church in the U.S. to form the new Presbyterian Church in America. When the United Methodist Church was formed in 1968, at least four nationally organized splinter groups and special purpose groups came into being as reactions against the church's new policies. Among Baptists, a host of new organizations sprang into existence, all inspired by dissent against liberal theological innovations: the Fundamentalist Baptist Fellowship, founded in 1961; the Progressive National Baptist Convention, also founded in 1961; the New Testament Association of Independent Baptist Churches, formed in 1965; the Sovereign Grace Movement, started in 1966; the Ohio Bible Fellowship, begun in 1968; and the Fellowship of Conservative Southern Baptists, organized in 1971. And within the Catholic church, the reforms associated with the Second Vatican Council (discussed in Chapter 5) led to the formation of numerous new organizations and special purpose movements, by far the most prominent of which was the Catholic Charismatic Renewal, founded at Notre Dame University in 1967. By the early 1970s this movement counted more than 350,000 among its members.

Added to the turbulence within established religious bodies was the considerable turmoil generated during the late 1960s and early 1970s by the so-called "new religions." Asian religious traditions generated a significant number of these movements. An example was the San Francisco Zen Center. With some 300 regular students in five locations, it was the focal point of the burgeoning interest in Zen Buddhism during the late 1960s. By the early 1970s, approximately 3 percent of the San Francisco metropolitan area claimed to have practiced Zen at one time or another and four times this many said they found Zen attractive.[25] Another movement of Asian origin that attracted large followings was Transcendental Meditation (TM). Initially made popular when several entertainment personalities joined the movement, it spread rapidly to virtually every major city in the country. In the San Francisco area approximately 5 percent of the population claimed to have practiced it at one time or another. And in the nation as a whole, some 4 percent said they had been participants.[26] Yoga groups, the Hare Krishna society, the Healthy-Happy-Holy Organization, and the Meher Baba movement also brought considerable numbers of followers to various offshoots of Eastern religions during this period.

Besides the more esoteric religious movements, a number of new organizations emerged with syncretic doctrines that were informed as much by popular psychology, science, and mysticism as by conventional religious traditions. One of these was the Inner Peace Movement, founded in 1964. Dedicated to self-realization, personal growth, and the exploitation of psychic energy, it spread to nearly 600 locations by the early 1970s. Another was the *est* movement (Erhard Seminars Training). Blending a brash, pragmatic self-help ideology with a mixture of psychic experience, self-awareness techniques, and social activism, it "trained" some 20,000 participants in the first three years of its existence. Dozens of other more localized, less widely publicized, and more informally organized personal growth groups also came into being during the late 1960s: Arica, Bioenergetics, Psychosynthesis, Rolfing, and Silva Mind Control, to name only a few. In the San Francisco area, one person in six claimed to have taken part in one or another of these kinds of groups by the early 1970s.[27]

Adding to the bewildering array of new movements that emerged during these years were thousands of communes, some with no more than a handful of members, others with members numbering in the hundreds as well as vast land holdings and highly successful economic enterprises. Scores of Satanic groups, covens, and occult groups also appeared about the same time. And there were movements like the Unification Church which, being generally more authoritarian in structure, also represented a clear departure from most of the established denominations. Altogether, the various new religions may have resulted in the organization of more than 3,000 local groups of one kind or another, with perhaps as many as a tenth of the entire population having participated in at least one by the early 1970s.

In terms of actual participation, the new religions scarcely constituted a major reshaping of American religion. Many age categories and many segments of the population were scarcely affected by these movements at all. The new religions, nevertheless, contributed an important symbolic dimension to the more general cultural upheaval of the 1960s. They served, in a sense, to redefine the outer limits of religious respectability. Like deviant sects and cults in the past, they provided instances of "abnormal" religious behavior that came to be widely discussed even in circles far removed from the centers of religious experimentation themselves. What constituted "liberal," "avant garde," or "innovative" religious orientations now came to include a wide range of not only Judeo-Christian theologies but also the practices of Eastern religions, mysticism, and quasi-religious "human potential" movements. And, just as with other forms of religious change during this period, opposition to the new religions also emerged. Particularly as the enthusiasm for countercultural activities began to wear thin in the 1970s, numerous anticult movements sprang up. Organized as special purpose groups, these movements heralded their objectives with names such as Ex-Moon, Sorting It Out, Project Yedid, the Citizens Freedom Foundation, and the Spiritual Counterfeits Project. Some merely provided information to anxious parents and friends; others became actively involved in deprogramming former cult members and in trying to limit the activities of new religious movements through legislation and the courts.

In comparison with the 1950s, then, the 1960s became a decade of sweeping upheaval in religious practices. Whereas the earlier period had been typified by the longstanding divisions between denominations, by conflicts between Protestants and Catholics, and by semilatent prejudices toward Jews, the 1960s witnessed the rise of a whole new set of issues around which positions "pro" or "con" could be taken: civil rights, antiwar activism, denominational mergers and schisms, new religions, among others. It was as if the bits of mosaic that had given shape to the religious topography had been thrown into the air, never to land in exactly the same positions as before. The patterns that became evident when they did land, however, were not determined strictly by forces within the religious community itself. To be sure, the enormous institutional resources of American religion and its commitment to become engaged in the important issues of the day contributed immensely to the reshaping that took place in these years. But this reshaping was also contingent on deep changes taking place in the broader society.

The Effects of Social Change

Any number of social influences can be identified for particular movements that contributed to the overall flux in American religion during the 1960s. Some of these movements, for example, capitalized on the drug culture—either promoting the use of mind-altering drugs or drawing members from the ranks of burned-out former users. Other movements became successful by deploying innovative fund-raising techniques. But these "movement-specific" kinds of explanations prove to be of little use in understanding why the 1960s as a whole became such a time of intense religious restructuring. Nor do they say much about which kinds of people lined up on different sides of the issues that surfaced and how these alignments contributed to the deep divide that appeared between religious liberals and religious conservatives. To answer these kinds of questions requires a broader look at the social changes that were taking place during the 1960s.

Changes in population, in the economy, and in the composition of the American public all provide plausible candidates to account for the religious restructuring of the 1960s. Population growth, for example, may have contributed to the religious upheaval of the decade by expanding the number of young people in the society and thereby creating a more clearly defined stage in the life cycle during which young adults could experiment with innovative religious beliefs and practices. Growth in the economy, similarly, may have given people free time, caused them to be restless with traditional religion's emphasis on other-worldly spirituality, and made it possible for new movements to finance themselves. A shifting population, increasingly located in cities and suburbs, may have exposed people to new ways of life and made it difficult for some churches to relocate facilities quickly enough to keep up with population trends. Or the growing regional migration, which appears to have contributed to the weakening of denominational boundaries, may have proved unsettling in other ways as well. Migration to the West Coast, for example, may have left people without available churches and synagogues, making them more susceptible to recruitment by the new religions that seemed to flourish in that region.

A comparison of trends in the 1960s with comparable trends in the 1950s, however, indicates that the two decades did not differ sufficiently on most of these changes to account for the notable increase in religious turbulence during the 1960s. The growth in population was actually higher in the 1950s than in the 1960s (19 percent as opposed to 13 percent). Economic growth was indeed faster in the 1960s than in the 1950s, as measured by annual increases in Gross Domestic Product (2.6 percent annually in the 1960s; 1.4 percent annually in the 1950s). But median family incomes (factoring out inflation) grew only 34 percent in the 1960s, compared with 38 percent in the 1950s. Moreover, the proportion of households with incomes above a threshold of $10,000 in constant dollars grew 36 percent in the 1950s, but only 16 percent in the 1960s. Other economic indicators also suggest that prosperity may have grown faster in real terms during the earlier decade. For example, the proportion owning homes rose from 55 percent in 1950 to 62 percent in 1960, but rose by only 1 percentage point by 1970. Automobile ownership increased 17 percentage points in the 1950s but only 5 points in the 1960s. And television ownership—often credited with adverse effects on religious participation—was clearly the growth phenomenon of the 1950s, rising from 9 percent of all households to 87 percent.[28] The growth in urban population, as a proportion of total population, also took place more rapidly in the 1950s than it did in the 1960s (up 12 percent as opposed to 9 percent). The only notable difference between the two decades was that the percentage of young people in the population did not grow in the first as it did in the second—indeed, it declined slightly (from 16.0 percent to 15.2 percent), compared to an increase in the 1960s from 15.2 percent to 19.6 percent.[29] But the significance of this growth cannot be understood without also taking into consideration another change that characterized the 1960s to a greater extent than the 1950s.

That change was the tremendous growth in science and technology, and with it, the enormous expansion of higher education. At the close of World War II, the U.S. government had decided to promote more actively than ever before the investment in higher education that had been initiated on a serious national scale in the 1890s. The G.I. Bill provided the means to this end: it allowed veterans to attend college at government expense at the same time that it helped to relieve the strain imposed on the economy by the sudden return to civilian status of the nation's armed forces. The experience of World War II had also confirmed the importance of science and technology to the nation's defense. The critical role played by the development of aviation and submarine technologies, and most of all by the Manhattan Project, convinced leaders that national security in the future could only be maintained by a strong commitment to education and research. In the 1950s, the nation's need for a vast program of science and technology was further dramatized by the Soviet Union's development of atomic weapons and in 1957 by its entry into the era of space exploration. During this period the United States' leadership in rebuilding a competitive world economy also pointed up the growing importance of educational expansion and technological advancement. By 1965, the country was producing $27.2 billion of goods annually for export (15 percent of the world total) and of this figure, 64 percent was in technologically intensive industries such as chemicals, aircraft, telecommunications, computers, electronics, and scientific instruments. By the same date, the United States had 500,000 scientists engaged in research and development, the highest proportion relative to the total labor force of any country in the world. And it was spending 2.9 percent of total Gross National Product on research and development (R & D), nearly twice the proportion that had been spent only a decade earlier.

Bringing about this high level of activity in science and technology—and sustaining it—required a vast expansion in higher education. In 1950, 2.6 million persons were enrolled in higher education and by 1960 this number had grown modestly to 3.6 million. But the 1960s were to be a decade of enormous expansion. By 1970, the figure was 8.6 million, an increase of 5 million (139 percent) in a single decade.

Demographically, these numbers had two sources. One was a considerable increase in the overall size of the college-age population: young people between the ages of 18 and 24 increased from 16.2 million in 1960 to 24.4 million in 1970. The other was a sizable rise in the *proportion* of eligible young people who actually attended college. This proportion rose from 22.3 percent in 1960 to 35.2 percent in 1970. Financially, the growth in higher education came about only by virtue of a huge investment by federal, state, and local governments. Altogether, expenditures on higher education grew from a mere $2.2 billion in 1950 to $5.6 billion in 1960, and then mushroomed to $23.4 billion by 1970. Almost overnight, sleepy colleges of a few thousand students turned into bustling "mega-universities" with enrollments in the tens of thousands. High-rise dormitories were thrown up to house the teeming masses of undergraduates. Run-down barracks from the war were converted to provide housing for graduate students. Labs were built. Thousands of young professors were hired. And liberal access to loans and scholarships lured droves of high school graduates to the joys of higher learning.

Even in the short run, the broader effects of this enormous social investment in higher education were clearly evident. Median years of schooling in the adult population grew steadily as a result of the influx of large numbers of young people who were considerably better educated than their parents. In science, the payoff was particularly apparent. By 1973, 39 percent of all scientific and technical articles produced in the world were being authored by U.S. scientists. Between 1946 and 1975, one of every two Nobel prizes in the world went to a scientist from the United States, compared with only one prize in seven prior to 1946. Nearly one in every ten federal government employees by the early 1970s was a scientist. And in the labor force at large the proportion of persons employed as professional or technical workers rose from 8.4 percent in 1950 to 14.5 percent in 1970, with perhaps as many as an additional 20 to 25 percent employed in support positions such as secretarial staff, office workers, sales representatives, and paraprofessionals.

In the cultural realm, the expansion of state-sponsored science, technology, and higher education was accompanied by dramatic shifts in attitudes and values. One of the more notable shifts occurred in the area of egalitarianism. As already seen, levels of anti-Semitism declined markedly during this period, Protestants became more tolerant of Catholics, and prejudices separating Protestant denominations from one another eroded to all-time lows. In addition, intolerance of blacks underwent a significant decline, new attitudes toward gender began to be evident, and support mounted for civil liberties in areas such as freedom of speech for Communists, atheists, and homosexuals. With regard to racial acceptance, for example, a poll in Texas in the early 1960s had shown that only 40 percent of the public was willing to eat in the same restaurant with blacks. By the early 1970s, this figure had risen to 80 percent. A poll in Detroit in the 1950s had shown that fewer than one person in two said they would not be disturbed if a black person moved into their block. By the early 1970s, three out of four said they would not be disturbed. Over the same period, the proportion of the public nationally who said they would be willing to vote for a woman for president rose from about a third to approximately two-thirds. Attitudes about the proper roles of men and women in the economy and in the home showed similar changes toward increasing egalitarianism.[30] Other studies showed pronounced increases in levels of tolerance for nonconformity of various kinds. For example, between the mid-1950s and the early 1970s, the proportion of the public who expressed tolerant attitudes toward socialists increased from about half to two-thirds, while the proportion expressing tolerance toward atheists grew from only a third to two-thirds.[31]

During the 1960s, a sharp liberalization of attitudes also took place on a wide variety of life-style issues, ranging from divorce and premarital sexuality to political and economic orientations. Between 1959 and 1973, for example, the proportion of the public who felt premarital sex was morally wrong dropped from nearly four out of five to less than one in two. Over the same period, studies in the Detroit area showed that disapproval of divorce dropped from 43 percent to only 18 percent. Even among Roman Catholics, disapproval of divorce had declined by the mid-1960s to the point that only about one Catholic in three thought divorce was wrong. On political attitudes, surveys showed consistent increases during this period in the numbers who thought governmental practices needed to be reformed. Approval of government spending for social services and for other welfare programs also rose steadily during the 1960s.[32]

Virtually every study, moreover, showed that the growing liberalization of American culture in these years was closely related to the rising influence of higher education. Some of this influence seemed directly attributable to the ideas that were being taught; for example, greater awareness of constitutional guarantees of civil liberties and deeper understanding of the relativity of cultural preferences. The remainder stemmed more from indirect sources—from the circuitous influences of more liberal elites in politics, the mass media, and the entertainment industry; from the greater geographic mobility associated with gaining an education and becoming employed in the professional-technical sector; and simply from the diversifying influences of living away from parents on college campuses amidst the turmoil and experimentation of the period.

In any case, the influences of higher education were sufficiently direct for polls and surveys generally to find differences in levels of education to be the best single predictor of differences in attitudes and values. A study of anti-Semitism, for example, found that fewer than one person in six among college graduates registered anti-Semitic attitudes, compared to more than half of those who had only completed grade school.[33] Another study, measuring levels of political tolerance, found that more than 80 percent of the college graduates interviewed fell into the tolerant category, compared with approximately half of the high school graduates, and only a fifth of the grade school educated respondents.[34] Still another study, concerned with worldviews more generally that might be conducive to liberal attitudes, found strong correlations between these worldviews and the likelihood that respondents had attended college or had been reared by college educated parents.[35]

So powerful, in fact, were the effects of higher education on a wide range of values and beliefs that speculation began to emerge in the 1970s as to whether a "new class" had come into existence. The rapidly expanding segment of American society who had college educations, said the proponents of this idea, were beginning to have distinct interests and a distinct ideology that set them off from the rest of the population. Egalitarian values with respect to civil liberties and the rights of minority groups, liberal attitudes toward government welfare spending, permissive views on sex and morality, and a generalized interest in knowledge and education were said to be the hallmarks of the "new-class ideology." These orientations were not only thought to be markedly stronger among college-educated and professional segments of the population but were also thought to serve well the particular class interests of these segments. Egalitarianism justified the elite position of the new class, allowing its members to speak on behalf of the "public interest" more generally. Support for government welfare spending provided jobs for the new-class professionals who could provide services for which the government would pay. Permissive lifestyle orientations—although the relation was not as direct here—were said to justify the sexual styles, gender equality, and attitudes toward families that went along with two-career households in the technological fast lane. Valuing knowledge and education, of course, legitimated the very credentials with which the new class claimed its status as an elite.[36]

Not surprisingly, these arguments drew criticism from all quarters—especially from the new class itself. Studies that used some measure of education or professional employment as a criterion for inclusion in the new class, however, did find sharp differences between its members and those in other walks of life on many of the predicted ideological themes. For example, a study based on data collected mainly in the early 1970s found that members of the new class were at least 20 percentage points more likely than the public at large to: express tolerance toward homosexuality, favor legalized abortion, hold egalitarian attitudes toward women, and disapprove of antimiscegenation laws. The study also showed significant differences between the new class and the general public on support for government spending in areas such as education, medicine, space exploration, environmental protection, and urban improvement.[37]

Education, therefore, seemed to be emerging as a fundamental basis of attitudinal divergence in American culture. The better educated tended to be more liberal on a wide variety of issues; the less educated tended to be more conservative. These differences, moreover, often overshadowed other subcultural differences, such as those rooted in ethnic origins, region of the country, or even income differences. Age differences were still notable, if only because the young were by and large much more likely to have been to college than the old. Professionals generally espoused the same kinds of values as the college educated more broadly. And on some attitudes—further pointing to the role of expanding government in all of this—government employees and persons in occupations in which government was the principal financial resource seemed to manifest new-class values despite levels of education.[38]

This was the larger social context in which the religious restructuring of the 1960s took place. The broader effects of rising levels of education were felt in the religious sphere as well. The effects of higher education in eroding denominational boundaries have already been examined. Educational differences were also to play an increasing role in other religious trends that were to figure importantly in the emerging division between religious liberals and religious conservatives. Trends in religious participation, in religious belief, in the status of clergy, in clergy-laity relations, in the composition of denominations, and in the relations between religion and educational attainment itself—all bore the imprint of the expanding education system.

One of the most noticeable trends in American religion during the 1960s consisted of declining levels of religious involvement. For the first time in a century and a half, church membership as a percentage of the total population peaked and began to edge gradually downward. Church attendance also turned downward. After peaking in 1958 at around 49 percent (people who said they had been to a religious service within the past week), it declined steadily, leveling off at around 40 percent in the early 1970s. The decline among Catholics was particularly pronounced. Many of the kinds of beliefs and attitudes that opinion pollsters tried to measure also registered a drop during the 1960s. The percentage of the public who felt that religion's influence was increasing, for example, dropped from 69 percent in the late 1950s to only 14 percent in 1969. Whether its influence actually was declining or not, the public at least perceived religion to be in decline. On some other questions, the public still registered a fairly high degree of commitment to religion in absolute terms, but still the trends over time pointed downward. For example, four-fifths of the public thought religion could answer all or most of "today's problems" in the late 1950s; by the early 1970s this figure was closer to three-fifths. People in these years also seemed to feel that their own commitment to religion was somehow not as vibrant or as certain as it once had been. In Detroit, a 1971 study, for instance, showed that 30 percent of the public felt they had recently become less interested in religion. This figure was up from only 7 percent in the late 1950s. The same study revealed that fewer than half of the Detroit public felt certain of God's existence, compared with 68 percent just prior to the 1960s.

Judging from indicators other than those obtained in public opinion polls, the influence of traditional religion also seemed to be declining relative to that of other social institutions. Scientific and technical books, for example, were beginning to constitute an increasingly large segment of the publishing industry. Religious publications, in relation, were declining. As a proportion of all books and pamphlets sold in the United States, religious publications fell from 6.8 percent in 1954 to 4.5 percent in 1972. The numbers of new religious books published showed a similar decline: from 6.8 percent of all new books published between 1950 and 1955 to 5.6 percent of the total between 1968 and 1972.[39] A pattern of relative decline was also evident in the relation between charitable giving to religion and charitable giving to education. In 1955, about $4.50 was donated to religion for every dollar donated to education. By 1970, this ratio had fallen to $2.90 for religion per dollar donated to education.[40] More generally, donations to religion showed only modest growth, especially after 1965. Between that date and the mid-1970s, charitable giving to religion grew by only 15 percent in constant dollars, compared with much larger increases in other categories of giving.

As higher education expanded to occupy a larger and larger role in American society, religion also came to represent a smaller and smaller share of the educational system itself. For instance, masters degrees in religion and theology comprised 2.2 percent of all masters degrees granted in 1955, but only 1.1 percent by 1975. Doctorates in religion and theology shrank as a proportion of all doctorates even more abruptly: between 1960 and 1970 alone, from 2.8 percent to 1.4 percent. Within the larger labor force, the numbers of clergy nearly kept pace—declining from only .30 percent of the total civilian labor force in 1960 to .27 percent in 1970. But their representation within the expanding new class of professionals and other knowledge workers fell noticeably in relative terms—from 4.2 percent of the professional-technical occupational category in 1950 to a mere 2.2 percent in 1970.

Another consequence of the growth of higher education was that an increasing share of the laity in most denominations were becoming college educated. Unless one was an Episcopalian, having been to college was extremely rare among the members of all denominations in the 1950s. Fewer than one Baptist, Lutheran, or Catholic in seven had ever been to college; only one Methodist in five had been to college; and even among Presbyterians the proportion was only one in three. By the early 1970s, at least one person in four had been to college in most denominations and in several the college educated comprised a clear majority. These proportions would likely have been even larger had it not been for the fact that college educated young people fled the churches in droves during the 1960s. Some turned to new religions. Others abandoned the churches in disgust because of disagreements with traditionalistic teachings on contraception, premarital sex, or the Vietnam War. Still others simply fell between the cracks, so to speak, as denominations found themselves unable to supply campus ministers fast enough to keep up with the exorbitant growth of campus populations.[41]

Even considering the defection of educated young people from the churches, rising levels of education among parishioners during this period contributed importantly to the growing turmoil that was beginning to be evident in the churches. For it was the growing proportion of college educated parishioners who provided the grass-roots support to new-breed clergy engaged in social activism. Clergy themselves tended to be considerably better educated than the typical person in the pew. And the growing activism among clergy generally took the form of "liberal" causes, such as racial equality and antiwar militancy. But the conflict generated by this activism, contrary to most of the popular accounts of this period, did not consist only of a "widening gap" (as one writer put it) of opposition between clergy and laity. It consisted more accurately of conflict between less educated segments of the laity who tended to hold more conservative views, on the one hand, and a coalition of clergy activists and better educated laity who supported liberal causes, on the other. Where education levels among parishioners were high—as they were, for example, in the Episcopal church even in the 1950s—lay support for clergy who spoke out on sensitive political issues, became involved in certain kinds of political activism, and facilitated political involvement among parishioners was quite high.[42] In other denominations, it was generally the better educated who most strongly supported clergy activism. For example, data collected as part of a national survey in the mid-1960s showed that only 23 percent of the sample who had graduated from college thought "clergy should stick to religion and not concern themselves with social, economic, and political questions"; in comparison, 63 percent of those who had only some high school education held this view. The study also showed that persons with higher levels of education were about 20 percentage points more likely to favor the idea of clergy participating in demonstrations or civil rights protests.[43] Without such support, other research showed, clergy were generally reluctant to become involved in social activism.[44] Partly, therefore, it was the presence of a larger segment of educated parishioners—who gave support to like-minded pastors—that contributed to the controversy evident in the 1960s concerning clergy activism.

Another notable feature of the role of higher education in American religion is that the very relation between education and religion seemed to change in the 1960s. In particular, participation in conventional kinds of religious activities began to slip noticeably among the better educated. Consequently, there was a considerable "education gap" in religious commitment by the end of the 1960s, whereas no such gap had been evident earlier.

During the 1950s, to be more specific, studies generally showed that college educated persons were somewhat more likely than the less educated to participate in organized religion. This tendency was attributed to the fact that better educated people seemed to participate to a greater extent in all kinds of voluntary associations. By the end of the 1960s, however, that well-established pattern had begun to change, as least in matters of religious participation. Attendance at religious services declined especially rapidly among the better educated. For example, between 1969 and 1970 alone, church attendance among the college educated fell by 6 percentage points, but among persons without college educations attendance levels remained constant. Other data, collected over a longer period of time, showed that regular church attendance among college educated persons dropped by 11 percentage points between 1958 and 1968, but fell only 5 points during the same period among persons who had not been to college. By the end of the 1960s, therefore, something new seemed to be afoot in the relation between higher education and religious participation. The better educated at this point were still about as likely as the less educated to attend religious services regularly. But for some reason religious commitment among the more highly educated had slipped to a considerably greater extent over the previous decade than it had among persons without exposure to higher education.[45]

On matters of belief, somewhat the same kind of change occurred. Studies in the 1950s showed the better educated holding about the same levels of conventional religious belief as the less educated, or moderately lower levels. By the early 1970s, belief among the college educated had declined much more dramatically than in the less educated population. For example, between 1957 and 1974 the percentages who thought religion could answer all or most of society's problems fell by only 6 points among those with grade school educations, but by 26 points among those with at least some college education.[46]

We shall come back to these changes in order to consider some of their possible explanations and implications. For the time being, however, it will suffice to observe that the growth of higher education in the 1960s appears to have had a multitude of implications for American religion. By the end of that period, the college educated were still participating in religion to about the same degree as those with lower levels of education. But they were beginning to differentiate themselves on many of the traditional tenets of the faith. And the better educated now constituted a more significant proportion of the laity in their churches than they had earlier. On the whole, they were younger, were likely to have been in college during the turbulent years of the 1960s, were better educated than their own parents, and often had the sympathetic ear of their pastors, whose level of education resembled their own.

These developments figure in virtually all of the social changes within American religion that have been mentioned thus far. It was the better educated, both among laity and clergy, who pushed religious organizations in a more socially activist direction, first in the civil rights movement and then in the protest movement against the Vietnam War. These were the persons who came to favor greater cooperation between the different faiths and denominations, who registered lower levels of prejudice and misgiving toward members of other faiths, and who themselves were more likely to switch denominations, to visit in other denominations, and to marry outside of their own faith tradition. In all likelihood, their support gave encouragement to the denominational mergers and more liberal confessional statements that were adopted during this period. The role of higher education in the new religious movements was also considerable. Most of these movements situated themselves near college campuses and recruited heavily from student and ex-student populations. Participants in groups such as Zen, TM, and yoga were better educated than average. Persons who viewed these movements favorably, even without participating personally, also tended to be above average in education and held worldviews which encouraged innovative social experimentation of all kinds.[47] Even those who joined some of the more authoritarian cults were often by-products of the expanding educational system: dropouts, members of the drug culture, hangers-on to campus communities.

The net result of the 1960s, therefore, was to create a new basis of cultural cleavage—a cleavage that fell largely along educational lines and that cut through most of the established religious organizations. Whereas ethnic and regional divisions had once been the chief basis along which religious communities had divided, educational levels now became an increasingly important mode of religious differentiation. To the extent that education was closely connected with income, prestige, power, and privilege in the past, it had always served as a mode of social differentiation. But the 1960s became a time of veritable revolution in the educational system and, perhaps more importantly, in the role that higher education came to play in the economy at large. Increasingly, education became not only a matter of individual outlook but a major means of stratifying the society into different subcultures, of promoting technology, and of maintaining the country's competitive position in the world economy. It was as if the very basis of social order underwent a transition—a transition from industrial to postindustrial society, as some put it—in which education became an increasingly valuable social commodity. Previously rooted in heavy industry, agriculture, old wealth, and traditional regional and ethnic cleavages, the society now became increasingly dependent on education and the various professions, services, technologies, and political arrangements associated with the advancement of education.

As with all such transitions, the transformation of American society in the 1960s was fraught with a high degree of strain. Symptoms of this strain included overcrowded campuses, generational tensions between young people and their parents, racial conflict, and even protest over government policy, especially in the controversy surrounding the Vietnam War. American religion was subject to these strains as well. Denominations that had been organized along regional, ethnic, and doctrinal lines suddenly faced divisions within their own ranks. These divisions led some members to work for greater cooperation with like-minded believers in other denominations. The same divisions led others to dig in and resist any such efforts. Still others were encouraged by the turmoil of the period to abandon established religious organizations entirely or to experiment with new avenues of spiritual fulfillment. By the end of the decade, only the bare outlines of a sharp division between religious liberals and religious conservatives were beginning to be visible. But the influences of higher education in the larger society, combined with the various forces favoring and opposing accommodation within the religious community itself, were beginning to give shape to this division.

Consolidation and Deepening Division

If the 1960s was a decade of social and religious upheaval, the period from about 1973 through the mid-1980s was a time of consolidation—of continuity in the major educational and religious patterns established in the 1960s—and of deepening division between religious liberals and religious conservatives. Continuities can be seen in this period both in religion itself and in the relations between religion and the educational system.

Within conventional religion, aggregate indices of religious strength remained virtually constant during this period. Church membership fell from 62 percent of the total population in 1974 to 61 percent in 1975 and remained there for the next decade. In 1980, 2,055 new religious books were published, representing 4.8 percent of all new books, compared with 5.0 percent in 1970. Sales of religious books actually made up a slightly larger share of the total in 1980 (10.3 percent) than in 1970 (9.2 percent).[48] Religious contributions remained constant throughout the decade at 1.0 percent of personal income. And church attendance during a typical week hovered around 40 percent or 41 percent from 1971 on.[49]

Measures of religious beliefs and attitudes also pointed toward a leveling out in the 1970s and 1980s, after the dramatic slumps of the late 1960s. Whereas only 14 percent of the public thought religion's influence was increasing in 1970, this figure rose to 31 percent by 1974, climbed further to 44 percent in 1976, hit 44 percent again in 1983 after having sagged somewhat in the late 1970s, and then rose to 48 percent in 1985.[50] Between 1973 and 1985 the proportion who indicated a great deal or a lot of confidence in the churches or organized religion held virtually steady, varying between 64 percent and 66 percent. The number who felt religion could answer all or most of today's problems was 61 percent in 1985, compared with 62 percent in 1974. And the number who said religion was very important to them held steady at around 55 percent, after having declined from 70 percent in 1965 and 75 percent in 1952.

During this period, Americans also continued to register exceptionally strong levels of commitment to relatively simple aspects of religious belief and practice, although some of the more specific tenets of religious belief showed the lasting effects of erosion occurring in the 1960s. By the mid-1980s, for example, approximately nine of every ten adults in the United States still claimed to pray—a third of these saying they prayed at least twice a day—a figure that was about the same as that in national polls dating back to the late 1940s. Seven in ten said they believed in the divinity of Jesus, in life after death, and in heaven, all figures that had scarcely changed at all from the early 1950s. On the other hand, belief in a tenet that was to become a kind of shibboleth in the division between religious liberals and religious conservatives—whether the Bible is literally true—had fallen below 40 percent by the early 1970s, after having been recorded at 65 percent in 1963, and remained at this low level through the mid-1980s. And despite the fact that a majority of the public believed in the divinity of Jesus, considerably fewer now believed it necessary to accept Jesus in order to be saved (38 percent in 1981, compared with 51 percent in 1964). Similarly, most people still claimed some belief in God, but fewer now held this belief with certainty than in the past (62 percent said they had no doubts about God's existence in 1981, compared with 77 percent in 1964).[51]

A few denominational mergers and sectarian reactions to these mergers appeared in the 1970s and 1980s, but by and large the period was quieter than the 1960s in these respects. One of the most publicized movements in the 1970s was the formation of the Association of Evangelical Lutheran Churches, a theologically liberal denomination involving 245 local congregations, which emerged in 1976 after a conservative faction captured control of the Lutheran Church-Missouri Synod and forced a number of the denomination's liberal seminary professors to resign their positions. Other significant mergers that were finally effected in the 1980s after years of negotiations were those uniting the northern and southern branches of the Presbyterian church and bringing together the American Lutheran Church and the Lutheran Church in America. As before, some of these mergers were accompanied by the emergence of splinter groups. But generally, the degree of schismatic activity fell considerably below that of the 1960s. For example, only 12 new sectarian groups came into existence in the 1970s, compared with 57 in the 1960s.

Most of the new religious movements still in existence by the 1980s had been founded sometime prior to 1972. One source lists 111 new religious organizations as coming into existence in the 1970s, but most of these were founded in 1970 or 1971, and even the total figure is well below that listed for the 1960s (184).[52] After the mass suicide of more than 900 cult members at Jonestown, Guyana, in 1978, and the emergence of a more vigorous anticult movement, many of the new religious movements adopted a lower profile. Consequently, evidence on the extent of their memberships and activities became more difficult to obtain.

Available evidence, though, suggests that new religious experimentation by no means died out; but it probably did not grow after the early 1970s either. National surveys conducted during that decade, for example, showed little change in participation rates between the mid-1970s and the end of the decade. About 1 percent of the public claimed to be involved in Eastern religions, about 4 percent said they practiced TM, and about 3 percent claimed they were involved in yoga. Given the small percentages, these figures were, of course, subject to considerable variation from sampling error.[53] More recent estimates have come from less systematic sources. They also suggest that participation in new religious movements is quite small relative to the larger population. Yet, in absolute terms, the numbers are scarcely inconsiderable. A relatively complete estimate of the numbers involved in one kind of new religious activity or another in the greater Philadelphia area, for example, indicates approximately 90,000 participants (out of a total population of more than 3 million). Follow-up research on people who were involved in new religions in the late 1960s and early 1970s also suggests that a very high proportion still pursue some kind of nonconventional religious philosophy, although actual membership in organized groups and in communal living arrangements has dropped off sharply.[54]

The fate of specific kinds of new religions has varied markedly since the early 1970s, depending greatly on leadership style and dominant beliefs. Many of the more authoritarian movements either fled the country or declined considerably as a result of litigation, public suspicion, or financial difficulties. Movements like the Children of God and Divine Light, for example, relocated many of their members in other countries, while the leadership of the Rajneesh community in Oregon fled the United States, and some of the leaders of movements like Synanon and the Unification Church were jailed. Many of the democratically led movements have fared better, although some of the more idealistic of these groups have found it difficult to sustain the levels of sacrifice required over long periods of time. The Farm, a highly successful communal movement in Tennessee, which was organized by lecturer Steve Gaskin in 1971, for example, underwent a massive internal reorganization in 1983 after nearly half its members defected. Today, its economic and political structure comes much closer to that of the larger society than was initially the case.[55] The most viable movements, however, have been ones such as TM, yoga, *est*, and various self-help groups that offer therapy, meditation techniques, and other kinds of courses on a relatively short-term basis without demanding total involvement or intensive changes in life style. Indeed, the proliferation of health food stores, esoteric book stores, meditation centers, and organizations offering courses on a for-pay basis suggests that new religious orientations may be increasingly organized as a commercial offshoot of the broader religious establishment.

The fact that new religious movements gradually ceased to attract the wider publicity they enjoyed in the early 1970s has also meant that they play a less vital symbolic role in American religion. The division between religious liberals and religious conservatives is to some extent reflected in publicized reactions to the new religions. Conservative religious periodicals occasionally run feature stories warning readers of the heresies of new religions (a favorite target being the so-called "New Age Movement") and study guides for anticult classes can be found in conservative bookstores. Liberal churches and liberal religious periodicals, in contrast, have been much more likely to ask what can be learned from the new religions. Taking a more tolerant attitude toward other religions in general, their response has often been to suggest ways in which to incorporate insights about meditation, mystical experience, holistic health, therapy, massage, and so on, into Christianity. For the most part, however, the new religions have played a much less prominent role in the religious tensions of the 1980s than in the early 1970s.

More visible by far have been the various movements on the religious right. Groups like Moral Majority, as well as the prominent role played by religious television, have become the controversial issues of the 1980s. These, to a much greater extent than any of the movements in the 1960s, have contributed to the polarization evident between religious liberals and religious conservatives. Because the emergence of these and related movements is itself a relatively complex feature of the restructuring of American religion, however, we shall postpone considering them until the following chapter.

While many of the tendencies in the larger religious organizations reflect continuities with the changes initiated in the 1960s, a more detailed breakdown of how different segments of the population stand with respect to these tendencies again requires a look at broader developments. The continued promotion of science and technology and the consolidation of educational divisions as a major source of social differentiation still constitute an important part of this larger picture. By 1980, 32 percent of the adult population (over age 25) had completed at least some college education, compared with only 21 percent in 1970. Total enrollments in higher education rose from 8.6 million in 1970 to 12.1 million in 1980. The proportion of young people age 18 to 24 who were in school rose from 35 percent to 40 percent. And expenditures on higher education from all sources increased from $23.4 billion in 1970 to $50.7 billion in 1980. Two-thirds of U.S. exports were still in high-technology industries and increasing attention was being devoted to developing these industries since they were the principal areas in which the country enjoyed a favorable export-import balance. Overall, total expenditures for R & D in the 1970s rose by 22.3 percent after inflation and an increasing share of these expenditures was being borne by the private sector. The new class, it appeared, was destined to play an ever greater role in American society. And, as will be seen in Chapters 12 and 13, science and technology were becoming increasingly important as part of the nation's legitimating myths.

The "education gap" in social attitudes and in religion that was becoming evident by 1970 became even more pronounced during the following decade. Those with college educations were considerably more likely to espouse religious views which in one way or another had come to be regarded as liberal orientations. The better educated were more likely in their own minds to identify themselves as religious liberals. And their views on church matters, social and moral questions, and political issues all tended to set them off from religious conservatives. Those without college educations, on the other hand, were much more likely to identify themselves as religious conservatives, to hold more traditional religious views, and to espouse a wide range of social and political attitudes that reflected a conservative orientation.

In a 1981 survey, for example, approximately half of the college educated American public identified themselves as "religiously liberal." In comparison, only one person in seven among those who had only grade school educations identified themselves this way. Views of the Bible, as noted earlier, were one of the issues on which the better and less educated divided most sharply. More than half of the grade school educated thought the Bible should be regarded as the literal word of God. Only a fifth of the college educated felt this way. People from different educational strata also took radically different positions on issues confronting the church. For example, 47 percent of the college educated thought it acceptable for homosexuals to be hired as clergy, compared with only 17 percent of those with grade school educations.[56] In an earlier survey devoted to issues confronting the Roman Catholic church, huge differences had also been evident between the different educational strata. Among college educated Roman Catholics, for instance, 48 percent said they approved of women being ordained as priests, compared with only 28 percent of the non-college groups. Similarly, three-quarters of the former said they approved of the changes in the church since the Second Vatican Council, compared with about half of the latter.[57]

Polls conducted in the mid-1980s have documented even more clearly the role of educational differences in the current divide between religious liberals and religious conservatives. In the study of religious liberals and conservatives mentioned at the beginning of the chapter, for example, persons with college educations were about twice as likely to be religious liberals as they were to be religious conservatives; conversely, persons with grade school educations were about twice as likely to be conservatives as liberals. Of all the social background questions in the study, education was the factor that most clearly discriminated between religious liberals and religious conservatives.[58]

Judging from other results, it is understandable why persons with different educational levels hold these different views about their religious orientations. Among college graduates, only one person in three thinks the Bible is absolutely true (contains no errors); among persons who have only attended high school the figure is closer to two-thirds. Of all college graduates, only a quarter say they have been "born again." The figure is approximately half among persons with high school educations. Half of the less educated sector says reading the Bible is very important to them, compared with only a quarter of college graduates.

In more subtle ways, educational differences also add up to quite divergent styles of religious expression. For example, college graduates are about three times more likely than persons without college education to put the Second Commandment (loving your neighbor) ahead of the First Commandment (loving God).[59] The better educated are also about three times as likely to think it possible to be a true Christian without believing in the divinity of Christ. Those with low levels of education, in contrast, are about twice as likely as college graduates to believe that being baptized is necessary in order truly to know God. The two groups also view Jesus and God in quite different ways. For instance, college graduates are about twice as likely as those without college educations to be most impressed by Jesus' compassion and forgiveness. The less educated, in comparison, are more likely to be impressed by Jesus' healings, miracles, and goodness. Those with higher levels of education are considerably more likely to attribute androgenous characteristics to God; those with lower levels of education, to emphasize the masculinity of God.[60]

More generally, persons with different levels of education also differ on a wide variety of social, political, and moral issues. For example, most of the polls that have asked about legalized abortion show nearly twice as much support among those with college educations than in the noncollege sector. On civil liberties items, such as allowing an atheist to teach, only a quarter of those who have graduated from college express disapproval, compared with 60 percent of those who do not hold a college degree. On national defense, more than four in ten college degree holders say the country is spending too much, compared with only a quarter of those without college degrees.[61] Differences of similar magnitude exist on most survey questions about pornography, homosexuality, and abiding by strict moral standards.[62] To the extent that religious organizations have generally regarded these as important issues to discuss, therefore, it is not surprising that a major division has emerged in these organizations between persons with high and low levels of education.

In addition to dividing people on social issues and on religious attitudes, the role of higher education can also be seen in some of the longer range trends that have been mentioned. It was suggested earlier, for instance, that religious participation rates declined more rapidly in the 1960s among the better educated than in the rest of the population. The full extent of these changes can be seen more clearly in light of additional evidence from the 1980s. Between 1958 and 1982, the most serious declines in regular church attendance came about among younger people with at least some college education. Specifically, there was a 19 percentage point difference between the two periods among college educated persons between the ages of 25 and 34. And there was a 21 point difference among college educated persons between the ages of 35 and 44. In none of the other categories were the differences this great. In other words, being a younger, better educated person in the 1980s was associated with relatively modest levels of religious participation, whereas the same kind of person in the late 1950s was likely to be much more active in religious involvement. Not only were there considerably more people with college educations by the 1980s, but these people were now less conventionally religious than their counterparts had been a generation earlier. Again, education seemed to have become associated with a kind of "gap" in religious commitment that had not been there prior to the 1960s.[63]

If the better educated were no longer as actively involved in religious organizations as they once were, their growing numbers nevertheless had become a significant influence in most denominations. By the 1980s, a majority—or very substantial minorities—of the members of most denominations carried college educations as part of their personal experience and brought with them many of the more liberal outlooks that went along with this experience. According to polls conducted in 1984, for example, 68 percent of all Episcopalians had been to college, as had an equal proportion of Jews. Among Presbyterians, six in ten had been to college. And better than four in ten had been to college in each of the following: American Lutheran Church, Lutheran Church-Missouri Synod, United Methodist, United Church of Christ, and Roman Catholic. Of the large established denominations, only Baptists continued to be comprised primarily of persons without college educations. And even among Baptists the percentage who had been to college was by no means inconsiderable: 29 percent among American Baptists, 30 percent among Southern Baptists.[64]

As the religiously active public became better educated, there was some denominational switching along educational lines as well. When people changed denominations, they tended to move toward denominations that most closely reflected their own levels of education. Among all denominational switchers, for example, 43 percent of those who had not been to college shifted either to one of the Baptist denominations or to a religious sect. In contrast, only 28 percent of the college educated switchers shifted to one of these groups. And on the other side of the scale, those who had been reared in one of these denominations were likely to "move up" to one of the better educated denominations if they themselves were better educated. For instance, 16 percent of the switchers who had been raised as Baptists but who had college educations became Episcopalians or Presbyterians. The comparable figure for former Baptists without college educations was 7 percent. Among former members of Protestant sects, the differences were even more pronounced: 31 percent of the college educated became Episcopalians or Presbyterians, compared with 8 percent of those without college educations. And the same was true among people reared in denominations with an ample mixture of different educational levels. Among former Methodists, 21 percent of the college educated became Presbyterians or Episcopalians, compared with only 10 percent of the non-college educated.[65]

Were these patterns to continue on any sizable scale, they would of course result in the division of denominations along educational lines. The better educated denominations would increasingly become the refuge of college graduates; denominations with large numbers of persons without college educations would attract even larger numbers of the same kind of people. This does not appear to be happening, however. As already seen in Chapter 5, the major denominations are becoming more similar to one another in educational composition rather than less similar. Several reasons explain why. One is that large numbers of church members still stay put rather than switching denominations at all. A second is that little switching seems to occur from better educated denominations to less educated denominations among those who themselves have lower levels of education. A third factor is that a sizable number of the better educated who switch denominations cease to affiliate with any denomination, rather than joining the better educated denominations. For instance, 16 percent of all former Methodists who switch and who have been to college list their current affiliation as "none." And 19 percent of the former Baptists with college educations do so. Consequently, the better educated denominations, such as the Episcopal and Presbyterian churches, have not grown in overall membership, even though the general population is becoming more highly educated. Finally, as was seen in Chapter 5, it appears that average education levels have grown faster among members of denominations that previously had the lowest education levels, perhaps simply because they had more "room to grow." The upshot, then, is that most denominations have substantial numbers of both the better educated and the less educated.

To the extent that rising levels of education have carried with them more liberal orientations, these views are now much more prominently represented in the major denominations than they have been in the past. Liberal theological orientations are more prevalent. Support for interdenominational cooperation is stronger. And reinforcement for liberal clergy who favor social activism, egalitarianism, and tolerant positions on issues such as pornography, homosexuality, ordination of women, and so on, is likely to be more pronounced. Often these shifts remain subtle, especially when they are clouded by the statements of powerful leaders at the top of these denominations. In other cases, the changes have been clear and decisive. Among United Methodists, for example, the proportion of laity who regarded individual salvation as the chief goal for the church to pursue dropped from 63 percent in 1958 to 55 percent in 1975 to 31 percent in 1983—with comparable shifts being evident in church policies as well.[66] Similarly, among Southern Baptists, rapidly rising education levels among pastors and members alike during the 1970s, as well as broader changes taking place in the South, led to wholesale questioning of the denomination's traditional stand on biblical inerrancy—which only in the 1980s came to be resisted by an even more powerful movement among conservatives in the denomination. Again, education was a decisive factor in shaping the ways in which Southern Baptists aligned themselves on these issues.[67]

Over the past quarter century, therefore, a noticeable move to the left has taken place in many sectors of American religion. In contrast with the solid centrism evident in the 1950s, many denominations have undergone a high degree of turbulence surrounding the civil rights movement, the anti-war protests, the counterculture, and a more general upgrading of educational levels with corresponding shifts in social values and religious orientations. At the same time, these shifts have not been so sweeping as to merely carry the day. They have generated countermovements and have been resisted by a strong enough constituency to have resulted more in polarization between the right and the left rather than a clear victory for either side. To understand fully the sources of this polarization, we must now turn to the changes that have taken place over the same period within the ranks of religious conservatives.

CHAPTER 8

Mobilization on the Right

THE DEVELOPMENT of a strong conservative thrust in American religion at the same time that religious orientations were moving to the left cannot be understood without examining both the internal dynamism of the religious right and the social forces to which it was tied. The tension between liberals and conservatives is itself an important part of the story. But the upsurge of religious conservatism cannot be understood simply as a reaction to the good fortunes—or even the excesses—of religious liberalism. Nor can the religious right be adequately appreciated if it is pictured as a kind of backwater phenomenon that is somehow removed from the main forces shaping American culture. To a very clear degree, the mobilization of the right in American religion was rooted in the same kinds of societal changes that gave rise to the religious left.

In the years immediately following World War II religious conservatives looked forward to a new era with the same kind of cautious anticipation that characterized religious leaders more generally. As mentioned briefly in the last chapter, the old separatist variant of American fundamentalism had come under serious attack by a new generation of conservative leaders who saw greater gains to be had from disciplined participation in the society than from withdrawal. The new leaders who were to shape the future of religious conservatism specifically repudiated the fundamentalist label and many of the connotations with which it had become associated. While they retained an emphasis on scripture, they declared the earlier movement to have been "blighted by religious froth," "acrimonious," and lacking in "brotherliness." The new label they chose to emphasize was "evangelicalism." Recognizing the interest in "evangelizing" the world that remained strong in most of the established denominations, they saw this thrust as both vital to the future of American Christianity in general and the key to the success of their own movement.

Organizing a National Movement

One of the first steps toward forging a national movement around the idea of evangelical Christianity had been taken amidst the war when nearly 600 religious leaders met in May, 1943, to found the National Association of Evangelicals (NAE). Those in the forefront of this organization saw the value of mobilizing a cooperative venture on a national scale that could counter the organizations with whom they disagreed. As Carl F. H. Henry was to remark a few years later, "If, as is so often remarked, the Federal Council of Churches is the voice of Protestant liberalism in America, Protestant evangelicalism too needs a single voice."[1] The NAE represented only a million members by the end of World War II, a tiny fraction of American Protestantism. It nevertheless gave the evangelical movement a national identity and provided a platform from which to launch a number of special purpose groups that were to become increasingly important in the years to come. These included the National Religious Broadcasting Association, which was to become increasingly important as radio and television ministries expanded; the National Sunday School Association, which played an important role in promoting educational activities in evangelical churches; the Evangelical Foreign Missions Association, a coordinating body representing 43 mission boards; the Commission for Church Schools, which focused on efforts to gain released time in public schools for religious instruction; and the Commission on War Relief (later renamed World Relief), which channeled charitable contributions to people in need around the globe.

Another significant organizational development in the new evangelical movement was the founding in 1947 of Fuller Theological Seminary in Pasadena, California. Endowed with a substantial trust fund by Charles E. Fuller's father, and instantly visible through the popular radio ministry of evangelist Charles E. Fuller himself, the seminary was widely lauded within the movement as a new force for training evangelical pastors and missionaries. As a byproduct, it also helped to forge a tighter national network among previously isolated centers of evangelical activity scattered around the country. It did so by recruiting faculty, administrators, and trustees from evangelical organizations nationwide. Among these recruits were Harold Ockenga from the prominent Park Street Church in Boston, Wilbur M. Smith from Moody Bible Institute in Chicago, Everett Harrison from Dallas Theological Seminary, and Carl F. H. Henry and Harold Lindsell from Northern Baptist Theological Seminary in Chicago. These men not only provided the nucleus of an important new center of evangelical activity in southern California, but also maintained strong connections with their former institutions, thereby forming the nucleus of a much broader national network.

Other connections also helped to transform American evangelicalism from a disorganized array of local efforts into a united national movement. The link between North and South, largely absent since the Civil War, was re-established, at first mainly by interaction between Moody

Bible Institute in Chicago and Dallas Theological Seminary. One of the key figures in this connection was Carl Amerding, formerly of Moody Bible Institute, who became a faculty member at Dallas in 1947. Another link that became stronger in these years was between eastern and midwestern evangelicals. Philadelphia and Chicago became the principal nodes in this connection. Here, a critical figure was William Culberston of Philadelphia, who became dean at Moody Bible Institute in 1942 and president in 1947. Another important figure was Philip E. Howard, Jr., editor of the conservative, Philadelphia-based *Sunday School Times*, who maintained increasingly close ties with Wheaton College outside of Chicago. It was Howard's daughter who became (as mentioned in the last chapter) the widow of slain missionary Jim Elliott and an increasingly vocal figure on the religious right herself. Another Howard offspring was to become prominent in Wheaton-based evangelistic work, especially in a new organization called World Vision. And still another sibling, after graduating from Wheaton, was to carry the evangelical connection back to the East Coast, becoming a faculty member at Gordon College in Massachusetts.

About the same time that the NAE was beginning to give religious conservatism a national identity, another movement called Youth for Christ was starting to give evangelicalism an articulate voice among the nation's high school students. Its method followed that of the great urban revivalists of the late nineteenth century. On Memorial Day, 1945, for example, it packed 70,000 people into Chicago's Soldier Field for a day of open-air preaching, commemoration of fallen servicemen, gospel music, testimonies, and rededication to the evangelical cause. By mid-1946 the movement had sponsored some 900 rallies in cities around the country, drawing attendance from as many as a million young people.[2] As much as it contributed to evangelizing high school students, however, Youth for Christ also became the occasion for growing interaction among evangelical leaders on a nationwide basis. Drawing on local leadership from Wheaton College and Moody Bible Institute in the Chicago area, it attracted prominent evangelical leaders from the Twin Cities (especially George Wilson, who was to play an important role in the Billy Graham movement), from Seattle (especially rally director Bob Pierce, who was to found the evangelical mission organization called World Vision), from New York (including Jack Wyrtzen, founder of Word of Life), and from southern California, Boston, Philadelphia, and North Carolina.

Youth for Christ was only one of many such organizations that were founded during this period. Reflecting the growing numbers of children and young people in the country as well as the churches' longstanding emphasis on education, many of these organizations focused on Christian training. The Child Evangelism Fellowship was one such movement.

Sponsored by Christian laity with experience at organizing evangelistic programs among businessmen and military personnel, its goal was to minister to children between the ages of 6 and 13. Other such organizations included Children for Christ, Word of Life Fellowship, High School Evangelism Fellowship, Miracle Book Club, Youth Jubilee Hour, and Voice of Christian Youth. An important impetus to these movements was the feeling among laity that denominational structures were becoming too bureaucratized, and in some cases too secular, to sponsor effective evangelistic ministries. As one New York lawyer who was active in several of these movements remarked:

> It is undoubtedly true that the branches of the visible church, hampered as they are with all their man-made rules and regulations, and shot through and through with criticism of the Bible itself, and with preachers who teach so-called science, literature and philosophy, rather than salvation, are losing out in the world today, so much that it seems that God is by-passing them and is having His work accomplished by choosing a people for His Name through all of these other agencies.[3]

Such was the mixture of foreboding and zeal that formed the basis of many of the new evangelical organizations.

Of all the organizations that began to give national shape to the evangelical movement, however, the most prominent became the network undergirding the Billy Graham crusades. Raised in North Carolina, schooled at Bob Jones University in Tennessee, Florida Bible Institute in Tampa, and Wheaton College in Illinois, Graham became an increasingly important bridge between northern and southern evangelicals. A Southern Baptist, he was married to a Presbyterian, had preached widely in independent Bible churches, earned the sponsorship of powerful conservative Northern Baptist leaders in Chicago, and had strong connections with leading business figures as well as evangelists and church leaders around the country. His interdenominational background, as well as his strong connections with interdenominational Wheaton College, made it easier for him to secure cooperation that crossed denominational lines. Graham's own roots as a preacher were in the rallies sponsored by Youth for Christ, and through these he forged his own regionally diverse team of sponsors and co-workers: Cliff Barrows from California, Beverly Shea from Canada, Torrey Johnson from Chicago, and George Wilson from Minnesota. Like others in the new wave of conservative leadership, Graham also steered consciously away from the term fundamentalist, preferring the label evangelical because it had a more dynamic, progressive, nondefensive connotation.[4]

These early gains notwithstanding, the evangelical movement was still quite weak in relation to the work being carried out by the established denominations. One of the most serious weaknesses stemmed from the fact that the evangelical movement drew its support mainly from scattered Protestant sects that were still quite small and deeply suspicious of one another. In 1946, for example, the 22 denominations of which the NAE was comprised averaged only 45,000 members apiece. In comparison, the 25 denominations represented by the Federal Council of Churches averaged about 1 million members each. Thus, it took the cooperation of about as many evangelical denominations to develop a coalition of 1 million members as it did the Federal Council of Churches to forge a coalition of 25 million members.[5] Another potential weakness lay in the fact that evangelicalism continued (as seen in the last chapter) to be a prominent emphasis within the established denominations themselves. Leaders of organizations like Youth for Christ and the Billy Graham crusades, in fact, depended heavily on these denominations for their support. It was, of course, encouraging to evangelical leaders to find their views so widely shared. But the identity of their own movement remained precarious by virtue of this very support. At any moment, their reason for existence might fade away. Only if a mainstream of American Protestantism turned decidedly to other concerns, as it in fact did in the 1960s, would the evangelical movement be able to make distinct claims of its own. For the time being, it functioned chiefly as a "parachurch" movement—as a cluster of loosely integrated special purpose groups devoted to the cause of evangelism.

Still, the seeds that were sown during this period represented the beginnings of a potentially fertile movement. Not only were the organizations comprising the evangelical movement rooted in skillful and energetic leadership, but the ideas around which the movement began to take shape also represented a dynamic thrust in American religion. From the beginning, evangelical leaders consciously steered away from the sectarianism, fragmentation, and theological strife that had reduced the effectiveness of their fundamentalist forebears. They acknowledged that negativism, confessional disputes, organizational inefficiency, and a badly remiss social conscience had left the fundamentalist movement in ill-repute with much of the American public.[6] They took heart in seeing themselves as the defenders of theological truth. But their energies focused less on defending timeless truths than on promoting a new spirit of interdenominational cooperation for the advancement of Christianity, a more constructive approach toward the complex relation between evangelism and social ethics, and a combination of up-to-date scholarship and firm commitment to the theological tenets of conservative Protestantism.

In keeping with the broader mood among postwar religious leaders, evangelicals tended to be more optimistic than fundamentalists had been about the possibilities of building on the religious values still prevalent in American society, rather than feeling it necessary to separate themselves from all nonevangelical influences. As Carl Henry put it, "the influences of Christian theism are still abroad with enough vigor that the usual solutions [proposed by nonevangelicals] are non-redemptive, rather than anti-redemptive, in character."[7] In his view, the prevalence of theistic values meant that evangelicals could cooperate with other groups in opposing war and racial injustice, in fighting moral decay, and in turning humanistic orientations toward a more religious perspective, rather than having to withdraw from these other groups.

This outlook held enormous advantages for the evangelical movement. At about the same time that the NAE was formed, the more separatist fundamentalists organized a countermovement called the American Council of Christian Churches, which insisted that members be denominationally separate from any of the organizations they regarded as being controlled by liberal or modernist influences, particularly those affiliated with the Federal Council of Churches. It attracted only a few thousand members. In contrast, the NAE permitted member congregations to maintain full membership in the association without withdrawing from denominations affiliated with the Federal Council of Churches. Its leaders recognized that many pastors and lay leaders in individual congregations held views similar to their own, but had valued their denominational affiliations strongly enough not to have formed separatist sects during the fundamentalist heyday in the 1920s. These, together with the smaller Protestant sects, they hoped, would form the basis of a broader evangelical movement than the fundamentalists had been able to mobilize. On theological grounds, the fundamentalists continued to argue that mainline denominations were so hopelessly filled with apostasy and idolatry that a stand consistent with scripture required complete separation. Evangelicals, in contrast, argued that it was more effective to stay in those organizations and attempt to purge their leadership of heresy rather than demand total withdrawal. This outlook gave the evangelicals far more strength in numbers than the fundamentalists. But, as noted before, it also presaged the nature of religious division that was to grow in decades to come. This division, rather than developing between denominations, was to emerge to a significant degree *within* denominations and even within local congregations.

If the issue of separation was to be decisive for the eventual development of relations between liberals and conservatives, the cultural and organizational grounds on which this issue depended deserve closer examination. Specifically, the conditions that made it more meaningful for evangelicals to adopt the position they took rather than the more separatist stance of the fundamentalists need to be understood. On the cultural side, fundamentalists thought of apostasy within the churches as monolithic, pervasive, and sufficiently extensive to have spoiled the entire apple barrel. Evangelicals thought apostasy was limited mainly to denominational bureaucrats and professors at liberal seminaries. Organizationally, these different points of view were in fact consistent with the denominational positions of the two groups. Fundamentalists came from separate denominations. They could only look across the fence at the policies they saw coming from their former denominational rivals and assume that the entire barrel had gone rotten. Evangelical leaders still operated from within the established denominations. Spokesmen such as Carl Henry and Harold Ockenga came from denominations such as the Northern Baptists and Presbyterians in which the leadership contained clearly liberal elements. But they could also see that this orientation was not shared by many rank and file members or even by other elements of the denominations' leadership. It was only natural, therefore, for them to argue for change from within rather than total separation.

Another important cultural difference between the two groups was that evangelicals tended to be more pragmatic, as evidenced by the fact that they were for the most part institution builders who were in command of considerable resources such as seminary professorships, journals, and pulpits in large congregations, and were theologically committed to the task of evangelizing the world rather than maintaining their own purity as an example to the world. To them, involvement with the secular world was mandated as a way of getting the job of evangelism done. It was also clear that a nonseparatist orientation contributed to the evangelicals' capacity to mobilize resources. They could appeal to individuals and whole congregations within otherwise liberal denominations. Lacking control of their own denominations, in contrast with the small denominations that fundamentalist leaders controlled, evangelicals found it imperative to form new organizations and to mold new means of communicating their ideas to people in many different denominations. Ironically, having to form innovative organizational structures, rather than being able to rely on their own denominations, also forced them to rely to a greater extent on the resources they could secure from other denominations. Interdenominational journals such as *Moody Monthly* and *Christianity Today* were founded in hopes of drawing readers from among conservative Christians of widely differing backgrounds. The doctrinal statements on which these journals were founded tended to emphasize only a few core tenets of Christianity, rather than wandering into mine fields of theological dispute. Interdenominational colleges, such as Wheaton, and seminaries, such as Dallas and Fuller, also depended for their very survival on evangelicals' willingness to work with leaders in established denominations. As Harold Ockenga remarked shortly after becoming the charter president of Fuller seminary: "We want our men to be so trained that when they come from a denomination, whatever that denomination is, they may go back into their denomination adequately prepared to preach the gospel and to defend the faith and to positively forward the work of God."[8]

Evangelicals also differentiated themselves from fundamentalism in placing greater emphasis on theological systematization and in stressing the importance of cooperation among their various component bodies. In calling for greater systematization of theological tenets, evangelical leaders had in mind the creation of a philosophically defensible biblical theology. They objected to the fact that fundamentalists had often been content to proclaim their doctrines as isolated tenets, integrated with one another only by being listed together as "fundamentals." Evangelicals thought this approach left the sophisticated person without any comprehensive basis for making theological judgments. Consequently, the fundamentalist was likely to adopt, reject, or incorporate particular doctrines willy-nilly into a secular philosophy. Evangelicals wanted their own theology to be a systematic worldview so that the sophisticated person could see value in the whole approach. This, they recognized, would be increasingly important as the population became better educated. In addition, although less apparent to evangelical leaders at the time, a systematic theology would require greater care in relating theology and ethics. The result was to be an evangelical movement that paid considerable attention to formulating views on social and moral questions. The other emphasis—on internal cooperation—was aimed intentionally at avoiding the divisiveness that had weakened the fundamentalist movement. This emphasis lay behind the many national organizations that soon came to characterize the evangelical movement. It also forced the movement to strip away much of the cultural baggage that had plagued its forebears, making it more adaptable and attractive in the new postwar cultural milieu. Issues such as preferred translations of the Bible, particular views of biblical prophecy, and even specific prescriptions in the realm of morality tended to be downplayed relative to central teachings of the Christian gospel.

In social location, finally, the evangelical movement was also poised to occupy a much more prominent position in American society than the fundamentalist movement had been. The earlier movement had been characterized correctly as a religious form that drew its greatest strength from areas that were "remote from the large metropolitan centers," "isolated from the eastern states," and in states with high levels of poverty and illiteracy. There were, of course, significant exceptions, such as the role of Princeton Theological Seminary early in the fundamentalist movement and the role of wealthy California businessmen in funding publication of the *Fundamentals*. But the strength of the fundamentalist movement had always resided mainly in the rural Midwest and South. In contrast, the evangelical movement from the start (at least outside the South) emanated from the major cities: Chicago, Philadelphia, Boston, Los Angeles. Its leaders came from large urban congregations and included seminary and college professors with good educations and skills in publishing and broadcasting. At the grass roots, constituents still tended to be relatively rural, less affluent, and less educated than the more liberally oriented denominations. But evangelicalism was poised to take advantage of trends toward urban and suburban growth, to capitalize on the rising numbers of young people and their growing involvement in higher education, and from the beginning it cultivated ties with business and community leaders.

Quiet Growth

The 1950s witnessed extraordinary expansion among evangelical organizations, just as it did among most of the major Protestant denominations. After a highly successful campaign in Los Angeles in 1949 that drew national publicity in the media, the Billy Graham crusades attracted larger and larger audiences in city after city. Soon Billy Graham was bringing national and even international recognition to the evangelical movement. With Graham as inspiration, and with the backing of longtime Graham supporter Henrietta Mears (herself a prominent Hollywood Bible teacher), a young California businessman named Bill Bright founded Campus Crusade for Christ—the name consciously modeled after the title of Graham's successful "Crusade for Christ" in Los Angeles. The movement was scarcely an original idea, taking its goal of "evangelizing the world in this generation" from the earlier Student Volunteers movement which had been organized in 1887 and had mounted successful campus ministries through the 1920s. Bright's experience in business, nevertheless, gave solid organizational guidance to the movement. And with the growth that was to occur on the nation's campuses, the movement was destined to play an increasingly prominent role among religious conservatives. Other campus organizations, such as Inter-Varsity Christian Fellowship, Nurses Christian Fellowship (an outgrowth of Inter-Varsity), and Navigators (a smaller, highly disciplined movement founded in 1933 and active among soldiers during World War II), also spread quietly from one college to another during this period.

The new opportunities for ministry on college campuses that appeared after World War II were rivaled only by the new fields that opened up for overseas ministries. With the return to peacetime conditions, and with the United States shouldering increasing responsibilities in diplomatic and economic relations, evangelicals saw a chance to revive the great missionary endeavors that had been initiated during the nineteenth century. No sooner had the war ended than evangelical mission boards began to be organized for this effort: the Evangelical Foreign Missions Association in 1945, United World Mission in 1946, Christian Missionary Fellowship in 1950, and World Vision in 1950. By 1952, some 18,000 North American missionaries were serving overseas, of whom approximately 8,000 were supported by evangelical organizations. By 1960, the total number of foreign missionaries had grown to more than 29,000, and the proportion sponsored by evangelical organizations had risen from 44 percent to 65 percent.[9]

The success of the evangelical movement during the 1950s depended greatly on the fact that its efforts focused specifically on the tasks of evangelism. Indeed, many of the organizations that comprised the evangelical movement could be described as special purpose groups devoted to the specific ministry of evangelism and missions. This focus gave the evangelical movement a clear identity and, insofar as its efforts at evangelization were often successful, drew new members to its ranks. While a number of these special purpose groups were of recent origin, they also benefited from imitating groups with much longer histories in American religion—groups such as the American Bible Society, Gideons International, the Student Volunteers, and the numerous missionary societies. In addition, it will be recalled from the last chapter that evangelism remained an interest of most of the established denominations during this period. As yet, the evangelical movement failed to be seen as a distinct rival to Protestant liberalism. Instead, many of the movement's organizations drew support from the larger denominations themselves. Youth movements, like Youth for Christ, were widely hailed as effective means of drawing young people into the churches. And ministries, such as the Billy Graham crusades, while viewed by many denominational officials with misgivings, generally thrived from the support given them by local churches and community ministerial councils. For ecumenically minded church leaders, these evangelical organizations actually comprised some of the more prominent examples of interdenominational cooperation. And for member bodies of the NAE, often too small to mount their own missionary programs or mass rallies or campus ministries on an effective scale on their own, the new evangelical organizations offered a powerful arm to which support could willingly be contributed. After the National Council of Churches began operations, the NAE increasingly sought to present itself as a more conservative alternative. But its appeals generally focused more on the necessity of devoting resources to the tasks of evangelization than trying to lure whole congregations or denominations into its camp.

As the Cold War unfolded, the evangelical movement (along with religious organizations more generally) clamored with increasing vigor against the threat to godliness posed by communists at home and abroad. This emphasis may have attracted some churchgoers into the evangelical fold, especially in the early years of the Cold War while religious leaders in some quarters were still advocating a "third way." However, it was the lingering elements of fundamentalism rather than the evangelical leaders who seized most firmly the appeals of anticommunism. Presbyterian fundamentalist Carl McIntire, for example, was instrumental not only in setting up the American Council of Christian Churches but also in launching an independent movement that had anticommunism among its chief objectives. A few years later, fundamentalists in southern California founded the highly successful Christian Anti-Communism Crusade. Another fundamentalist movement that tried to combine anticommunism with extremist religious zeal was Billy James Hargis's Christian Crusade. Educated at Ozark Bible College in Arkansas, and later pastor of churches in Missouri and Oklahoma, Hargis resigned the pulpit in 1950 to work full-time in the crusade against communism. "God bear me witness," he has written, "I would rather win souls to Christ than fight Communism any day, but a man has to do what God calls him to do. When God calls a man to do a specific ministry, he had better do it."[10] Like most of the other organizers of vigorous movements against communism, Hargis found that his greatest appeal was to fundamentalists in small independent churches who had already made a strict break with mainstream culture and who expected the wrath of God to descend on America at any moment in the guise of Soviet totalitarianism.

Besides the growth of evangelical special purpose groups, membership in conservative sects and denominations also expanded greatly during the 1950s. Assemblies of God, for example, added more than 2,000 new congregations, resulting in an 18 percent increase in total membership between 1952 and 1962. The Church of the Nazarene grew by approximately 1,000 congregations, an increase of 37 percent in total membership. And the already huge Southern Baptist Convention expanded its numbers by 28 percent, adding more than 2 million members and 4,000 new congregations in the process. Particularly significant, as mentioned in Chapter 5, was the growth in this denomination outside of the South itself. At the start of World War II, only 14 Southern Baptist churches had been in existence outside the South. By 1960 there were nearly 700 churches outside the South with a total membership of 175,000.[11] In proportional terms, several smaller denominations registered even higher rates of increase. For example, the Pentecostal Holiness Church grew from little more than 40,000 members to nearly 60,000 members, an increase of almost 50 percent. And the Evangelical Free Church nearly doubled its members, from 19,000 to almost 37,000. Aggressive evangelism, as well as high fertility rates and strong denominational retention rates among young people, appear to have been the principal sources of this growth.

Some of the splinter groups that split off the mainline denominations during the 1950s also contributed to the overall strength of the evangelical movement. In 1950, founders of the Baptist Missionary Association broke away from the American Baptist Association after a controversy had erupted concerning the seating of delegates to the denomination's assembly. A year later the Baptist Bible Fellowship came into existence after a dispute involving the leadership of the World Baptist Fellowship. This group, however, was eventually to contribute more to the revival of fundamentalism than it was to the broader evangelical movement. Two new denominations evolved out of the already conservative Lutheran Church-Missouri Synod. One was the Orthodox Lutheran Church, organized in 1951; the other was the Concordia Lutheran Conference, founded in 1956 by congregants in the West and Midwest who wished to place greater emphasis on biblical inerrancy. Within Presbyterianism, the Evangelical Presbyterian Church came into being in 1956. After two subsequent mergers in the 1960s and 1970s, it eventually came to form part of the largely evangelical Presbyterian Church in America. Another small Presbyterian denomination, calling itself the Upper Cumberland Presbyterian Church, split away from its parent denomination in 1955 when the larger body decided to join the National Council of Churches. During this period, several small denominations also broke away from the Congregational Christian Churches and the Methodist church in opposition to proposed mergers.

In addition to increasing memberships and organizational activity, the evangelical movement also succeeded in developing several new outlets for its ideas that were to become increasingly significant in the coming years. As television came on the national scene, evangelical preachers quickly began experimenting with the new media. Most still found radio better suited to their budgets and presentational styles. A little known faith healer in Tulsa, Oklahoma, however, found his services attracting increasing attention and by 1955 Oral Roberts's programs were being broadcast weekly on 95 television stations and the revenue taken in was sufficient to employ a staff of 180 auxiliary workers. Three years later another little known evangelist, named Rex Humbard, began broadcasting from a new facility in Akron, Ohio, called the Cathedral of Tomorrow, with seating capacity for nearly 3,000 participants. And Billy Graham's "Hour of Decision" became one of the first religious programs to break into prime-time viewing space.

Another significant vehicle for promoting evangelical ideas was the founding in 1956 of what was to become the premier periodical for conservative Protestants—*Christianity Today*. Conceived of as a deliberate alternative to liberal theology, secularism, modernism, and the corrosive decay of scientism, the magazine was also carefully differentiated from fundamentalism. Its editorial policy stressed evangelism and biblical inspiration, but avoided identification with fundamentalist organizations, literalist views of scripture, and particular versions of church government, eschatology, or the sacraments. It focused on the primacy of individual salvation in the Christian gospel, but also acknowledged the importance of infusing Christian values directly into the culture, polity, and society. Drawing its editorial staff from a wide assortment of denominations, Christian colleges, and youth ministries, it stood as a symbol of the new coalition among conservative Protestants.

By the end of the 1950s, then, the evangelical movement was well established as part of the postwar structure of American religion. Having shucked off most of the earlier trappings of fundamentalism, it commanded a relatively impressive array of nationally organized special purpose groups and represented some of the fastest growing denominations in the country. As yet, it had not become embroiled in political controversy. Nor had it gained much attention from the mass media or from the leaders of the more established denominations. It was poised to exercise greater influence in American religion in the future. But the character of that influence was to take some unexpected turns during the turbulent 1960s.

The Pull to the Left

In distinguishing itself sharply from fundamentalism, evangelicalism had been able to some extent to maintain itself as one of the centrist elements in American religion during the 1950s. It clearly spoke with a more conservative voice than did the leaders of denominations that espoused neo-orthodoxy or in some ways harked back to the "higher criticism" of the nineteenth century. Yet it could legitimately claim to be the successor of the mainstream of evangelical thought throughout much of American history. And even in the postwar period it could claim to have responded positively to the beginnings of the nation's buildup in higher education and expansion in world affairs. For all these reasons, therefore, it was not out of the question that some evangelicals should move from the center toward the left during the 1960s rather than toward the right.

The decade of the 1960s confronted evangelicals, as it did the nation at large, with a time of anguished self-examination and social redirection. On the one hand, demographic and political factors conspired to add considerably to the overall membership of the evangelical movement taken broadly. Successful recruitment, large families, and high retention rates among young people continued to create huge gains for many of the conservative denominations. Assemblies of God churches, for example, grew at a rate of 9.2 percent annually between 1958 and 1975.[12] During the same period, Nazarenes grew 3 percent annually, the Salvation Army grew 3.2 percent annually, and the Southern Baptist Convention grew 2.3 percent per year. By 1967, the Southern Baptist Convention had surpassed the Methodist church as the largest single denomination, marking nearly three decades of phenomenal growth in virtually every category. Enrollments in Southern Baptist Sunday schools stood at more than twice the rate of three decades before; total membership was two and a half times higher; and the number of children attending vacation Bible schools was six times higher. In other ways, evangelical organizations also registered marked growth during the 1960s. For example, the Wycliff Bible Translators, an evangelical organization devoted to missionary translation work, expanded its staff from approximately 700 in 1958 to more than 1,700 in 1970. As clergy activism developed in the mainline denominations, evangelicals also found their ranks swollen by conservative reactions within these denominations. Though the extent of actual defection should not be overemphasized, special purpose groups sprang up by the dozens among disaffected mainline parishioners, giving new impetus to conservative inclinations that had long failed to gain organizational expression. Conservative organizations among Presbyterians, such as Presbyterians United for Biblical Concerns and the Presbyterian Lay Committee, have been referred to earlier. Responding to the efforts underway in the denomination to reformulate the denomination's creedal statement, these organizations soon became active in opposing grants to black power groups and resolutions condemning the Vietnam War as well. The Forum for Scriptural Christianity played a similar role in the Methodist church.

The 1960s also witnessed the formation of a number of new evangelical denominations, many organized by conservative parishioners and clergy dissatisfied with the growing activism of the National Council of Churches and World Council of Churches. In 1962 the Association of Free Lutheran Congregations split away from the denominations that were uniting to form the American Lutheran Church, not only in opposition to the impending merger, but also in protest against the World Council of Churches. In 1965 the Association of Independent Methodists formed in opposition to the growing social activism of the southern Methodist church as well as its impending merger with the northern branch. A year later the Sovereign Grace Movement emerged, drawing individuals from both Baptist and Presbyterian backgrounds who were concerned about the growth of liberalism within these traditions.

Apart from the formation of actual splinter groups, there was also evidence of growing unrest on the part of individuals and local congregations who were distraught by the liberal activism in which their denominations had become engaged. In May, 1960, the First Baptist Church of Wichita, Kansas, decided to withhold funds from the American Baptist Convention in order to protest what it perceived as growing socialism within the denomination and in the National Council of Churches. Two months later, by a vote of 739 to 294, the church decided to withdraw entirely from the denomination. The following year Episcopal churches in Arizona and Texas drafted protests against their denomination's growing political involvement and role in "hastening us on our way toward the Total Welfare State." In the same year two large congregations in California called on the Presbyterian church to dissociate itself from the communistic activities of the National Council of Churches. And over the next five years, a growing number of congregations—Baptists, Presbyterians, Methodists, Lutherans, Episcopalians—passed similar resolutions expressing grievances over clergy activism, political pronouncements of the denomination, theological liberalism, and the activities of the National Council of Churches.[13] To many in the forefront of the evangelical movement, these signs of dissent merely confirmed the correctness of their own early misgivings about the National Council of Churches.

There was also, however, a tendency in the opposite direction afoot within the evangelical movement. That movement was rooted in the larger social trends to which evangelicals, like the rest of the nation, were exposed during the 1960s. Greater regional integration, residential migration, serious changes in race relations, shifting attitudes on public issues, and especially the growth of higher education were all to have a decided impact among evangelicals. Between 1960 and 1972 the proportion of members in evangelical Protestant sects who had been to college tripled. Even by the latter date, this proportion was still well below the national average—but not nearly as far below as it had been in 1960. At that date, evangelical sect members were only a third as likely as people in the nation as a whole to have attended college. By 1972, they were underrepresented among the college educated only by a margin of 0.8 to 1 in comparison with the public at large.[14] In self-perception, too, a dramatic shift also took place during this period. In 1960, only 13 percent of the members of evangelical sects thought of themselves as part of the "middle class." By 1972, 37 percent did—a figure not far short of the 45 percent who did in the general population. In short, evangelicals were participating in the broader educational upgrading that was happening in the society as a whole.

While it was still the case, as seen in the last chapter, that those with less education remained more conservative religiously and on most social opinions, the rising levels of education among evangelicals were producing a more diverse mixture of social opinions within the ranks of evangelicals themselves. Specifically, a growing minority of evangelicals were beginning to combine conservative religious orientations with relatively liberal perspectives on other issues. By 1968, for example, evangelical Protestants were almost as likely as liberal Protestants to favor desegregated housing and to say the United States had been wrong in getting into the war in Vietnam. In absolute numbers, somewhere between a third and a half of all evangelical Protestants had come to view the civil rights movement with favor, while a slight majority had come to disapprove of the Vietnam War.[15] Part of this tendency was a result of the broader mood of activism and reform in the society at large. And part of it was attributable to the growing numbers of evangelicals who were exposed to the liberalizing atmosphere of the nation's campuses. At any rate, evangelicals themselves as well as other observers of American religion became increasingly aware of this tendency by the end of the 1960s.

Among evangelical leaders a growing and vocal minority began to espouse liberal positions on issues of the day. Outspoken critics of the Vietnam War, for example, such as evangelical Senator Mark Hatfield of Oregon, began to challenge the more hawkish sentiments of an older generation of evangelical leaders. Black evangelicals brought the conservative attitudes of their white counterparts on the civil rights movement into question. New periodicals directed at liberal evangelical constituencies, such as the *Post-American* (later, *Sojourners*) and *New Freedom* (later, *The Other Side*) began to attract attention. And even among more established evangelical leaders and in established evangelical journals the call began to go out for greater attention to social issues, greater concern for the downtrodden, and greater support for social activism. For the first time in many years, the implicit bond between evangelical religion and conservative politics began to be questioned. One evangelical writer, for example, stated flatly that the yoke between evangelicalism and political conservatism had become "a disservice to Christ," a burden that prevented the Christian message from exercising its "fullest effectiveness."[16] Another evangelical, himself pastor of an inner-city church, urged fellow evangelicals to engage in more "political struggles with the establishment" in order to appeal more effectively to people in the ghetto.[17] Still another spokesman, a high official in the Billy Graham association, addressing a large gathering of evangelical clergy in 1969, argued that evangelicals must totally repudiate efforts to link the gospel with anticommunism, work devotedly for the cause of racial justice, and reappropriate the "revolutionary" characteristics of the Christian message.[18] A Catholic observer, listening to the strange new sounds emanating from evangelical throats, remarked that it was now "evident that the evangelicals had come into the secular city and acknowledged their responsibility for it."[19]

Within the ranks of evangelicals, therefore, a new split was beginning to appear that resembled the one evident within the mainstream denominations. As educational levels increased, a growing segment of the evangelical elite began to move toward the left on political and social issues, while the majority of evangelicals with lower levels of education remained solidly conservative. The "new breed" of evangelical liberals came mainly from the seminaries, from evangelical colleges, and from evangelical students in secular universities. They were by no means the dominant voice in American evangelicalism. But their voice came increasingly to be heard as part of the image which evangelical leaders presented to their own constituencies and to the larger public.

One consequence of the rising levels of education among evangelicals was a tendency for some of the new breed to abandon conservative denominations for more liberal denominations in which their social and political views gained more support. As seen in the last chapter, persons who switched out of the conservative denominations and who had college educations were more likely than average to join liberal denominations, such as the Presbyterian or Episcopal churches, or to become unaffiliated. Those data were from the 1980s. Data from the 1960s showed some tendency for conservative Protestants to move toward liberal denominations as well. For example, a national study conducted in 1966 showed that conservative Protestants in urban areas in the North were considerably more likely to switch to liberal denominations than were liberal Protestants to switch to conservative denominations. This tendency, the study also showed, was not evident in more culturally isolated areas, such as the South or rural areas.[20] For the most part, however, denominational switching was not pronounced enough to deprive evangelical denominations of their better educated, more liberal members.

A more serious consequence of the pull to the left during the late 1960s was to open up a potentially serious cultural gap between the evangelical left, on the one hand, and fundamentalists and politically conservative evangelicals on the other. During the 1950s, fundamentalists had remained on the fringes of the larger evangelical movement, often content to ride along on its coat tails. There was enough political and social conservatism within the broader movement to give them some hope of realizing their own agendas. The new liberalism being articulated by younger evangelicals in the late 1960s, however, was disquieting to fundamentalists. Repudiation of anticommunism was, to their ears, a dangerous move toward the slippery slope of creeping socialism. Editorials in liberal evangelical journals calling for fundamentalist colleges in the South to desegregate were even more threatening. Evangelicals, fundamentalists charged, were even growing soft on their views of the Bible.

These concerns began to surface in a variety of attacks on the evangelical left from the fundamentalist right. Although still relatively minor, these attacks were launched with greater vigor and on different targets than had been the case in the past. Fuller Theological Seminary, for example, became the target in 1963 of a fundamentalist attack directed at its alleged softening on the inerrancy of scripture. Fundamentalist leaders such as Bob Jones, Carl McIntire, and Billy James Hargis openly denounced Billy Graham and other moderate evangelical leaders for their views on civil rights and Vietnam. In the South, presidential contender George Wallace began picking up third-party votes from conservative Protestants who in years past had remained firmly in the Democratic stable. Splinter groups also began to appear—now representing fundamentalist discontent with evangelical denominations. The Fundamental Baptist Fellowship and the New Testament Association of Independent Baptist Churches broke away from the Conservative Baptist Association in protest against the "new evangelicalism" in the parent body. Out of the conservative Lutheran Church-Missouri Synod came the Lutheran Churches of the Reformation and the Federation for Authentic Lutheranism, both protesting the liberalism they saw creeping into their denomination. From the Southern Methodist Church, itself a conservative holdout against the broader merger within Methodism in the 1930s, came the archconservative John Wesley Fellowship and the equally conservative Francis Asbury Society of Ministers. And out of the Independent Fundamental Churches of America, a 1930 fundamentalist offshoot of the Congregational church, came the even more conservative Ohio Bible Fellowship.

It was also during these years that a new wave of fundamentalist or politically conservative evangelical special purpose groups began to appear on the social horizon. Three of these were specifically concerned with promoting creationism and the teaching of creationism in public schools—views that most of the liberal evangelical leaders had quietly set aside somewhere along the way. The Creation Research Society was founded in 1963 to support research projects and publications. The Bible Science Association emerged in 1964 to lobby for creationism to be taught in the schools. And the Institute for Creation Research came into being in 1970 to promote inclusion of creationism in textbooks. Other movements appeared to promote a combination of fundamentalist religion and archconservative political views: the American Christian Action Council, formed in 1968; and Americans for God, also formed in 1968, to cite two examples. In reaction to the more permissive views on sexuality, as well as the experimentation with communes, homosexuality, and the like that had become evident as part of the youth culture, new organizations also began to appear—quite separate from the current evangelical establishment—to promote a return to traditionalistic Christian views of home and family. These included United Parents Under God, an organization founded in 1970, and Life Action Ministries, a Michigan-based organization formed in 1971. It was also at this time that special purpose groups began to appear within conservative denominations to counter the liberalizing trends seen developing in these denominations. One that was to have increasing importance in the coming decade was the Fellowship of Conservative Southern Baptists, organized in 1971 to promote conservative views on biblical inerrancy and other issues facing Southern Baptists. As yet, most of these groups had relatively small constituencies. They were overshadowed by the more pressing issues currently facing the country, such as the black power and antiwar movements. And they were still the work of "outsiders" who had few connections with any of the established national leaders of the evangelical movement. But their appearance was symptomatic of the division that was beginning to be present between liberal evangelicals and their more conservative grass-roots counterparts. Their appearance also presaged developments that were to become increasingly important in the 1970s.

The other effect that the leftward leanings among educated evangelicals had during the late 1960s and early 1970s was to create confusion within the ranks of the more vocal leaders of American evangelicalism. Especially during the early 1970s, after events in Southeast Asia and in Washington had conspired to vindicate the criticisms of many on the left, established evangelical leaders found themselves in a position of not knowing exactly what to say. *Christianity Today* had remained a staunch supporter of government policy in Vietnam until the very end. It had also been critical of clergy activists and had championed the moderate policies of Richard Nixon. Billy Graham had been more closely identified with Richard Nixon than with any other president. Older evangelical leaders like Carl F. H. Henry and Harold Ockenga had favored a policy in Vietnam even more militant than the government had followed. Suddenly, these positions all seemed out of vogue. Clergy activism had won the support of government officials and had brought a relatively peaceful climax to the civil rights movement. The antiwar protesters succeeded in convincing the government to withdraw troops from Vietnam. And the Watergate disclosures were casting Richard Nixon and his administration into an increasingly bad light. Established evangelical voices wavered. Some fell silent. Others tried to articulate a make-do attitude toward the changes that had taken place. Still others acknowledged they had been mixing religion and politics and from their sad experience drew the lesson that evangelicals had better be more circumspect about making political statements in the future.

The Triumph of New Voices

By the early 1970s, therefore, the stage was set for a major realignment to take place within American evangelicalism. The older generation of evangelical leaders that had nurtured the movement into a national presence during the 1950s now found themselves out of step with a younger elite of liberal evangelicals, on the one hand, and an emergent ultraconservative clientele, on the other hand. Some moved in one or another of these directions; others simply lost their voice entirely. Among the better educated segment of evangelicals, a beachhead of liberal opinion had been established. Many of the rank and file, in turn, were beginning to have doubts about the direction in which evangelicalism seemed to be heading. As was the case among more liberal constituents in the larger, established denominations, the 1970s were to perpetuate and deepen some of these tendencies. Among religious conservatives, the 1970s were also to produce a new set of voices capable of mobilizing a strong reaction against religious liberals.

For the growing numbers of college trained young people who remained identified with evangelical religion, the 1970s perpetuated what many observers were to characterize as accommodation to the secular culture. Not only were evangelicals beginning to take on the educational and attitudinal characteristics of the rest of the population, but it was also becoming increasingly respectable to tag oneself as an evangelical. In 1976, for example, a Gallup survey discovered that a third of the public were willing to identify themselves as "born-again" Christians.[21] The election of Jimmy Carter to the presidency later the same year—a man who openly described himself as a born-again evangelical Christian and yet who held a degree in nuclear engineering and espoused liberal causes—seemed to confirm the fact that evangelicalism had "arrived."

Studies of evangelicals pointed up the many ways in which they were beginning to adapt to the dominant trends in American culture. For one thing, their sheer numbers seemed to attest to their increasing success. Having begun with about 1 million members in the 1940s, the NAE now boasted more than 3.5 million members. Campus Crusade for Christ had grown from a one-man operation in the 1950s to a sprawling international movement with more than 12,000 full-time staff workers. Inter-Varsity Christian Fellowship now had chapters on more than 800 campuses across the country. Navigators boasted a staff of 2,200 in the United States, with another 400 serving abroad. In the 1950s, only four of the top ten largest seminaries had been evangelical institutions (all denominationally sponsored, three by the Southern Baptist Convention); now all but two of the top ten were run by evangelicals.[22] Evangelical denominations continued to grow at a pace far above that of the more liberal denominations. For example, the Southern Baptist Convention grew by more than 2 million members between 1970 and 1985, the fastest growth both in absolute and in relative terms of any of the large denominations. Smaller evangelical denominations sometimes experienced phenomenal growth during this period: Evangelical Free churches, for example, nearly tripled in membership; and Assemblies of God churches more than tripled. Evangelical denominations also seemed to be the most effective at mobilizing resources. In 1980, for example, Pentecostal Holiness churches sported 33 clergy and 27 church buildings for every 1,000 members; Nazarenes claimed 16 clergy and 10 buildings per 1,000 members; Evangelical Free churches had 16 clergy and 9 buildings per 1,000 members; and Assemblies of God churches had 13 clergy and 6 buildings per 1,000 members. In comparison, Methodists had only 4 clergy and 4 churches for the same number of members; Presbyterians, 6 clergy and 4 churches; Episcopalians, 5 clergy and 3 churches; and Lutherans, 3 clergy and 2 churches. These differences meant that, compared to other denominations, evangelicals were being cared for by a much higher ratio of professional staff and that they were clustered in smaller congregations in which intimate fellowship was easier to achieve. Evangelicals were also much more conscientious about giving generously to their churches. Among Southern Baptists, for example, 37 percent claimed to give at least 10 percent of their incomes to the church, compared with only 15 percent among Lutherans, 12 percent among Methodists, and 8 percent among Catholics.[23] Another survey showed that 50 percent of all evangelicals gave at least a tithe to their churches, compared with only 16 percent of the public at large.[24]

Despite the fact that many evangelicals were clustered in small, intimate congregations, most of the nation's largest congregations were also to be found within evangelical ranks by the end of the 1970s. Calvary Chapel in Santa Ana, for instance, claimed more than 9,000 on its rolls by 1978 and more than 30,000 in the region named it as their primary spiritual center. In the same region, more than 8,000 belonged to the Melodyland Christian Center in Anaheim, and over 7,000 members were claimed by the First Baptist Church in Van Nuys, California.[25] These, along with churches of similar size in Dallas, Phoenix, Indianapolis, and Atlanta, gave evangelicalism an impressive presence in local communities and often gained national prominence as well.

As much as anything else, however, the growing prominence of evangelicalism in American culture during the 1970s was a product of the mass media and the polling industry. An earlier generation of evangelicals, or an even earlier generation of fundamentalists, had had to rely on denominational membership statistics or estimates of the numbers of members represented by organizations such as the NAE. With the new publicity that evangelicals began to acquire during the Carter years in the 1970s, pollsters began to create new definitions of what it meant to qualify as an evangelical. Suddenly, it could be touted that a third of the population regarded themselves as evangelicals. Or by more stringent criteria, such as holding a literal view of the Bible, proselytizing, *and* having had a born-again experience, about one person in five could be counted as an evangelical. By virtue of the capacity of opinion polling to define aspects of the culture, therefore, evangelicals came to be regarded as a force some 30 to 40 million strong.

At the same time that their numbers were growing, evangelicals were also coming to resemble the broader society in a variety of ways. By the early 1980s, approximately one in three had been to college among members of evangelical denominations. Using the definitions of evangelicalism established by pollsters, the proportion of evangelicals who had been to college increased during the last half of the 1970s alone from about one in six to one in five.[26] Whereas a small minority of clergy in the previous generation had gone to college, approximately two-thirds now had college and seminary degrees. And attitudes increasingly reflected these changes. According to a major national study of evangelicals conducted in 1978, one in three no longer thought of the devil as a personal being. An equal number said they used alcoholic beverages. One in five condoned premarital sex and homosexuality.[27] Another study, conducted a few years later among students at leading evangelical colleges, pointed toward changes of even more dramatic proportions. Only about a third of these students still believed the Bible should be taken literally. Fewer than half thought "heavy petting" was wrong (compared with four out of five in a comparable study conducted in 1961). And approximately three in ten scored as "liberals" on a range of social, economic, and political questions.[28] Yet another data source showed that among younger evangelicals in the nation at large with at least some college training better than three-quarters expressed tolerance on civil liberties questions toward groups such as atheists, Communists, and homosexuals.[29]

These tendencies all pointed toward a growing rapprochement between religious conservatives and religious liberals, rather than the emergence of a great divide between the two. The liberalization that was taking place among evangelicals, however, was not to be the major force that would shape relations between the two groups. As a relatively small, relatively educated minority of the larger evangelical population moved to the left, a new set of issues—and a new set of leaders—came increasingly on the scene.

At about the same time that the older generation of evangelical leaders was suffering from the perplexities of Watergate and the American debacle in Vietnam, a different group of leaders was beginning to capture the major means of disseminating evangelical ideas. The older generation had relied heavily on religious magazines, on a small cluster of evangelical colleges and seminaries, and only to a small extent on television. The new leaders capitalized primarily on the television networks and used these resources to build up their own empires of colleges, seminaries, publishing houses, and direct-mail operations. Rex Humbard, as previously noted, got his start in Akron, Ohio. By 1969, he was purchasing air-time on 68 television stations. By 1972, his programming was being carried on more than 300 stations.[30] Jimmy Swaggart's start came in an Assembly of God church in Baton Rouge, Louisiana. His programming would eventually be seen on more than 1,000 television stations and would bring in enough revenue to support the Jimmy Swaggart Bible College and a $30 million World Ministry Center.[31] Pat Robertson, Jim Bakker, and Jerry Falwell were other names that would become household words as a result of successful television ministries. By the early 1980s, Robertson would be able to boast ownership of the fifth largest cable television operation in the country, secular or religious, some 4,000 employees, and a house valued at close to half a million dollars. Bakker would be pulling in more than $100 million annually from his PTL (Praise the Lord) network. And Falwell, recipient of revenues of an equal size, would head up broadcasts in some 172 markets as well as pastoring a church with 21,000 members.

Along with Oral Roberts, Robert Schuller, and a few others, these "televangelists" were to become increasingly prominent among the leaders of the conservative evangelical movement. None of the newcomers was part of the old evangelical elite centered around Wheaton College, Fuller Seminary, and *Christianity Today*. With the exception of Pat Robertson, who had attended law school, none was particularly well educated. Bakker, for example, dropped out of North Central Bible College before graduating; Humbard took only a few correspondence courses in Bible beyond high school; and Falwell graduated from Baptist Bible College in Springfield, Missouri, after dropping out of Lynchburg College.[32] The ascendancy of these leaders was also symptomatic of a demographic shift within American evangelicalism that went deeper than the mere rise of religious television. With the exception of Humbard in Ohio and Schuller in California (who fell on the fringes of evangelicalism anyway), all were headquartered in the South. Bakker broadcasted from Charlotte, North Carolina; Swaggart, from Baton Rouge, Louisiana; Falwell, from Lynchburg, Virginia; Robertson, from Virginia Beach. A solid geographic constituency contributed greatly to success in carving out television market zones. In addition, these men came chiefly from the fastest growing evangelical denominations—Baptists and Pentecostals—unlike the earlier generation of evangelical leaders who had emerged mainly from the more conservative wings of the northern Baptist and Presbyterian denominations. Unlike the earlier leaders, the new generation was also much more comfortable with the label "neofundamentalist," or simply "fundamentalist." Falwell used these terms deliberately, but the other leaders tended to identify with the same tradition. They did not have direct links with the fundamentalists left over from the disputes earlier in the century. For example, they did not claim ties with Carl McIntire or Billy James Hargis. But their rhetoric was often much the same, albeit decidedly less separatist. They were more likely to preach biblical inerrancy than simply the view that God inspired the Bible. They were more outspoken on matters of dress, sexual propriety, and the use of alcohol. And they represented a much more militant group of opponents to communism and of advocates of free enterprise.

The rapid growth of religious television programming in the late 1970s has generally been attributed to changes in FCC rulings. These changes made it possible for television stations to count as a public service broadcast time sold, rather than donated, to religious broadcasters. Those who were able to pay for broadcast time soon began to replace others (mainly local churches) who had relied on free air-time. Cable hookups, aggressive fund-raising techniques, direct-mail campaigns, and other factors undoubtedly contributed to the rise of the conservative television broadcasters as well. At any rate, the audience for these programs appears to have grown considerably by the end of the 1970s. A study done in 1963 had found that only 12 percent of all Protestant churchgoers regularly watched religious television programs or listened to these programs on radio. Studies conducted in the late 1970s, in contrast, suggested that as many as a third of the public might have viewed religious television programs during the past month, while one person in two claimed to have tuned in at least once during the past year.[33] By 1984, estimates of the total number of regular viewers of religious television programs were placed conservatively at approximately 13 million.[34] That number nearly equaled the membership of the United Methodist, Presbyterian, and Episcopal churches combined.

Those who watched religious television included persons from all segments of American society. But viewing tended to be concentrated heavily among older persons, people living in the South where the programming was most readily available, and persons with lower-than-average levels of education. One national survey, which examined religious television viewing in depth, found that 48 percent of all viewers of religious programs within the past month were age 50 or over, compared with 31 percent of nonviewers; 37 percent of viewers lived in the South, compared with 27 percent of nonviewers; and 38 percent of viewers had not graduated from high school, compared with 23 percent of nonviewers.[35]

Viewers of religious television programs, according to research studies, also tended to be overwhelmingly conservative, both religiously and on social attitudes. Six viewers out of ten, for example, held the Bible to be literally true, compared to only a quarter of nonviewers. Two-thirds of all religious television viewers said they had tried to convert someone to belief in Jesus Christ, compared with only a third of nonviewers. Among viewers, more than half had had a born-again experience, compared with a quarter of nonviewers.[36] Seven out of ten regular viewers would require having prayer in public schools, about 30 percent more than among nonviewers. Four in ten identified themselves as being "far right" politically, compared with only one in four among nonviewers.[37] Not surprisingly, much the same kinds of attitudes are expressed on the religious television programs themselves. Nine programs in ten refer to the Bible, usually with references to the literal reality of the devil, Hell, the Second Coming, or some other tenet of evangelical theology; one in three makes critical references to liberal churches; one in three also discusses politics or the government; one program in four discusses the evils of sexual promiscuity; and one in five talks approvingly of school prayer.[38]

Television ministries, then, became one of the important new forces shaping American religion in the 1970s. They advanced conservative social and religious ideas, and they appealed to people with similar attitudes. Religious television also became an effective fund-raising tool. By 1979, for example, Jim Bakker was taking in $52 million annually; Pat Robertson, $46 million; Jerry Falwell, $46 million; Rex Humbard, $30 million; and Jimmy Swaggart, $20 million.[39] As many as 5 of every 7 dollars had to be plowed back into the television ministries themselves to pay for air-time and to send out additional solicitations.[40] But the money left over paid for sizable projects of other kinds as well. Jerry Falwell built a university and theology school; Pat Robertson, a graduate school of communications; and Jim Bakker, a Christian amusement park.

Also contributing to the institutional base of religious conservatism in the late 1970s were a number of new "megachurches" and hundreds of Christian schools. The basis for Falwell's television ministry was a huge church in Lynchburg, Virginia. Falwell was also linked to the Baptist Bible Fellowship, a loose coalition of some 3,500 independent congregations that included some of the largest in the country. These and others, such as Schuller's enormous Crystal Cathedral in California, Humbard's independent congregation in Akron, and James Kennedy's in Fort Lauderdale, provided a strong platform from which conservative preachers could launch a broad variety of programs. Acknowledging virtually no controls from the outside, in contrast with the situation that faced most ministerial entrepreneurs in the established denominations, these pastors were free to use their vast resources for virtually any activity the local market would bear. Within the major evangelical denominations, these kinds of churches also became increasingly important as centers of power. In contrast to an earlier generation in which denominational leadership had come mainly from theological seminaries, church politics now seemed to revolve increasingly around the leaders of large churches. As one observer noted, writing about the Southern Baptist Convention:

> Baptists . . . looked to the pastors of large churches for theological guidance. These churches usually had memberships exceeding 1,000—often several times larger. The pastors of these megachurches invariably stressed evangelism and seemed unanimously committed to a highly conservative theology. Speaking frequently at various conferences and supervising large staffs of younger ministers who later took charge of other churches, these pastors came to have a tremendous following.[41]

The author went on to note that all of the recent Southern Baptist presidents were pastors of megachurches. In addition, these and other conservative churches were increasingly becoming involved in running Christian schools and in using these schools to create employment, generate revenue, and propagate their ideas. By 1978, almost 6,000 Protestant-supported Christian schools were in existence, employing some 66,000 teachers, and counting pupils in excess of 1 million. In that year, these schools represented about one-third of all nonpublic schools and about one-fifth of all pupils enrolled in nonpublic schools. Moreover, the growth since 1971 had been phenomenal: a 47 percent increase in numbers of schools, a 113 percent increase in numbers of teachers, and a 95 percent increase in enrollments.[42]

The growing influence of a more conservative element within American evangelicalism, however, was as much a function of trends in the culture at large as it was of institution building by evangelical entrepreneurs. Prior to the mid-1970s the majority of religious conservatives, as already mentioned, had decried political activism among clergy and had stayed somewhat aloof from political activities themselves. Study after study conducted during the 1960s and early 1970s documented this fact: the more conservative one was religiously, the less likely it was that one would be involved in political activities.

One survey of the literature in 1973 concluded that "active involvement in political issues appears so alien to the laity they may well regard those who engage in it as not of their own church, that is, as deviant from their conceptions of proper religious behavior."[43] Another study asked a panel of 25 leading social scientists, historians, and theologians to rank religious groups, first in terms of theological conservatism, and then in terms of concern about social and political issues. Those at the top of the first list were almost always placed at the bottom of the second.[44] Studies based on attitude surveys also demonstrated that parishioners and clergy alike who held evangelical or fundamentalist views were less likely to join political groups, less likely to write to political officials, less likely to vote, and less likely to favor church groups that spoke out on political issues.[45]

By the late 1970s, these patterns were beginning to change. A national study done in 1976, for example, showed that born-again churchgoers were just as likely as other churchgoers to be registered to vote and to say they planned to vote. Two years later, another national survey found that evangelicals were indeed considerably more likely than nonevangelicals to say religious organizations should be making public statements on political and economic issues. Other studies, conducted during the 1980 presidential election, suggested that evangelicals had begun to vote in higher proportions than other segments of the population—a finding that surprised pollsters not only because of evangelicals' history of nonparticipation but also because their characteristics such as rural residence and lower levels of education generally militated against voting. Studies of clergy during this period also suggested that evangelical and fundamentalist pastors were beginning to mobilize politically. A study conducted among North Carolina clergy in 1978, for example, found that theologically conservative clergy were actively preaching against the equal rights amendment, against abortion, in favor of school prayer, and in support of the views of particular political candidates in much higher numbers than were clergy with more liberal theological inclinations.[46]

Several factors seemed to be contributing to this new-found political interest among religious conservatives. One was that evangelicals, as already mentioned, were becoming better educated and more mainstream in ways that might make them more likely to participate in politics like other members of the broad middle class. Another change was linked directly to the presidential candidacy of Jimmy Carter. The presence of a born-again Christian on the ballot, as well as the widespread publicity that his candidacy gave to the evangelical sector, provided evangelicals with a sense of political entitlement that they had not felt for a number of years. Suddenly it was respectable to be a born-again Christian. Suddenly the media wanted to know what born-again Christians thought on political issues. Suddenly it was part of one's Christian duty to exercise the responsibilities of citizenship. Magazines like *Christianity Today* recovered from their earlier confusion and began running editorials encouraging their readers to become involved in political issues. The NAE basked in the sensation of having its "proverbial lights . . . exposed from underneath their bushels." Billy Graham began cautioning fellow evangelicals that they must exercise their new prominence wisely. And other writers began urging readers to take seriously the new opportunities they had to influence the political sphere.[47]

More than their changing social status (which still affected a minority of evangelicals) or even their newly gained sense of political entitlement, however, the political rebirth that religious conservatives experienced in the late 1970s was a result of a change in the issues on the political scene. Questions about public morality, abortion, and the relations between church and state all began to reappear as matters of political debate. The new voices that were being heard on religious television and from conservative special interest groups played an important role in adding these questions to the national agenda. But other conditions in the culture also played their part.

The Watergate episode did much to revitalize public discussion about morality. Coming at a time when the nation was still reeling from the Vietnam experience and was wallowing in a severe economic recession as well, Watergate served as a kind of public ritual in which broader issues of values and conscience could be discussed.[48] Among the many messages that Watergate communicated, one of the most powerful was the folly of trying to separate morality from public life. The political health of not only an incumbent president but of the entire nation came to be seen more clearly as a product of decency and honesty. In turning Richard Nixon out of office, the public in effect called for a cleansing of the national moral order. And in electing Jimmy Carter, the candidate of decency and high moral virtue, it in a sense restored the feeling that the nation would be great as long as it was also good. The "campaign of good intentions," as Carter's victory was called, not only succeeded in bringing unity back to a divided nation but also effected a sense of national atonement and redemption.

Greater clarity about the relation between morality and public life also resulted from the Supreme Court's 1973 decision on abortion. While some saw it as a matter strictly of civil liberties, many (especially in the evangelical community) recognized it as a statement by the Court that questions of morality could not be divorced from the agencies of government. Even though the Court, like most other public institutions at the time, championed a private conception of morality that respected the right of each individual to make moral choices, the very act of deciding on such issues gave a different message. It communicated that morality really was too important to be decided by individuals alone. The state would, therefore, intercede whenever it felt the need.

From these and other sources, the wall that had been built up between private morality and public institutions began to break down. Law schools began offering courses in ethics to guide barristers in thinking about difficult moral issues. Business schools and medical societies also instituted courses on ethics. Professional associations began passing resolutions stating ethical guidelines for their members. The government itself became increasingly active as well. Between 1974 and 1978 more than 20 congressmen were investigated for unethical or immoral conduct. In 1977 both the House and Senate adopted codes of ethics and created select committees on ethics. In the same year President Carter proposed a comprehensive Ethics in Government Act. During this period the Justice

Department also took an increasingly active role in investigating the conduct of public officials allegedly engaged in unethical or illegal behavior. While only 63 officials had been indicted by federal grand juries in 1970, this number rose to 255 by 1975 and increased further to 337 in 1976. And in the national media, articles and editorials dealing with morality and ethics registered more than a 50 percent increase and began to address an increasingly wide range of institutional sectors.[49] The media also began to feature much more prominently articles about sexual morality and abortion. By one estimate, the number of articles on abortion in the late 1970s was about four times as high as in the early 1960s, while the number of articles on "sexual ethics" was more than five times as high.[50]

By the end of the 1970s, what had once been a rather sharp symbolic boundary between private morality and collective life had become so ambiguous that writers and public figures began openly challenging the earlier privatistic notions. In an editorial in the *Washington Post* just prior to the 1980 election, for example, Meg Greenfield wrote: "We have refused to view practically any indecency, outrage or pathological assault on our sense of rightness in any way except as a civil-liberties problem—protecting the abstract right of the sickos to come to dinner."[51] In the same vein, the *Wall Street Journal* charged that the earlier separation of morality from public life had "come to stand for the proposition that it makes no difference to the well-being of the polity whether, for example, the populace is heterosexual or homosexual, the traditional family is preserved or not, some 'lifestyles' are considered exemplary or not."[52]

To most evangelicals, statements such as these were scarcely new. Evangelicals had always seen a close connection between private morality and the collective good. One had only to read the stories of God's judgment on the children of Israel to know that personal acts of immorality could become the basis for horrible acts of divine judgment. God would, by the same token, not permit American society to go unscathed if people persisted in ignoring what was abhorrent to the laws of God. In a much quoted passage, in fact, the Book of Proverbs made this abundantly clear: "Righteousness exalteth a nation; but sin is a reproach to any people."[53] Morality had never been a strictly individual matter for evangelicals. And now they found the same sentiments being expressed in high places, from the nation's capitol to the *Wall Street Journal.*

Morality was also an issue around which evangelicals could mobilize. If they had become divided over Vietnam, or if they disagreed about race relations, national defense, social welfare, and a host of other issues, they nevertheless exhibited virtual consensus on questions of morality. Fewer than one in ten was willing to condone abortion; all but a handful were deeply opposed to homosexuality and pornography. Extramarital sex was unthinkable and premarital sex was bad enough. And the more strongly one felt about evangelical beliefs, the more likely one was to feel strongly about these issues as well.

"Faith and morals," were in fact, as one conservative evangelical put it, "two sides of the same coin."[54] Believing as they did that the Bible was the inerrant word of God and to be taken literally, word for word, evangelicals saw in the Bible a clear set of moral guidelines that they should try to follow. Being assured of salvation did not itself depend on following these guidelines to the letter—salvation was simply an act of faith in which one accepted Christ and became born again. But a saved Christian could scarcely expect to reap the benefits of a Christian life if he or she did not try to please God by following the injunctions laid out so clearly in scripture. To fail was to admit that one had not fully yielded to the claims of Jesus. Consequently, moral disobedience was a sure way to make oneself feel guilty and separated from God. As data from one national study showed, 85 percent of all evangelicals felt they would feel "very bad" about themselves if they were "tempted into doing something immoral"; only 1 percent said they would feel no worse about themselves.[55]

Now that morality and politics were being discussed in the same breath, evangelicals found it only natural to condone political activities that appeared to uphold standards of morality. The two were so closely linked, in fact, that many evangelicals probably failed to see that for the first time in many years they were becoming politically involved. Rather, they considered they were merely taking a public stand on matters they knew to be morally mandated as part of scripture. In any case, evangelicals' convictions about morality motivated them more clearly than anything else to take a more active role in politics. A survey conducted in 1980 by the Opinion Research Corporation, for example, found that 72 percent of those who thought morals had been deteriorating felt religious groups should be having more political influence. In contrast, only 13 percent of those who thought morals had not deteriorated felt religious groups should have greater influence.[56] This study did not examine the opinions of evangelicals separately, but other data did. In a 1978 Gallup study, 68 percent of the evangelicals who thought abortion (taken as an indicator of conservative moral views) was never acceptable felt the churches should try to influence legislation, compared with only 50 percent of those who thought abortion was acceptable. In other words, the more strongly one was opposed to abortion, the more likely that person was to favor political action on the part of religious organizations. Among liberal Protestants, however, just the opposite pattern was evident. Only 33 percent of those who felt abortion was never acceptable thought the churches should try to influence legislation, compared to 46 percent of those who felt abortion was always acceptable. Pretty clearly, morally conservative evangelicals wanted their churches to speak out because they figured what was said would support their own views. In contrast, morally conservative members of liberal churches did not want their churches to speak out because they figured the positions taken would not support their views.

If moral politics was the issue around which religious conservatives could be mobilized, the new leaders associated with religious television and large independent fundamentalist churches were quick to recognize this potential. The more centrist evangelical leaders of the 1950s and 1960s had generally taken a quiet stance toward moral issues. They had certainly favored strict moral rules according to biblical guidelines, but had often downplayed these rules in order to give a more central place to the gospel message itself. Theirs was, they hoped, an upbeat message about God's love and forgiveness. Too often in the past this message had been obscured by long lists of rules. The more important issue was to bring people into the Christian fold. After that, moral lessons could be learned in quiet ways such as Bible study, personal devotions, and Sunday school classes. The new leadership that emerged in the late 1970s took a much more militant view. Harking back to a greater extent to Old Testament lessons about God's dealings with entire nations, they argued that moral standards needed to be upheld not only in the closets of private devotion but in the cloisters of public legislation. "Our nation has begun to reject God's absolute laws and we have proudly insisted on a life of independence from Him," Jerry Falwell intoned. "We must humble ourselves, pray, seek His face, and turn from our wicked ways. We must repent that we have not fulfilled our function as the 'salt of the earth.' We must repent for neglecting to speak out for God in our land. And we must repent for our personal sin in our own homes and lives. Only then will our nation experience the forgiveness and healing of God."[57] For leaders like Falwell, morality was a major public issue. And it was broadly defined, not just as a set of rules forbidding fornication and alcohol, but as a matter of godly thinking on a whole range of political, economic, and social questions. In a radio broadcast on homosexuality, for example, Falwell asked rhetorically: "Is it any wonder that we are the laughing stock of the world? Is it any wonder that nations and terrorists thumb their noses at this once proud land?" To others, declining moral standards were responsible for social ills, ranging from crime to declining SAT scores.

If public morality was indeed the mainstay of national strength, evangelicals could hardly stand by, knowing that God had given them both the answers and the opportunity to voice their answers, while the social fabric decayed. In the biblical prophets evangelicals found dramatic examples of persons who had been called to speak out against moral decay, and the new group of conservative spokesmen who rose to national prominence during this period consciously adopted these models. In prophetic tones Texas evangelist James Robison explained, for example: "God has given me the role of pulling down and destroying anything that is raised above God or in place of God or that limits God's work in the nation, the church, or the world. That means the idolatry of excessive government or the idolatry of appetites and entertainment and pleasure, or anything else that gets between an individual and God."[58]

As the embodiment of morality in public life, Jimmy Carter became a frequent target for these invectives. Through Carter the link between evangelicalism and politics, and between politics and morality, had been dramatized. He was one of their own, and evangelicals felt a kind of obligation on his part to uphold their points of view. When he did not, they felt a deep sense of betrayal. In his book *The New Right: We're Ready to Lead*, fund-raiser Richard A. Viguerie lamented: "Not only has the Carter administration ignored the born-again Christians, it has actively and aggressively sought to hurt the Christian movement in America."[59] In response, Viguerie argued, evangelicals should become involved with more conservative political groups.

While the secular right, like Viguerie, railed at Carter for having left them out of the political spoils, the growing cadre of religious conservatives drew on other imagery. (Both were offended by Carter's apparent lack of nerve in failing to oppose abortion and promote Christian schools and prayer in public schools, and in allowing feminists and gays to be represented at his White House Conference on Families.) But the religious conservatives drew their language from deep within the Protestant tradition. They harked back to Reformation doctrines describing two kingdoms, one spiritual, one political. They would grant the political kingdom authority over all aspects of the temporal world, even to the point of arguing that Christians must be law-abiding, responsible citizens. But they would work against the political kingdom if the holders of temporal power chose to violate divinely instituted moral principles. Hence, Jerry Falwell could admonish his viewers to "be subject to the higher powers" in all walks of life, from paying taxes to obeying the speed limits, and yet reserve the right actively to challenge any act of these powers deemed to be in violation of biblical morality. "Jimmy Carter," he remarked in 1976, "is now my President and he will have my respect and support. I will pray for him daily." But, Falwell went on to warn, "I will oppose him when he violates moral codes which in my opinion are in . . . Scripture."[60]

The story of how Falwell and others mobilized an increasingly vocal set of political action movements in the late 1970s has been told often enough that only the bare essentials need to be repeated here. In 1976 Falwell began testing the potential for a national movement by organizing

"I Love America" rallies on the steps of state capitols around the country. Students from Falwell's Liberty Baptist College in Lynchburg were sent to speak and sing, while a network of pastors from the Bible Baptist Fellowship did most of the local advance work. By 1978 Falwell's rallies were having considerable success, as were fund-raisers at Liberty Baptist College and special appeals on his syndicated religious television broadcasts. About the same time, other religiously conservative activists were beginning to play an increasing role in local political skirmishes. As far away as Florida, California, and Washington state, local clergy were joining battle over Christian schools, homosexuality, and pornography, while closer to Washington, D.C., mailing lists were quietly being amassed and computerized. The organization known until 1985 as Moral Majority (then renamed "Liberty Federation") came into being in 1979, with Falwell at the head and an advisory board comprised of leaders from both the religious right and the political right. Moral Majority was closely linked (through interlocking directorates) with two other prominent organizations that also came into existence in 1979: Christian Voice and Religious Roundtable. Together, these organizations and several others that had also been formed in the late 1970s—Prayers for Life, Intercessors for America, Concerned Women of America, the National Christian Action Coalition, and Family America—constituted the nucleus of what was to become known as the New Christian Right.

From the beginning, these organizations courted support from evangelicals through direct-mail campaigns, telephone hot lines, mass rallies, and especially religious television broadcasts. For a time, Falwell employed a Madison Avenue advertising agency to coordinate direct-mail blitzes with his television broadcasts, consciously experimenting with different appeals by rotating on a week-to-week basis from straight evangelical religion to missionary appeals to moral issues to political themes. The moral and political issues on which the various New Christian Right organizations came to focus most heavily included opposition to the equal rights amendment, opposition to pornography, opposition to homosexuality, opposition to abortion, and support for prayer in public schools.

In relation to the 30 or 40 million people in the United States who might have considered themselves evangelicals at the time, Moral Majority—which became the most visible nationally of any of the New Christian Right organizations—experienced relatively little success. According to a national poll conducted in 1982, 51 percent of all evangelicals had heard of Moral Majority, but positive sentiments toward it were outnumbered by negative feelings or indifference by a margin of 3 to 2. And only 1 evangelical in 7 had ever contemplated joining the organization.[61]

Evangelicals did, however, give wide support to the platform of issues that the New Christian Right organizations sought to advance. Viewers of programs by Falwell and other television preachers, for example, registered dissatisfaction with the current trends in moral standards by a margin of better than 5 to 1. They also listed "high moral standards" as one of the top goals the churches should be pressing for, placing it ahead even of goals such as evangelism, fellowship, and worship.[62] On more specific attitudes and orientations, heavy viewers of religious television programs described themselves as political conservatives rather than political liberals by a ratio of 4 to 1. By a similar margin, frequent viewers said they favored tougher laws against pornography. An even larger proportion thought homosexuality was always wrong.[63] Among evangelicals more generally, as already seen, opposition to sexual experimentation was nearly universal, as was support for strict moral standards. One study of these attitudes also discovered very high rates of consistency, such that support for one kind of moral issue could generally be counted on as evidence of support for others as well.[64]

Whether or not the New Christian Right actually succeeded in drawing the opinion of evangelicals farther to the right, it clearly succeeded in placing these issues at the forefront of their attention. This feat was accomplished partly because the New Christian Right leadership had access to a much wider and more effective range of communications media than did the leadership that had been associated with the centrist or left-oriented evangelicals. It was also facilitated by the fact that an increasing segment of the evangelical leadership more generally were drawn into the New Christian Right's coalition, if not as supporters of specific groups, then at least as supporters of the same kinds of political moral issues. By the early 1980s, for example, the NAE's Washington office had come out so strongly in favor of conservative moral issues, conservative political candidates, and conservative political issues ranging from national defense to tax laws that some liberal members in evangelical churches were beginning to question whether they should continue to support the organization. A host of prominent evangelical writers and speakers had also fallen into step with the New Christian Right. For example, Francis H. Schaeffer, a popular evangelical philosopher, had turned increasingly from intellectual analyses of worldviews toward making pointed statements about abortion and advocating that evangelicals consider using civil disobedience to get their way. Shaeffer's son was even more militant, becoming a frequent participant in anti-abortion marches and publishing vitriolic newsletters denouncing moderate evangelicals for not joining his cause. Tim LaHaye, then a pastor in California, left off writing about Christian personality types in order to become active, first as board member of Moral Majority, and later as national president of the American Coalition for Traditional Values. Other converts to the new conservative activism included the evangelical child psychologist James Dobson and Bill Gothard, a specialist in the problems of teenagers.

The New Christian Right also set in motion a series of public controversies in which evangelicals increasingly became pitted against religious liberals concerning the proper relations between church and state. These consisted less of purely technical questions about the constitutionality of particular positions than they did of symbolic struggles concerning the definition of basic concepts. In the process, the very meaning of terms such as "religion," "morality," and "politics" came to be contested, as did the content of these conceptual categories and the proper connections among them.

Waging Symbolic Warfare

The war in which New Christian Right leaders engaged in the late 1970s and early 1980s was not symbolic—at least to them—in the sense that it had no real importance, but because it was a struggle to define cultural categories. It was about symbols and it was waged with symbols. Since the early 1970s, old boundaries that had separated religion, morality, and politics, or at least told how they were to be related, had become ambiguous. Conservative evangelical leaders had become captains of an impressive religious army by articulating the relations among these words in ways that made sense, both to their constituencies and to many in the society at large. But the very ambiguity in these words made it possible for critics to propose their own definitions and to attempt cultural reconstructions favorable to other points of view. Most hotly contested were the relations between morality and politics, on the one hand, and religion and morality, on the other. Morality became a kind of no man's land into which both sides launched forays. In the process, its meaning also was very much open to question.

Conservative evangelical leaders had been well served by the blending together of morality and politics earlier in the decade. They now found it in their interest to define morality as broadly as possible. For if it was not quite acceptable for clergy to engage in the dirty business of politics, it was entirely proper to speak on issues of morality. Within their own narrow constituencies, they could generally rely on biblical teachings or on claims of divine revelation to create this connection between morality and a broad range of public issues. In order to enlist a larger following and to legitimate their claims in the broader public arena, however, they found it necessary to play more by political rules than by religious rules. Two approaches, both part of the ways in which claims are legitimated more generally in modern democratic systems, proved to be the strategies of choice. One involved following norms of procedural rationality in linking their own moral views to the political realm; the other involved drawing connections between these views and notions of the public interest.

The connection between morality and procedural rationality, in a general way, had already been established by the various Supreme Court decisions and congressional committees that had begun to deal with questions of ethics and morality. By adhering to proper judicial and legislative procedure, these activities demonstrated that moral questions affecting the entire society could legitimately be decided by the organs of state. Perhaps it was not possible to "legislate morality," as the popular phrase had it, but it was possible to render authoritative decisions even on such controversial, and seemingly private, questions as abortion and public prayer. Without much of a trick of imagination, these decisions gave precedent for assuming that moral positions could be legitimated by going through the proper motions of making judicial or legislative decisions. In other words, evangelical leaders scarcely saw it as a breach of religion's separation from the state to make appeals to the state over questions of morality. Nor did they see it as an enhancement of the state's powers. They were merely doing what the courts and legislatures had already been doing. In addition, conservative leaders also began to dramatize their own adherence to the norms of procedural rationality. They staged events that showed they "knew the ropes" and could be counted on to play by the rules. Activities such as the Washington for Jesus rally, the formation of lobbying groups, endorsement of bills such as the family protection act, and public appearances with political candidates and officials all served this purpose. Whether any of these activities had a chance of succeeding was not the issue. Their value was symbolic. They showed evangelicals that their leaders knew what to do—that their own moral visions had just as much right to be placed on the national agenda as anyone else's. As Jerry Falwell put it: "Someone often asks - can morality be legislated? The answer is yes. All civilized societies are governed by the legislation of morality—based upon a code of ethics agreed upon by consensus."[65]

The other standard way in which moral issues could be legitimated was by linking them with some notion of the public interest. In the 1960s, liberal activists had done this by claiming to speak on behalf of the poor and by arguing that social welfare programs would contribute toward making the whole nation a "Great Society." Now it was the conservatives' turn to make similar claims. Again, evangelicals had within their own biblical tradition ample reason to believe that godly morality would make for divine blessings on the nation as a whole. But other language was needed to legitimate these claims in the political arena. The name "Moral Majority" was, of course, an attempt to speak for the society at large. And New Christian Right publications frequently referred to public opinion polls to argue that a majority of the American public did, in fact, favor curbs on abortion, pornography, and so on, and that most Americans abided by the traditional family values that the movement championed. To claim favor with the majority, as time would prove, was not the most effective strategy, however. After nearly two decades in which the rights of various minority groups had been won at a costly price, it was comforting to many constituents to think that they now had a movement advocating the interests of the great "silent majority." But this language also struck a note of heavy-handedness, even totalitarianism. It seemed to say that the civil liberties of minorities need not be respected as long as the majority made up its mind. More effective were patriotic and nationalistic images. For a long time, broadcasts of Jerry Falwell's "Old Time Gospel Hour" began with the American flag and closed with pictures of the Liberty Bell. Advertisements for Moral Majority announced: "We care for America and for Americans." *Moral Majority Report* carried pictures of the Capitol and, once budgets increased sufficiently, began to appear with front material in red, white, and blue. Later, when the Liberty Federation came into being, the timing coincided nicely with restoration work on the Statue of Liberty. Other New Christian Right organizations, like religious special purpose groups more generally, declared their value to the nation at large by using "America" and "national" in their titles and by incorporating words connoting broad core values into their slogans, such as "freedom," "life," and "family."

In addition to these symbolic strategies, conservative leaders also sought to legitimate their vision of morality as part of the broader political arena by appealing to the values of reason, logic, evidence, and knowledge that went along with the more general prominence of higher education in American society. Falwell was typically introduced as "Dr. Jerry Falwell" and according to sources close to his organization took great pride in being the founder and chancellor of a growing university. Pat Robertson repeatedly made known to the media that he was a graduate of Yale Law School (but generally did not disclose his failure to pass the New York State bar exam). Both leaders spoke widely on the nation's campuses and reported to readers of their material how much they had been abused and yet how well they had managed to score in debates with secular intellectuals. Opinion polls, both based on random samples and contrived as petition campaigns among loyal followers, also provided proof for the correctness of many of the movement's assertions. Even in publications criticizing secular knowledge, such as Tim LaHaye's widely distributed *Battle for the Mind*, constant references were made to polls, research studies, scientific publications, and the like. Leaders were generally careful in the use of these kinds of legitimation not to push them to the point of alienating their relatively less educated constituencies. Indeed, much poking of fun at the pretensions of secular academics also tended to be mixed in. But the symbols of secular knowledge could scarcely be ignored as a means of legitimating moral claims.

In all of this, the religious right consistently used the language of morality to present its claims, arguing that morality was a very large domain and that liberals were simply amoral or immoral rather than merely holding different political views. Some issues were, in fact, matters that evangelicals had long held to be violations of biblical moral standards. Through the workings of the American political system, they had become politicized. But they remained no less subject to divine law. Jerry Falwell remarked, for example, that homosexuality "was a moral issue long before it became political." Abortion, he argued, had traveled the same road: "Today, it is political, but it was a moral issue."[66] On other issues, New Right leaders seemed willing to stretch biblical conceptions of morality to fit their purposes. Richard Zone, a leader of Christian Voice, wrote in a direct-mail solicitation: "We can talk about a balanced budget as a moral issue because the Bible says 'you should not live in debt.' " Ed McAteer of Religious Roundtable denied that his organization expressed partisan views at all, claiming instead that it was "a coalition of concerned national leaders who have one concern—the moral rebirth of America."[67] On the other hand, the question of whether something was political or moral could be sufficiently ambiguous to serve other purposes. After the government had decided, against the opposition of some conservative evangelical leaders, to set in motion a process that would turn the Panama Canal back to Panama, for example, Jerry Falwell confessed: "I was against the giving up of the Panama Canal, but I didn't get involved because that was solely a *political* issue."[68] Still, the domain of morality was one that the religious right sought to claim for itself, arguing that liberals simply were not concerned about morality. As Jerry Falwell remarked in a Moral Majority letter: "I believe that the overwhelming majority of Americans are sick and tired of the way the *amoral liberals* are trying to corrupt our nation from its commitment to freedom, democracy, traditional morality, and the free enterprise system."[69]

Critics of the New Christian Right, for their part, sought to disconnect as far as possible the notion of morality from politics. They argued that morality, after all, was private and that what the conservative leaders were doing was really pushing political interests. Mark Hatfield remarked: "What I react against is the equating of a political issue with one's morality or one's ethics or one's relationship to God."[70] Others were more extreme in their criticisms, raising the spectacle of right-wing preachers exploiting political force. "Their agenda," proclaimed an American Civil Liberties Union solicitation, "is clear and frightening: they mean to capture the power of government and use it to establish a nightmare of religious and political orthodoxy."

What both sides recognized, of course, was that the symbolic boundary between morality and politics was crucial. If the boundary was blurred, and if the category of morality was allowed to spill over into the public domain, then evangelicals had a right to take action and to do so with moral conviction. If the boundary was clear and impermeable, keeping morality in the private domain, then evangelicals were merely meddling in matters that had better be left to those who knew more about politics.

The boundary between religion and morality took on similar ideological importance. As far as evangelicals were concerned, it was useful to draw a close connection between religion and morality, especially by citing biblical injunctions in support of moral claims. Once the New Christian Right began to mobilize broader interests, however, evangelicals discovered that it was not always the best strategy to validate moral claims with religious arguments. After all, critics could argue that religion was supposed to keep separate from the state. Nasty investigations by the Internal Revenue Service could be initiated if religious organizations claiming tax-exempt status became directly involved in political issues. Even among evangelicals there were lingering doubts about the propriety of mixing religion and politics. The problem was sufficiently troublesome, despite leaders' claims that their focus was really on morality rather than on politics anyway, that some effort had to be made to differentiate religion from morality. In discourse intended to be heard outside their own circles, New Right leaders increasingly drew a distinction between two aspects of their religious faith: morality, on which there was apparently broad agreement among various conservative religious groups, thereby mitigating the accusation that sectarian religion was involved in politics; and theology, which admittedly was subject to different interpretations and therefore should be kept out of politics. This distinction gave New Right leaders the ammunition they needed to fend off accusations that they were really out to impose their own peculiar religious views on the nation. As Jerry Falwell explained to an interviewer in 1981: "Our task is not to Christianize America, it's to bring about a moral and conservative revolution."[71] It was also a useful ploy for forging a coalition among pastors and laity from many different denominations. Describing efforts to mobilize clergy against homosexuals in California, Tim LaHaye provided a candid illustration of the distinction's usefulness when he wrote: "Knowing pastors as we did, we all recognized that the only way to organize them was to make it clear that our basis of cooperation was moral, not theological."[72] The same distinction proved useful in dealing with the press, as Moral Majority discovered in repeated efforts to deny that it was a religious organization. For instance, full-page advertisements carried in the *Washington Post*, the *Wall Street Journal*, and the *New York Times* in 1981 declared that "Moral Majority, Inc. is not a religious organization attempting to control the government." Instead, the advertisement declared, the organization represents "millions of Americans who share the same moral values."[73]

On the other side, opposition tactics from the left involved efforts to push the notion of morality as far into the religious corner as possible, thereby demonstrating that religion was being illegitimately dragged into politics. People for the American Way, for example, ran broadcasts that concluded "There's got to be something wrong when anyone, even if it's a preacher, tells you that you're a good Christian or a bad Christian depending on your political point of view." The same broadcast linked religion and morality with privacy and individual diversity. Other critics relied on the symbolism of religious absolutism—Ayatollah Khomeini and the mullahs of Iran, Christian soldiers, holy wars, fundamentalist dictatorships—to suggest that any consensus about morality in politics was inconceivable except in the form of religious totalitarianism.

In the course of these symbolic struggles, the nature of morality itself was particularly subject to redefinition and counterdefinition. One subject around which much debate surfaced was the question of whether morality should be regarded as essentially private or as public. That is, should it be considered primarily a matter of individual choice, or should it be thought of as a function of collective values and linked to the health of the society as a whole? The abortion issue provided an especially heated controversy around which this broader debate could focus. New Right leaders saw abortion as a moral evil bringing danger to the well-being of the entire society. Jerry Falwell wrote: "For six long years Americans have been forced to stand by helplessly while 3 to 6 million babies were legally murdered through abortion on demand . . . when a country becomes sick morally, it becomes sick in every other way."[74] In contrast, opponents of Falwell's position saw the matter as a moral decision that must be left up to the individual (indeed, the label "pro-choice" characterized this view). An article published in *Playboy* in 1981, for example, took the New Right to task, arguing: "That minority of the populace that opposed abortion was free to have all the babies it wanted."[75]

On this and other issues, liberals and conservatives defined morality in dramatically different ways, often by framing their discussions in different symbolic contexts. Those who regarded morality as a matter of private choice generally spoke about individual cases, for example, citing women whose health was endangered by not having access to a legal abortion. They emphasized the right of individuals to make their own choices, making frequent references to the First Amendment, and arguing that individuals were capable of exercising reasonable discretion over their own lives. They also painted graphic images of the invasion of people's privacy, with pictures of government agents headed by Bible-brandishing preachers invading the sanctuary of a couple's bedroom. Conservatives, on the other hand, framed morality as much as possible in public contexts. Demonstrators posed for pictures in front of the nation's capitol carrying infant dolls crucified on huge wooden crosses. Leaflets spoke of abortion as a "national sin." Other moral issues were described as matters of such grave importance that the nation stood at a crossroads—a "point where moral Americans who still believe in decency, the home, the family, Bible morality, the free enterprise system, and all the great ideals that are the cornerstone of this great nation must rally together and make their voice heard across this land and in the halls of Congress and the White House."[76] Or, as a solicitation from Anita Bryant Ministries opposing homosexuality illustrated, moral deviance was not simply a matter of private choice but was creeping into all the society's major institutions: schools ("they want to recruit our school children"), churches ("ordaining homosexual preachers"), television, and law.

The two sides also differed fundamentally over the question of whether morality should be thought of in a priori terms—as an absolute—or whether moral views were socially derived. This division was crucial, for it determined whether or not moral claims should even be subject to discussion and negotiation. And it was especially crucial in dividing religious liberals, who often shared some of the same moral viewpoints with the New Right, from religious conservatives. While there were substantive disagreements as well, liberals often railed at the tactics used by Moral Majority and other organizations. What they objected to most strongly was the unwillingness of conservatives to make moral issues a matter of reasoned discussion. Conservatives wanted to clean up problems that were all too apparently evil in the sight of God. Liberals preferred the forum of open discussion, rather than claims of divine revelation. As one group of liberal church leaders wrote: "The churches have consistently expressed their belief that our corporate health depends on hearing the call to love God and neighbor. . . . But . . . these truths must and can win their way in the open forum of ideas. They are not to be imposed from above."[77]

By the early 1980s, then, the lines separating religious conservatives from religious liberals had come to be drawn with a wide brush. Evangelicals were still distinguished from religious liberals, in statistical averages, on characteristics such as education, age, and region of residence. Their numbers had grown considerably, both in real terms and through the magic of public opinion polls, so that they now constituted a much more visible alternative to liberal religion than they had in the 1950s or 1960s. After being pulled temporarily to the left in the late 1960s, a new leadership group had arisen that was much more conservative, and closer to the earlier fundamentalist movement, than the evangelical leaders of previous decades had been. These new leaders in effect succeeded in becoming the national voice for religious conservatism. Even those within evangelical ranks who disagreed with their tactics agreed with many of their views on moral issues. And those who disagreed commanded relatively few of the resources and media channels that were needed to make themselves heard. In this sense, the New Christian Right increasingly came to define the larger public image of American evangelicals. As the media saw it, what New Right leaders said must be the conviction of millions of evangelicals at the grass roots. The struggle to forge a national political movement, to win political battles, and to define the very terms on which these battles were fought, moreover, created an increasingly bitter rivalry between religious conservatives and religious liberals.

CHAPTER 9

Fueling the Tensions

CLOSER CONSIDERATION of the perceptions and controversies that animate liberals and conservatives reveals the depth of the chasm that has appeared between the two. As noted already, liberals look across the theological fence at their conservative cousins and see rigid, narrow-minded, moralistic fanatics; conservatives holler back with taunts that liberals are immoral, loose, biblically illiterate, and unsaved. But how seriously should these rivalries be taken? Do tensions between religious liberals and conservatives actually run deep? Or are they merely the work of a few highly articulate pressure groups such as Moral Majority and People for the American Way? What are the broader social and political controversies that have contributed to these tensions?

ACROSS THE DIVIDE

According to national data collected in 1984, religious conservatives and religious liberals view one another with a distinctly skeptical attitude. To be exact, 64 percent of those in the study who identified themselves as religious liberals said there was either a "fair amount" or "great deal" of tension between religious liberals and religious conservatives; among conservatives, the figure was 68 percent.[1] When asked, without any prompting, to describe members of each group, both sides thought of some favorable things to say: for example, liberals said conservatives were dedicated to their churches and tried to live by the Bible; conservatives said liberals were open-minded and tried to help people. But more negative images also came pouring out: conservatives thought liberals were not very religious or dedicated to the Christian faith, took an "anything goes" attitude toward religious and moral issues, tended to be too outspoken, and yet accepted uncritically everything their denominations told them; liberals, in turn, described conservatives as closed-minded, inflexible, intolerant, and egoistical.

The study probed more deeply into the perceptions of religious liberals and conservatives toward one another by presenting the persons interviewed with lists of phrases, asking them to say which phrases applied to people with conservative religious views and which ones applied to people with liberal religious views. On the list describing religious conservatives were 7 distinctly negative phrases (out of a total of 19): "intolerant of other religious views," "overly strict on moral issues," "fanatical about their beliefs," "too concerned about their own salvation," "close minded," "too rigid and simplistic," and "too harsh an emphasis on guilt, sin, and judgment." Liberals picked out these phrases most often to describe conservatives. Indeed, half of the liberals chose 4 or more of these critical phrases to describe conservatives. And five liberals out of six chose at least one of the 7. The list presented as possible ways of describing religious liberals contained 6 negative or critical images (out of a total of 17 phrases): "morally loose," "do not truly know Christ," "knowledge of the Bible is shallow," "not interested in sharing their faith," "tend to be unloving in their attitude," and "don't believe in the Bible." Conservatives emphasized these negative views much in the same way that liberals chose negative views of conservatives. A third of the conservatives said that at least 4 of these 6 phrases applied to liberals, and another third said that at least 1 of them did.

These kinds of images, like the more traditional stereotypes that have divided Christians and Jews or Protestants and Catholics, probably contain a grain of truth. For instance, a conservative Christian who regards the Bible as a divine book to be taken as literally true, word for word, is likely to think there is good reason for saying that liberal Christians do not show proper respect for the Bible—especially when four out of five liberal Christians fail to regard the Bible as being literally true. In return, liberal Christians who believe that faith in the Bible must be tempered with reason, personal experience, and historical knowledge have some cause to regard conservatives as narrow-minded when close to two-thirds of all religious conservatives view the Bible as literal truth. There is, in short, a factual basis for the negative views that religious liberals and conservatives hold of one another. And yet, the history of religious prejudice has so often shown that grains of truth become deserts of misunderstanding. Holding negative stereotypes provides an excuse for dismissing another group categorically, rather than trying to understand what it has to offer. Criticizing an out-group becomes a way of justifying one's own group. Rather than trying to appreciate different ways of expressing religiosity, one simply dismisses other points of view. Cultural divisions raise their heads from the murky waters of conceptual ambiguity, setting in motion waves of ill-feeling and currents of misgiving.

In the present context, the connection between negative stereotyping and other kinds of misgiving is abundantly clear. Liberals, for example, disproportionately registered negative feelings toward target groups such as "evangelicals," "fundamentalists," and "charismatics." Both ends of the theological spectrum also thought their opponents had too much influence, especially over religious agencies, the government, and the schools. It is not surprising that people should think this way, given the public statements their leaders have made. "Tall steeples, no people," was the phrase one pastor of a large conservative church used to characterize his liberal counterparts. "They've kept only the bath water and thrown everything else out," declared a liberal cleric in an impassioned sermon about fundamentalists. Recounting the "inflexibility," "intolerance," and "passion for annihilation" among evangelicals, another liberal pastor said it made him think of "the Great Inquisition and the Dark Ages."[2] "Shilly-shallying," a conservative pastor told an interviewer. "We want no association with churches that can't get serious about preaching the Christian faith."

Most kinds of prejudice attenuate considerably once people actually do associate with one another. That, at least, has been the tendency when blacks and whites, Christians and Jews, have taken the time to communicate. It was also the solution mentioned most often when conservatives and liberals were asked what they thought would be most helpful in promoting greater mutual understanding. The experience of the two groups, however, sadly belies the effectiveness of this solution. Tension, it appears, is rooted more in the presence of contact than in its absence. Among conservatives, antiliberal stereotypes were three times as likely among those who said they had been in contact with liberals "a great deal" than it was among conservatives who had had little or no contact with liberals. And among liberals, 60 percent of those with the highest level of contact with conservatives held anticonservative feelings, compared with fewer than 40 percent of those with the lowest levels of contact.[3] Among both groups, negative impressions did diminish in settings involving intimate communication; for example, in prayer fellowships. Unfortunately, however, these kinds of settings were not the most common sources of contact. Instead, each group was most likely to have had contact with the other "among friends or neighbors," "among family or relatives," "at work," or "in a former church." All of these settings resulted in higher than average levels of negative stereotyping.[4]

Education has been the other major factor in combating prejudice of more traditional varieties. As shown in Chapter 5, denominationalism and stereotypes separating Christians and Jews and Protestants and Catholics have eroded dramatically over the past four decades with the rise of higher education. In the present context, religious leaders and the general public alike share confidence in the efficacy of greater knowledge to bring about an easing of tensions between religious liberals and conservatives. Higher levels of education as such, however, do not seem to promote greater understanding. Among conservatives, college graduates were slightly *more likely* to hold antiliberal stereotypes than were conservatives with lower levels of education.[5] And among liberals—perhaps because they tend to be better educated than conservatives—this tendency was even stronger: 64 percent of the college graduates held anticonservative stereotypes, compared with 40 percent of the high school graduates, and only 30 percent of those who had not completed high school.

These results, then, give some sense of how deeply rooted the current divisions between religious liberals and conservatives are. Each side holds negative views of the other. This is not true of all religious liberals or of all religious conservatives. But a majority on both sides have something negative to say about the other side. Negative feelings and misgivings about the power of the other side are also expressed fairly widely. The most common kinds of contact, moreover, accentuate these attitudinal barriers rather than mitigating them. And the better educated one is, the more one is likely to hold negative views of the other religious group, whether one is conservative or liberal. These divisions also reflect the fact, as seen in Chapter 7, that religious liberals and conservatives do differ from one another on a number of beliefs and values. The two groups, as seen there, also divide strongly along educational lines. Worth underscoring, too, is the fact that approximately two-thirds of the American public *believes* there are deep tensions between religious liberals and religious conservatives—a belief that seems to have become a self-fulfilling prophecy for many Americans.

Denominationalism (Again)

Clearer perspective on the cleavage between liberals and conservatives can be gained by looking at this division in relation to the barriers separating denominations. Since the latter were examined in some detail in Chapter 5, we need only recount several of the major conclusions. First, much evidence pointed up trends toward greater interaction across denominational lines and a reduction of the social and attitudinal barriers separating members of different denominations. Second, the members of most of the major denominations now display a large amount of diversity on most social issues and on educational levels. Third, denominational affiliation alone helps little in predicting how people will stand on current social issues; education levels, in contrast, separate people dramatically on a number of social, political, and moral issues. Since religious liberalism and conservatism correspond closely to educational differences and to attitudes on many specific issues, we might guess that education has become a more important basis of cleavage in American religion than has denominationalism.

We have already seen that negative images and negative feelings between religious liberals and religious conservatives range higher than do many of the feelings and attitudes that separate the major denominations. It is also worth pointing out that the division between religious liberals and conservatives is one that *cuts across* denominational lines, rather than pitting one set of denominations against another. For example, among Southern Baptists the ratio of liberals to conservatives is almost exactly even (1.04 to 1.00). Among Methodists, the same is true (1.15 to 1.00). And among Catholics, liberals do not outnumber conservatives by many (a ratio of 1.38 to 1.00). This is one reason, by the way, why so many liberals and conservatives claim they have contact with one another; they often worship in the same church.

Where the two groups differ most is in the kinds of special purpose activities to which they belong. We saw in Chapter 6 that special purpose groups on which participation data are available tend to divide into two groups. Bible studies, charismatic groups, healing ministries, prison ministries, and world hunger programs constitute one distinct set. Antinuclear coalitions, social protest activities, holistic health groups, positive thinking seminars, and group therapy constitute the other. For convenience, we might label the first set "evangelical," since these activities are more common among evangelicals, and the second "humanistic," since none of them purports to be uniquely religious in emphasis. By a margin of 43 percent to 18 percent, religious conservatives are more likely than religious liberals to be involved in at least one of the evangelical kinds of groups. In contrast, liberals outstrip conservatives by a margin of 14 percent to 8 percent in being involved in at least one of the humanistic groups. Also of note, participants in evangelical groups are more likely to harbor antiliberal stereotypes than are participants in humanistic groups (11 percent versus 6 percent). And participants in humanistic groups are more likely to hold negative views of religious conservatives than are participants in evangelical groups (42 percent versus 26 percent). Among both liberals and conservatives, moreover, participation in their respective kinds of special purpose group seems to reinforce negative views of the other side.[6]

The *relative* weight of denominationalism, on the one hand, and of differences between religious conservatives and liberals, on the other, is most clearly seen by looking at the effects of both *simultaneously* on such matters as religious values and social or moral issues. This allows us to see whether differences of religious opinion are more likely to flow along denominational lines or along the fracture separating religious liberals from religious conservatives. With the data at hand, we can make these comparisons for Baptists, Lutherans, Methodists, and Catholics on a number of religious and social issues: views of the Bible, being born again, valuing religious fellowship, Moral Majority support, spending on social welfare, and so on. Presenting all the results would be tedious, but several overall conclusions can be drawn. On the whole, denominational differences by no means drop out of the picture, even when the differences between religious liberals and conservatives are taken into account. But the gap separating liberals and conservatives generally tends to be wider than that separating any of these denominations. It also tends to be quite consistent on all issues and for all denominations, whereas the differences between denominations tend to vary much more according to specific issues.

A few examples will illustrate these conclusions. On an issue such as holding to a literal view of the Bible, we would expect the major differences to be between religious conservatives and liberals. And this is consistently the case: among Baptists, conservatives are 15 percentage points more likely to view the Bible literally than are liberals; among Lutherans, the gap is 40 points; among Methodists, 27 points; and among Catholics, 36 points. Still, denominational differences prevail as well. Conservative Baptists, for example, are 21 points more likely than conservative Catholics to hold this view; liberal Baptists, 42 points more likely than liberal Catholics. On an issue such as "growing into a deeper relationship with God," we would have no particular reason to think that conservatives and liberals would differ, but might expect that denominational traditions would distinguish people according to how important this value was held to be. Among conservative Methodists, for example, only 56 percent said this was "very important" to them, whereas among conservative Lutherans 92 percent said it was very important. Still, in three of the four denominational categories, a difference remained between conservatives and liberals: 17 points among Baptists, 52 percent among Lutherans, 13 percent among Catholics.

The fact that denominations group together in different ways on particular issues can also be seen by considering a few examples. On views of the Bible, the value of proselytizing, support for prayer in public schools, and opinions of Moral Majority, for example, conservative Baptists and conservative Lutherans resembled one another but were relatively distinct from conservative Methodists and conservative Catholics. Yet on attaching importance to church services and fellowship groups, conservative Lutherans stood out, while conservative Baptists were more like conservative Methodists and conservative Catholics. Among the religiously liberal, Baptists and Methodists resembled one another in valuing prayer and salvation relatively more than liberal Lutherans or Catholics. But liberal Baptists and liberal Catholics were more like one another than either of the other two groups in favoring social welfare programs. In contrast, 36 of the 40 comparisons that were possible showed consistent and significant differences between religious liberals and religious conservatives.

These results help put into perspective some of the conclusions from previous chapters about the nature of the divide that has arisen between religious liberals and religious conservatives. As the boundaries separating denominations have been lowered, religious leaders on both the right and the left have found it easier to recruit constituencies that cut across denominational lines. Supporters of antinuclear coalitions can draw participants from all the major denominations because there are religious liberals in all these denominations and because interdenominational cooperation is a plausible, if not attractive, strategy. Leaders of groups like Moral Majority, as well as the television preachers more generally, are also able to draw on wide constituencies because there are religious conservatives in every denomination. Given the negative opinions that the two sides harbor toward one another, it is probably safe to say, moreover, that many parishioners feel closer to people in other denominations than they do toward people at the other end of the theological spectrum. Thus, conservative Baptists and conservative Catholics may share more in common than conservative with liberal Baptists. And liberal Methodists may have greater empathy with liberal Baptists than they do with conservatives in their own denomination. With denominations still in charge of many of the significant resources that church people need to promote their views (from finances to parliamentary procedures to retirement plans and legal control of church property), it may not be surprising, therefore, to see the kinds of conflicts and special interest groups that have sprung up in many denominations between liberal and conservative factions.

The declining prejudice (at least overt prejudice) among Christians toward Jews must also be given due significance. On the liberal side, Protestant leaders have seen Jews as their natural allies, just as they did earlier in the struggle against Catholics. Not only have Jews been consistent supporters of strict separation between church and state, but they have also espoused liberal views on many of the issues that the New Christian Right has championed and have been deeply suspicious of fundamentalists and the New Right in particular. In a 1984 survey, for example, Jews registered unfavorable impressions of Moral Majority by a margin of 69 percent to 7 percent favorable. In contrast, the American Civil Liberties Union (one of the principal opponents of Moral Majority) was given favorable marks by a ratio of 42 percent to 13 percent unfavorable.[7] As interfaith barriers have diminished in significance, and as tensions between liberals and conservatives have grown, the alliance between liberal Christians and liberal Jews has been all the more possible to promote. In addition, changes among Jews have tended increasingly to cast this as an alliance among "liberals" rather than an interfaith alliance as such. An increasingly large proportion of Jews have come to identify themselves as "just Jews" rather than Jews in a religious sense, and this tendency has been especially prominent among Jews with liberal political orientations and higher levels of education. An added consequence of this shift in public identity, however, has been that religious conservatives can now express some of their animosity toward Jews as antiliberalism, rather than openly as anti-Semitism. Indeed, the trends in American society that have placed overt anti-Semitism beyond the bounds of respectable discourse have probably contributed to the tendency among conservative Protestants to express their conflicts with Jews as antiliberalism. In addition, the growing level of sophistication that New Right leaders have brought to bear on public discourse in differentiating between religion and morality has also had direct implications for their relations with Jews. It has been possible, on the one hand, for New Right leaders to maintain that Jews are wrong *religiously* (as well exemplified in Baptist leader Bailey Smith's 1980 remark, "God Almighty does not hear the prayer of a Jew"). And yet, on *moral* grounds, conservative Christian leaders have been able to argue that they strongly supported the morality of a strong pro-Israel policy and have sought out (albeit with limited success) alliances with Orthodox Jews on issues such as abortion and pornography and with Jewish neoconservatives on issues such as welfare spending and national defense. In sum, then, the changing relations among Jews and non-Jews appear to have contributed both to the cross-religious alliances among liberal Christians and Jews and to the (potential) alliances among conservative Christians and Jews at the same time that they have become part of the growing tensions between liberals and conservatives.

Divisive Issues

In addition to the broader changes in American society that have already been traced in previous chapters, the flames of tension between religious liberals and religious conservatives have been fanned by a spate of controversial issues that have moved to the center of the political stage mainly since the mid-1970s. Some of these—abortion, school prayer, pornography, homosexuality—have already been mentioned. We need to look again at these issues, however, to see more precisely their role in the chasm currently separating liberals and conservatives.

Within each of the major denominational categories we have been considering, conservatives and liberals showed sharp differences as of 1984 on most of the issues that have animated the New Right and its critics on the left. In each of the three Protestant denominations and among Catholics, two out of every three self-identified conservatives said they were in favor of "tougher pornography laws." In comparison, liberals were divided about equally between support, opposition, and indifference to such laws. Abortion on demand was strongly opposed by a majority of the conservatives (and mildly opposed by most of the remaining conservatives); it was opposed by no more than a quarter of the liberals. Voluntary prayer in schools, opposition to homosexual teachers in schools, and government spending on social programs also divided liberals from conservatives in each of the denominational categories. Overall, the issues that discriminated best between the two (in order of strength) were: government spending on social programs, abortion on demand, homosexual teachers in schools, view of Moral Majority, and pornography laws. These issues, in fact, divided liberals and conservatives more strongly than did most of the theological and religious orientations examined in the study.[8]

Not only did liberals and conservatives differ in their opinions on these issues; how strongly they felt about these issues also contributed to their overall evaluation of the other side. Conservatives who felt strongly about particular issues were more likely to hold negative views of liberals; liberals who felt strongly reciprocated in their views of conservatives. To take some specific examples: 26 percent of the conservatives who strongly approved of Moral Majority scored high on antiliberal sentiments, compared with only 5 percent of the conservatives who strongly disapproved of Moral Majority. Similarly, a quarter of the conservatives who strongly opposed homosexual teachers in schools scored high on antiliberal stereotypes, but none did among conservatives who thought homosexuals should be allowed to teach in schools. On the other side, liberals were much more likely to harbor negative images of religious conservatives if they were liberals who felt strongly about these issues. Three-quarters of the liberals who strongly opposed Moral Majority held negative images of religious conservatives; only a third did among liberals who felt more positive toward Moral Majority. Approximately the same differences were evident between liberals who strongly supported the right of homosexuals to teach in schools and liberals who opposed this view.

The upshot of these results is that the presence of controversial issues as part of the broader national agenda, coupled with groups mobilized specifically around these issues, has clearly added to the attitudinal tensions between religious liberals and conservatives. Much of the trouble, admittedly, must be credited to deeper histories of theological and social differences. But these differences have not erupted into open conflict in a cultural vacuum. Within the ranks of religious liberals and conservatives alike, it is the presence of a sizable minority with very strong opinions about particular social and moral issues that contributes most to the acrimony toward the other side.

This point can perhaps be recognized more clearly by stepping back again momentarily into the political arena of the late 1960s. In that period, as deeply divided as the nation was, the major issues around which political controversy focused scarcely provoked divisions between religious liberals and religious conservatives in the same way that the issues of the late 1970s and 1980s have done. One of the significant reasons for this is that the two major controversial issues —race relations and Vietnam—divided religious people in somewhat different ways. On race relations, the cleavage cut through the middle of most of the larger denominations. Those with theologically conservative views tended to resist racial integration more than did those with theologically liberal views. But, taking these differences into account, the so-called liberal denominations did not differ markedly from the so-called conservative denominations.[9] In contrast, polls show that the Vietnam War provoked differences between denominations more than it did between people with liberal or conservative religious attitudes. On public opinion concerning the war, members of conservative denominations were more likely to support U.S. involvement whether they themselves held theologically liberal or conservative views; and members of liberal denominations were less likely to support the war, no matter what their theological preference. These patterns were especially apparent among regular churchgoing Protestants. For instance, national survey data on this group gathered in 1968 revealed that members of liberal denominations were significantly different from members of conservative denominations on Vietnam (33 percent versus 50 percent thought the country should have become involved), but not on race relations (27 percent versus 30 percent thought blacks should stay out of white neighborhoods). In contrast, the same study showed that individuals who were theologically conservative with respect to the Bible did not differ significantly from individuals who were theologically more liberal when it came to the Vietnam War (35 percent versus 42 percent supported getting involved). But the two groups did differ from one another significantly on the race question (28 percent versus 15 percent approved of whites keeping blacks out).[10]

Looking at exactly the same kind of data for the issues that had come to dominate the national agenda by 1980, however, showed a different pattern. Among regular churchgoers, denominationalism had largely dropped out as a distinguishing factor (as other evidence has already shown). For example, members of liberal Protestant denominations differed from members of conservative Protestant denominations by only 10 percentage points on abortion and by only 6 points on a question about gender discrimination. In comparison, the differences between individuals with theologically liberal and theologically conservative views (toward the Bible) were consistent and considerably stronger: 20 points on abortion, 12 points on gender discrimination.[11]

In sum, the issues that divided religious people in 1968 cut in different ways; the issues that divided them in 1980 reinforced one another. In the earlier period people within a particular denomination might agree with one another on Vietnam but were likely to be internally divided over race relations. And people who were themselves theologically conservative (or liberal) might agree with kindred spirits over race relations but were more likely to be divided denominationally over Vietnam. Thus it was less likely that a single cleavage would emerge as a major basis of religious differentiation. In the 1980s, in contrast, most of the major issues that animated religious leaders seemed to divide the theological world neatly into two opposing camps.

Feminism and Ordination

Although reference has just been made to the issue of gender discrimination, its powerful role in fueling the tensions between religious conservatives and religious liberals demands that we consider it in greater detail than many of the other issues already discussed. One of the reasons for its importance is that women have traditionally played an especially prominent role among churchgoers. Another is that the feminist movement which flourished in the 1970s began to alter those patterns. A third is that the struggle to change denominational policies so that women could be ordained resulted in the erection of serious ideological barricades between religious liberals and religious conservatives.

The prominent role played by women churchgoers can be seen readily in most attitude surveys asking about religious participation and religious beliefs. According to recent national surveys, only half as many women (6 percent) as men (11 percent) claimed to be without any religious faith.[12] By a margin of 46 percent to 35 percent, women were more likely than men to report having attended religious services within the past seven days. Two-thirds, compared with fewer than two-fifths among men, said they read the Bible (at least once a month). And by a margin of 57 percent to 37 percent, women were more likely than men to report having given a lot of thought to developing their faith. Indeed, significant percentage point spreads differentiated women from men on almost every kind of religiosity measure: women were 18 points more likely than men to say their religious commitment had been a positive experience; 17 points more likely to say their relation to God was a very important source of self-worth; 16 points more likely to say they would read religious literature when faced with personal problems; 15 points more likely to report they tried to seek God's will through prayer; and 14 points more likely to indicate that religion on the whole was very important in their lives.[13]

That women should demonstrate greater commitment, on the average, to religion than men do can be interpreted as part of the traditional set of roles which women have played until very recently: mother, housekeeper, guardian of traditional values, participant in voluntary associations, marginal to the labor force, marginal to sources of social status such as education and professional occupations. Religion's role in secular society has run in many of the same channels: an extension of the family, a promoter of traditional values, relegated to the private sphere, associated with localistic values, peopled frequently by the down and out. Not surprising, many have argued, that women should have found religion to their liking. If one needs to get away from the children for a while, or to seek solace in the comforts of other-worldly promises, houses of worship are the place to go.[14]

Less commonly recognized is the fact that gender differences in religious commitment seem remarkably immune to the changing roles that women have begun to play. For instance, higher levels of education and greater rates of participation in the labor force among women should presumably wipe out some of the differences in religious commitment that have been evident between women and men. When women with college educations are compared with men of similar educational attainment, however, the differences persist. Even when *younger* women with college educations are compared with younger, college educated men, no reduction is evident. Nor do the differences dissipate much when younger, college educated, full-time participants in the labor force are compared with their male counterparts.[15]

On the whole, then, it appears that gender differences in religious commitment may be more deeply rooted than has often been thought. Over the long haul, the changes in gender roles that have taken place in American society in recent decades may lead to greater similarities in the levels of religious commitment among women and men. For the time being, however, religion remains an activity that can scarcely be ignored. Rather than being simply a peripheral issue that can be relegated to the dark corners of the past, religion remains a vital aspect of the public and private lives of the vast majority of American women. As just seen, nearly three-quarters consider themselves church members. Half attend religious services at least once every week and more than two-thirds attend at least once a month. Four in ten claim they pray more than once a day. Seven in ten say their relation to God is very important to their self-worth. And three-fourths consider their religious faith the most important influence on their life.

If American women continue to register high levels of religious commitment overall, sharp differences in these levels can be observed, nevertheless, between women with feminist orientations and women with more traditional gender orientations. From the beginning, the feminist movement that grew to national proportions during the 1970s drew a more favorable response from segments of the population in which religious commitment already tended to be weak: the young, the better educated, women with professional careers, those with more secular orientations toward life. A study conducted in California in 1973, for example, showed that only 38 percent of those who explained events in terms of traditional beliefs about God said they favored equal rights for women, compared with 64 percent of those who explained events with a combination of ideas from secular sources such as the social sciences, literature, and humanistic psychology.[16] Rooted as it was among the better educated, feminism functioned much like the liberal, egalitarian values of the "new class" more generally. It ran counter to the more traditionalistic values that had been prominent in the churches during the 1950s.

To the more conservative parishioners in the churches, the feminist movement seemed too much a part of the recent counterculture, too closely associated with sexual experimentation, too much in sympathy with abortion and permissive moral standards to arouse support. "I would associate [feminism] with across-the-board liberality, a weak view of [biblical] inerrancy, a lenient view of abortion and capital punishment," one churchgoer told an interviewer. Another, commenting on feminists who wanted to introduce nonsexist language into religious services, remarked: "They're open to homosexuality and they lean toward favoring pro-choice over pro-life on abortion."[17] To feminist leaders, these kinds of responses only reinforced suspicions that the churches were enemies in the struggle rather than potential allies. As one leader lamented: "The churches have contributed an enormous amount of money, time and organizing toward the goal of crushing us, especially on the issues of abortion and the ERA."[18]

As the movement progressed, feminism did gradually acquire some support within many religious organizations. Members of liberal denominations, clergy and church bureaucrats in these denominations, and women with better educations and politically liberal outlooks became especially influenced by the claims of the feminist movement. Even a few evangelical writers began to contribute to the feminist cause. For the most part, though, feminism deepened the divisions that were already becoming evident between religious conservatives and religious liberals.

Had feminists championed only the broader issues, the churches might have been able to duck some of the controversies that developed. But feminism also became an issue of particular interest to the churches because it raised afresh many of the demands that had been simmering for several decades concerning the proper position of women in church leadership roles. Efforts had been underway in many denominations and interfaith agencies since the 1940s to reconsider theological proscriptions against ordaining women as members of the clergy. At the popular level, polls conducted in the late 1940s had shown that there was as much support for including women in the clergy as there was opposition, and this support was as strong as it was for women's inclusion in other professions, such as medicine, law, or politics.[19] Progress toward actually incorporating women into the clergy, however, was relatively slow because the idea ran counter to notions of apostolic authority in many denominations and could not be pressed through legal means because of First Amendment guarantees against state interference with religion. By the end of the 1960s a number of the major denominations had revised their theological guidelines to permit women to become ordained as professional clergy. It was not until the end of the 1970s, however, that women began to pursue careers as clergy in large numbers. Between 1972 and 1980, female enrollments in theological seminaries increased 223 percent while male enrollments grew by only 31 percent. As a result, by 1981, 22 percent of all seminary students were women, as were 31 percent of those enrolled in professional programs in seminaries. During this period the rate of increase in the proportion of all "religious workers" (as defined by the U.S. Census) who were women was actually higher than that for any other profession except law, and by 1980 the proportion of clergy who were women was higher than for law or medicine.[20]

Beyond the specific impact that these changes had on the composition of the clergy itself, the drive to ordain women had several far-reaching effects on American religion. Coming as it did at a time when the broader feminist movement was generating both support and opposition, revisions in denominational policies to permit women to be ordained often generated controversies that paralleled those raised by the larger movement. On both sides of the ordination question, special purpose groups sprang up within the churches. Some of these groups gradually began addressing feminist issues more generally. In addition, participation rates in the churches began to divide along lines of how feminist or nonfeminist a person was. And religious conservatives began to see feminism as part of a more general ideological package to which they needed to voice opposition, while religious liberals increasingly saw it as a matter of moral and theological urgency.

Churches in which permission for women to be ordained was either slow in coming or not forthcoming at all became the staging grounds on which the most enduring special purpose groups became mobilized. Failing to achieve their initial aims quickly, these groups sometimes began championing a whole range of feminist issues and branched into other controversial areas of religious policy as well. The Women's Ordination Conference, organized in 1974 to promote women's ordination in the Catholic church, provides one case in point. Although it focused initially on ordination, its agenda steadily expanded during the 1970s. By 1982, it had issued calls not only for inclusive ordination but also for the church to condemn all forms of sexism and for Christians everywhere to work for "justice and equality for women." Over the same period it worked actively to encourage the national bishops' council to endorse the equal rights amendment and in 1983 secured a promise from the council to write a pastoral letter on women in church and society. A similar example is provided by a movement called Ezrat Nashim, founded in 1972 by women within Conservative Judaism to press the Rabbinical Assembly to allow women to participate fully in religious observance, synagogue worship, and decision making in governing bodies. Through the networking and conferences of this group, the Jewish Feminist Organization came into being two years later. Its goals were considerably broader, including an end to sexism in all areas of Jewish life and political action to give women a greater voice in Jewish communities.

Despite the fact that these and other organizations gained considerable support, the broader social trends in the 1970s did not favor an active partnership between feminism and religious involvement. The slow pace at which many religious organizations moved toward implementing change, together with broader social differences in the type of clientele most easily attracted to the churches, led to wide disparities between the religious involvements of feminists and nonfeminists. A study of Catholic women, for example, showed that only 26 percent of those with feminist orientations and at least some college education attended church regularly, compared with 49 percent of those with nonfeminist orientations and comparable levels of education. By a margin of 20 percent to 40 percent, the feminists were also less likely to express confidence in the church's leadership.[21] Other evidence documented the same kinds of differences among most Protestant denominations, although some significant exceptions were apparent. In data collected in the late 1970s, Baptist women with feminist orientations were 16 percentage points less likely to attend church regularly than were Baptist women with nonfeminist orientations. Among Lutheran women the difference was 15 percentage points. And among women in Protestants sects, it rose to 21 points. The exceptions were the two predominately liberal denominations—Presbyterians and Episcopalians—and Jews (all of which contained a majority of women with feminist orientations, unlike the other denominations in which these views were in the minority). Among Presbyterians and Jews, feminists were no less likely to attend church regularly than were nonfeminists. And among Episcopalians, feminists were 11 percentage points *more likely* to attend regularly than were nonfeminists.[22]

The exceptions indicated that feminism and religion need not, as if by some historical law, run contradictory to one another. The Episcopal church, for example, not only reacted to the changing interests of women, but also played an active role in sponsoring gender consciousness-raising groups for both sexes, provided counseling and other services for women making the transition from one kind of identity to another, and generated awareness of sexism in traditional theological language and liturgy. The broader tendency, however, did appear to run against feminist involvement in religious organizations. Early socialization did the job in some cases by orienting potential feminists away from the churches, if only by virtue of being reared in households where religious observance was not practiced. The experience of attaining higher education, as we have seen, led students to take more liberal orientations toward social and moral issues and (for various reasons) to turn away from conventional religion. These experiences also provided the occasion for many younger women with higher levels of education to become positively oriented toward feminism. Then, in some cases, churchwomen who became more oriented toward feminism actually became less actively involved in religion, switched to denominations in which they felt more at home, or defected from religion entirely. Whatever the exact sequence, the result was that many religious organizations (with the few exceptions mentioned) tended to be populated by women who did in fact lean away from feminist orientations, and these women tended to be among the most active members in these organizations. At the grass-roots level, therefore, many churches were probably better able to mobilize sentiment against feminism than in its favor.

The fact that pressure groups within the churches continued to mobilize on both sides of the feminist issue, nevertheless, meant that conservatives and liberals alike were forced to pay attention to it. And in many cases, it appears, the question of ordination and of feminism more generally was seen as part of the deeper differences separating the two. Commenting on conflicts within the Methodist church, for example, one minister told an interviewer: "Conservatives think of themselves as manning the barricades against [liberals] on lots of issues—they are typically anti-gay rights, pro-life, believe in biblical inerrancy, and would be violently opposed to a gay pastor or a woman pastor."[23] Or as one churchwoman who defined herself as a religious conservative expressed it: "Having a woman as pastor generally indicates a liberalism which denies the authority of Scripture." Asked more pointedly whether the two went together, another churchwoman admitted that having a woman pastor was tantamount to abandoning the Bible in a way that "opens the door to other culturally relative views."[24]

In many instances, views such as these were held privately by parishioners who went along with their church's decisions on women's ordination rather than trying to stir up dissent. By the end of the 1970s, however, the broader religious climate had become sufficiently fraught with controversy over issues of particular interest to women that special purpose groups and political interests were beginning to make headway in mobilizing churchwomen to take more active positions on their views. Women with conservative views, it appears, became particularly susceptible to inclinations that caused their religious participation to spill over into the political realm.[25] Data from national surveys, for example, showed that women who attended religious services more frequently were, in general, significantly more likely to score high on political participation in the 1980 and 1984 presidential campaigns.[26] During the 1980 election the Reagan campaign and conservatives more generally appear to have capitalized on the churches as a resource for political mobilization with more success than their opponents. Women who showed the strongest positive relations between church attendance and political participation included: opponents of the equal rights amendment, women who felt the government should provide fewer welfare services, women who felt government had grown too powerful, and registered Republicans. Those who voted for Carter showed a negative relation between church attendance and political participation. In contrast, those who voted for Reagan showed a positive relation.[27] The 1984 election continued much the same pattern established in the 1980 election. Reagan supporters and Republicans were the most likely to show positive relations between church attendance and political participation. Like Carter's before him, Walter Mondale's supporters in his presidential campaign were *less* likely to participate in politics if they went to church regularly than if they did not. Conservatism also appeared to reinforce the relation between church attendance and political participation. For example, those who favored increases in defense spending and who thought women's place was in the home were more likely to be politically involved if they were religiously involved, whereas their liberal counterparts did not show these patterns.[28]

Overall, then, the dominant tendency in the 1980 and 1984 elections appears to have been one in which religion played more of a role in mobilizing political activity among conservative than among liberal women. This was the case, at least, in the population at large. Adding to the divisions between conservative women and liberal women, however, was the fact that both sides were represented by special purpose groups which displayed an increasing tendency to mix religion and politics.

On the conservative side, several antifeminist movements emerged which had clear political objectives as well as close ties with religious groups. The most visible of these was Concerned Women for America, founded in 1979. Described by its leaders as "a positive alternative to the militant feminism that threatens American society," its stated objectives included:

> (1) to inform women in America of the erosion of our historical Judeo-Christian moral standards; (2) to expose movements seeking to weaken the family; (3) to educate women in the principles for living according to the Word of God; (4) to organize the Christian women of America into a united prayer action network for the nation and its leaders; (5) to train volunteer lobbyists in our "535" Program to make our views known both in Congress and in State Legislatures; (6) to provide representation on family and moral concerns in Washington, D.C., for the concerned women of America; and (7) to provide legal defense to preserve religious freedom.[29]

Specific issues on which Concerned Women lobbied included abortion, pornography, parental rights, national defense, free choice in education, and the free enterprise system. In addition to its explicit concern for religious values and frequent reference in its publications to God and Christ, the movement was closely allied with both the religious and political right. Its president and founder, Beverly LaHaye, was the wife of Tim LaHaye, Moral Majority board member and president of the American Coalition for Traditional Values. Other members of Concerned Women's advisory council included the wives of Jerry Falwell, Senator Jesse Helms, and television evangelists Jimmy Swaggart, James Kennedy, and Jack Wyrtzen.

In addition to movements like Concerned Women that were organized by and specifically for women, other conservative organizations constituting the New Christian Right involved large numbers of women and were specially concerned with gender issues. In studying the pro-life movement in California, for example, Kristin Luker found that the leaders were overwhelmingly women with strong religious convictions and close ties with conservative religious organizations.[30] At the national level, conservative activists like Phyllis Schlafly and Connie Marshner were closely involved in the development of Moral Majority, Christian Voice, Religious Roundtable, and other New Right organizations, all of which took strong stands against the equal rights amendment and styled themselves as "pro-family" supporters.

More generally, the role of religious television also appears to have been especially important in mobilizing support among women for conservative political causes. Not only were women more likely to watch religious television programs than were men, they were also more likely to watch these programs for longer periods of time each week, to send in money, to have positive attitudes toward them even if they did not watch personally, and to support many of the political issues favored by the television preachers.[31] The role of religious television in providing a common identity and an outlet for political inclinations was especially important for women whose lives were otherwise isolated because of small children, nonparticipation in the labor market, or old age. The significance of this role was also amplified by the fact that local churches often did not favor direct political participation or else contained too much political diversity to encourage organized political involvement. A survey of women in evangelical Protestant churches in New Jersey, for example, showed that supporters of Moral Majority were relatively scattered and in most churches did not enjoy a substantial critical mass.[32] Under these circumstances, the capacity of religious television, combined with direct mailing and telephone hookups, to link individuals directly with a national political movement became all the more important.

On the liberal side, special purpose organizations for women have enjoyed a long history as part of most denominations' formal structure and have for many years included certain kinds of political issues among their agenda. One of the oldest of these organizations is the International Association of Liberal Religious Women, founded in 1910, the objectives of which include not only the promotion of liberal religious ideas and ecumenical cooperation among religious women but also the promotion of peace and, more recently, equal rights for women in all countries. Another is Church Women United, founded in 1941 as an ecumenical movement including both Protestants and Roman Catholics, currently represented in every state by more than 2,000 local organizations. Since the 1960s, it has taken an increasingly active role in national and international political activities. In the late 1970s and 1980s, actions taken by the movement's executive council included: support of the sanctuary movement for refugees from Latin America, support of New Zealand's declaration of its waters as a nuclear-free zone, opposition to the U.S. government's decision to mine Nicaraguan harbors, adoption of a resolution deploring apartheid in South Africa, sponsorship of civil disobedience at the South African embassy in Washington, D.C., and lobbying against the MX missile and federal funding of contra operations in Nicaragua.

Many of the liberal Protestant denominations, as well as groups within the Roman Catholic church and among Jews (as suggested earlier), have also witnessed a rise in political consciousness and political mobilization among women as part of the movement toward greater inclusion of women in clergy and other leadership roles. In part, this development is the result of the politicization of women clergy and seminary students as part of the struggle for inclusion itself. Finding ideological support for their cause in the broader feminist movement, many of these leaders have gone on to challenge other manifestations of gender bias within their churches and to support broader initiatives for legislative and political reform.

By the 1980s, therefore, a relatively wide variety of women's movements were in operation under specifically religious auspices and yet with distinctly liberal political issues as part of their objectives. These movements fell primarily into three categories: movements having bureaucratic sponsorship from organized denominations or other religious bodies, movements organized separately from any established religious bodies but subscribing to established Judeo-Christian beliefs, and movements organized around other religious beliefs and usually expressing self-conscious opposition to the Judeo-Christian tradition.

An example of the first was the United Churches of Christ Coordinating Center for Women in Church and Society. Sponsored by the hierarchy of the United Churches of Christ, its activities consisted chiefly of publishing a quarterly newsletter containing articles and announcements on political issues ranging from toxic waste disposal to economic justice for the elderly; cooperating with other national organizations in lobbying on political issues; maintaining a support network among clergywomen; sponsoring various conferences and publicizing literature; and promoting religious and political involvement among women at the grass-roots level through chapters in local churches. Similar organizations were in existence among women in the Church of Christ, Methodist church, Episcopal church, Presbyterian church, and among Roman Catholics.

Illustrative of the second kind of movement (lacking sponsorship of an established religious body) was the Coalition on Women and Religion. Organized in 1973 in Seattle, it represented women of all faiths and was dedicated primarily to furthering the spirituality of women. Its activities included endorsing local and national legislation on issues such as the equal rights amendment, abortion, and the displaced homemaker's bill; supporting ordination of women clergy; preparing study materials on religious and cultural attitudes toward women; sponsoring workshops and panels; making television appearances; and sponsoring a credit union for women and a shelter for abused women and children.

The third category included a wide variety of post-Christian, occult, witchcraft, mystical, Buddhist, meditative, and therapeutic movements. Mostly small, and because of opposition from anticult groups relatively apolitical and oriented toward maintaining a low public profile, some of these groups were nevertheless active in promoting political consciousness among women and occasionally became involved in political activities. One such movement, organized on a national scale, was the Grace of God Movement for the Women of the World. Organized in 1970, it was operating by the mid-1980s in more than 100 locations and was offering a wide variety of training programs, including courses in political consciousness-raising and courses designed to alter traditional conceptions of gender.

Judging from the survey results mentioned earlier, women's movements combining liberal political and religious goals have not been as successful in mobilizing participation in electoral activities as have conservative movements. Yet in some ways this failure may be attributable to the broader, and more radical, reforms many of them seek. Rather than focusing primarily on specific candidates or referendums, these movements have been concerned with fundamental reorientations of language and self-identity as well as political attitudes. Much of the published literature that has emerged from the religious wing of the feminist movement has been concerned with recasting basic religious symbols and practices in more inclusive language. Trial liturgical experiences, curriculum materials for the instruction of children, role-modeling through the inclusion of women in clergy and other leadership positions, as well as consciousness-raising groups and personal counseling have all been part of the broader programs of these movements and organizations. Basic to all these activities is the assumption that the political cannot be separated from life and that life involves conceptions of self and reality which transcend, and yet permeate, the political.

The Broader Role of the Political

In the case of women, then, it is evident that feminism and other issues came to be divisive for religious conservatives and religious liberals partly because they mobilized religious practitioners in different directions politically. The tensions between these two groups were also fueled more generally by the ways in which religious people began participating in the political arena during the late 1970s and 1980s. We have already considered the formation of special purpose groups such as those associated with the New Christian Right during this period. The relations between religious involvement and political participation at the grass roots during this period are also instructive to consider.

If we step back in time, again, to the late 1960s, we discover several dominant patterns in the relations between religious commitment and political participation. We see, as already noted in Chapter 8, that religious conservatives tended to be less active politically than either their liberal counterparts or their own successors in the late 1970s. Data collected nationally during the 1968 presidential campaign demonstrate this pattern clearly. These data feature more active kinds of political involvement, such as attending political meetings and working in the campaign, rather than merely being registered to vote or expressing a desire for churches to speak out on political issues. In 1968, people who took a nonliteralistic view of the Bible tended to be significantly more politically involved than those who approached it from a more conservative perspective, particularly if these conservative views were held by members of evangelical or fundamentalist Protestant denominations. Specifically, one-fifth of the theological liberals in both mainstream and evangelical denominations scored high on a scale of political activism, compared with one-sixth of the more conservatively minded members of mainstream denominations, and only one-tenth of the conservatives in evangelical denominations. There was, however, a tendency for regular churchgoers to be more politically active than irregular churchgoers or nonattenders in all kinds of denominations and among people with both liberal and conservative theological views. In other words, greater levels of religious involvement seemed to be compatible with political involvement, no matter what kind of church was involved.[33]

Also of significance in 1968 was the fact that the two political issues around which church people were most likely to mobilize tended to work at cross-purposes with one another. These were the civil rights movement and the Vietnam War. As shown previously, church people divided along different lines on these issues, thereby preventing some of the polarization that might have been present had the two issues divided people in the same way. In addition, the two issues also generated different kinds of relationships between levels of religious and political involvement. On civil rights, religious involvement seemed to be conducive to political participation in the public at large (unlike the pattern for clergy) among persons who opposed the movement, but not among people who favored it. For example, there was a significant positive relation between church attendance and political participation among people who thought the civil rights movement was moving too fast, but not among people who thought it was moving about right or too slow. There was also a significant positive relation between church attendance and political participation among people who thought the government should keep out of school integration, but not among those who wanted the government to press for integrated schools. Similarly, those who favored segregated housing showed a positive relation between religious and political participation; those who favored integrated housing did not.[34]

On Vietnam, on the other hand, it was the doves rather than the hawks who showed the strongest relations between church participation and political participation. Specifically, those who said the United States should have stayed out of Vietnam in the first place showed a significant positive relation between church attendance and political participation; those who said the United States was right in getting involved in Vietnam showed no such relation. Also, those who favored pulling out of Vietnam and those who favored an immediate withdrawal showed the same positive relation between church attendance and political participation; those who favored a complete military victory and who wanted the government to take a stronger military stand did not. It is, of course, difficult to draw firm conclusions from this kind of correlational evidence, but it appears that in 1968 the churches were mobilizing people in several different directions. From the same data, we also see that positive relations between church attendance and political participation were evident among both Democrats and Republicans, among people of all different educational levels, and among young people to an even greater extent than among older people. In short, political participation had not yet begun to flow along lines that reinforced sharp divisions between conservatives and liberals; as yet, it ran in relatively diverse channels. All that was to change by the 1980s.

The transitional state of religion in relation to political activity during the early 1970s could be seen in the patterns of relations during the 1972 and 1976 presidential election campaigns. In 1972, many of the complex relations between religious involvement and political involvement seen in 1968 were still in evidence. On the one hand, younger people, political liberals, and those who favored greater equality for women showed positive relations between church attendance and political participation. On the other hand, those who opposed busing to achieve school integration also showed such relations. Republicans and Nixon voters showed positive relations; McGovern voters showed a negative relation. None of these relations, however, was very strong. By 1976, the relations between religious involvement and political involvement had virtually disappeared. While levels of political participation remained about as high for the nation as a whole as in the previous two elections, active church attenders were now no more likely to be political participants than infrequent churchgoers. The only subgroups of the population for whom the two kinds of participation were still related were political liberals (more politically active if infrequent churchgoers), and those who felt the government was too powerful (more political if frequent churchgoers). There was also beginning to be some tendency for people opposed to abortion to be more politically active if they were regular churchgoers, but as yet this tendency was weak and in absolute terms such people remained much less politically active than those with more favorable views toward abortion. Overall, then, the 1972 and 1976 elections suggested that political participation alone was not yet falling into any distinct pattern that either reflected or reinforced the growing division between religious liberals and religious conservatives.

The picture during the 1980 and 1984 presidential elections showed contours that had been absent in all three of the previous elections. Once again, church attendance was positively associated with higher rates of political participation: by a margin of 20 percent to 13 percent in 1980, and 20 percent to 15 percent in 1984. Now, however, the relation was consistently limited to subgroups of the population with conservative views. Among those who identified themselves as political conservatives in 1980, for example, a significant positive relation was evident between church attendance and political participation, but no significant relation was evident between attendance and participation among political liberals. On other conservative issues, the pattern was similar: those who sided with conservative issues such as disapproving of the equal rights amendment, favoring an increase in defense spending, favoring cuts on social welfare services, saying that minority groups should help themselves rather than depending on government for help, and opposing abortion all displayed a positive relation between church involvement and political activity. Those who took liberal positions on these issues showed no relations between church attendance and political engagement. Not surprisingly, those who sided with the Republican party in 1980 and those who voted for Reagan also manifested a consistent positive relation between churchgoing and political participation, while Democrats in general and Carter supporters in particular showed no such patterns. In 1984, the relations were much the same. Republicans and Reagan voters were significantly more likely to have participated actively in political endeavors if they were regular churchgoers than if they were infrequent church attenders; Democrats and Mondale voters did not show this kind of effect. And on other issues, particularly abortion, gender equality, and defense spending, churchgoing also seemed to reinforce political participation among conservatives but not among liberals.

Whether these relations between churchgoing and conservative political activity came about as a result of conscious organizational tactics or from a more subtle mood prevalent among conservative churchgoers is difficult to determine. Certainly organizations such as Moral Majority, as well as Reagan himself, courted the political participation of conservative churchgoers, while Democratic candidates and liberal church leaders were more likely to argue for separation of church and state—or at least to ignore the potential for mobilizing churchgoers. The fact that persons with more liberal views, both politically and religiously, were on average less actively involved in religious organizations may have also made it easier for conservatives to use these organizations as a political platform. It is also worth noting that the differences in styles of political involvement may have reflected in some measure differences in the kinds of resources at the disposal of religious conservatives and religious liberals. Conservatives not only tend to be more actively involved in their local churches, but are also more likely to be members of small churches or small denominations with relatively high degrees of local autonomy. And if they are members of large, centrally organized denominations they are likely, with several exceptions, to be decidedly more conservative than the church bureaucrats at the top of these hierarchies. For conservatives to become politically involved at all, therefore, they may have to organize through the leadership provided by the more active members of their local churches or through the grass-roots organizing activities of political leaders or television preachers. Religious liberals, in contrast, are more likely to belong to large denominations with well-established national bureaucracies. These bureaucracies are themselves more likely to be staffed with persons favoring liberal religious and political views. And there may be sizable numbers of special purpose groups devoted to bringing pressure on these hierarchies to make statements on selected political issues. The style of political involvement in these organizations, therefore, may take the form of official denominational pronouncements on political issues, endorsing political platforms, or lobbying through national agencies.

For present purposes, however, the important feature of the relation between religious and political involvement is the degree to which this relation had come by the beginning of the 1980s to reinforce the cleavage between religious liberals and religious conservatives. A decade earlier, the mobilizing potential of the churches seemed to run in pluralistic directions as far as political constituencies were concerned. By the 1980s, this mobilizing potential seemed to all run in the direction of political conservatism. To the extent that political participation gave religious people a public profile, therefore, this profile tended to be primarily colored in conservative hues. Despite the fact that religious conservatives might be highly diverse in other ways, such as denominational affiliations, this political uniformity contributed to their being perceived as a monolithic entity. And liberals, on the other side, could readily argue that religious conservatives were not only aligned against them on theological grounds but constituted a political bloc as well.

Quite apart from personal experiences, then, the public image that came to characterize American religion in the 1980s was one in which deep polarization between two monolithic camps seemed to be an accurate appraisal. In the media, this image clearly reinforced the perception of a basic cleavage dividing religionists from one another. Indeed, the media itself played an important role in fueling the tensions between liberals and conservatives, especially by painting conservatives in categorical terms and by publicizing vociferous reactions on the part of religious liberals. Not surprisingly, those on both sides who took their cues from the media were even more inclined than others to hold negative stereotypes of the other faction. With political issues at stake as well as religious views, the media could scarcely contain its efforts to picture the entire controversy in much the same way that it usually depicted the conflicts between political interest groups. And yet, as the evidence suggests, and as the material still to be considered in the next chapter indicates, the division between liberals and conservatives often rested on grounds about which the media knew little.

CHAPTER 10

Civil Religion: Two Cheers for America

WE HAVE concentrated thus far on what might be called the "institutional" aspects of American religion, including both its organizational manifestations and expressions of personal faith, and have attempted to trace the major ways in which these aspects have been restructured in recent decades. The religious quest, however, manifests itself not only in the beliefs of individuals, expressed privately and in organized groups, but also—as Durkheim argued some years ago—in the character and identity of entire societies.[1] The "why?" questions that seem inherently a part of human consciousness concern not only the meaning and purpose of our individual lives but also the meaning and purpose of our existence as a people.[2] We seek answers to the question, "What is the identity and direction of America?" just as we do about our personal missions as careerists, breadwinners, and family members. It has, therefore, been evident to many observers of America that the faith of its people includes important tenets which concern the nation *as a people.*

These tenets of faith are not always framed in explicitly religious language. The richness of America's religious heritage ensures that religious values often remain pertinent to the nation's definition of itself. But this heritage intermingles with other myths having no explicitly religious content. It is this intermingling, complex as it may be, that shapes public opinion and the perspectives of policy makers.

The tenets of America's legitimating creed naturally bear some relation to the religious opinions and practices of the American people. If religion is deeply valued in the private sentiments of its people, the nation's public culture is also likely to reflect the value attached to these sentiments. And if organized religion undergoes a series of restructuring events—if it becomes polarized—then the legitimating myths of the nation at large may also be subjected to certain tensions and modifications. Yet it also seems self-evident that the content of public discourse about America represents a reality distinct from any of the more personalized convictions that its citizens may hold.

Public religion, as an element of the political culture, consists in part of public utterances about the nation and in part of unspoken assumptions that provide the background for these utterances. On the one hand, a measure of how America defines itself is present in the kinds of arguments that intellectuals, public officials, and religious leaders deem appropriate to include in public discourse about the nation. It is in the context of such discourse that policies actually become articulated, defended, and debated. On the other hand, the unspoken assumptions prevailing in the culture broadly (often elicited only by poll takers) constitute the matrix of shared understandings that make possible the meaningful and plausible utterance of particular statements.[3]

Much of the content of public discourse focuses on specific policies, events, and personalities. These matters often appear to resolve themselves into purely substantive and technical issues. At the same time, there is a deeper level of understanding at issue in public discourse—a level of implicit and explicit claims about the character of the nation itself, the propriety of its actions, and the nature of its place in history and in the world. These constitute an extremely important dimension of public life, for they provide the assumptions on which the nation is legitimated.

The Problem of Legitimation

"Man was born free, and everywhere he is in chains," wrote Rousseau in his *Social Contract*.[4] But the principal question Rousseau sought to address in that treatise is perhaps not as familiar: not "how can we escape this misery?" or "why does such evil persist?" but "what can render it legitimate?" Rousseau's fundamental concern was with the fact that no society, as he understood it, could be governed effectively unless its governing system was deemed to be a proper expression of authority.

Rousseau clearly recognized the essential relation between questions of legitimacy and religion. The myths with which a society is legitimated must be powerful and authoritative, must arouse the public's devotion, and must give the society an awareness of its origin and destiny. Religious convictions can play a vital role in sustaining these legitimating myths—or they can be weak and divisive, so that they gradually lose place to stronger and more powerful secular myths.

The special relevance of religion to the legitimation of democratic societies lies in the fact that legitimation, in an ideal sense, must play a dual function if a democratic society is to be strong and enduring. On the one hand, legitimation means tacit acceptance of the nation and its policies by citizens and other relevant actors, as well as a degree of loyalty to, or conviction about, the nation's methods and goals. On the other hand, legitimation involves an articulation of transcendent purposes or ideals in relation to which the nation can be judged. In the first sense, legitimation quiets dissent that might become socially disruptive; in the second sense, it may evoke questions that help correct the society's course and ensure its viability over the long run. In democratic societies both of these functions rest more on the persuasiveness of legitimating beliefs, including religious convictions, than they do on the powers of coercion.

Legitimating myths are often portrayed as purely domestic matters—as a kind of political culture or civil religion that gives a nation its identity, promotes civil harmony, creates cultural cohesion, and satisfies the public that its government is governing properly. Legitimation is, in this sense, a matter of garnering support from the populace by appealing to certain common values, such as religious beliefs, or by governing in accordance with certain commonly accepted procedures. As long as the populace gives tacit assent to the governing system, that system may be regarded as legitimate. In the extreme, symptoms of crisis in the legitimating myths consist mainly of internal dissent or strife that cannot be resolved through ordinary means. This view of the nature of legitimation corresponds well with a long tradition of Western political theory, from Locke and Rousseau to more recent writers such as Talcott Parsons and the West German sociologist Jürgen Habermas. Yet there is another dimension to legitimation that is often neglected in these discussions. That is the international dimension.

Nations seldom legitimate themselves with reference only to internal traditions and values. They compare themselves with other nations and develop myths about their identity and standing relative to other nations.[5] Legitimation always involves differentiation. The myths a nation lives by differentiate it from other nations, define its relationships with other nations, and explain why it is unique among nations. Much of what gives a nation legitimacy consists of explanations about its relative power, privilege, and wealth. Being a good and decent nation often means having a standard of living that is the envy of other nations, or a defense system that cannot be challenged, or a governing system that other nations try to emulate. Consequently, any discussion of America's legitimating myths needs to take account of this broader dimension.

America's legitimating myths have developed over more than two centuries during which the nation has, with few reversals, beaten its enemies, given aid to its friends, maintained domestic tranquility, attracted millions of immigrants, and seen its star steadily rise in the galaxy of economic and political power. Its legitimating myths have closely reflected this history and its religious traditions have been deeply intertwined with these myths. Whether religiously inspired or secular, these myths have been influenced by the nation's position of prominence and privilege in relation to the rest of the world.

But ever since World War II, America's position in the world has been changing. The social infrastructure in which its legitimating myths have been grounded has been shifting, particularly since the late 1960s. Economic and political realities have grown more uncertain at the same time that they have become more complex—and the future promises no reversal of these trends. Thus questions arise about our legitimating beliefs which require careful examination: Are the continuities in these myths strong and enduring? Or are there signs of crisis and change?

One Nation Under God

Robert Bellah has written that the key ingredients of America's legitimating myth include a civil religion and a highly utilitarian secular ideology.[6] The civil religion consists of Judeo-Christian symbols and values that relate the nation to a divine order of things, thus giving it a sense of origin and direction. The utilitarian ideology, emanating from Enlightenment political philosophy, provides the nation with a sense of proper governmental procedure, as well as fundamental guiding values such as life, liberty, and the pursuit of happiness. Together, these cultural traditions have at various times in the past legitimated great national crusades. Periodically, they have combined to check the excesses of political expediency by subjecting the nation's programs to the harsh light of transcendent values. But they have also contended with one another for political supremacy.

Civil religion continues to serve as an extremely visible dimension of American culture. In recent election campaigns presidential candidates have often appeared to stumble over one another in their haste to demonstrate loyalty to some branch of the Judeo-Christian tradition. Inaugural addresses, now as in the past, pay ritual obeisance to the divine judge; prayers at all major political functions invoke God's presence and blessing; and, despite constitutional restrictions, much mixing of religious and political symbols continues on major holidays. America's civil religion portrays its people, often in comparison with people in other countries, as God-fearing souls, as champions of religious liberty, and in many instances as a nation that God has consciously chosen to carry out a special mission in the world.[7]

American civil religion is, nevertheless, deeply divided. Like the religion found more generally in the nation's churches, it does not speak with a single voice, uniting the majority of Americans around common ideals. It has instead become a confusion of tongues speaking from different traditions and offering different visions of what America can and should be. Religious conservatives and liberals offer competing versions of American civil religion that seem to have very little of substance in common.

On the conservative side, America's legitimacy seems to depend heavily on a distinct "myth of origin" that relates the nation's founding to divine purposes. According to this interpretation of American history, the American form of government enjoys lasting legitimacy because it was created by Founding Fathers who were deeply influenced by Judeo-Christian values. Although their personal convictions on occasion may have strayed from this standard, men like Washington, Franklin, Witherspoon, and Adams knew the heart of man from a biblical perspective so that they understood what kind of government would function best. Francis Schaeffer wrote of the Founding Fathers in his book *A Christian Manifesto*:

> These men truly understood what they were doing. They knew they were building on the Supreme Being who was the Creator, the final reality. And they knew that without that foundation everything in the Declaration of Independence and all that followed would be sheer unadulterated nonsense. These were brilliant men who understood exactly what was involved.[8]

Like many other evangelicals, Schaeffer had become actively involved in New Right politics, and therefore held strong views about the ills confronting American culture. But these ills were, in his view, a byproduct of the nation's abandonment of the Judeo-Christian vision, a result of the subversion of this vision by a materialist-humanist worldview, not any fault in the basic principles on which American government had been founded. America's conformity, even in principle, to biblical ideals was a lasting source of legitimacy.[9]

The idea that American government was founded on biblical principles actually represents a somewhat more temperate view of the relation between America and God than the one often heralded during the nineteenth century and that is still voiced by some evangelicals. That earlier view tended to picture America in millennialist terms, in Ernest Lee Tuveson's apt phrase, as a "redeemer nation."[10] America was not only called of God, but existed as a "chosen people," brought into being for the final fulfillment of God's purposes on earth. As the strength and size of the nation grew, and as its farms and cities prospered, writers could scarcely hide their conviction that the kingdom of God was indeed coming to pass and that it was happening in America. Melville's much-read novel of the mid-nineteenth century, *White-Jacket*, described Americans as "the Israel of our time" and the nation as a "political Messiah" sent as an advance guard to "bear the ark of the liberties of the world."[11] Whitman's epic poem *Passage to India*, extolling the natural beauties and human accomplishments of the American continent, drew an even more direct connection between the nation's wonders and God's purposes:

> Passage to India!
> Lo, soul, seest thou not God's purpose from the first?
> The earth to be spann'd, connected by network,

The races, neighbors, to marry and be given in marriage,
The oceans to be cross'd, the distant brought near,
The lands to be welded together.[12]

The new realities of the first half of the twentieth century, in which nearly every decade was blemished either by war or economic depression, dampened much of the enthusiasm that religious and secular writers had once expressed about the millennial future of America. Yet, as America increasingly found itself at the forefront of world military and economic leadership, some of the traditional zeal continued to be voiced. A favorite theme was the slogan "One Nation Under God," which carried more than one level of meaning, connoting both a unified nation and an "only," "best," "leading," or "special" nation under God. Norman Vincent Peale, in a book with this slogan as its title, argued that America had received a unique calling from God at the beginning of its history which continued to be expressed in the special zeal and spiritual quality of its people.[13] In another book by the same title, evangelical writer Rus Walton arrived at the conclusion that even the American constitution had been "divinely inspired."[14]

In the late 1960s and 1970s, as the nation's military involvement in Vietnam inspired a mood of questioning about America's purposes, defenders of the American way seemed to become even more explicit in their efforts to find divine legitimacy in American history. Edward Elson asserted that America could not be understood except as a "spiritual movement" with God as its source and the Holy Spirit guiding its development.[15] Christian businessman George Otis, echoing the same theme, wrote: "God's hand was in the founding of this country, and the fiber of Christ is in the very fabric of America."[16] With similar conviction, Dale Evans Rogers contended that America "was in the mind of God before it became earthly reality" and that it was still "a part of His purpose for mankind."[17]

In emphasizing the close historical connection between America and God, evangelicals and fundamentalists assert the importance of religious values which they themselves still uphold. Their version of American history points to a time when such values were evidently taken quite seriously. By implication—and sometimes directly—the proponents of this interpretation suggest that these values should again be taken more seriously, thus restoring a way of life in America with which evangelicals and fundamentalists could feel comfortable.

The distinction between personal convictions and the religious story of the nation remains sufficiently sharp in evangelical teachings that any kind of militant religious nationalism tends to appear atypical. Priorities generally focus on personal salvation, spiritual growth, biblical knowledge, and the affairs of local religious communities instead of God's providence in American history. Even Jerry Falwell alludes only occasionally in his books and sermons to America's collective relation to God. Insofar as conservative civil religion can be associated with evangelicals and fundamentalists, therefore, it appears to consist of a background assumption rather than an explicit object of devotion.

Although America is closely identified in conservative civil religion with biblical faith, spokespersons for this tradition have often been careful not to equate the two. A sharp distinction has been drawn between divine mandate and the material expression of that mandate. Frequently, this distinction has been formulated with reference to the classical theological demarcation between the kingdom of God and the kingdom of man. As a transcendent ideal, the kingdom of God calls into judgment any specific nation or people. Variously conceived of as a description of heaven, or as a kingdom that will be established on earth only after the present age has passed away, the kingdom of God is above all not to be confused with any currently existing nation, including America. Senator Mark Hatfield emphasizes that the evangelical Christian who opts for a career in politics must be careful to "obey God rather than men" and be wary of any thinking that too readily equates the biblical ideal with political decisions. The problem with confounding biblical faith and national pride, he warns, is that an idolatrous civil religion develops which "enshrines" the political order, and "fails to speak of repentance, salvation, and God's standard of justice."[18] Jerry Falwell also asserts flatly that "America is not the kingdom of God."[19] Other conservative spokesmen even warn against a too tacit acceptance of the idea that America was founded on purely Christian principles. The evangelical writers Robert Linder and Richard Pierard suggest in their assessment of American political religion that this idea "not only shocks the sensibilities of many believers, but also casts doubt on the infallibility and immutability of divine truth itself."[20]

Yet conservative civil religion generally grants America a special place in the divine order. Falwell goes on to say, "The United States is not a perfect nation, but it is without doubt the greatest and most influential nation in the world. We have the people and the resources to evangelize the world in our generation."[21] Tim LaHaye, head of the American Coalition for Traditional Values, makes the same point negatively: were it not for America, he asserts, "our contemporary world would have completely lost the battle for the mind and would doubtless live in a totalitarian, one-world, humanistic state."[22]

The idea of America evangelizing the world is in fact a much-emphasized theme in conservative civil religion. God's purpose for America is to use its advantaged position to preach Christianity to all nations—a task that in some evangelical eschatologies represents the final work that must be accomplished in order to hasten the "second coming" of Christ to this earth. America's wealth and power is thought to be God's supply of resources for carrying out this important task, as well as a token of divine "good faith" to those willing to shoulder the task. This view is particularly prominent among conservative Christian groups with a strong missionary emphasis. For example, Bill Bright, founder of Campus Crusade for Christ, writes: "God has given this country unlimited resources and manpower and finances. [He] . . . has called America to help bring the blessing of His love and forgiveness to the rest of the world."[23]

Despite formal separation between the kingdom of God and the kingdom of man, the "two kingdoms" doctrine in conservative civil religion also confers a strong degree of divine authority on the existing mode of government. Although no human government can ever fully conform to God's ideal, government is nevertheless established by God as a means of maintaining social order. Thus ordained, it should not be questioned or openly challenged, except in those rare instances when it violates the Christian's right to worship. Kenneth Kantzer, former editor of *Christianity Today*, explains, "It is imperative . . . that we recognize government's divinely ordained duty. . . . Dangers can arise from the abuse of these duties, but this does not negate their validity as ordained by God and deserving of our support."[24] In the American case this argument generally carries conservative connotations, since evangelicals have been able to point to the freedom of religion they enjoy under democratic government, especially in comparison with other countries.

In addition to its views on government, conservative civil religion generally includes arguments about the propriety of the U.S. economic system. These arguments grant capitalism a high degree of legitimacy by drawing certain parallels between capitalist economic principles and biblical teachings. Economist George Gilder, who identifies himself as an evangelical Christian, has argued, " 'Give and you'll be given unto' is the fundamental practical principle of the Christian life, and when there's no private property you can't give it because you don't own it. . . . Socialism is inherently hostile to Christianity and capitalism is simply the essential mode of human life that corresponds to religious truth."[25] Elsewhere he remarks, drawing a calculated reference to the apostle Paul's teaching on love, "the deepest truths of capitalism are faith, hope, and love."[26]

Jerry Falwell has also been an outspoken apologist for U.S. capitalism. He asserts, "I believe in capitalism and the free enterprise system and private property ownership. . . . People should have the right to own property, to work hard, to achieve, to earn, and to win." For Falwell, this is not simply an assertion of personal opinion, but a position that has divine sanction: "God is in favor of freedom, property ownership, competition, diligence, work, and acquisition. All of this is taught in the Word of God in both the Old and New Testaments."[27]

Others, with perhaps less obvious agendas than Falwell, also assert the existence of a certain affinity between Christian doctrines and American capitalism. Television preacher Pat Robertson draws directly on Gilder's work to arrive at the conclusion that "free enterprise is the economic system most nearly meeting humanity's God-given need for freedom."[28] Similarly, Christian writer Ronald H. Nash, arguing against a dangerous leaning toward socialism which he perceives in liberation theology, suggests that capitalism is the preferred system because it is impossible to have "spiritual freedom" without "economic freedom."[29]

As with arguments about American government, arguments in conservative civil religion about the propriety of capitalism often appear with greater ambivalence than these statements by Gilder and Falwell, in particular, would suggest. Instead of defending the absolute rectitude of capitalism by giving it divine sanction, evangelical spokesmen are prone to argue only for the *relative* merits of the American system. In such arguments, comparisons with other countries and with other economic systems become especially important. Capitalism acquires legitimacy mainly in contrast to the evils seen in Marxist or fascist systems. Senator Bill Armstrong, a self-proclaimed evangelical Protestant, provides an illustration of this logic: "Our form of government is vastly preferable to Marxism. But that doesn't prove that Christ would be a capitalist. I think Christ is indifferent to issues of that type, with one exception. I think he would approve of those institutions of government or economy that foster human liberty. So I take it for granted that Christ would not approve of the arrangements in Nazi Germany or in the Soviet Union."[30] By this logic, the United States is favored mainly because it takes sides with God against these other systems.

How commonly are these views held by the general public? Although several studies have explored opinions concerning the issue of civil religion, none has been representative of the country at large. Nor has any detailed investigation of the subject been made. Thus any answer to this question is inescapably less than satisfactory. A 1975 survey in North Carolina suggested that civil religion—actually, some questions concerning the tendency to mix religion and patriotism—was relatively widespread in the region as a whole, but especially so among self-identified religious conservatives, members of fundamentalist denominations, residents in rural areas, and persons with lower levels of education.[31] A 1981 survey in the Dallas-Fort Worth area gave somewhat mixed results. While a large majority of the residents in this area thought political leaders should believe in God and uphold religion, relatively few (about one in five) considered holidays such as the Fourth of July to be religious as well as patriotic.[32] Neither of these studies examined any of the more complex relationships between religious beliefs and beliefs about capitalism or American democracy.

In other studies some indirect evidence has been found that suggests a general tendency for conservative or traditional religious beliefs to reinforce support for American political and economic practices among those who hold these beliefs. For example, a national survey conducted in 1980 that divided the public into five categories ranging from low to high on levels of religious commitment found that those in the higher categories were more likely to agree "that the most important national problems, such as energy, inflation and crime can be solved through traditional American politics."[33] The same study showed the religiously more highly committed to be more supportive of a strong military force and more willing to believe that "America offers an opportunity for financial security to all those willing to work hard." Another national poll found that levels of overall satisfaction with "life in this country today" varied positively with membership in conservative religious denominations, holding evangelical beliefs, and attaching high importance to religious and spiritual values.[34]

With Liberty and Justice for All

On the other side, few spokespersons for the liberal version of American civil religion make reference to the religious views of the Founding Fathers or suggest that America is God's chosen nation. References to America's wealth or power being God's means of evangelizing the world are also rare and religious apologetics for capitalism seem to be virtually taboo. A liberal version of American civil religion does exist, but it draws on a different set of religious values and portrays the nation in a very different light from the conservative version.

The liberal view of America focuses less on the nation as such, and more on humanity in general. According to this interpretation, America has a role to play in world affairs, not because it is a chosen people, but because it has vast resources at its disposal, because it has caused many of the problems currently facing the world, and because it is, simply, part of the community of nations and, therefore, has a responsibility to do what it can to alleviate the world's problems. Rather than drawing specific attention to the distinctiveness of the Judeo-Christian tradition, liberal civil religion is much more likely to include arguments about basic human rights and common human problems. Issues like nuclear disarmament, human rights, world hunger, peace, and justice tend to receive special emphasis. The importance attached to these issues is generally not legitimated with reference to any particular sacred mandate, but simply on the assumption that these are matters of life and death—perhaps for us all. Nevertheless, religious faith often plays an important part in the discussion, differentiating liberal civil religion from purely secular or humanist beliefs. Faith plays a role chiefly as a motivating element, supplying strength to keep going against what often appear as insuperable odds. The example of the biblical prophets, who spoke out for peace and justice, is frequently mentioned as a source of strength and hope.

The interplay of these various themes is evident in many of the social statements that mainline denominations have promulgated to clarify their position on America's place in the contemporary world. The statement on "World Community: Ethical Imperatives in an Age of Interdependence," adopted by the Lutheran Church in America at its biennial convention in 1970, provides an illustration of the kinds of arguments often employed in these statements. The thrust of the Lutheran statement is to emphasize America's interdependence with the rest of the world and, therefore, the special responsibilities which Americans should accept in working for human rights, international security, and economic justice. Biblical injunctions per se occupy a relatively small portion of the document. The primary assertions with which the argument is legitimated tend to focus on obvious universal concerns. For example: "Men are beginning to sense that if they do not soon devise some means of living together they will surely perish together."[35] Or as the church's accompanying pastoral handbook argues, the task of global reconciliation is "imperative" and "urgent" because "there is no alternative to it short of the extinction . . . of the 'human experiment.' "[36] Manifestly religious arguments are also included, but in a secondary capacity that reinforces the more universalistic appeals. For example: "Concern for human survival, fulfillment, and community flows from the very heart of the Christian faith. The church has long proclaimed both mankind's natural oneness 'in Adam' and eschatological oneness 'in Christ.' " The remainder of the statement outlines a number of concrete problems and issues that need to be addressed, concluding with a final motivational appeal that the "God-given mandate" to build a world community be given high priority. And the pastors' handbook, which deals at greater length with economic and political proposals, ends by affirming the hope that all branches of the human family "may discover in new and tangible ways their oneness in Him who is the Truly Human."

Because of their awesome destructive potential, nuclear arms have occupied an especially prominent place in liberal civil religion. As one writer has acknowledged, "In virtually every large gathering of mainline or liberal Protestants these days, preoccupation with the awful possibility of nuclear war sooner or later rises to overshadow whatever the meeting was supposed to be about."[37] Liberal clergy have so often taken the lead in seeking solutions to the arms race that the peace movement has come to be identified in many circles as a religious issue. In a 1982 survey of a national sample of Presbyterians, for example, two-thirds agreed strongly with the statement "peacemaking is not simply 'another political issue' but is a basic aspect of the Christian faith."[38]

The National Conference of Catholic Bishops, in its 1983 pastoral letter "The Challenge of Peace: God's Promise and Our Response," also saw a strong connection between the arms question and religion. Much of the debate elicited by this document, and by similar statements from Protestant bodies, has centered on the problem of identifying "realistic" solutions to the arms race. The question has been less one of arriving at consensus about the biblical mandate for peace than of agreeing on practical steps toward achieving that goal.[39] Nevertheless, an implicit assumption in the debate is that the United States has a special responsibility to work for arms reduction as well as international peace, and perhaps more importantly, that basic religious principles exist that should guide such efforts. For many religious leaders the peace movement represents an application of a special kind of civil religion which defines and legitimates major courses of action for the American people as a collective entity.

Other crusades that have typified the liberal version of American civil religion include civil rights, international justice, and ecology. Liberal religious periodicals have kept these issues in the forefront of their readers' attention. For example, *Christian Century* during a single six-month period in 1982 published a total of 136 articles on topics such as nuclear weapons, social issues, economic issues, and peace (compared with only 22 articles on the Bible, 9 on evangelism, and 9 on prayer). A survey of Presbyterian clergy conducted during the 1970s also illustrates the priority given to such causes. When asked to rate various goals for the nation, the clergy gave top priority to having America serve as an example of liberty and justice to all nations. Also ranked near the top were international conservation of scarce resources and reducing disparities between poor and wealthy nations. Spreading American capitalism ranked at the bottom of the list. The survey also showed that eight of every ten pastors saw national pride as a hindrance to the work of the Christian church in the world, while fewer than a third thought America was currently a blessing to mankind throughout the world.[40]

The rhetoric of liberal religious leaders often includes references to the biblical tradition in support of its concern with peace and justice. Addressing more than 3,000 clergy and lay leaders gathered in Washington to protest the nuclear arms race in 1983, Jim Wallis, editor of *Sojourners* magazine, alluded repeatedly to the Christian values on which their movement was founded: "As the crisis we face becomes ever more clear, so do biblical passages about the oppression of the poor, the arrogance of power, and the idolatry of military might. Christians are remembering that the Gospel is to be good news to the poor and that the children of God are to live in the world as peacemakers."[41] Yet in making these appeals, liberal religious leaders offer little that specifically legitimates America as a nation. Instead, they appeal to broader values that transcend American culture and, indeed, challenge some of the more nationalistic assumptions it incorporates. As Father John Langan of the Woodstock Theological Center suggests, what seems to be needed most is a "clear delineation of the moral claims of the solidarity that binds us together as human beings sharing a common destiny under God. Such a delineation necessarily involves a critique of individualism and self-reliance in our national culture."[42]

A critique of this sort was a prominent feature of the Catholic bishops' "Pastoral Letter on Catholic Social Teaching and the U.S. Economy," issued a few days after the 1984 national election. Calling both Catholics and non-Catholics in the United States to a greater commitment to alleviating the suffering of the poor, the bishops were openly critical of America's practices in relation to their understanding of the Christian tradition. "We live in one of the most affluent cultures in history where many of the values of an increasingly materialistic society stand in direct conflict with the gospel vision," they charged. "Our contemporary prosperity exists alongside the poverty of many both at home and abroad, and the image of disciples who 'left all' to follow Jesus is difficult to reconcile with a contemporary ethos that encourages amassing as much as possible."[43] The letter stopped short of raising questions which might have been interpreted as challenges to the legitimacy of American democracy or American capitalism as such. But it fell squarely in the lineage of civil religious pronouncements calling the nation to closer conformity to its own ideals. Crediting the American tradition with great accomplishments in the past, the bishops proposed a "new American experiment" that would strengthen its citizens' resolve to work for economic justice, inspire them with ideals transcending the accumulation of material possessions, and engage the country as "a nation founded on Judeo-Christian principles" in the sacrifices necessary to bring justice and peace to the world.

The liberal version of American civil religion taps into a relatively deep reservoir of sentiment in the popular culture about the desirability of peace and justice. According to a 1982 Harris survey, 98 percent of the American public said they would like to see "a sharp decline in the number of people who suffer from hunger," 97 percent said they would like to see "a decline in terrorism and violence," 96 percent said they would like to see "a real easing of tension between the U.S. and the Soviet Union," 95 percent hoped for "a decline in racial and religious prejudice," and 90 percent wished to see "an end to the production, storage, and testing of nuclear weapons by all countries on earth."[44] The same survey, however, indicated that most Americans have little confidence that these goals will actually be realized in the foreseeable future. The percentages of respondents who thought each of the changes asked about would happen in their lifetime ranged from 40 percent down to 16 percent. "The problem," concluded the authors of the study, "is not so much a lack of motivation by the people of this country, but the inability of those vested with power and responsibility to fulfill the hopes and aspirations of the people." If anything, then, religious leaders who champion these causes may detract from the legitimacy of the current U.S. system rather than contribute to it.

Possibly for this reason, and possibly also because of the difficulties in realizing accomplishments in the pursuit of peace and justice, liberal religious leaders have sometimes presented themselves as a small prophetic remnant that is either rejected or ignored by the majority of the culture. Sociologist Donald E. Miller has aptly characterized the prophetic vision which underlies many of the causes in which liberal churches attempt to become involved:

> These persons will attempt to abolish idolatry in their midst. . . . They will follow in the tradition of the Hebrew prophets: feeding the poor, caring for widows and orphans, attacking economic systems that produce injustice. They will constitute a true community: unselfishly concerned for each others' needs and rejoicing in a love freely expressed. They will worship grandly and yet will also organize effectively, combating the evils of this world. They will be disciplined persons, almost sectarian in their attitudes and commitments, but choosing to live fully immersed in this world rather than withdrawing from it.[45]

Miller acknowledges that a more likely scenario for most people in liberal churches may be a kind of social club atmosphere which makes them feel good about themselves. Yet his description captures well the ideal that motivates many of the spokespersons for the liberal version of civil religion.

Both the liberal and conservative wings of American religion, therefore, have a vision of where America should be heading. But the two visions frequently appear to be at fundamental odds with one another.[46] Each side inevitably sees itself as the champion of higher principles, against which present conditions often seem wanting.

The two sides, in fact, appear to have become differentiated along a fracture line that has long been apparent in discussions of civil religion. That line reflects the inherent tension between symbols expressing the unique identity of a nation and those which associate the nation with a broader vision of humanity. As Bellah notes in his initial essay on the subject, civil religion in America seems to function best when it apprehends "transcendent religious reality . . . as revealed through the experience of the American people"; yet, the growing interdependence of America with the world order appears to "necessitate the incorporation of vital international symbolism into our civil religion."[47]

Perhaps it is not terribly surprising that these twin objectives can be accomplished more easily by two, relatively distinct civil religions than by one. The conservative tradition has in recent decades made clearest use of those symbols which are unique to the American experience; e.g., the mythologies of the Founding Fathers, of God's calling to the nation, of America's heroic accomplishments, and of the unique mission which America has to fulfill in the world. The liberal tradition, in contrast, has often been accused of neglecting these uniquely American symbols, but has given concerted emphasis to the international symbols that derive from a vision of the commonality of humanity.

The two versions of America also correspond in a general way with the ambivalent character of the American state. On the one hand, the relatively long period in American history during which the nation was able to enjoy virtual isolation from the rest of the world has resulted in the orientation of a segment of the bureaucratic state toward nationalistic concerns. On the other hand, America's rise to global power in the twentieth century has forced the state to act not only on behalf of narrow U.S. interests, but also as a potential contributor to the common good in global terms. These dual functions have sometimes been sufficiently different that particular agencies have come to be identified clearly with one or the other. But more commonly the two have been ambiguous enough that different advisory groups, administrators, and policy proposals have provided their chief manifestation. Under these circumstances, both versions of American civil religion have found proponents within the state who were willing to exploit them for purely political purposes.

In consequence, the two visions of America have been the subject of disagreement and polarization more than they have of consensus and mutual understanding. A few leaders have managed successfully to borrow ideals from both camps. For example, Senator Mark Hatfield has been a leader in the disarmament movement while retaining a religious identity as an evangelical. Jim Wallis has also combined these two orientations, although his outspokenness on the disarmament issue has alienated him from many of his fellow evangelicals. On the other side, writers like Richard John Neuhaus, Peter L. Berger, and Michael Novak have adopted some of the views of the conservative version of American civil religion, while retaining a more liberal theological position than most evangelicals would support. But such cases appear to be the exception rather than the rule.

It is more common to find the two camps taking openly hostile positions toward one another. In his Washington address, for example, Jim Wallis minced no words in criticizing New Right apologists:

> The new wave of activism in the churches provides a very different image of Christians from that presented to the public by big-time television preachers and their New Right allies. These evangelical nationalists exalt America at a time when we need to be humbled. They call for unrestrained economic growth in a world where resources are running out. They extol the virtue of wealth and power when most of the world is poor and powerless. They fan the national frenzy of fear and hostility by calling for more military spending when we are already on the brink of destruction. As such, they have corrupted the original Gospel message and the radical impulses of Christian movements throughout history.[48]

In return, spokesmen for the Right have been quick to label Wallis and others sharing his views as "socialists," "communist sympathizers," and "radicals."[49]

The problem this hostility poses for American religion as a source of national legitimacy is that neither side can claim effectively to speak for consensual values. Each represents a constituency, but holds—especially in the other's view—no assumptions on which all can agree. Any claim one side makes is likely to be disputed, leaving much of the public in doubt about the credibility of either. Religion, therefore, becomes (as indeed it has often been characterized in the press) "sectarian" rather than providing a basis of unity.

The full import of this propensity becomes apparent in relation to classical understandings of legitimacy in sociological theory. In the Durkheimian tradition, which continues as one of the more important contributions to these understandings, consensus or near consensus on basic societal values gives these values special weight because their plausibility is not likely to be eroded by questioning and debate. They become, as it were, sacred or inviolate. Clearly, the present tendency in American religion is to erode this sense of de facto authority. It is one thing to assert that the Founding Fathers were divinely inspired if everyone assumes this was the case; quite another if such claims, as presented by one religious faction, are disputed by another.

Conflicting interpretations notwithstanding, large segments of American culture continue to presuppose certain shared assumptions about religion and about the place of religion in the democratic process. The competing interpretations of American civil religion actually converge at a number of points. They agree with one another in asserting the importance of religious values to the political process; both assume the existence and importance of transcendent values in relation to which the nation may be judged; they agree on the relevance of certain biblical principles, such as compassion, equity, and liberty (while disagreeing on the priorities given to these principles); and they in fact draw on a common heritage of Judeo-Christian symbols and stories. The sheer existence of differing, even hostile interpretations need not result in total decay as far as the legitimating power of religious symbols is concerned. The Civil War period, after all, appears to have witnessed an empowerment of American civil religion at the same time that religious bodies were subjected to unprecedented division.[50] So it has been in recent decades. Were it not for the presence of competing interpretations, civil religion on the whole might well have been considerably less salient than it is.

Where the rub comes is that American civil religion does not operate in a vacuum. In a society which is not only deeply religious but also decidedly secular, other values and assumptions stand as ready alternatives to the civil religion. Faced with conflicting interpretations based on religious premises, spokespersons for the American creed have the option of turning to other arguments on which there may be greater consensus. Indeed, religious leaders themselves may fall back on purely secular values in attempting to find firmer ground from which to launch their religious arguments.

As the debate in American religion has intensified, the different versions of civil religion, therefore, have continued to be voiced as motivational appeals and as alternative stories of America. Among those at either end of the spectrum, these appeals seem to play both a canalizing and an energizing function with respect to specific policies and programs. But in the eyes of many middle-of-the-roaders, both sets of arguments may have lost plausibility by virtue of being too much disputed, leaving room for secular ideologies to play an enlarged role in legitimating the nation.

Freedom to Choose

As an illustration of the diminishing persuasiveness of religious arguments in the culture at large for legitimating the U.S. system, it is instructive to consider some of the arguments that in recent years have boldly sought to take their place. Michael Novak's *The Spirit of Democratic Capitalism* is particularly instructive because it introduces theological arguments at a number of points and in some ways offers itself as a Christian defense of capitalism.[51] At times Novak comes close to providing a biblical apologetic for the American economic system. For example, although he admits that "Judaism and Christianity do not *require* democratic capitalism," he goes on to assert that "without it they would be poorer and less free."[52] But this statement clearly stops short of suggesting any inevitable connection between Western religion and capitalism. Indeed, Novak acknowledges that capitalism has appeared in areas of the world not under the influence of Christianity and that Christianity has been strong in areas with noncapitalist economic systems. He also admits that Christianity is a universalistic religion that will likely outlast American capitalism or any other economic system.

In the bulk of his argument Novak retreats, perhaps unwittingly, to a purely secular defense of capitalism which suggests only that capitalism has been good for Christianity by undergirding American affluence and freedom. Going a step farther, he actually reconstructs the essence of Christianity so that it becomes a kind of watered-down version of affluence and freedom—which capitalism seems to have upheld. In specific, the Trinity becomes a vision of the importance of individualism over against the constraints of community; the Incarnation becomes a reality principle that warns us against the utopian hopes of socialism; the value of many biblical narratives is that they "envisage human life as a contest"; the doctrine of Original Sin serves mainly to convince us that no economic system can ever be free of some evil; the doctrine of the Two Kingdoms becomes an argument for laissez faire; and the principle of love in the Judeo-Christian tradition mainly suggests that we should respect the freedom of the individual. Novak's theological understanding can perhaps be questioned, but there is clearly a strong component of secular ideology here, perhaps considerably more than there is of biblical tradition.

If Novak has subtly confused civil religion with secular ideology, others have openly denounced civil religion in favor of secular arguments that to them seem more persuasive. For example, the Catholic bishops' pastoral letter on economic justice was roundly criticized by defenders of current economic policies. Writing in the *New York Times*, economist Leonard Silk took explicit issue with the bishops' religious arguments and suggested subjecting these arguments to "higher standards" of efficiency and self-interest.[53] Robert J. Samuelson, writing for the *Washington Post*, declared that the bishops were simply engaged in an act of "economic make-believe."[54] Echoing the same sentiment, columnist George F. Will charged the bishops with "child-like innocence," "vanity," "flight from complexity," and a "comic sense of moral bravery."[55]

Perhaps equally illustrative of the growing tendency for pragmatic, secular arguments to replace religious values as a basis of legitimation was an episode of competitive graffiti reported to have taken place in deeply religious, but economically strapped, Johnstown, Pennsylvania, during the recession of 1982. On one of the soot-covered stone walls outside the town appeared the familiar fundamentalist slogan, "Jesus Saves." To which another sign a few yards down the road replied, "Shinto Invests!"[56]

One of the most frequently voiced secular arguments that has been advanced to legitimate America links the nation with the value of freedom. The American system, simply put, is good and decent because it upholds individual freedom. Both democracy and capitalism are said to provide necessary conditions for the survival of freedom. This has been a particularly powerful argument because it focuses on what is popularly regarded as an extremely important value as well as a very common assumption about the nature of reality. Historian David Potter has written in his book *People of Plenty*:

> Americans have always been especially prone to regard all things as resulting from the free choice of a free will. Probably no people have so little determinism in their philosophy, and as individuals we have regarded our economic status, our matrimonial happiness, and even our eternal salvation as things of our own making.[57]

The belief in freedom also provides advantageous comparisons with other countries, and of course relates present conditions to some of the high ideals on which the nation was founded.

As a legitimating value, freedom is often combined with some version of American civil religion. In the conservative view, it is likely to be included as one of the biblical principles that the Founding Fathers built into the Constitution or as one of the conditions which the American system upholds so that religious people may worship as they choose without fear of intervention by any secular authority. In the liberal view, freedom may be colored by other religious connotations, such as freedom from fear or freedom from want, either of which may be interpreted as manifestations of the redemptive process outlined in the Christian gospel. Freedom is a concept sufficiently inclusive to be easily incorporated into these other worldviews.

Clearly the idea of freedom cannot in any way be regarded as a strictly secular ideology in conflict with religious myths of America. Tocqueville's observation a century and a half ago concerning the essential harmony between freedom and religion in the United States still seems apt: "The Americans combine the notions of Christianity and of liberty so intimately in their minds that it is impossible to make them conceive the one without the other."[58] The question does need to be considered, however, of how these different ideas are combined. At one end of the spectrum, freedom may be combined with religious values in a way that places it in an unambiguously secondary position. An example might be the belief that worship of God is the highest value to which humans should aspire and that a free society is simply a means which facilitates the attainment of that end. At the other extreme, freedom may itself occupy the position of an ultimate value. In this view, religion might simply function as a kind of story that illustrates the importance of freedom or a cultural resource that helps maintain a free society.

The fact that most Americans believe in God *and* in freedom makes any number of complex legitimating arguments possible. In many of these religion may play a substantial role, but there is also strong indication that freedom often receives greater prominence. In comparisons between religious values and freedom the latter receives wider valuation; freedom, rather than religious values, serves as the guiding principle which requires no additional justification or definition; and in public discourse freedom—devoid of religious connotations—appears as one of the more acceptable defenses of the American system. Certainly it has become more common for Americans to conceive of freedom apart from religion than Tocqueville believed it to be in the nineteenth century.

The keen sense of importance which Americans attach to the value of freedom was evident in a 1981 Gallup poll which asked a sample of the public to rate the importance of a series of values on a scale from one (low) to ten (high). In all, 59 percent of the respondents gave "freedom to choose" the highest possible rating; another 36 percent gave it a rating between six and nine. Not a single respondent rated it lower than five. The powerful attraction of freedom was also evident from the responses given to other values on the list. Freedom was rated extremely important by larger percentages than were any of the following: "following God's will," "living up to your full potential," "a sense of accomplishment," "having an interesting and enjoyable job," "helping people in need," "an exciting stimulating life," "a high income," or "social recognition."[59]

Freedom, held in such high regard by the American public, provides an excellent value with which to legitimate the American way of life. In 1983 a national survey asked, "Generally speaking, what are the things about this country that you are most proud of as an American?" All of the most frequently given responses concerned freedom: freedom in general (mentioned by 36 percent of the respondents), freedom of speech (9 percent), and other specific freedoms (17 percent).[60] Another survey in the same year asked, "What are you proudest of about America?" Sixty-nine percent said "freedom or liberty."[61]

In *Capitalism and Freedom*, a book that has become required reading in many colleges and universities, Milton Friedman, an economist and winner of The Nobel Prize, has spelled out the essential connection between freedom in general and the U.S. economic system in particular. Government, he argues, must be limited to prevent it from infringing on the individual's freedoms; that limitation is provided by the private sector. Free enterprise thus ensures "an effective protection of freedom of speech, of religion, and of thought."[62] Through the competitiveness of free enterprise the ability of "bad people" to do harm is effectively limited. Moreover, "the great advantage of the market . . . is that it permits wide diversity." As a result, one can choose freely from a great range of products, books, jobs, and life styles. The key to protecting our freedom, therefore, is to uphold the free operation of the market system.

George Gilder's *Wealth and Poverty*, which ranks among the top ten books subsidized by the U.S. Information Agency for foreign distribution, articulates additional connections between freedom and capitalism. One of the great virtues of U.S. capitalism, he suggests, is that it has been successful in creating wealth, and wealth "confers freedom" because it "does not have to be spent on any particular good."[63] Indeed, the capitalist's primary motivation is not to amass wealth for its own sake, but to enhance his own freedom and the freedom of others. Capitalists should, therefore, be seen not as greedy individuals but as benevolent altruists who take risks in order to give others the gift of freedom.

These are by no means new ideas in the history of Western capitalism.[64] But their force appears to remain strong. According to opinion polls, Americans believe that a close relationship does indeed exist between their freedoms and the free enterprise system. A 1976 poll, for example, posed the question, "Some people say that a free market economy is necessary for personal liberty and democracy and that if you take away the free market we will lose liberty. Other people say that the two aren't really related and we can be free and democratic in any kind of economy. Is a free market economy essential to freedom or not?" In all, 59 percent said they thought it was essential, only 17 percent thought it was not essential (the remaining 24 percent said they were unsure).[65]

These opinions receive frequent reinforcement in the press. "Capitalism equals freedom equals individual self-perfection," is a frequently articulated theme, says one columnist.[66] "Freedom, capitalism, and economic development go hand-in-hand" is another commonly expressed theme.[67] In this view, the best way to produce wealth, and therefore to give people greater freedom, is to let the free enterprise system follow its own dictates. As George Will suggests, "American capitalism is the most efficient anti-poverty machine the world has seen."[68] Or as another columnist summarizes, "Most of us do not see the economy as an end in itself but as a means to other desirable ends: greater prosperity, less suffering, more freedom."[69]

Other studies indicate that Americans compare their own country favorably with virtually every other country when it comes to freedom. A 1984 Gallup survey asked, "For each of the following countries please tell me if you think the people of that country now have a great deal of freedom, only some freedom, very little freedom, or no freedom at all?" Four out of every five respondents in the United States said they thought people in the United States had a "great deal" of freedom. By comparison, Canada was the only other country that Americans viewed about as favorably (78 percent thought people in Canada enjoyed a great deal of freedom). Only 60 percent gave this response with reference to the United Kingdom, and the responses for other advanced industrial democracies ranged even lower: France (44 percent), Japan (37 percent), West Germany (32 percent), and Italy (30 percent). For countries like the USSR, Poland, China, and Iran, only 1 or 2 percent thought there was a great deal of freedom.[70]

The moral capital to be gained from Americans' satisfaction with their freedom has not gone unrecognized by government leaders. As Hodding Carter III, State Department spokesman under the Carter administration, once observed: "The central desire of men and women is for enough freedom to allow for some development of themselves as individuals—free of the state and free of repression." In his view America's "chief weapon" in the battle for respect from other countries was the fact that we protected such freedoms.[71] A similar view was expressed by a high-ranking military official who remarked: "We are mankind's last real hope for freedom. Indeed, it is our democracy . . . which will make the real difference—which will determine whether mankind continues to live a meaningful life, albeit marked with unpleasantries—or whether mankind ceases to live any kind of life at all."[72]

As a legitimating myth, the relation between freedom and America includes two additional properties which, like civil religion historically, make it particularly powerful. One is the fact that freedom is relatively intangible and, therefore, not easily disconfirmed. Just as it is difficult to disprove that God holds America in special esteem, so it is hard to disconfirm the idea that American life maximizes freedom. Unlike most economic indicators, such as GNP or disposable income, freedom is largely in the eye of the beholder. Even opinion polls reveal only what people think about it, not the actual extent to which freedom exists. Americans can thus persuade themselves that their level of freedom is high, especially in comparison with obvious counterexamples (such as totalitarian systems), without pinning down too precisely what freedom means or how they know it is present.[73] The second property which makes freedom a strong legitimating myth is that it reinforces the belief that we are in charge of our own lives and, therefore, are morally accountable for what we do.

On an individual level, participation in the marketplace or in the democratic process can be understood as a kind of exchange relationship between the individual and society. The individual, in roles such as producer, consumer, or citizen, contributes labor, money, or votes to the society. In return, the individual receives wages, products, or political representation. But apart from these tangible returns, the individual also derives a certain sense of moral worth from having fulfilled some of his or her social obligations. Part of what convinces us that our political or economic system is worth supporting is this sense of moral worth.

Superficially, this view appears to contradict textbook descriptions, particularly of the economy, which emphasize purely rational, utilitarian relations between supply and demand or between the individual and society. But the founders of modern economic theory clearly recognized the moral character of the marketplace. Adam Smith, the great eighteenth-century spokesman for laissez-faire economics, was as interested in moral philosophy as in economic theory. To Smith, the freely functioning market was an instrument of human betterment, for as buyers and sellers pursued their private interests, an "invisible hand" guaranteed that prosperity would accrue to them all. What was good for the pin maker was, in Smith's view, good for England. After all, the pin maker contributed to the good of society by making pins. If he withdrew from the market, hoarded his pins, or took an extended vacation, he not only damaged his personal interests as a businessman but failed to keep the public trust as well. His moral obligation, therefore, was to participate in the market.

Such arguments may no longer carry the weight or conviction they once did, but neither have they altogether disappeared. Older notions of character and virtue may have given way to modern concepts of the self; yet people still need to think of themselves as moral individuals, and the market remains a primary arena in which to demonstrate moral responsibility. Public voices regularly call on consumers to conserve energy, buy American goods, regulate spending habits, and avoid hoarding and speculation—all for the good of the society. Even presidents and their advisers present economic policies in moral terms—often as the moral equivalent of a war against the enemies of a free society. In these and in other ways, behavior in the marketplace takes on moral significance. Because individuals' actions can affect the very well-being of society, they represent more than strict economic calculation; they are a way of discharging both civil and social responsibility.

That people do in fact derive a high degree of self-worth from their participation in the marketplace is again suggested by the results of opinion surveys. Contrary to the popular, perhaps only half-serious view that people work because they have to and would quit immediately if finances allowed, opinion surveys suggest that work is actually a major source of personal worth. According to one national study, five out of every six adults considered their work important to their basic sense of worth as a person; over half said it was very important. Valuing one's work, receiving satisfaction from work, and feeling productive were also strong correlates of self-esteem as measured by other scales.[74] Another national study found that more than 90 percent of the public believed their work "contributes to society" and felt "a sense of dedication" to their work.[75]

If people prefer to think of themselves as being morally upright, it then becomes natural for activities that promote this sense to evoke strong commitment and to appear legitimate. In this way, the legitimacy of the system which provides such activities is reinforced. The sense that one is morally upright can be sustained, however, only if some degree of freedom is also perceived.

What freedom to choose does, even if that freedom is voluntarily relinquished, is to make it possible for individuals to be held morally responsible for their actions. Responsibility for an action can be imputed to an individual only if he or she could have chosen to do otherwise. The person ordered by a prison guard to dig a ditch can scarcely take credit for having "decided" to dig. But if that person voluntarily chooses to engage in some task, the moral credit is clearly his.[76]

The fact that the market system is frequently associated with the idea of freedom is, therefore, doubly important. Not only does it link the economy to a virtually unquestioned value; it also undergirds the market's capacity to provide moral worth. If the market is to sustain loyalty by nurturing individuals' perceptions of themselves as good and decent persons, it must demonstrate to them that they are free to discharge their moral obligations by participating in the economy. Like religious conceptions of America which imbue citizenship with a sense of moral duty, the ideology of freedom, in this way, also supports a sense of moral commitment to the American system.

America "Number One"

But there is also another component to the secular legitimating ideology currently prevalent in America. As if freedom were not in itself enough—or perhaps because other more tangible reminders are necessary to convince us of our virtues as a people—a materialistic ideology is frequently advanced in defense of America's position in the world. This ideology is blatantly pragmatic, like much of the culture more generally. It asserts simply that America is right because it is rich. Undisguised by any references to historic values or cultural ideals, the pragmatic myth asserts that we are virtuous because we are so successful.

A more traditional version of the relation between American success and American virtue—one that ironically is reported to have been frequently voiced by President Nixon—is the idea expressed by the slogan, "America is great because America is good."[77] The pragmatic myth turns this slogan around: America is good because America is great.

It has been argued that this myth grew into prominence during the nineteenth century. As the nation became richer, pragmatic justifications apparently became more compelling, besides being more compatible with the prevailing worldview accompanying commerce and industry. Unlike the earlier civil religion of Puritan New England, the new ideology put greater stock in the intrinsic merits of success, and generally downplayed the ambivalence toward materialism that had been stressed in religious teachings. According to Robert Bellah, "The end result, which was not evident until the late decades of the 19th century and the early decades of the 20th, was a conception of the meaning of human life, summed up in the word 'success,' so narrow that Franklin and Jefferson seem giants of complexity in comparison."[78]

Whether this myth was in fact a nineteenth century development or not, the further rise of the United States to world prominence in the twentieth century seems to have given added plausibility to the greatness-is-goodness thesis. Emboldened not only by industrial expansion but by military victories in the Caribbean and in Europe early in this century, American leaders became more outspokenly proud of their own accomplishments and more firmly convinced of the moral superiority of American culture. The nation's expansion served as justification not only for its own way of life but also for a more active role in spreading its values to the rest of the world. Edward N. Hurley, head of the U.S. Shipping Board during World War I, for example, remarked with confidence: "Great power may be used either for good or for evil. If possessed by the United States we may be sure it will be used for good."[79] Others saw American economic and military power increasingly as a force that could not rightly be restrained in a world desperately seeking to learn from the nation's example.

Reinhold Niebuhr, writing during the heady, self-congratulatory years immediately following World War II when Americans happily took pride in the accomplishments of their economy and armed forces, underscored the growing tendency to legitimate ourselves on purely pragmatic grounds. "[I]t is natural," he observed, "for men and nations to assume that obvious success and obvious power are the proofs of an inner virtue." Yet in Niebuhr's view this was not only faulty logic but also a dangerous cultural tendency. As he went on to caution, "Our power will be used the more justly, if we recognize that our possession of it is not a proof of our virtue."[80] We should instead, he suggested, understand our power and plenty either as an accident of history or as an unmerited gift of God's grace. Few, it would seem, have heeded Niebuhr's admonition.

Writing in 1965, Elwyn A. Smith asked, "What are the components of the American myth?" His answer, though given critically, reflected what in his view was the common perception both among Americans themselves and among Europeans as they viewed America from a distance: "Abounding health, overwhelming competence, an inexhaustible supply of money, crushing military power, tremendous political strength—you name it, the Americans have it."[81]

Critics of this ideology have argued that it is rooted in individual self-interest of the kind that apparently became even more prominent during the "me-decade" of the 1970s, and that it is essentially self-serving, egoistic, and lacking in respect for others' rights, for justice and equality, or for the common good. They note a strong degree of self-interest in most national elections and argue that political candidates often stoop to legitimating their programs on strictly utilitarian, "pocketbook" arguments. Speaking with an obvious element of hyperbole to a conference at the University of Southern California shortly after the Reagan inaugural in 1981, Robert Bellah asserted, for example, that "the people who surround Ronald Reagan have no sensibility. For them there is literally nothing in this world except looking out for 'number one.' "[82]

Yet opinion polls consistently show that Americans' faith in their country depends on the state of the economy and their own position in the economy more than anything else. Implicitly pragmatic, the public expresses satisfaction with the country when the economy is strong, and withdraws that faith when the economy is weak. For example, in 1984, at the height of an economic upswing, 50 percent of those polled in a Gallup survey said they were satisfied with the way things were going in the United States; yet only five years previously, when the economy was at the bottom of a recession, only 12 percent gave this response.[83] The same polls also reveal that Americans' satisfaction with the country depends almost entirely on their own economic standing. Thus in 1984 the same Gallup survey found that professionals and business managers were overwhelmingly favorable toward the country, whereas manual workers were mostly dissatisfied. Similarly, persons with incomes of $40,000 or more were twice as likely to express satisfaction than were persons with incomes of less than $10,000.

If anything, then, the two versions of American civil religion—one conservative, one liberal—have, by virtue of their very tendency to dispute one another, become less capable of providing the broad, consensual underpinnings of societal legitimation that have usually been associated with the idea of civil religion. This is not to say that religious beliefs have no place in the repertoire of America's legitimating myths. For many Americans, the nation's effectiveness in promoting religious commitment remains one of the surest signs of its greatness and essential goodness. For many others, even secularized notions of freedom, success, and other high principles, such as equality and democracy, may have some vague understanding of Jewish and Christian theology as their ultimate reference point. But one can scarcely understand the legitimating myths of a society so deeply secular as the United States by looking only at specifically religious language. Substantial segments of the population and of its most vocal leadership, as the foregoing has shown, dispute the conservative vision of America, while equally substantial sectors challenge the vision presented by religious liberals. Certainly neither vision of what America is and should be enjoys the kind of de facto legitimation that comes with simply being taken for granted. Instead, secular mythologies seem to be gaining a more powerful position, if only by virtue of being so widely and implicitly assumed in public discourse. Freedom to choose and the expectation of material success that comes with thinking of America as "Number One" probably undergird patterns of social behavior as well as decisions about public priorities at a deep level simply because they are so much a part of the "American way of life" that we often fail to question them. And yet, these myths of legitimation also rest on precarious foundations.

CHAPTER 11

From Civil Religion to Technological Legitimacy

AMERICA'S secular legitimating myths, not to mention the ethical problems that Niebuhr, Bellah, and others point to, present difficulties because they depend on a certain degree of supremacy in the world. The pragmatic "rich-is-right" ideology, in particular, works only if the United States can continue to dramatize its wealth and power relative to all other nations in the world community. The capacity to maintain that degree of supremacy, though stronger in some years than in others, has by all indications eroded in the decades since World War II. And with this erosion have arisen questions about the very basis of America's secular legitimating myths. To gain a more complete understanding of religion's place in the larger repertoire of such myths, we must consider the extent of this questioning and the kinds of alternative myths that may be gaining increasing acceptance.

It is difficult now to recall fully the flush of confidence that dominated American culture in the years immediately following the nation's victory in World War II.[1] Despite the more serious counsels of "sober serenity" (discussed in Chapter 3), periodical literature in those years sometimes projected a degree of optimism which would seem unwarranted only a decade or two later. A 1948 editorial on "America's Greatness" in *Christian Century*, for example, spoke unabashedly of America's glory: "We are a nation that boasts of bigness. We have the biggest army and navy, the biggest skyscrapers, the biggest harvests . . . even the biggest mountains and waterfalls and sunsets." The editorial went on to venture a glimpse of the nation's future:

> It can be more than a Great Power; it can be the Greatest Power. Its fleets can command the seven seas, and its airforces can impose the American will on every continent. It can come closer to setting up a world empire, in the Roman sense, . . . than has any other nation in all of history. Even Russia cannot stop us—not while we have sole possession of the atom bomb.[2]

Being a "Christian" editorial, the article did warn that material greatness should not be allowed to overshadow the nation's sense of spiritual purpose. But nowhere was there the kind of doubt that was to appear in the coming decades.

Isolationism and Mild Euphoria

Less than a half century later, observers of America's "greatness" strike a rather different note. Gone is the confidence that the United States can shape the world in its own design. Gone too is the certainty that it can achieve everything it desires even within its own borders. And underneath these uncertainties questions have begun to be raised about the myths with which U.S. hegemony in the world has been legitimated. As one of the leading foreign policy teams concluded in a 1983 article in *World Politics*, "the country has undergone such a substantial change—from the world's preeminent superpower to one whose status has now been challenged militarily, politically, and economically—that breakdowns have occurred in the underlying value consensuses on which its unity had rested."[3]

Other writers note a sense of pessimism and doubt about the nature of American capitalism and its relation to the American system of government. Michael Novak points out that "a shrewd observer cannot fail to note a relatively low morale among business executives, workers, and publicists." Democratic capitalism, he fears, "seems to have lost its spirit."[4] *Business Week* editors in 1984 appeared to agree with Novak, noting in a gloomy cover story that in the 1950s the United States "could outproduce anybody," whereas now "the rest of the world has caught up in its ability to produce goods."[5]

Among the concerns that have been raised are basic questions about the viability of the U.S. free market and whether it will be able to compete effectively in the world economy without greater intervention by the state. Political scientist Robert S. Walters, for example, notes that "America's altered position in the global economy and increasing doubts in key industries regarding the market mechanism are raising anew serious questions about the proper role of the state in the economy."[6] Jürgen Habermas goes further, suggesting that the complexities of the debate over the proper relation of the state to the free market constitute a major "crisis of legitimation."[7] And Bellah suggests, perhaps with undue cynicism, that Americans in particular seem to be engaged in "a last desperate attempt to believe that unfettered free enterprise can save us."[8]

Stanley Hoffman, a political scientist at Harvard University, has captured the mood of the 1980s so clearly that a portion of his description seems worth quoting at length. According to Hoffman, the prevailing view in the United States of its place in the world represents a major departure from the views that have historically guided our sense of destiny and identity.

> [T]his new mood fits neither of the two archetypes of American attitudes toward the outside world that prevailed in the past: the High Noon sheriff who restores order so that the good people can do their business unharmed by evil ones, and the missionary who is out to cure bodies and souls among the miserable and suffering. What is missing today are the sheriff's willingness to step in and shoot it out, and the missionary impulse itself. All that is left of both are self-righteousness and a sense of moral and material superiority. . . . The militancy of the two archetypes has given way to the complacency of happy self-contemplation. The mood is one of mild euphoria, a sort of holiday during which people want to forget about the hectic chores and the heavy headaches of ordinary days, and merely relax and enjoy themselves.[9]

Hoffman suggests that this mood was especially evident at the 1984 Olympic Games in Los Angeles, where we were temporarily able to forget about the problems of the world and simply focus on ourselves and our successes.

What Hoffman persuasively argues is that Americans have (perhaps for the better) lost faith in their ability to solve the world's problems. The result has not been simply an upsurge of pessimism. It has rather been a new kind of isolationism, not the confident isolationism of the nineteenth century, but a "head-in-the-sand" isolationism that revels in our own successes while failing to face up to the new complexities of the world system. This attitude allows the nation to maintain some semblance of pride in itself, but creates a lack of concern, and even a naive form of nationalism, that greatly damages our relations with the rest of the world. The result, he suggests, is a "growing resentment at America's apparent indifference to misery and injustice, and at its condescending conviction that what is good for America will trickle down and be good, ultimately, for others." Even if America succeeds in maintaining its own standard of living, therefore, it is likely to fail at maintaining the credibility of its myth about itself in the eyes of the rest of the world. For "even where the natives are friendly, or a bit envious of America's return to growth and to optimism, they are offended by the cosmic ethnocentricism that seems to come with success."[10]

Hegemony on a Slippery Slope

It is not surprising that observers of American culture should note a sense of doubt about its legitimating beliefs. The objective position of the United States in the world has in fact changed markedly over the past quarter century. This change has been particularly evident in foreign policy. From the end of World War II until about 1968 the prevailing view in U.S. foreign policy was one of optimism about the nation's capacity to build a new world order and to "contain," if not "roll back," the forces of communism. That image came to a relatively abrupt end with the inability to bring the Vietnam War to a successful conclusion.[11] As a result, U.S. foreign policy through the decade of the 1970s was characterized by a renewed sense of the desirability of peaceful coexistence with the Soviet Union, with a greater interest in arms control talks, and with lingering unease about entering into foreign military commitments. Although that decade was imbued with some degree of optimism that detente and limited commitments could guarantee the success of American interests, these hopes soon ran up against events that cast American policy in an even less certain framework. Beginning with the loss of Iran as a trusted ally in the Middle East, followed by the hostage crisis, Soviet intervention in Afghanistan, and fears of creeping socialism in Latin America, the United States' position in world affairs steadily deteriorated through the early years of the 1980s, leading to a resurgence of efforts by conservatives to rebuild the defense budget and re-establish American military supremacy.[12]

As late as 1983, the number of Americans who considered the military defense system of the United States to be weaker than that of Russia outnumbered those who felt it enjoyed superiority by a margin of two to one.[13] Defense Department officials readily reinforced these fears, showing that Soviet outlays for military purposes had risen dramatically compared to those of the United States. According to their figures, Soviet military expenditures in 1960 were only three-quarters those of the United States, but by 1970 the Soviets had achieved parity, and by 1980 were spending approximately 50 percent more than the United States.[14]

Economic indicators also pointed to a period of sustained decline between the 1950s and 1980s, at least in America's position relative to other leaders in the world economy. Gross domestic product per capita in West Germany rose between 1960 and 1980 by 16 percentage points relative to that in the United States; in France, by 23 percentage points; and in Japan, by 38 percentage points.[15] In 1960 the United States produced 35 percent of the world's energy; by 1980 this proportion had declined to 25 percent. Over the same period, the United States' net merchandise trade balance slipped from $4.9 billion to a deficit of $25.3 billion.[16] Writing in the *Washington Post* shortly after the 1984 election, a time when many indicators actually pointed toward economic prosperity, Henry Kissinger, former national security advisor, summed up the situation as follows:

> When America ended its isolation after World War II, an atomic monopoly gave America a margin of security unprecedented in history. As late as 1950 the United States produced 52 percent of all the world's goods and services. America by itself represented the global balance of power. American alliances were in effect unilateral guarantees; recognized problems could be overwhelmed with resources.
>
> By the late '60s these conditions were disappearing. Nuclear parity was upon us. As Europe and Japan recovered and other nations industrialized, America's percentage of the world's gross national product was declining. By 1970 we produced about 30 percent of the world's goods and services; today the figure is around 22 percent.[17]

The changing position of the United States has also been reflected in its growing financial dependence on the world economy. Over the past two decades an increasing share of capital investment in the United States has come from foreign sources. In 1960 foreign direct investment in the United States amounted to only $6.9 billion; by 1980 this figure had grown to $68.4 billion—a nearly tenfold increase.[18] At the same time, domestic savings in the United States failed to keep up with the rate of domestic savings in most other industrialized countries. For example, in 1982 the savings rate in the United States was only 6 percent, compared with 11 percent in Canada, 14 percent in West Germany, and 22 percent in Japan.[19]

Another indication of the nation's rising dependence on the world economy is the change in its exports and imports. As recently as 1970, only 9.3 percent of American production was exported, whereas by 1980 this figure had increased to 19 percent. Similarly, in 1970, only 9.3 percent of the goods used in America were imported, whereas by 1980 this figure had increased to 22 percent.[20] Economist Robert Reich estimates that as of 1980, more than 70 percent of all the goods produced in the United States had to compete with foreign-made goods, up from only 8 percent in the early 1960s.[21] Reich also points to a number of areas in which this competition appears to be seriously eroding America's commercial advantage: declining shares of U.S. products in the world market in basic industries such as automobiles, industrial machinery, agricultural machinery, and metal-working machinery; noncompetitive labor rates; declining advantages in productive efficiency; and increasing use by foreign competitors of standardized production lines, the key to America's competitive edge until recently.

America's declining position in world affairs also appears to have registered itself in world opinion. According to recent polls, even in countries that remain the United States' closest allies, public opinion is deeply divided. Gallup surveys in 1982, for example, showed that in the United Kingdom 46 percent of those polled held a favorable opinion of the United States, while 44 percent expressed an unfavorable opinion; in France, the ratio was 55 percent favorable to 32 percent unfavorable; in West Germany, 73 percent favorable to 24 percent unfavorable; in Italy, 63 percent favorable to 21 percent unfavorable; and in Belgium, 49 percent favorable to 22 percent unfavorable.[22] The same series of surveys asked "How much confidence do you have in the U.S. to deal wisely with world problems?" No more than a small minority in any of the countries said they had a great deal of confidence: 6 percent in the United Kingdom, 4 percent in France, 16 percent in West Germany, 17 percent in Italy, and 7 percent in Belgium.

Whether America's declining world position has begun to erode confidence among its own citizens seems to be more of an open question. Some opinion polls indicate that the American people still overwhelmingly think highly of their country. A Roper poll in 1981, for example, asked, "Earlier on in American history, many people around the world thought the United States was the very best place in the world to live. Do you think it still is, or not?" Ninety percent thought it was; only 8 percent thought it was not. The same survey also asked, "Do you think the United States has a special role to play in the world today, or is it pretty much like other countries?" Eighty-one percent thought it had a special role; only 14 percent thought it was like other countries.[23]

Other polls, depending on the sample and the question asked, have shown more qualified confidence in the American system. In a 1982 national sample of high school seniors, 66 percent agreed with the statement, "Despite its many faults, our system of doing things is still the best in the world"—meaning that a sizable minority either disagreed or were unsure.[24] A 1983 Roper poll of a sample of the adult U.S. population found that only a bare majority (52 percent) were "generally optimistic" about "our system of government and how well it works," while 21 percent said they were "generally pessimistic" and 27 percent said they were uncertain. Compared with a similar poll conducted in 1977, these figures represented a 7 percentage point increase in pessimism and a corresponding decline in optimism. The 1983 survey also asked people's opinions about "the soundness of our economic system over the long run." Again, only about half the public expressed optimism (49 percent), while 23 percent expressed pessimism, and 28 percent indicated uncertainty.[25]

Plausibility in Question

In addition to the undercurrent of doubt expressed in such global assessments, more specific tenets of America's legitimating myth also appear to manifest signs of at least potential erosion. This is especially true of the pragmatic myth which legitimates America on the basis of its economic and military successes. As the ability to achieve these successes has eroded, doubts have inevitably arisen about the efficacy of our way of life.

Japan's success as an economic competitor has been particularly vexing. Despite the fact that many aspects of Japan's success remain unexplained, one consequence of this success has been an apparent undermining of the pride that has traditionally been associated with America's work ethic.[26] At a deeper level, questions have also arisen about the relations between the self-interest on which the American system is based and the common good. In Tocqueville's formulation self-interest was effective in the American case only because it was, as he put it, "rightly understood"—that is, tempered by moral virtues that channeled self-interest toward the service of the common good.[27] Or, as Bellah has suggested, market relations operate effectively only within the framework of a "moral ecology" that binds us to the common good and prevents the unfettered pursuit of self-interest.[28] The question now is whether that moral ecology still exists or whether self-interest has become purely self-serving.

On one side of the issue, apologists like Novak argue that American self-interest is indeed tempered by self-restraint, altruism, philanthropic concerns, and an adherence to moral virtue. "American economic elites," he asserts, "have been remarkable in the world for their involvement in affairs of citizenship and their involvement in affairs of morals and of culture."[29] On the other side, critics like Bellah fail to take comfort in such generalizations, arguing instead that the moral ecology which made the American system work historically has begun to break down. "Both romantic cultural particularism and radical secular individualism," Bellah says, "have contributed to this end."[30] Cultural particularism has, as in the case of the contending versions of American civil religion, been so fraught with sectarianism that it has been unable to inform public debate, especially on matters involving the state. And radical individualism has evolved into a consumerist mentality which manifests little concern for the rights of others or for higher standards of justice and equality.

Chiding Americans for abandoning the altruistic virtues which should normally temper self-interested pursuits, the columnist Meg Greenfield has charged that many of the affluent simply hang a "Do Not Disturb" sign on their wealth. Indeed, rather than justifying affluence by showing kindness to the poor, it has become commonplace, she believes, to use the example of the poor as an excuse for clinging ever more tightly to our possessions:

> *Our* well-being, not that of the poor, becomes the moral imperative. Since the days when our mothers told us to think of the starving Indians and eat our spinach, through the years of the four-course charity banquet (have a chocolate-covered kiwi for the poor), to this moment of nouveau trickle-down economics, we have been geniuses at using the plight of the poor as an excuse for having something else to eat—or drink or drive or wear or perhaps invest at 11¾ percent.[31]

Novak's suggestion that self-interest in the United States continues to be tempered by a strong altruistic orientation gains support, perhaps, from such visible manifestations of altruism as the annual United Fund drive, emergency relief aid for Bangladesh or Ethiopia, media events such as "Live Aid" and "Hands Across America," and the involvement of business elites in patronizing the arts. Yet within the culture at large both popular opinion and evidence of other kinds point to a decline in charitable activities. When asked in a 1981 Roper survey if people are less willing now than 25 years ago to help their neighbors, 72 percent of those sampled said "yes." Sixty-one percent said people are also less willing to help their elderly parents, and 58 percent said there was less willingness to volunteer to help with youth activities.[32]

Other studies indicate that a majority of the public is cynical about the altruistic motives of business and government leaders, and suggest that the public's perceptions of unbridled, calculating self-interest among these leaders and their institutions has risen to a high level over the past several decades. A Roper poll found that 76 percent of those sampled thought business executives in large corporations tended to act mostly in their own self-interest, while only 16 percent thought these executives acted more in the public interest. The same survey showed that 50 percent of the public regarded "selfishness, people not thinking of others" as one of the major causes of problems facing the United States. This was in fact the highest percentage for any of the causes of problems asked about except for "a letdown in moral values."[33]

As for trends in these attitudes, Harris surveys have shown relatively steady increases in cynicism toward those in power as well as more general feelings of alienation. In 1971, for example, 33 percent of the public agreed that "most people with power try to take advantage of people like yourself"; by 1983 this figure had risen to 65 percent. In 1966, only 45 percent of the public felt that "the rich get richer and the poor get poorer," whereas by 1983 this proportion was 79 percent. Conversely, in 1966, 55 percent of the public expressed a great deal of confidence in the country's "major companies," but by 1982 this figure had dropped to a mere 18 percent. Overall, Harris's composite "alienation index" indicated that the proportion of Americans who felt alienated from centers of power and wealth increased from 29 percent in 1966 to 40 percent in 1971, to 57 percent in 1976, to 62 percent in 1982.[34]

Apart from such trends in public opinion, the legitimacy of any system thought to be based on the unbridled pursuit of self-interest is at best likely to be precarious within the context of American culture. Both in liberal democratic political theory and in the biblical tradition self-interest has always been regarded with considerable ambivalence. Despite the divisions evident in American civil religion, religious leaders (especially on the left) continue to mount criticisms of the utilitarian ethos on which some defenders of the American way rest their claims. As social ethicists Prentiss Pemberton and Daniel Finn observe:

> Christianity has always denounced any attempt to base social organization on self-interest alone. Behind this stance is an appreciation of the power of human sinfulness. In its critique of every social and economic system, Christian ethics points out the way those persons with power . . . can subvert the usual checks and balances, can gain their own ends, and can legitimate this by showing how "just" it is since they are not breaking any laws.[35]

The biblical tradition, although at many times bent to support utilitarianism, has provided an alternative set of values against which to judge actions based on self-interest. Pemberton and Finn point out that the biblical tradition tends to associate values with collectivities which have a higher authority than that given to personal preferences. It calls for a public morality that transcends individual inclinations, and upholds such values as human dignity, social justice, and the rights of future generations over against purely market-dictated concerns for efficiency. It also persistently raises questions about the uses to which property is put, as well as the inevitable temptations of greed, both of which challenge the materialistic basis on which market decisions are made.

Put differently, the weakness of the success ethic as a legitimating creed is that it offers nothing transcending concrete achievements. Legitimacy comes to rest on the pragmatically evaluated performance of government policies. Faced with any time of collective trial or need for the public to make sacrifices, serious questions about the legitimacy of the policies demanded would inevitably arise. Under these circumstances, the success ethic would either have to be supplemented with other values or else new seekers of power would have to convince the public to accept their proposals on purely self-interested grounds.

Freedom Revised

In comparison with the utilitarian myth, arguments linking the American system with freedom have probably continued to enjoy much greater vitality. These arguments are neither so purely materialistic nor are they as subject to disconfirmation by the eroding position of the United States in world affairs. As long as it can be shown, if only by negative comparison, that religious freedoms are greater in the United States than in many other countries, that the right to vote is being upheld, and that individual freedoms of life style, speech, career, and personal expression are protected, then the idea of freedom continues to legitimate the American system. Yet there are also subtle ways in which the meaning of freedom has changed.

The nineteenth-century legacy of the word "freedom" in the American context closely associates it with freedom of opportunity and, in even more specific terms, with upward mobility. Freedom meant an absence of caste, aristocracy, or government restrictions which might have prevented the individual from pulling himself up by his own bootstraps. It meant the possibility of achieving the legendary climb from rags to riches. Looking back on the 1880s from the vantage point of the 1980s, Oscar Handlin could assert:

> In practical terms opportunity meant social mobility, the chance for individuals to rise uninhibited by the shackles of status. Some began life with advantages others lacked—inherited wealth, favored family connections, attractive appearance. At the other extreme, poverty, broken families, and isolation handicapped others. But neither advantages nor handicaps were decisive. Many a scion, born into a wealthy home, saw a fortune slip away. Many a lad from the slums advanced to a place of distinction in business or the professions.[36]

The number who actually advanced to "a place of distinction" was small even then. But at least the myth of freedom as possibility for upward mobility served as a plausible legitimating argument.

Closely associated with that meaning of freedom was the image of America as a land of freedom for the immigrant. For the millions of immigrants who streamed through Ellis Island to establish residence in the

United States, and perhaps equally for those who already claimed the United States as their native land, America was good and decent and just because it saved these millions from lives of tyranny and impoverishment.

For some, this image still continues to serve as part of the legitimating myth of America. Novak, for example, takes pride in the fact that "the sound of incoming feet is still heard on our shores," and suggests that "for millions, the United States is still the land of opportunity."[37]

But neither the image of freedom as upward mobility nor the vision of America as a land of freedom for immigrants remains as clear as it once was. Handlin goes on to decry the ways in which government has had to intervene to help minority groups achieve any kind of upward mobility. A "vast deterioration" has occurred, he believes, in the possibility of moving up in the American system strictly on the basis of one's own hard work and personal skills. Similarly, Robert Lekachman, author of *Greed is Not Enough: Reaganomics*, counters Novak, pointing out that "by comparison with the American past, there is much less opportunity than there used to be."[38] Nor has it been possible to sustain the myth of an open door for immigrants in view of the restrictive legislation that has virtually cut off immigration since the 1920s, and even less so when only scattered church groups, whose leaders face constant legal intimidation, seem willing to grant political refugees asylum from terrorism and death squads.

Opinion polls suggest that the image of America as a land of opportunity is by no means dead, but these studies also reveal that a large minority of Americans doubts its validity, and that many others believe it is less applicable now than it was in the past. In 1981 a CBS poll asked respondents, "Do you think it's possible nowadays for someone in this country to start out poor, and become rich by working hard?" Sixty-nine percent thought it was possible, compared with only 29 percent who thought it was not. A similar question in a 1982 ABC poll asked, "Is it true that if you work hard, eventually you will get ahead?" Fifty-eight percent said it was; 42 percent said it was not. These responses perhaps demonstrate that a belief in the possibility that at least some people can experience upward mobility is by no means dead. But other polls reveal a widespread impression that these opportunities are becoming more limited. For example, a 1981 Roper poll posed the question, "Compared to twenty-five years ago in this country, do you think it is easier or harder for an individual to get ahead financially?" Only 19 percent said "easier"; 74 percent said "harder."[39]

Americans may continue to reflect nostalgically about the time when immigrant masses "yearning to be free" were welcomed to this country. But if polls are to be believed, contemporary attitudes deny the validity of this image too. When asked in 1982 whether they would like to see the number of immigrants allowed to enter the country decreased or increased, a national sample of the American public overwhelmingly said "decreased": 66 percent versus 4 percent. The same survey found that recent immigrants were much more likely to be perceived as a bad influence on the country than as a good influence. For example, by a margin of 59 percent to 9 percent Cubans were perceived as a bad influence; Puerto Ricans were similarly perceived by a margin of 43 percent to 17 percent; Haitians, by a margin of 39 percent to 10 percent; and Vietnamese, by a margin of 38 percent to 20 percent.[40] Had polls been conducted a century ago about Irish or Italian immigrants, much the same kinds of prejudice would likely have been registered. Nevertheless, such attitudes today do little to augment the image of America as a land of freedom.

Many observers consider that these traditional images of freedom are being replaced by a new connotation which equates freedom chiefly with "freedom of choice." In a sense, the modern supermarket with its myriad consumer products from which to choose has come to be the symbol of freedom, perhaps even more so than the traditional flag-waving Fourth of July parade. Freedom means the opportunity to choose from a variety of products, to select a full complement of goods that meet our individual needs and desires. It means having the financial resources with which to purchase any gadget of seeming use in our quest for personal development and self-expression.

But this meaning of freedom comes perilously close to being dependent, like the utilitarian myth, on the success of the economy in producing ever more gadgets and an ample income with which to purchase these gadgets. In broader terms, it also appears to be dangerously narrow, selfish, and materialistic.[41] As one observer remarks, "Too often when we Americans speak of freedom, we sound as if freedom meant having access to the hedonism of the consumer market, or as if freedom were synonymous with license."[42]

While the concept of freedom may still suggest a cherished ideal, therefore, its meaning may have become compromised by the materialistic ethos of American success to the point that it no longer associates the nation with an untarnished virtue. Especially in countries where the standard of living is only a fraction of that in the United States, America's freedom may seem less than worthy because of the excesses sanctioned in its name. Some years ago, in one of his poems about America, Robinson Jeffers warned:

> The states of the next age will no doubt remember you,
> and edge their love of freedom with contempt of
> luxury.[43]

The problem Americans face in attempting to legitimate their system strictly on the basis of freedom does not appear, as European observers have often supposed, to be one of reconciling freedom with increasingly complex social institutions, such as the bureaucratic state. Habermas's concern for the conflict between free-market ideology and state intervention in the economy, for example, seems not to be shared by many at the popular level. Debate surfaces with some degree of regularity about the extent and desirability of state intervention. But this debate seldom acknowledges any conflict between the expansion of the interventionist state and a basic commitment to freedom in politics, economics, or other spheres. Indeed, state intervention is often portrayed as a legitimate means of advancing free enterprise and free choice.

The problem is rather one of legitimating particular collective choices on the basis of freedom alone. In the extreme, the value of freedom functions to define the outer limits of acceptable social practice, thus legitimating defense budgets to protect the society from conquest by totalitarian regimes and establishing legal guarantees against coercive infringements of basic civil rights. But within the sphere defined by the absence of such extreme violations, the value of freedom says virtually nothing about the kinds of choices that should be made or the criteria for arriving at collective decisions.

The moral imperative defined by the value of freedom is to make a choice. But freedom is by and large neutral as to what that choice should be. As a result, two kinds of cultural tendencies are reinforced. One is an extreme relativism which places freedom itself on such a high pedestal that no other value considerations can be entertained. By this logic, the act of choosing—or being in a position of detachment so that one can choose—becomes valued more highly than the substance of the choice itself. The other tendency is for norms of expediency or material enhancement, in the absence of any explicit consideration of values, to become the determining principles of social life. Either alternative can militate against public discourse about socially transcendent values, particularly discourse aimed at arriving at a collective consensus which might necessitate some sacrifice of individual choices, and leads easily to the kind of hedonism against which Jeffers and others have repeatedly warned.

Jeremiads and the Apocalypse

The relative decline of America and its changing myths of legitimacy have also figured prominently in the restructuring of its civil religion. The bifurcation that has taken place between conservative and liberal interpretations of American civil religion has at once been propelled and contained by these broader developments. Two effects stand out in particular.

The first has been a tendency for the two versions of American civil religion to respond differently to the perception of the nation's decline. The conservative response has been typical of the pronouncements of religious leaders during previous times of national trial. It translates indicators of the nation's decline into symptoms of evil which are heaping God's wrath on America—or at least preventing the nation from realizing the fullness of God's rewards. An episode such as the hostage crisis in Iran, for example, evokes jeremiads about the nation's moral decline, the lack of godly commitment among its leaders, and liberals' blindness to such evils as homosexuality and abortion. Such arguments have often been voiced by evangelists and revivalists to inspire greater commitment to religion at a personal level. In recent years they have also played a role in legitimating collective action on the part of conservative political coalitions such as the New Right. In his introduction to Richard Viguerie's book *The New Right: We're Ready to Lead*, Jerry Falwell, for example, stated clearly his conviction that America was in decline: "At this present hour, there can be no questioning the retrogression of America's stability as a free and healthy nation." The problem, he went on to say, was equally clear: "Americans have literally stood by and watched as godless, spineless leaders have brought our nation floundering to the brink of death."[44]

The liberal response to America's changing world position has generally taken this change as a sign of the need for a new realism in economic and military policy. If America was unable to have its way in Vietnam, for example, the problem was not one of moral turpitude but simply an outcome which vindicated the liberal view that it had no right to be there in the first place. No longer able to shoot it out with the bad guys, to use Hoffman's metaphor, America should work through diplomacy and negotiation for a lasting peace. Rather than try to reassert its economic or military superiority, it should take a more modest place in the community of nations, engaging in compromise in the broader interests of humanity. Indeed, the danger most clearly envisioned is that conservative fanatics, perceiving America's decline, will attempt to rebound through an aggressive arms race that could lead the world directly into the apocalypse.

The differing responses to America's decline have in one sense, then, heightened the division between conservative and liberal interpretations of American civil religion. Reacting to a perception of real or impending crisis, both sides have intensified their pleas for a redirection of American values. Yet at the same time, other features of American culture have worked to prevent this division from turning into an even more extreme type of conflict.

The creedal dogma which champions freedom of choice has probably played a dampening role in the division between the two versions of American civil religion. Although both sides have sought to identify themselves as the true proponents of freedom, the broader effect of this value has probably been to deter either side from gaining broader support for its claims in the public sphere. The reason is that the ethos of choice, especially radically relativized choice, turns moral discourse into a mere discussion of personal preferences. Not only is the legitimating capacity of each side weakened by the explicit delegitimating counterclaims of the other, but both sides are also weakened by having their claims treated—by many public leaders and much of the media—as nothing more than personal taste.

Coupled with the hedonistic success ethic, radical freedom of choice further erodes the mobilizing potential of either version of American civil religion by championing privacy in opposition to public involvement. The difficulty with either kind of civil religion is that it demands sacrifices: in the form of public restraints on private morality, or as demands on personal time and resources to become involved in causes of peace and justice. Neither is likely to mobilize a high degree of commitment—as did, for example, a Timothy Dwight or Abraham Lincoln—because the demands of privacy make stronger claims. As Richard Neuhaus observes in reviewing a number of public controversies, "Much of the course of public reasoning in America can be read from the fact that our highest appeal is no longer to Providence but to privacy."[45]

Technology as Myth

If many of the traditional legitimating myths have begun to show some signs of erosion, either from a declining infrastructure or from subtle shifts in their meaning, there is, nevertheless, a new myth to which many give unquestioned allegiance—technology. Though scarcely a religion, it presents itself with religious force, combining seemingly inevitable developments in the social infrastructure with belief in the unassailable sanctity of these developments.

Technology is particularly well qualified to serve as a basis for legitimating myths. Rather than being a mere philosophy or free-floating ideology that has to be maintained primarily by the powers of belief and persuasion, it is a vast institution. Even to call it an institution is somewhat misleading, because it is generally not recognized as such, but is regarded simply as a basic feature of modern life. Much like the medieval church, or in a later period, the all-pervasive "market," it organizes and influences virtually every aspect of society. It commands vast resources, is a major concern of the modern state, affects the power of nations in the international arena, and generates its own culture.

Peter Berger has observed that a good way of legitimating something is to make it seem so natural, so much a part of the taken-for-granted "nature of things," that it is never questioned.[46] In short, achieve legitimation through reification. This has been a common way of legitimating social arrangements in the past. Karl Polanyi has shown how the "marketplace," for example, became reified in the nineteenth century.[47] Its specific historical manifestation was equated with the entire generic phenomenon of "economy." Thus, since all societies had had economies, it was argued that the market system must be inevitable.

In a similar fashion, a tendency now exists for technology in its peculiar twentieth-century manifestation to be confused with technology as a broader generic phenomenon. In the latter sense of the word, technology can be defined as "that form of cultural activity devoted to the production or transformation of material objects, or the creation of procedural systems, in order to expand the realm of practical human possibility."[48] But that sense, which can be applied equally to the wheel or the space program, is often equated with semiconductors and lasers and all that is new in American technology.[49] Consequently, it seems only natural that we should have technology and that we should attach great importance to its development. Technology becomes legitimate—something so much a part of the nature of things that we do not question it. To extend this legitimacy to the nation, or to its political and economic system, all that has to be done is to show that the nation does a decent job of fostering technology. Like legitimating a regime as "defender of the faith," America gains legitimacy from technology by proving itself a worthy supporter of what must by all indications be sacred.

In the past, dominant modes of societal legitimation have never existed simply as belief systems. They have consisted of vast networks of organizations, resources, and power relations. The doctrine of religious universalism in the Middle Ages, for example, made sense when it was used to legitimate dynastic claims and great monarchies because it was firmly grounded in the very fiber of community life, from the rituals governing peasant production, to the status hierarchies imposed on the production of culture. The marketing mind of the nineteenth century may have been compelling, if Polanyi's thesis is correct, by virtue of the subtle fallacy of logic on which it was based. But it was also rooted in trading empires and foreign relations and the very system of creating wealth. So it is today with technology.

Scientific technology is increasingly produced, diffused, and administered through complex networks of organizations that function as technical systems. These webs of interlocking organizations, oriented toward such technical problems as cancer research or chemical warfare, employ thousands of persons with advanced technical educations, consume millions of dollars of public and private funds, and necessarily involve the state in a close alliance with industry and universities.[50] As such, they provide a natural bridge between perceptions of technology and images of the modern state. Science historian Langdon Winner writes, "It is no surprise . . . that technical systems of various kinds are deeply interwoven in the conditions of modern politics. The physical arrangements of industrial production, warfare, communications, and the like have fundamentally changed the exercise of power and the experience of citizenship."[51]

For advanced industrial societies, technology is of course increasingly recognized as a key determinant of their position in the world economy. Leaders of these countries, meeting for summit talks in Versailles in 1982, for example, agreed on the necessity of greater expenditures for science and technology for the welfare of all industrialized nations.[52] In 1984 alone France mounted a massive program to remain competitive in such potentially lucrative fields as biotechnology and telecommunications; Britain launched a program to increase its labor force's capacity "to cope with, and use effectively, the new technologies which pervade all branches of economic activity"; Quebec announced a major new technological thrust that would increase levels of funding for programs in engineering; and Japan declared as official government policy its intention of shifting from a "trade-oriented state" to a "technology-oriented state."[53]

Responding to these initiatives, educators in Europe and Japan, as well as in the United States, have increasingly called for a renewed emphasis on teaching science and technology, often at the expense of programs in the humanities and at the cost of introducing a new element of utilitarianism into the educational system as a whole.[54] What distinguishes these proposals is not their interest in science as such, but the new sense of practical economic urgency with which they are advanced. Kenneth Prewitt of the Social Science Research Council has observed, "In an earlier era, discussions of scientific literacy focused more often than not on whether nonscientists could achieve an aesthetic appreciation of the complexity, beauty, order, and ever-deepening mystery of science." But now, he suggests, "the major issue in the current clamor . . . is about the technical skill-level of U.S. workers."[55]

Along with other industrialized nations, the United States has come to depend heavily on high technology for its competitive edge in the world economy. The reality of this dependence was underscored by President Reagan in a 1982 memo to members of Congress:

> Science and technology are essential to the accomplishment of the goals of this Administration and the needs of the American people for jobs, enhanced national security, increased international competitiveness, and better health and quality of life. The continued advancement of both theoretical and applied scientific knowledge is of vital importance to continued human progress and the resolution of the complex problems facing the world in the years ahead.[56]

By the following spring, more than 200 bills aimed at encouraging technological growth were pending before Congress.[57]

In international trade the rising U.S. dependence on technology has been signaled by the fact that between 1960 and 1980 the U.S. trade balance in products requiring intensive R & D rose from a surplus of $5.9 billion to a surplus of $52.4 billion. Over the same period, trade in other manufactured products slipped from a net deficit of $0.2 billion to a deficit of $33.5 billion. As of 1980, U.S. exports of high-technology goods exceeded imports by a ratio of two to one.[58] Robert Reich notes that the United States will have to move yet further into high-technology areas in the future in order to maintain its competitive advantage. Precision castings, specialty steel, special chemicals, sensing devices, fiber-optic cable, fine ceramics, lasers, large-scale integrated circuits, and advanced aircraft engines represent, in his view, the major industries that can make use of America's lead in precision engineering and that can be counted on to remain secure against low-wage competition from developing countries.[59]

The United States can rightly be regarded as a world leader in the production of science and technology, not only for economic purposes, but also for symbolic purposes. According to the 1983 report of the National Science Board, the United States had more scientists and engineers relative to the total labor force than any other industrialized country. Given the total size of its labor force, this meant that the nation had by far the largest pool of scientists and engineers in the world—more than double the size of its nearest competitor (Japan). The same report also indicated that the United States spent more money on R & D than any of its allies, devoted one of the highest percentages of its GNP to R & D, derived one of the largest shares of R & D funds from taxes, devoted one of the largest percentages of business domestic product to industrial R & D, and alone produced more than one-third of all scientific and technical articles in the world. Since World War II, the United States has been the recipient of more than 100 Nobel prizes in science, three times as many as its nearest competitor (the United Kingdom), and more than a dozen times as many as the Soviet Union.[60] Indeed, the United States has led other countries in nearly all categories of scientific and technological output.[61]

More Objective Than God

In view of these accomplishments it is not surprising that much of America's myth about itself and about its position in the world has come to involve science and technology. Sociologist Robert Nisbet writes, "Technology for many Americans is not simply a good thing; it is in its way millennialist, offering happiness beyond earlier dreams to the world, and with America leading the way."[62]

Technological accomplishments reaffirm our sense that we are a special people and that we have something special to offer the world. As contributors to these accomplishments, we convince ourselves that civilization is progressing and that we are leaders in creating this progress. Science and technology provide us with a sense of destiny and give us, in political scientist Sheldon Wolin's words, "objective proof for the existence of progress"—proof which in his opinion is "certainly more objective than Anselm was able to give for the existence of God."[63]

There is, indeed, a kind of mythic quality about science to which we link ourselves as a nation when we view such "advances" as space launches, mechanical heart transplants, and the latest generation of American-produced home computers. Science mythologically connects us, not with the past as mythology has done traditionally, but with the future. It is through science and technology that we see ourselves drawn toward some inevitable, yet mysterious, future. The advance of technology seems to us predetermined, relentlessly leading us toward some goal that it, not we, has established. As historian Daniel Boorstin points out, "We feel the surprises, the discoveries themselves, are somehow the work not of men and women but of the machines."[64]

Opinion polls uniformly demonstrate that the public's faith in science and technology is incomparably strong. To many people, technology seems to be the key to America's greatness. A 1979 Harris survey asked, "What will make a major contribution to America's greatness in the next 25 years?" Leading the list of responses were "scientific research" (mentioned by 89 percent of the respondents) and "technological genius" (73 percent). In comparison, only 57 percent selected "deep religious beliefs," 31 percent mentioned "government spending for social programs," and 24 percent listed "welcoming refugees from the world."[65] Another national survey in 1979 asked people to mention two factors "that contribute the most to U.S. influence in the world." At the top of the list was "our technological know-how" (46 percent); another 22 percent mentioned "our scientific creativity"; whereas, by comparison, only 15 percent mentioned the nation's "religious heritage."[66]

The same survey asked people whether they thought the "benefits of scientific research outweigh its harms" or whether the harms outweighed the benefits. By a margin of 70 percent to 11 percent, respondents opted for the benefits outweighing the harms (this percentage rose to 87 percent among college graduates). A slightly different wording of the question in another survey a year before also demonstrated overwhelming faith in science and technology: 60 percent thought science and technology had done more good than harm for the country, 28 percent thought the good and harm were about equal, while only 5 percent thought the harm was greater than the good.[67] This question was repeated in 1980 and 1982, again showing about two-thirds of the public with favorable attitudes toward technology versus fewer than 5 percent with negative attitudes.[68]

Americans' confidence in scientific technology, indeed, seems to be more widespread than in any other Western industrialized country. In a 1981 cross-national study of 13 western European countries, for example, respondents were about 1.6 times more likely to say that scientific advances were helping rather than harming mankind; in the United States, respondents were about 3.6 times more likely to give this answer.[69]

Another type of question also illustrated the high degree of faith attached to technology by the American public. Asked in annual Roper polls since 1973 to select the leading causes of problems in America, fewer than one in ten persons in any of the surveys selected "too much technology." Indeed, this response always ranked at the bottom of the 12 causes included in the list.[70] In contrast, a different survey asked people to indicate what was helping the nation's economy grow: here, leading the list of 13 items, was "the current state of American technology, know-how, and innovation."[71]

One of the interesting features of the American faith in technology is that this faith seems to be virtually immune to criticism or to doubts that might arise from the risks accompanying technology. For example, the accident in 1979 at the nuclear reactor located on Three Mile Island near Harrisburg, Pennsylvania, seems to have had little impact on the public's attitudes toward technology. Relatively stable responses to questions about technology, such as those just cited, were reported both before and after the incident. Indeed, even attitudes toward nuclear power were little affected, despite massive changes in government policy which greatly restricted the growth of the nuclear power industry. One year before the Three Mile Island incident a Harris survey found that 55 percent of the public favored building more nuclear power plants in the United States; an identical survey conducted a month after the incident showed that this figure had declined only to 52 percent.[72]

Technology also seems to play a valuable role in legitimating American business. Despite the cynicism many people express toward business leaders, particularly with reference to problems of selfishness, corruption, and dishonesty, they nevertheless willingly justify high profits in business on the grounds that such profits are necessary in order to keep technology moving forward. For example, 50 percent of the public in a 1978 survey, when asked what would happen if businesses failed to make high profits, agreed that "the American economy will lose its place as a technological leader in the world."[73]

Again, the international dimension figures importantly in Americans' assessments of their technology. At a time when it no longer remains as clear that Americans work harder than people in other countries, and when there is nagging doubt about the nature of the American economy, Americans still take comfort in the fact that they are "number one" in technology.[74] In a 1982 survey respondents were asked to indicate which of five countries—the United States, France, West Germany, England, or Japan—ranked highest on a number of dimensions. The one dimension on which Americans ranked their own country highest was "the most advanced technology." By comparison, America was ranked inferior, especially to Japan, on every other dimension, such as having "the hardest working employees," "workers having the most pride in their work," and "the highest quality products."[75]

With attitudes like these among the general public, it is not surprising to find public leaders drawing frequently on the technological myth to legitimate America and its way of life. This seems to be a favorite theme in patriotic speeches by national leaders. For example, Admiral James Watkins concluded an address in 1983 by asserting, "America has always prided itself in its ability to research, develop and effectively employ new concepts, being in the forefront of applied scientific advancement. This has been a national strength and has helped maintain us as leader of the western world and defender of freedom."[76] Employing similar rhetoric, U.S. Air Force Chief of Staff Charles Gabriel remarked in a public address, "We depend on the high quality of our people and on superior training, tactics, and technology to give us the critical edge in combat. We will hold onto this edge . . . through the dedication of our people, and through our determination to exploit technological change to its fullest."[77]

Such rhetoric appears to play an especially prominent role when American leaders find themselves addressing international audiences. In a 1982 address to the General Assembly of the United Nations, Secretary of State George Shultz proclaimed:

> Historians in the future will surely marvel over the accomplishments achieved by human beings in the last half of this century. We have expanded the frontiers of thought—in science, biology, and engineering; in painting, music, and mathematics; in technology and architecture—far beyond the point anyone could have dared predict, much less hoped for. We know much today about the oceans and forests and the geological strata that lock in the story of our past. We know more about a baby—or the brain—than was accumulated in 10 millennia before our time. We are learning to produce food for all of us; we are no longer helpless before the threat of disease; we explore our universe as a matter of course. We are confronting the nature of nature itself.[78]

For Shultz, the editorial "we" only dimly masked the message that it was the United States, not the community of nations as a whole, that was responsible for these feats. As he pointed out, the fact that Americans were "a practical and pragmatic people" was chiefly responsible for their great strides in technology.

If public leaders have been quick to exploit America's technological leadership for symbolic advantage, leaders of business have been no less eager to demonstrate their place in this symbolic universe. Through advertising and slogans, as well as public addresses, businesses utilize the technological myth to legitimate their nation, the American economic system as a whole, and their specific role in the American system. From slogans like "Technology is creating tomorrow. You can invest in tomorrow . . . today" (a mutual fund advertisement), to "Gee! No, GTE!" (a slogan for an advanced technology firm), or the familiar, if dated, "Better living through chemistry," Americans are taught that technology is good, and that American business is good because it is the source of technology. Nothing, it seems, sells quite as well as science and technology—automobile tires are marketed as "high-tech" radials; even toothpaste is "scientifically formulated." As one corporate executive admitted, "Happily, the majority of Americans eventually board the technology train, either as passengers enjoying the convenience of the ride or as informed travelers who have some notion of where the train is headed."[79]

Increasingly, technology is presented in commercial advertising both as the source of a good life and as the solution to the nation's economic problems. "Like a talisman," remarked a *Business Week* editorial, "high tech is being called on to spawn new industries to meet ever stiffening foreign competition, revitalize decaying smokestack industries, and put . . . workers back on the job."[80]

The distinction that frequently becomes blurred in public rhetoric about technology is the distinction between ethos (a norm or means) and worldview (an end in itself). As ethos, technology may be regarded as a mere methodology or necessary means for achieving other desired ends; as worldview, technology becomes a set of limiting assumptions which shapes the choice of ends itself. The reason this distinction becomes blurred in public discourse is that higher values are almost always given tacit recognition as justifications for the advancement of technology—to achieve world peace, promote national security, make life easier, discover more about the nature of nature, etc. But the reasons for selecting precisely these values are generally left unspecified, as are the exact connections between particular technological proposals and their implicit objectives. Consequently, it is seldom clear that the more general values were not selected only because they seemed compatible with available technologies; nor is it possible to know whether full consideration was given to alternative means.

The mythologization of technology, therefore, comes at the point when a full range of public values cannot be seriously debated because technical considerations have already ruled some of them out. The problem is not inherent in the nature of technology itself, nor in the expanded role which technology has come to play in modern societies. Technology becomes increasingly prominent as a legitimating myth because the expansion of the technological infrastructure makes it more difficult for public discourse to remain truly open to a full range of intrinsic values.

Apart from the purely logical problem of confusing ethos and worldview, technology is also amenable to ideological exploitation because it corresponds so well with the nature of the modern bureaucratic state. To the degree that the bureaucratic state needs to be reconciled with the ideal of a free market economy in order to enjoy legitimacy, this reconciliation is quite commonly achieved by pointing to the state's activities in the realm of science and technology. Promoting research and development can be deemed a legitimate activity of the bureaucratic state since such projects frequently require expenditures on too large a scale to be accomplished through private investment, and since many R & D programs fall into the category of "collective goods" from which the entire public presumably benefits (e.g., defense, medicine, space, communication). Yet the benefits of R & D programs are also widely regarded as having broadly positive effects, as knowledge is disseminated, for the private sector as well. Programs that might otherwise be met with skepticism, therefore, can be sold—and in turn heralded as signals of proper governmental responsibility—by locating them within the category of "technological advancement."

What gives technology much of its legitimating power, in addition to the fact that each new discovery seems to dramatize its worth, is that its development is portrayed as being inevitable. We cannot go back. Technology has become our destiny. "The door . . . has been opened and it could no more be slammed shut than could the doors opened by Gutenberg's printing press, Galileo's telescope, Fulton's steam engine or the Wright Brothers' first flight," says a NASA administrator.[81] "The clock cannot be turned back," echoes the chairman of one of the nation's largest banks.[82] Or, as one historian of technology warns, writing from a more analytical perspective, "Technological development has come to be viewed as an autonomous thing, beyond politics and society, with a destiny of its own which must become our destiny too."[83]

The relationship presumed to exist between technology and science further tends to reinforce the belief that technological development is inevitable. Our approach to technology is different from our approach to the arts, philosophy, or even religion. The determining factor in these other areas seems increasingly to be personal preference—the arbitrary expression of taste, choice, and the particular values to which one has been socialized. Technology, in contrast, seems to depend on the laws of nature uncovered by science.[84] It is these discoveries that make technology possible, we convince ourselves; and then, by a curious feat of logic, we conclude that knowledge discovered must inevitably lead to new technology.[85] Even technology which on the surface seems foolish or undesirable must be developed because "if we don't, someone else will."

Frequently, the inevitably of technology becomes a self-legitimating ideology which, as Habermas has cautioned, creates a kind of "technical reason" which limits our ability to think about social problems except in the terms set by technology.[86] Does technology cause pollution, safety hazards, health risks, and other side effects? If so, "only technology itself," responds the president of another large corporation, "can save us from the undesirable side effects."[87] This logic is what critics of technology have termed the technological fix: "an attempt to answer a social or human problem using technological devices or systems without any attempt to modify or alter the underlying social or human problem."[88] Is there economic injustice? Then use technology to expand the availability of goods rather than attempting to redistribute wealth. Is there conflict among nations? Then develop ever more destructive weapons so that their very destructiveness will (we hope) serve as a deterrent.

The technological fix appears to be fairly much a part of public policy and public opinion. Policy makers frequently appear to rely on technological solutions to redress social ills, rather than engaging in serious debate about deeper values of peace, justice, equity, and well-being. What they perhaps realize intuitively is that public confidence in scientists and scientific research can nearly always be counted on for support.[89] Policy makers' decisions, in turn, educate the public to look first, if not only, to technological options.[90] Judging from a 1982 poll of high school seniors, nearly two of every three young persons now believes that "when things get tough enough, we'll put our minds to it and find a technological solution." This proportion represented an increase from only a bare majority who felt this way in the mid-1970s.[91]

The Avenue to Freedom

Somewhat ironically, given its apparent inevitability, technology is also widely portrayed as the avenue to enhanced freedom, acting both directly and indirectly. Directly, it creates new choices, new possibilities that previously seemed unthinkable—new gadgets, new amusements, new defense systems, new health possibilities, new industries, and new kinds of jobs. We have only to make decisions among the many opportunities set before us. Technology also seems to enhance freedom because it requires, as well as contributes to, knowledge—one of the bases classically thought necessary for true freedom. By this logic, America's technological contributions mean that it is apparently a society which is free and therefore fosters knowledge and creativity. Indirectly, technology enhances freedom, if by default, because it seems so utterly indifferent or neutral to the kinds of freedoms that the individual enjoys. "He can listen to the music he likes," writes social philosopher Jacques Ellul, "dress as he likes, take on completely aberrant religious beliefs or moral attitudes; none of these things challenge the technological system."[92] In other words, technology does not limit our freedom; its development is not contingent on certain life styles or choices—or so it seems.

Once the meaning of freedom has become restricted to the idea of choice, then technology becomes the obvious means of maintaining and expanding our freedom. The images of freedom portrayed on television and reported in the newspapers invariably imply that freedom is ours because we have been given new options by technology: freedom to communicate warmth to loved ones—via the wonders of ITT long-distance fiber optic technology; freedom to range the open countryside where all cares fade into a glorious sunset—in a new Datsun ZX Turbo; freedom to enjoy life longer despite heart disease—just around the corner due to the generosity of Humana's mechanical heart research program; freedom now to give every woman the "right to choose"—by supporting access to abortion technologies; freedom at last from the terrible fear of nuclear holocaust—by spending $24 billion on "star wars" research. Like the historic connections once seen between "liberty" and the American and French revolutions, now freedom is symbolized by the computer revolution, the information revolution, the medical technology revolution, and the video revolution.

In a subtle, but perhaps important, way technology has, therefore, become linked with that most fundamental value—freedom—on which Americans rely to legitimate their way of life. If the marketplace gradually redefined freedom to mean freedom of choice, technology now begins to replace the marketplace as the main source of that kind of freedom. Not simply the modern supermarket, with its panoply of choices, but the Electronic Candy Store, filled with word processors and software, becomes the symbol of our expanded freedom to choose.

This is not to suggest that technology can operate effectively without the market. But increasingly it is not the market as such, but technology, that is recognized as the dynamo driving the American economic system. According to former science policy advisor Harvey Brooks, "Technology is not demanded by the market. The market really does not demand anything that does not exist, and so the market really only begins to act after the technology exists."[93] Or as one corporation chairman predicts, "The victories which we have to win in the marketplace of the 1980s and beyond are victories which will be won in the laboratories and testing grounds of American science and technology."[94]

Finally, as if to complete the picture, technology has like other legitimating institutions in the past begun to create its own version of the self—"technological man"—who finds his way of life legitimate because his very identity has been shaped by that way of life. In his book *Technological Man*, Victor Ferkiss argues that it is high time we simply made peace with technology and consciously adopted this new identity. Our concept of self should, he suggests, incorporate a new naturalism, a new holism, and a new immanentism. With the new naturalism we become part of the natural world, equal with it and its technological creations. With the new holism we become more aware of our dependence on nature and technology. Conceived of as parts of a natural process or system, our lives take on meaning only as parts of that system. With the new immanentism we come to believe that life is ultimately not governed by some creator-god outside the natural world, but by forces within the system of nature itself. "Technological man," he says, "must so internalize these ideas and make them so much a part of his instinctive world view that they inform his personal, political and cultural life."[95]

Ferkiss's notion of what it will take to reconcile ourselves fully with technology may seem extreme. Yet it in part represents the kind of self-identity that other writers have suggested is already characteristic of many in the technological society. Scientists N. Bruce Hannay and Robert McGinn observe that "modern technology has increasingly become an important source of personal identity and self-esteem." In their opinion, "religion, race, class, sex, and nationality [have] become progressively less able to serve that function in achievement-oriented, post-traditional society." Consequently, "the items of technology an individual possesses and in which he or she is reflected have, along with work, become increasingly important sources of identity."[96] More critically, another writer concludes, "It is not facetious to call our system of technologically stimulated production and consumption a religion. An economic process defines for millions of Americans what it is to be truly human, what the meaning of life is, how to avoid guilt."[97]

Eternal Passion and Eternal Crime

How effective technology will be in legitimating America to the world obviously remains to be seen. Certainly it is a legitimating myth that differs substantially in content from traditional civil religion, or from the pragmatism and emphasis on freedom in America's secular ideology of the past. But like those earlier myths it contains a sense of continuity with the past, a link with destiny and freedom, and a sense of pride in America's position in the world that seem to be potentially persuasive.

The economic importance of technology to the American way of life seems already to be an established fact. What a greater acceptance of the technological myth may accomplish is, as Ferkiss suggests, more willing acceptance of that reality. Once technology comes fully to be accepted not only as an economic fact, but also as a desirable state of affairs, we may be in a better position to make the sacrifices it will inevitably require of us—to become better technicians, to spend our leisure time enjoying the particular pleasures it provides, to devote our surplus income to purchasing its products, to reshape our educational institutions in a way that keeps us ahead of foreign competition in the technological race, and to mold our children to become better at math and engineering and to enjoy the aesthetics of a well-constructed bridge more than a classical work of art.

Still, the suspicion cannot be entirely avoided that our freedom as a people may ultimately depend more on maintaining a critical perspective toward technology than on accepting it completely as our guiding myth. At the Amsterdam World Assembly of Churches, held in the immediate aftermath of World War II to consider how churches of all denominations could cooperate in rebuilding a stable world order, technology was identified as one of the most likely sources of social *disorder* in the years ahead. The assembled delegates acknowledged technology's potential for alleviating poverty and creating a better infrastructure for communication among the nations. But they also cautioned of the dangers implicit in accepting it too uncritically: "There is no inescapable necessity for society to succumb to undirected developments of technology, and the Christian church has an urgent responsibility today to help men achieve fuller personal life within the technical society."[98]

Critics, even in high places in the political and scientific establishments, have continued to sound the alarm that America may be sacrificing its birthright of freedom and integrity for a mess of technological pottage. Senior White House advisor John McLaughry, for example, has cautioned that "a narrow scientific vision that ignores the holism of human life, the considerations of ecology, and matters not susceptible to empirical measurement is a limiting and potentially destructive way to approach economic and technological questions."[99] Similarly, David F. Noble, curator of the Smithsonian Institution and historian of American technology, has suggested that the view which regards technology as the only means of achieving progress is in reality "a bizarre and relatively recent Western notion invented to disarm critics of capitalism."[100]

But such voices represent only a minority and appear to have grown fainter as time has gone by. At the dawn of the industrial era, workers optimistically joined the ranks of Luddite machine-wreckers in hopes of regaining some control over the world they had lost.[101] Today, Luddites exist only in the imagination of their novelist creators, appealing to the modern ambivalence toward technology in a way that roams safely within the bounds of fantasy. Like Edward Abbey's "monkey-wrench gang," they win symbolic victories in fanciful acts of high-tech vandalism, but ultimately fail to stand in the way of technological change.[102] At a fundamental level, the ability to offer critical opposition to technology is similarly impaired because, as Noble points out, the opposition "suffers from a fatalistic and futuristic confusion about the nature of technological development." Moreover, he suggests, this confusion "is rooted in, and reinforced by, the political and ideological subordination of people at the point of production, the locus of technological development."[103]

The tendency to legitimate America—to seek ideological security in an increasingly complex and uncertain world—by avowing the urgency of technology and exaggerating the importance of America's lead in its development promises only to deepen its mythological effects. The ambivalence that is perhaps an inevitable consequence of a force as powerful as technology can lead, under favorable conditions, to a balance between love and hatred, between adulation and fear. It can temper material dependence on technology with a cultural distance which preserves the capacity to raise critical questions about its uses and direction. But the ideological exploitation of technology to justify economic programs and to regain a sense of euphoria about the nation's supremacy in the world threatens radically to undermine that critical balance. Given thoughtful guidance, technology can serve as a valuable tool; given license for its own excesses, it can become an awesome master.

Almost a hundred years ago, at a time when the locomotive still symbolized the dangers of technology unchecked, the French novelist Emile Zola painted a stark projection of where technology could lead:

> On and on it went, soulless and triumphant, on to the future with a mathematical straightness and deliberate ignorance of the rest of human life on either side, unseen but always tenaciously alive—eternal passion and eternal crime.[104]

CHAPTER 12

A Broader Context: Politics and Faith

WHEN ALL is said and done, then, what picture emerges? How do we assess the changes that have taken place in American religion during the decades since World War II? Apart from the specific developments themselves, is it possible to see in these changes some broader patterns which conform to—or deviate from—the theories we have at our disposal for understanding modern religion?

It was suggested at the outset that discussions of secularization provide little in the way of helpful insights about the recent restructuring of American religion—at least not discussions of secularization that envision a simple linear decline in the social prominence or cultural influence of religion. Both the aggregate trends and the complex developments that have been examined belie such formulations. Some indicators of traditional religiosity in the United States (belief in the literal inerrancy of the Bible, for example), to be sure, have declined in absolute terms over the past two or three decades. But many other religious beliefs and practices have remained remarkably stable. And even those that have shown some decline must be interpreted with caution in view of the short span of time involved. More to the point, the patterns that have been traced in preceding chapters indicate greater complexity and greater internal variation than such notions about secularization generally admit.

There are, however, more complex theories—theories of religious and cultural evolution—that bear relevance to the present discussion. Rather than depicting secularization as a simple decline in the importance of religion, these theories emphasize qualitative changes in the character of religion. They depict broad evolutionary stages in the development of modern religion and provide clues about its possible future. These are, of course, speculative frameworks, based as much on stylized notions of intellectual currents as on factual evidence about either the past or present. Nevertheless, they can be useful as a starting point for thinking about recent changes in American religion from a broader perspective.

Evolutionary Patterns

One need not accept the strong statements that some theorists have made about cultural evolution (let alone "sociobiological" evolution) to find value in theories that have tried to organize what we know about historical development according to some broad evolutionary schema. The virtue of such theories is that they provide general frameworks which highlight certain aspects of the modern situation and permit comparisons to be made with earlier periods. In tracing broad processes of social and cultural change, these theories also offer some guidance in thinking about the possible direction of changes in the future. It is, of course, necessary to recognize that such theories depend to a great extent on the kinds of values and presuppositions built into the larger cultural environment from which they emerge. One finds, for example, that the present period is often portrayed as an infinitely better arrangement than anything that has been experienced previously—or, in other cases, that the present period is fraught with deep crises which nearly spell doom for modern society, but that new ideas are just now being formulated which will save humanity from sure destruction. Obviously, value judgments of this kind must be recognized for what they are rather than confusing them with the historical record itself. In providing an Archimedean point from which to view the major contours of an entire cultural epoch, however, such theories can be enormously useful.[1]

In varying ways, the leading theories of religious evolution all stress the importance of greater self-awareness with respect to symbolism—or to culture, we might say—as a feature of modern religion. There is, in fact, much evidence that religious culture since World War II has become increasingly a focus of self-conscious reflection and discussion, at least at some levels. Theological reflection has, for example, converged to a remarkable degree with some aspects of the social sciences in its concern for the symbolically constructed character of reality. Wolfhart Pannenberg, professor of theology at Munich, in a passage strikingly social scientific in tenor, observes: "It is only by symbols and symbolic language that the larger community to which we belong is present in our experiences and activities."[2] And he goes on to argue that the church not only uses symbols but is itself symbolic. In a similar manner, Yale theologian George A. Lindbeck writes, "A religion can be viewed as a kind of cultural and/or linguistic framework or medium that shapes the entirety of life and thought."[3] Both writers develop their arguments, not from metaphysical first principles, but from anthropological considerations about the nature of symbolism. In applications of discourse analysis and deconstructionism, other theologians have taken the investigation of religious symbols even further.[4]

At the popular level, evidence of greater self-consciousness about the nature of religious symbolism is naturally less apparent. To broach the subject of mythology or textual criticism remains a mark of extreme heresy among the third of the public who believe that the Bible is not only divinely inspired but to be taken literally. Yet there are also indications that a substantial number of believers have achieved some degree of mental differentiation between their faith and the symbols with which it is expressed. For example, among those who believe the Bible to be divinely inspired, only half regard it as absolutely free of errors. Or for another example, a study of Lutheran church members showed that only one member in three felt it possible to prove the existence of God, and of these only about half felt this could be done from evidence in the Bible.[5] These tendencies, along with some of the evidence discussed in Chapters 7 and 9, suggest that some of the difference between religious conservatives and religious liberals may be understandable in terms of variation in levels of cognitive differentiation between religious symbolism and the truths underlying these symbols.

Studies of new religious movements are also particularly replete with evidence of the self-conscious application and manipulation of symbols. Because many of these movements grew from small groups in which symbols were either invented or synthesized from other sources, members tended to be keenly aware of their power. Being in a position to remake their own rituals and ideologies, and seeing the immediate effect of these symbols on group life, they quickly developed a heightened sense of "symbolic consciousness." Movements which sought to block out the effects of taken-for-granted constructions of reality through meditation, drugs, or religious experiences also sharpened their members' sensitivities to the nature of symbolism.

The possibility that greater self-consciousness about religious symbolism is accompanied by a greater emphasis on personal interpretation and a decline in tacit acceptance of official creeds also finds support in a variety of evidence. In the Lutheran study mentioned previously, only half of the respondents felt God had given clear, detailed rules for living that applied to everyone; most of the remainder felt that individuals had to figure out how to apply God's rules to their own situations. The study also included an effort to determine how much agreement existed between individual members' views and the official theological positions of the church, first by interviewing theologians to determine what the official positions were, then by surveying pastors to see if these positions were taught, and finally by surveying members about their own beliefs. The core theological tenets of the church, as described by its theologians, consisted chiefly of three simple propositions: that Christ was fully God and fully man, that Christ was crucified to forgive our sins, and that men and women are sinners whom God loves and is giving new life. These tenets were uniformly accepted by the clergy and, partly because of the prescribed schedule of sermon topics, emphasized from the pulpit. Yet the laity survey found that only one member in three affirmed all three of these propositions. On other teachings, such as the church's views of baptism and communion, agreement was equally low. Given these tendencies, it may not be surprising (as seen in Chapter 5) that denominational boundaries seem to be weakening.

The evidence is less clear with respect to the claim, propounded in some evolutionary theories, that modern religion is principally characterized by a collapse of the dualistic worldview which distinguishes God from man, the supernatural from the natural, this world from a world beyond life. Upwards of 90 percent of the American population affirms some belief in the existence of God. Such affirmation scarcely answers the question of whether there has been, as some theorists suggest, "a massive reinterpretation" of the nature of God. But more refined questions suggest that a sizable number of Americans still express their faith in dualistic terms. For instance, nine persons in ten believe Jesus Christ actually lived, seven in ten believe he was truly God, and six in ten think one must believe in the divinity of Christ to be a Christian. The results of studies documenting consistently high levels of belief in life after death, heaven, and Christ's presence in heaven also point to the survival of a strong element of religious dualism in American culture. Indeed, the persistence of these beliefs seems to be one of the more stable elements of American religious culture, in contrast with the serious restructuring that has taken place in many other beliefs and practices.

But if dualism continues, evidence also suggests that God has, in a sense, become "subjectivized" rather than existing as a metaphysical, transcendent, or omnipotent being. A study conducted in the San Francisco Bay area in the 1970s found, among persons who said they definitely believed in God, that eight out of ten believed in God's influence on their personal lives, but only about half felt God influenced social events.[6] In the Lutheran study only three in ten believed that God "shapes events directly through nations and social affairs."

A good deal of speculation—and some research—has also suggested that God is relevant to contemporary Americans mainly because the sense of God's presence is subjectively comforting; that is, religion solves personal problems rather than addressing broader questions. This is true, perhaps particularly so, among evangelicals who in the past at least tended to emphasize God's sovereignty in all things. Now, however, much of evangelical literature focuses mainly on emotional and psychological concerns.[7]

While it may be, then, that a high degree of supernaturalism remains in

American religion as a formal tenet, the operational relevance of the supernatural may have largely collapsed into the interior concerns of the self. This conclusion also tends to be supported by the high degree of interest surveys document in questions of personal meaning and purpose, and in the number of quasi-religious self-help movements that have developed since the 1960s.

At the level of religious organization there is also much to support the contention in evolutionary theories that religious expression has become increasingly differentiated from traditional religious institutions. High rates of denominational switching and interdenominational marriage, reduced levels of denominational identity and cross-denominational tensions, as well as pervasive amounts of contact across denominational lines (as seen in Chapter 5) all point toward a declining monopoly of specific religious traditions over the enactment of religious convictions. Evidence on the numbers of individuals who consider themselves religious, or who hold certain tenets of faith, and yet do not belong to religious organizations or attend regularly points in a similar direction.

At the most general levels of societal integration and legitimation the evidence, while subject to alternative interpretations, suggests the continuing relevance of religiously inspired ethical concerns, but also reveals the diminishing weight of religious arguments as such, relative to the weight these arguments carry at the individual level. In many respects, the most obvious religious development with respect to societal integration has been the rise of the New Christian Right (Chapter 8). On the surface this movement—and the countermovements it has elicited—suggest a continuing tendency for religious values to find their way into the public domain as a part of debates over societal goals. Liberals and conservatives alike have resorted to religious arguments in defense of claims about public morality and the role of the state in defending public morality. Yet the very dissension that has been produced by the religious right points up the difficulties of gaining any kind of broad consensus around traditional religious values. Tacit agreement has been achieved mostly with respect to the underlying rational-legal procedures to which political action must pay heed. Moreover, as suggested in Chapter 11, secular myths having to do with individual freedom, material success, and perhaps especially the wonders of technology may be an even more powerful source of societal legitimation than traditional religious arguments by virtue of being grounded in many assumptions that are so nearly taken for granted that they enjoy a virtual de facto status as taboo.

Evidence suggests that rationality, natural science, and the social sciences have all exercised a negative effect on traditional religious beliefs and practices. Not only do scientists—and especially social scientists—demonstrate radically low levels of religious commitment, but scientific and social scientific meaning systems also appear to operate as functional alternatives to traditional theistic ideas for a number of people, and technical rationality plays an increasingly important legitimating function in the wider society. Highly publicized reactions to science and social science on the part of religious conservatives, as evidenced by lawsuits concerning the teaching of evolution in public schools and court cases challenging the influence of "secular humanism" on school textbooks, suggest that the forces of "secular rationality" have by no means carried the day. And yet, the very grounds on which these controversies have been fought—arguing for the "scientific" basis of creationism, making use of the rational-legal procedures supplied by the modern court system, and drawing on social scientists for "expert testimony"—all point to the considerable degree to which even religious conservatives have accommodated to the norms of secular rationality.

At the same time, a clear case cannot be made in support of evolutionary claims that the sciences have so reduced the physical and social contingencies of modern life as to make religious worldviews largely irrelevant. To the contrary, the sciences seem only to have contributed to a greater degree of sensitivity about such contingencies. Indeed, modern society is inevitably confronted with the paradoxes of its own contingency. Thus the concerns that continue to inspire deep religious discussion, such as the prospect of nuclear annihilation, rights of the unborn, euthanasia, world hunger, Third World dependence, etc., are clearly the evidence of lingering contingencies in a technologized world.

At a more theological or philosophical level there is, however, a very significant development that evolutionary views help to illuminate. That is the manner in which religion itself has been redefined in the face of advances in the realm of natural reason. Modern definitions of religion have come to focus increasingly on symbolism and meaning. Writers such as Clifford Geertz, Peter Berger, and Robert Bellah conceive of religion as a special kind of symbol system which evokes a sense of ultimate, transcendent, encompassing meaning. But what this conception does, in addition to drawing on the social sciences, is to save religion from the onslaught of post-Enlightenment positivism. Specifically, this feat is accomplished by positing religion as a type of symbolism concerned with the meaning of the whole of life. The meanings of anything less—of selected aspects of the world—can be identified by the contexts or frameworks in which those aspects are located. But the meaning of the whole lies beyond any specific context; as Wittgenstein observed, "The meaning of the world lies outside of the world."[8] Thus the world of facts with which the empirical sciences deal must be seen ultimately in another context—a context given meaning by religious symbols—which is beyond the scope of the empirical sciences.

It is, therefore, not irrelevant that modern religion tends to be defined the way it is. Not only has there been a greater degree of differentiation between symbols and truth, but there has also been an increasing degree of differentiation among kinds of symbols. As a result, religious symbols have been put beyond the reach of rational and empirical criticism by identifying them with a different type of reality construction. Some of the difference evident between religious liberals and religious conservatives may be understandable in these terms, especially if some part of the more liberal population can be assumed to have differentiated in their religious discourse between symbolism oriented toward holistic meanings and symbolism subject to empirical criticism.

Evidence also suggests that, despite considerable erosion of religious practices in other areas, manifestations of attempts to communicate with the divine remain strikingly prominent in the United States. Prayer in particular seems to have remained a strong feature of contemporary life in comparison with other kinds of religious behavior. For example, one of the Gallup surveys mentioned earlier showed that 60 percent of the American public personally considered prayer to be very important and another 22 percent regarded it as fairly important; by comparison, only 39 percent thought reading the Bible was very important, 38 percent thought attending religious services was very important, and 28 percent thought it very important to belong to a close religious fellowship group. Other surveys have documented high levels of interest and involvement in prayer, a high degree of belief in the efficacy of prayer, and a strong tendency to regard prayer as actual communication with God.

Apart from prayer, evidence also suggests that sensing a relationship with God continues to be highly valued and that many people in fact feel they are close to God. The Gallup survey showed that "growing into a deeper relationship with God" was considered very important by 56 percent of the public and fairly important by an additional 26 percent. In another Gallup survey, 64 percent of the public felt their relationship to God was very important to their own sense of self worth and nine out of ten expressed satisfaction with this relationship.

It has been observed with some interest that modern religion seems to depict God chiefly as an all-loving being, thus reducing much of the motivation for salvation from damnation that was present in historic Christianity. This depiction may in fact serve a positive role in sustaining the plausibility of communication with an invisible God in the modern era; that is, communication may be easier to sustain when God is envisioned, not as distant judge, but as lover and friend—as an intimate "God within." At any rate, indications are clear that contemporary imagery regards God in such terms. Eight of every nine persons say they feel that God loves them; 80 percent say they feel close to God; and, negatively, only 16 percent say they have ever felt afraid of God.[9] In the Lutheran study cited earlier, nine in ten said God loved them and was giving them new life; only a quarter felt they were sinners under the wrath and judgment of God. And evidence from a 1984 National Opinion Research Center survey indicates that, although images of God as judge and king persist, substantial numbers of Americans lean toward more intimate images such as lover and spouse.[10]

The idea, promulgated in some recent evolutionary theories, of the church as a kind of counterculture devoted to maintaining the plausibility of communication with God also appears consistent with a variety of evidence. Although this is by no means a new role for the church to fulfill, it is a role that the church seems to have carried on with surprising success as the culture has become increasingly secularized. To be sure, the religionless Christianity of humanistic ethicalism is evident in many mainline churches. But the importance of the religious community gathered for worship and fellowship with God is also strikingly evident. Protestants and Catholics alike have shown increasing interest in liturgy as the heart of such communal activity. Pannenberg writes: "The rediscovery of the Eucharist may prove to be the most important event in Christian spirituality of our time, of more revolutionary importance than even the liturgical renewal of our time." As the sense of guilt and sin which became prominent in the teachings of the Protestant reformers erodes, he suggests, the church will increasingly find its reason for existing that of serving as a symbol of wholeness in a broken world. This is the purpose of the Eucharist: to dramatize communion with God and to evoke the healing presence of God in the world. Moreover, he suggests that the Eucharist can be interpreted in distinctly modern terms as a symbol that dramatizes freedom by casting ossified structures in doubt and that enhances adaptiveness and communication by emphasizing openness and provisionality: "The human predicament of social life is not ultimately realized in the present political order of society, but is celebrated in the worship of the church, if only in the form of the symbolic presence of the kingdom to come."[11]

The typical congregant may well not participate in "the worship of the church" with the sense of sophistication that Pannenberg suggests. Yet in some form the church—whether liberal or conservative—does continue to attract participation largely as a place in which to experience the closeness of God and the communion of fellow worshippers. Among the gratifications derived from church mentioned most often in a national survey of regular church attenders, for example, were: feeling close to God (77 percent), the experience of worshipping God (60 percent), and a sense of companionship or fellowship (54 percent).

If the foregoing is any indication, then, American religion demonstrates many of the characteristics that theorists have identified with modern culture. Many religious beliefs and practices remain much in evidence, contrary to simpler predictions that have envisioned a sheer decline in religious vitality. These beliefs and practices may have retained their vitality in fact by accommodating to the contemporary cultural situation. In becoming more oriented to the self, in paying more explicit attention to symbolism, in developing a more flexible organizational style, and in nurturing specialized worship experiences American religion has become more complex, more internally differentiated, and thus more adaptable to a complex, differentiated society.

Although evolutionary theories are scarcely designed to account for short-term changes, they can help us more fully to understand some of the restructuring that has taken place in American religion since World War II. Specifically, the characteristics of religious liberalism seem to conform for the most part to the depiction of modern religion in these theories. Greater room for interpretation of doctrinal creeds, self-conscious syncretism of symbolism from several of the world's religions, a more privatized form of religious expression, mixtures of social scientific and theological reasoning, and a more universalistic style of legitimating myth have all been associated with religious liberalism. The conservative side, from this perspective, can be viewed both as a reaction to the liberal mode of cultural accommodation and as a partial mode of accommodation itself. Thus, religious conservatives may cling to a more communal, creedal, particularistic style of religious expression. But they have in subtle ways, like their liberal counterparts, also become more privatistic and more influenced by the sciences, by procedural modes of legitimation, and by the attractions of technology. Indeed, efforts to portray religious conservatives in relation to some evolutionary schema of modernization have often disagreed on whether reaction or accommodation has been the dominant motif. In either case, the relatively sharp increases in science, in higher education, and in technology since World War II provide some basis for arguing that these kinds of responses from the religious community should have been expected. Evolutionary theories, then, may provide valuable clues about the directions in which religious restructuring is moving, even though they fall short in accounting for its more specific contours.

For several reasons these are fairly speculative conclusions, however. In the first place they have to be defended largely without comparable evidence from other times or places. Some of the characteristics of American religion that bear directly on these theories can be shown to have intensified even in the short period since World War II. But many of these characteristics can legitimately be questioned as to whether they are truly unique to the recent period, whether they are intensifying, or whether they might also have characterized Western religion a century or even a millennium ago.

Another difficulty is that evolutionary theories tend to be cast in such broad terms that data can be readily manipulated to support them even when the same data might also be viewed from a less sympathetic angle. What counts as evidence of increasing differentiation and what might be regarded as counterevidence often seems less than clear. Some theorists indeed have argued specifically against trying to make such connections with concrete historical examples, suggesting that evolutionary theories are better viewed as normative guides toward the future than as testable theories. Thus it may be that American religion seems to have accommodated itself to modernity only because of a selective interpretation of the facts.

This criticism, however, should not overshadow the positive role that evolutionary perspectives can play. If we admit that their purpose is not to provide us with testable hypotheses, then we can make use of them, as suggested earlier, to illuminate what might otherwise seem to be disparate or insignificant developments. We are led to think about the possibility that some signs of apparent decay in American religion may actually have beneficial consequences for its survival over a longer period. For example, the decline of orthodoxy may be associated with a rise in personalized religious interpretations which make religion more adaptable to changing circumstances. We are also led to think about the relations among certain developments and the significance of these developments in a wider context. If it is true that American religion is becoming more highly differentiated, then greater effectiveness in dealing with new distinctions, with new understandings of symbolism, and with new kinds of religious organizations, may be especially important.

The more serious limitation of existing evolutionary approaches to religion is that they fail to illuminate much about the relations between religion and the broader social environment. Most of these approaches relate religious evolution to the growth of complexity and subsystem differentiation in the larger society. But few draw explicit connections between these two levels of development, that is, connections that would indicate how a particular form of religious differentiation might be related to a specific example of societal complexity. And since evolutionary theories usually leave open possibilities for maladaptive reactions, it becomes exceedingly difficult to pin down what constitutes complexity and what the effects of complexity may be.

Beyond this general problem, mechanisms of cultural change are seldom identified either. At times it appears that theorists regard religious evolution, like other dimensions of cultural evolution, as resulting from its own internal dynamics. Previous symbolic structures set the constraints and provide the opportunities for new cultural developments. Thus one is forced to look mainly at the internal logic of Christianity, the legacy of Reformation Protestantism, and theological debates of the eighteenth and nineteenth centuries to understand what has shaped the character of American religion. Implicit in this approach is the view that institutional differentiation has progressed to such a high degree that religion is no longer significantly affected by anything other than developments within the religious institution itself.

In the American case evolutionary theories are most deficient in interpreting religious characteristics in relation to elements of the broader social fabric. Most of the empirical characteristics that fit in one way or another with these theories do not apply uniformly to the entire population. Many of them pertain most clearly to the young and to the better educated—factors which suggest the growing prominence of these characteristics. But the theories provide little help in answering questions such as, why education, and why now? Nor do they cast into sharp relief, except in very general statements about adaptation and reaction, the kinds of conflict that have emerged between religious liberals and religious conservatives. To say that differentiation marches forward may be an accurate appraisal of long-term tendencies, but the seeming inevitability attributed to this process fails to suggest the more specific tensions that develop in the short run or the precipitating events that engender these tensions. Greater differentiation between values and behavior or between the kingdom of God and institutional programs, for example, can scarcely be understood in any adequate way apart from the specific societal pressures that reinforce these changes.

What is needed, as a complement to highly abstract evolutionary theories, are concrete historical comparisons from which to gain a sense of the kinds of environmental factors—as well as the kinds of internal institutional responses—that may result in religious restructuring. The recent period in American history has been fraught with rapid changes in education, in technology, and in the character of the state. To understand how these developments have affected religion in the past, and how they may shape American religion in the foreseeable future, comparisons are needed which draw on concrete historical material.

Historical Comparisons

Our attempt to supply historical comparisons must of necessity be very abbreviated. We cannot hope to provide in any systematic way an answer to the question of how the period since World War II in American religion may be similar to or different from other times of religious restructuring. Insofar as we have argued that the present period has been subject to larger processes of transition in the society, however, we can obtain some perspective on the nature of this transition by considering it in relation to two other periods that were notable for their effects on the development of modern religion.

One such period—the one that most theorists of cultural evolution identify as perhaps the most critical epoch in the emergence of modern religion itself—is the Reformation. Another—also given special prominence in most theories of cultural evolution—is the Enlightenment. We need not assume that the process of religious restructuring in the United States since World War II in any way rivaled the cultural changes that characterized either of these historic periods. We can, however, gain perspective on our own time by stepping back momentarily into these periods and looking at the ways in which changes in religion were conditioned by broader forces in the social environment.

One conclusion that emerges almost immediately from looking at these earlier periods of religious ferment is that religion cannot be understood very well if attention is limited only to arguments about disembodied ideas (symbols) or even abstract conceptions of organizations and actions. Religion has an organic quality, a communal and moral dimension, that binds people to one another and creates close dependencies between them and their environments. Even in a society as deeply conditioned by individualism as the United States, religious adaptation invariably involves (as the foregoing chapters have given ample testimony) complex interactions between religious communities as collectivities and the changing character of these collectivities' social and cultural environment.

To say this is only to recognize that the concept of moral community—which was so important to Durkheim's view of religion—needs to be rediscovered and reconsidered. Religions become embodied as moral communities—as networks of deeply felt obligation to one another and to collective rituals and beliefs, all of which provide a sense of belonging, even security, to the participants. The very beliefs and ideas of which any religion is comprised reflect and dramatize these moral obligations; thus, even a focus on belief requires more than an abstract consideration of ideas.

In seeking to make sense of the Reformation, historians have been led increasingly, not to the seminaries nor to the halls in which the great disputations were held, but to the manors and villages. This was where upwards of 90 percent of the population lived on the eve of the Reformation. It was in these rural settings that the Reformation ran up against insuperable odds, causing it to become an almost exclusively urban phenomenon. With the exception of some of the Anabaptist groups which were persecuted in the towns and ultimately found refuge on some of the larger estates in eastern Europe, the peasantry and rural villagers remained almost wholly uninvolved in the Reformation. This was so because the established church was deeply integrated into the moral fabric of rural life. Except in some of the less densely populated areas of Poland and Lithuania, the average parish encompassed no more than about fifty square kilometers and thus could easily be traversed in less than a day. Villagers met face to face at the local church; its bells served as an important mode of communication; and daily life depended heavily on the church calendar. Religion was also deeply integrated into the local community. Its rites—even the ordering of processionals and arrangements of pews—dramatized the status relations between peasants and landlords. Peasants enacted deference, landlords received honor, and both renewed their sense of duty and obligation.

One must realize, of course, that the moral communities undergirding religion in the sixteenth century no longer sustain it today except in remote or isolated instances. Geographic mobility, urbanization, and occupational specialization have all eroded the relationship between religion and communities of residence. Yet there is much evidence to suggest that religion continues to find its strength in moral communities and in the dramatization of moral obligations. As mentioned earlier, a recent national survey showed that 57 percent of the U.S. adult public felt that "being part of a close religious fellowship group" was either very important or fairly important. About one person in three in the United States belongs to some kind of Bible study group, prayer fellowship, therapy group, or religious movement, while twice this many continue to maintain some affiliation with a denomination or religious organization. And, as the evidence in Chapter 6 suggested, special purpose groups in American religion have flourished since World War II, often to be sure, with purely rational goals in mind, but yet they clearly function as moral communities for many of their participants. The United States may well be an exception among industrialized countries in the extent of its religious activities. But even if religious communities are declining in importance, is not community itself an aspect of social structure that needs to be included more systematically than it has been in most theories of religious evolution?

There is, however, another level at which social structure becomes relevant to the examination of religious change. Even if one form of religious adaptation begins to erode because of some disruption of the moral community sustaining it, that erosion does not in itself account for the rise of some new mode of religious adaptation. Studies such as those advanced recently by some American sociologists of religion, which naively "explain" the rise of new religions by looking at the demise of established religions, fail to grasp this point. By the same token, accounts of the recent growth of religious conservatism which throw the burden of explanation on the so-called "demise" of liberal religion fail to be compelling because they omit consideration of any of the broader societal developments that may have conditioned both responses. At crucial junctures in the past the evolution of modern religion was determined not so much by the decline of old religions but by structural changes that created new resources—resources that played a prominent part in the institutionalization of new ideologies.

The Reformation again provides an example. An earlier generation of religious historians was content largely to explain the rise of Protestantism as a response to growing weaknesses, apathy, corruption, and secularity within the church. These accounts have now fallen into disrepute. A more recent generation of historians has found little evidence that the church was more corrupt in those areas that became Protestant than it was in areas that remained Catholic. If anything, the church was stronger or at least religious enthusiasm ran higher in those areas that became Protestant, a factor that may have been of positive importance in the rise of Protestantism.

More generally, the recent historiography of the Reformation points to the importance of social resources both in areas where it became institutionalized and in areas where it was successfully resisted. The religious traditions of peasant life were extremely resistant to change not only because they fulfilled needs for security and sociality at the grass-roots level, but because peasant communities were the basis of a vast infrastructure that channeled resources to the church. If the church was a vital ingredient in the life of the peasantry, it was even more so for the nobility. Not only did the church symbolically dramatize the nobility's social position, it also reinforced their position materially through a system of regressive taxation in which peasant tithes contributed to the state's treasuries which in turn exempted the nobility from taxation. During the first half century of the Reformation, the nobility generally lent its considerable resources to the defense of the church, often making armed attacks on local towns that were in danger of succumbing to the new heresies.

However, social resources were also instrumental in giving the Reformation its own vitality. The sixteenth century witnessed an exceptional degree of material and economic expansion. After serious losses of population dating from the middle of the fourteenth century, demographic recovery was gradually achieved during the last half of the fifteenth century and became a major stimulus to economic growth in the sixteenth century. In many areas local economies began to flourish again as new modes of agriculture were implemented. But it was long-distance trading that created the most significant social changes. The Rhine valley, Low Countries, coastal cities of Denmark and Sweden, and England—precisely the areas that led the way in adopting the Reformation—participated most extensively in this commercial expansion. Towns in these areas grew in wealth, population, and power as a result of the trade which passed through them. Tolls, mines, artisan trades, shipping, and the finishing of raw goods created new sources of income which no longer derived from the presence of the nobility. These were the new resources that allowed Protestant armies to be raised, that gave towns the wherewithal to defend themselves and to shoulder the costs of their own relief and charity systems, and that created incentives for changing the mode of worship and tithing.

What is suggested by these considerations is not a simple materialistic explanation of the Reformation. Neither the content of its ideas nor the convictions of its adherents seem to have been shaped very much by material conditions. Nor did commercial expansion have an entirely straightforward or direct effect on the churches. Yet, like any social movement, the Reformation depended on a certain supply of social resources for its very survival, and these resources were in turn amplified in northern Europe by more general conditions of growth.

The conditions surrounding the diffusion and institutionalization of the Enlightenment were not entirely different, despite the lapse of a century and a half. During much of this intervening period the European economy had suffered severe setbacks. From roughly the 1680s until the American and French revolutions the European economy again experienced a period of unprecedented economic expansion. Although the Dutch role in leading this expansion had faltered badly by the beginning of the eighteenth century, France and England, including Scotland after 1707, and increasingly Prussia, grew to new heights in foreign trading, manufacture of luxury items, military strength, and domestic security. The new modes of cultural expression that began to flourish in Paris, London, Edinburgh, and Berlin came not from the established churches, which in each case were seriously weakened by internal divisions as well as increasing subordination to the state, but from the salons and coffee houses frequented by the new urban "public" and from the scientific and literary academies that provided new means of cultural production. When one traces the rivalries that existed among these academies, the nature of patronage and public employment, and the histories of publishing and reading habits, especially in comparison with countries such as Austria, Spain, and Russia, one cannot help but be impressed with the massive social resources that contributed to the making of the Enlightenment. And so, in considering the social conditions underlying the recent restructuring of American religion, the overall supply of relevant social and cultural resources would seem to be a factor worthy of close attention.

Yet in neither the Reformation nor the Enlightenment was the institutionalization of different (and presumably more "modern" or "adaptable") cultural forms simply the result of an undifferentiated growth in social resources wrought from a fortuitous wave of commercial expansion. In both periods the role of mediating social structures—structures that channeled and translated crude material resources—cannot be ignored. For anyone schooled in Marxist theory the role of social class as a mediating structure, of course, comes to mind. And this factor becomes all the more important in view of the popularity that class theories have attained in some quarters with respect to the conflicts and cleavages evident in American religion. In the historical literature, there is in fact a long tradition of Marxist scholarship that relates both the Reformation and the Enlightenment to changing class relations.

Historians have left virtually no stone unturned in examining the role of class relations in the Reformation and Enlightenment. Their efforts, though still inconclusive in some respects, have failed to uncover even a shred of evidence that clearly supports a strict class interpretation. Despite the fact that the Reformation occurred mostly in cities and towns, for example, detailed studies of places such as Strasbourg, Nuremburg, and Lyon have turned up no evidence that the bourgeoisie was any more prone toward adopting the reformers' teachings than were artisans, the poor, or even urban members of the nobility. Even the role of the bourgeoisie in its more traditional conception as urban residents fails as an entirely satisfactory explanation of the Reformation, since heavily commercialized towns existed in Poland, France, and Spain, just as they did in central and northern Europe and England, yet none of the former became officially allied with the Reformation. Similar problems are also encountered in attributing the Enlightenment to the rise of the bourgeoisie. The nobility played a prominent role in supporting science and enlightened literary culture in France, England, Scotland, and Prussia; the bourgeoisie either resisted this role or were largely indifferent in Holland, Sweden, the coastal trading cities of France, and industrial districts of England. Writers (Rousseau, for example) who came to be the champions of later democratic revolutions in which the bourgeoisie gained new freedoms were no less characteristic of the Enlightenment than were defenders of monarchy and aristocratic privilege (Montesquieu and Voltaire, for example). And even strict economic analyses of the period show such high degrees of overlap between the bourgeoisie and nobility as to cast doubt on the wisdom of emphasizing class conflict between the two.

In part, the lesson to be drawn from these historical cases is that explanations focusing on social class have faltered because they have too readily projected analyses of industrial societies into the context of pre-industrial societies. While there were in fact conflicts among status groups in both the Reformation and Enlightenment periods, these conflicts have often been obscured by treating them as if they could be understood with concepts from the nineteenth century such as "bourgeoisie" and "proletariat." Similarly, the religious divisions characteristic of the recent period in the United States have (as shown in Chapter 7) been influenced by changing relations among status groups, but again, to translate these changes into prototypical Marxist categories is likely to miss the dynamics of what actually transpired.

The Reformation and Enlightenment cases suggest another potentially important lesson for the analysis of religious restructuring. Although it has until recently been relatively neglected in sociological work, the state appears to provide a more promising area of investigation for understanding the processes by which new cultural forms become institutionalized. The state, indeed, exists as the chief agent in modern societies that mobilizes social resources and channels them in particular directions. Its role in directing, obstructing, or shaping market forces even in democratic societies is becoming increasingly well known. Its role in shaping and legitimating the means of cultural production also seems worthy of exploration. In both the Reformation and the Enlightenment the state's role was a decisive factor in determining which areas of Europe came to institutionalize the production of new cultural forms.

The pattern evident in the Reformation involves an interactive relation between economic expansion and the autonomy of states relative to the traditional ruling class. The central regimes in England and Scandinavia, territorial princes in northern Germany, and municipal magistrates in the German, Swiss, and Dutch regions all gained autonomy in their fiscal and administrative relations with the aristocracy as a result of commerce, tolls, shipping, and mining, as well as local conditions which in some areas weakened the hold of the nobility even in rural areas. France, Poland, and Spain, in contrast, remained clearly dependent on the nobility. The important conclusion is that the regimes in areas that became officially Protestant had considerably greater autonomy from the nobility than in those areas that remained Catholic, and thus were better placed to exert their influence on behalf of the reformers.

By the time of the Enlightenment, the scope and character of the state had changed considerably, of course, but again the relation between the state and the ruling class became a particularly interesting influence on Enlightenment scholarship. Because of the enlarged structure of the state, the dynamics of this relation and its influence on cultural production were actually felt to a great extent within the institutions of the state itself. France, Prussia, and England, as well as Scotland after the union with England, all underwent a tremendous expansion in the bureaucratic sector of the state during the first half of the eighteenth century. And the growth of central bureaucracy was a major factor in stimulating scientific academies, in promoting universities or other academies in which civil servants could be trained, and in creating a geographically concentrated public with common literary and political interests. Further, an important byproduct of this growth was what many contemporaries saw as a "constitutional crisis," or at least a fundamental new consideration in balancing the legislative and representative functions of the nobility, parliaments, and courts against the powerfully enlarged interests of the bureaucracy itself. Perhaps more than any other single theme, this is the question that runs through the writings of such otherwise diverse figures as Montesquieu, Hume, Pope, and Defoe. All were to a serious degree motivated by the need to write for an informed public whose corporate interests were clearly shared but yet whose interests could not be articulated simply with traditional perspectives amidst the complex vortex of contemporary politics.

Restructuring in the American Context

It remains, then, to bridge the gap between these historical examples and the question of religious restructuring in the United States in these closing decades of the twentieth century. It should perhaps be said as a brief caveat that speaking of *religious* restructuring may be to frame the question in a somewhat misleading manner. One cannot help but notice, in comparing the development of the Reformation with the Enlightenment, how much less religion as such mattered by the eighteenth century. And this is even more the case if one examines the rise of new ideologies in the nineteenth century. Religion was, of course, affected in all three periods, but the more recent movements were to a greater extent both separate from the churches as such and focused much more directly on the state itself. Thus it may be that a consideration of contemporary ideological change would focus more fruitfully on a broader range of developments than those confined only to religion. Nevertheless, it does seem evident that religious developments also remain important to examine in themselves. And this is especially the case in the United States where even traditional or institutionalized religious expressions remain powerful.

Some parallels with the two earlier periods, particularly the effects of rapid economic expansion and the role of the state, are sufficiently obvious to warrant attention. To say this, however, is to suggest nothing of value unless further specification is added. Certainly the period since World War II, or even before, has witnessed much growth both economically and in the social role of the state. As suggested in the foregoing chapters, economic growth in the period after World War II provided the material resources that made possible much of the adaptive expansion of churches and other religious organizations, while the state's growth created a steady succession of new challenges and entitlements to which religious communities actively responded. One can link the declining significance of denominationalism and the growth of special purpose groups, as well as many of the liberalizing trends in American religion, to the correlates of economic expansion: higher education, professionalization, science and technology. But one must also credit the state with an active role in these changes. The state initiated and mobilized the resources for growth in higher education, and actively promoted the transition to a more highly technical mode of economic production. In the same way, the state played a direct role in many of the specific episodes that evoked responses from the religious community: the civil rights movement, the Vietnam War, the Watergate episode, Supreme Court rulings on school prayer and abortion, FCC and Internal Revenue Service decisions affecting religious television, to name only a few. As the state expanded its regulative functions, and as more and more decisions came to be made by central administrative and judicial agencies, some sectors of the religious community responded positively, pressing the government to do even more, while other sectors mobilized to oppose these incursions.

Although the United States may be unique among industrialized countries because of its high degree of organized religiosity, some sense can possibly be made of the religious changes it has experienced in recent decades which may be of more general interest as well. It appears, in particular, that many of the highly diverse religious movements and countermovements that have characterized the nation since the 1950s can be understood in general terms within the context of broader economic and political changes that have greatly restructured the fabric of American social life. Nothing as profound as the Reformation or the Enlightenment can be identified, to be sure, but a serious degree of polarization has begun to emerge that may have sweeping ramifications for the future of American religion. The expanding social presence of the state has in no way determined the character of this cultural cleavage, nor even dictated that a cleavage of this kind should have developed. And yet, the state's role has been evident either implicitly or explicitly in most of the developments we have examined.

The area in which the state has most directly intervened in cultural production in the United States, we have argued, is the realm of higher education. Stimulated by international competition in science and technology, the federal government has fostered huge increases in the social role of higher education both by increasing absolute levels of funding and by shouldering an ever larger share of what were once private and local expenditures on higher education. These changes have been reflected, in turn, in a growing sector of the occupational structure which depends heavily on highly specialized training and which works mainly with science, advanced technology, education, and information processing. Described in some of the literature as a "new class," this sector is not so much a distinct class as it is a differentiated class fraction whose values and interests differ sharply both from the less privileged and from less educated members of the social elite. As the size of this "knowledge" sector has increased and as its position in both the economy and the state has become more important, a kind of vertical cleavage has developed which cuts through many traditional communities and modes of social differentiation, including both gender differences and ethnicity.

For American religion, this cleavage has become increasingly apparent as a new basis of differentiation not only between, but also within, major religious bodies. Many of the movements, organized and unorganized, which climaxed around the time of the social unrest of the Vietnam War reflected this cleavage. And the more stable period since 1973 has witnessed a widening gap between the two fractions, one of which tends to identify itself as religiously liberal no matter what specific denomination is involved; the other of which has taken a much more conservative orientation toward religion and has increasingly exercised its influence in American politics as well. At present, the two sides seem to be deeply divided, comprising almost separate religious communities whose differences have become far more important than those associated with denominational traditions. Both communities have educated elites who articulate theological and political opinions, although the liberal wing tends on the whole to be much more fully integrated into the knowledge sector than the conservative wing. Like earlier denominational rivalries, the present conflict between the two groups has given added vitality as well as visibility to organized religion as a whole. And yet, the very terms of religious discussion are increasingly being dictated by norms of technical rationality, as evidenced in such diverse developments as televised religion, creation science, the church growth movement, and religious nuclear disarmament campaigns. If American religion currently shows signs of both survival and revival, then, it also appears to be accommodating itself in perhaps irreversible ways to the dominant ethos of scientific technology.

In some respects the current cleavage in American religion represents an adaptive pattern that is contingent on its own unique resources as well as the unique role that the state has come to play in American society since World War II. Had it not been for the buildup of financial resources in church coffers during World War II and the even greater demand for new facilities after the war, the great "surge of piety" of the 1950s might not have been experienced and the capacity of religious organizations to adapt to the radical social upheaval of the 1960s might have been considerably weaker. The broader cultural resources that were deeply integrated into the religious heritage also facilitated this capacity to adapt. Religious leaders articulated their own visions of how their organizations should respond to the challenges of the future and did so with relative freedom from the dead weight of institutional precedents. The capacity to motivate action on the basis of mixed optimism concerning the promise and perils of the future led religious communities into an active engagement with the secular society rather than an alarmed or passive withdrawal from it. And confidence that religious education, preaching, and public pronouncements could in fact make for a better world reinforced this engagement.

As political issues such as the civil rights movement and the antiwar protests—and later, the feminist movement, the controversy over abortion, and the politics of public morality—impressed themselves with increasing prominence on the broader society, religious organizations mobilized their members both collectively and as individuals. Special purpose groups were founded, often in direct response to new initiatives by the state, for the purpose of uniting specific fragments of the religious community who now shared common interests. The tactics adopted by these groups often reflected the latest in political and organizational technology. And yet, the response was also conditioned by a deeper predisposition—one with roots in American history, in perceptions of the religious struggles in which people were engaged in countries around the world, and in the Judeo-Christian heritage itself. This was a predisposition to view all government activity with some suspicion and, therefore, to mobilize most actively around adversarial causes.

Politics and Faith

Engagement by religious movements in the political sphere, perhaps ironically, has often resulted in an expansion rather than a contraction in the power of the state. Civil rights protests resulted in entitlement legislation which required massive bureaucracies and public expenditures. Pressures on the part of religious groups to bring about greater social and economic justice have played a positive role in encouraging the formation of federal welfare programs. Even lawsuits aimed at promoting a return to traditional moral standards have sometimes threatened to give the courts greater power in determining the life styles of the American people. Closer examination of the relations between political orientations and political mobilization among the members of churches and other religious organizations, however, reveals that almost every issue since the late 1960s that has animated the energies of religious people has been associated with a feeling that the power of government was becoming too great. In 1968, for example, there was a significant positive relation between church attendance and political involvement among people who felt the government was becoming too powerful, but no such relation existed among people who were content with the growing power of government. Furthermore, the positive relations (discussed in Chapter 9) between religious and political involvement among those who opposed the Vietnam War were restricted to those who felt, more generally, that government was becoming more powerful. Similarly, the positive relation between religious involvement and political involvement among those who opposed racial integration, again, was limited to people who feared the growing strength of government.

In the 1980s, although the issues were different, the same patterns prevailed. During the 1980 elections, for example, active churchgoers were much more likely to become politically involved than less active churchgoers—but only if they thought government was becoming too powerful. Those who thought the government should be providing fewer welfare services were especially likely to show this kind of relation—again, if they thought government in general was becoming too powerful. The same was true on other issues as well: for example, defense, abortion, and the equal rights amendment. In virtually every instance, religious activity had more of a mobilizing effect in the political arena if specific orientations to the issues were combined with the feeling that government needed to be put back in its place.[12]

It is, of course, difficult to determine why this tendency has been such a prominent feature of the relation between politics and faith in the United States. Certainly it may reflect the high value that Americans have come to place on religious freedom—which, from the kinds of historical narratives now emerging, is likely to be understood chiefly as freedom from government interference. Even religious conservatives, who according to their more liberal detractors would wish to see a government-imposed form of totalitarian morality, are likely in their own rhetoric to define their objectives more in terms of restraining the hand of government than of courting its power.

The adversarial stance of religious groups toward government expansion may also be a function of the fact that religious organizations have for the most part carried out their tasks in the private sector. Consequently, any significant penetration of the private sector by government represents a diminished sphere of activity in which religious groups may be able to operate. This potential for conflict between religion and state is especially apparent if it is recalled, as shown in Chapter 2, that up until the end of World War II religious organizations played a substantial role in providing for many of the social services that government has more recently begun to appropriate for itself. By some indications, religious organizations had been responsible in the period just prior to World War II for approximately 15 percent of all hospitals, 42 percent of all homes for the aged, and at least a third of all institutions of higher education. These services not only contributed substantially to the public welfare but also provided tangible ways in which religious organizations could attract participation (for donors and recipients alike). With the significant growth of government in all of these areas since World War II, the relative role played by religion has become much less important. Not surprisingly, many have argued, religious organizations have had to develop other kinds of appeals; for example, the more privatized, therapeutic offerings that were mentioned earlier. Less easy to document has been whether this expanded role of the state has actually resulted in any overall decline in the strength of religious organizations.

At best, such effects would be difficult to measure. One relevant kind of information, however, comes from examining the relations between overall levels of government activity and overall levels of religious membership. Taking total government expenditure (federal, state, and local) as a measure of government activity, and comparing the 48 contiguous states in both 1952 and 1981, we find that increased government activity has a significantly *negative* effect on church membership—an effect that cannot be explained away by differences in region, race, religious composition, urbanization, or geographic mobility.[13] The proclivity of religious organizations to mobilize in adversarial politics, therefore, may in part stem from the adverse effect on these organizations of state expansion.

If there has been a common tendency for religious organizations to function as Caesar's adversaries, the direction in which these activities have been mobilized has varied greatly depending on the specific theological, social, and moral orientations of the organizations involved. Otherwise, it would be difficult to understand the sharp differences that have emerged between religious conservatives and religious liberals. The circumstances leading up to, and reinforcing, this cultural cleavage have, as the foregoing has shown, been highly complex and have involved characteristics internal to the religious community itself as well as pressures from the larger society. To suggest that the changing role of the state has contributed to the widening gap between religious liberals and conservatives, therefore, must be taken within this broader context. Nevertheless, at least some of the tension between the two religious communities must be attributed to the manner in which the state has functioned in recent decades.

Much of the state's growth since World War II has, as suggested in previous chapters, been linked closely with broader features of the world economy. Especially when viewed in this broader context, the state's changing social role appears to be related to what many regard as a transitional period in the world economy itself. From the laissez-faire, decentralized, firm-oriented capitalism of the nineteenth century, the U.S. economy has shifted increasingly toward a regulated, centralized, state-sponsored form of production in which technology and information become crucial to sustained economic growth. As shown in the last chapter, some of the impetus for this transition has come from the increasingly competitive world market in which the United States must participate. In addition, the various fiscal crises which plagued industrial societies earlier in the century, particularly the Great Depression of the 1930s, led the state to take an increasingly active role in matters of public relief, welfare services, medical benefits, old age assistance, redistributive and counter-cyclical spending, and a variety of domestic social functions. Overall, the state has come to play a much greater role in the economy than in the period prior to World War II. Military interests, mobilized by competition with the Soviet Union, have also contributed to its rising prominence, as have a number of other trends, such as growing professionalization, an increasingly large service sector in the broader economy, and processes of rationalization within the state bureaucracy itself.

This transition, however, has not been smooth. Like earlier transitions from feudalism to mercantilism and from mercantilism to industrial capitalism, the present transition has been fraught with unforeseen economic and political challenges. It has meant significant alterations in the power and privilege of various class fractions and has, accordingly, been advanced wholeheartedly by some and resisted just as strongly by others. As with any shift from a familiar social arrangement to an as yet unknown mode of social and economic organization, different models have competed as definitions of the future. And these have reflected both the familiar traditions of the past and the interests that status groups projected for themselves in the future. Laissez-faire models still compete with ideas of central planning, as the platforms of different political candidates illustrate. A mixture of industrial and post-industrial programs clearly remains, sometimes involving competition within the same corporation between departments devoted to different product lines. Government policy vacillates between combinations of free market competition and varieties of state-planned or state-regulated economic programs. And interest groups can usually be found on both sides of these policy debates. The present transition—in which the United States has been deeply involved since the collapse of the institutions that governed world trade during the nineteenth century under the shield of the *pax Britannica*—cannot, therefore, be understood as a simple shift from point A to point B. It needs to be seen as a series of moves that come in fits and starts, that often involve combinations of both A and B, and even involve competing visions of B itself.

Much of the consequent uncertainty in the economic and political realms may seem remote from the world of religious convictions—until it is remembered that American religion is, as Weber recognized (and as we tried to demonstrate in Chapters 2 and 3), heavily oriented toward an inner-worldly asceticism which connects it closely with ethical, social, and inevitably economic and political concerns. The major ingredients of the broader political and economic transition are also ones in which American religious groups have been vitally interested. Consider, for example, the connections between conceptions of religious freedom and arguments about economic freedom (some of which were discussed in Chapter 10); the religious conceptions of social justice that have influenced the development of the American welfare state; the intensive historic involvement of American religion in higher education and, as previously noted, other social services such as hospitals and old-age programs and the changes in this involvement that have come about as a result of state efforts to build a system of public higher education; the threats that many conservative religious groups perceive from the advancement of science; and the ambivalence toward capitalism itself that is generated by religious concepts of stewardship, equality, peace, love, and ultimate worth. The shift from one kind of political economy to another has generated religious responses—and counterresponses—on all of these issues.

Returning, then, to the cleavage that has developed between religious conservatives and religious liberals, it should not appear surprising that some of the cultural uncertainty in the broader political and economic realms has contributed to this development as well. Certainly such periods of transition like this have resulted in religious movements and countermovements in the past (the 1830s and 1840s being a prominent example in American history) and the present period seems to be no exception. Neither the conservative community in American religion, nor the liberal community, can be correlated in any one-to-one fashion with the different positions that have prevailed in discussions of political economy. For example, conservatives cannot be placed strictly on the side of classical laissez-faire economics, for they scarcely oppose government intervention to uphold their own version of public morality and seldom vote in ways that strictly favor an industrial rather than a postindustrial model of the economy. Religious liberals, for their part, seem closer to a laissez-faire model of government on issues of church-state separation than do religious conservatives. Nevertheless, both sides gain periodic reinforcement for at least some of their positions from the more general debates that characterize the political arena. As shown in Chapter 10, both sides have a distinctive view of the larger society, including a civil religion that not only legitimates certain kinds of political issues but also provides their own organizations with a positive role to play in relation to the public interest. From time to time, as the recent fortunes of New Christian Right leaders have shown, religious conservatives find themselves being courted and applauded by political factions whose interests include not only such issues as pro-life and antipornography but also such programs as tax reforms and incentives for business. At different times, liberal religious constituencies find their perspectives being championed by political factions which not only endorse clear separation of church and state but also attempt to promote nuclear disarmament initiatives and proposals for mitigating economic injustice. Neither side has to depend entirely on its own resources to legitimate itself or advance its particular positions. Both sides can depend on some support from public leaders who badly need their votes in opposing other political factions. Some of this competition revolves strictly around partisan politics. But neither the issues nor the ways in which religious constituencies vote conform strictly to partisan identities. Much of the tension involves deeper questions about the way in which the state itself should relate to the economy and the larger society. In this manner, then, the cleavages that are often prominent in the political sphere reproduce themselves in the religious sphere as well.

The ways in which American religion has been restructured since World War II, therefore, have been conditioned by the cultural, social, and political environment in which it functioned and by the internal resources with which it was able to adapt to these challenges. As the social role of the state has expanded, American religion has been exposed to the vagaries of political life in ways far more complex than at almost any time in its history. And these political influences have functioned both directly and indirectly to reinforce the changes internal to the religious community that we have sought to examine. Although these influences have made themselves felt simultaneously with the Supreme Court's espousal of a strong policy of "strict neutrality" toward religion, the policies the state has initiated have been anything but inconsequential for American religion.

NOTES

Chapter 1

1. Douglass and Brunner, *Protestant Church*, 200.
2. Tocqueville, *Democracy in America*, 2: 116.
3. Douglas, *Purity and Danger*, 165.
4. Norman O. Brown, *Love's Body*, 247.
5. Addressing complex questions has required the use of many different kinds of evidence and methods of analysis. Some of the evidence is of the kind that cannot adequately be examined with quantitative methods. Other pieces of evidence rest entirely on quantitative materials. Throughout the discussion an effort has been made to keep the argument as readable as possible. The more technical and statistical types of evidence have usually been presented in summary form, focusing on substantive conclusions; often the more technical aspects of these analyses have been published in separate reports or papers or have been put in footnotes. Similarly, a deliberate effort has been made to keep the discussion relatively free of technical jargon and obscure social science language.

Chapter 2

1. Fosdick, *Faith for Tough Times*, 114.
2. See *Emerging Trends*, Dec. 1985, 1, for Gallup figures on church attendance since 1939. Because of variations in sampling, early figures fluctuate considerably, for example, from 41 percent in 1939 to 37 percent in 1940.
3. In comparison, French data showed that only 33 percent in that country attended religious services regularly. *Public Opinion Quarterly* 10 (1946): 434.
4. Clarence Seidenspinner, "Religion on the Bandwagon," *Christian Century*, 24 Sept. 1947, 1141.
5. Kean, "God, Gods, and Dr. George Gallup," 17-19; the other figures were: England, 83 percent; Holland, 80 percent; Sweden, 80 percent; Denmark, 80 percent; and France, 66 percent.
6. Barnett, "God and the American People," 37, 230-34.
7. Thomas, *Religion and the American People*, survey conducted for the *Catholic Digest* in 1952.
8. Herberg, *Protestant-Catholic-Jew*, see especially Chaps. 1 and 5.
9. Figures cited in this section are from annual volumes of the *Yearbook of American Churches*; denominational minutes and handbooks; and Frank S. Mead, *Handbook of Denominations*.

10. Laski, *American Democracy*, 283.
11. Historians of American religion have routinely pointed out the limitations of these and other historical figures on religious membership. For crude comparative purposes, however, the numbers provide relatively useful indications of denominational size and trends in membership. Some recent uses of these data by sociologists have also suggested possibilities for analyses at state and county levels.
12. The most useful study of these organizational aspects of American religious history is that by Primer, *Protestants and American Business Methods.*
13. Useful sources on Catholic history in the United States include Hennesey, *American Catholics* and Dolan, *American Catholic Experience.*
14. Bernard G. Richards, "Organizing American Jewry," *Jewish Affairs*, 1 Oct. 1947, 3.
15. For a useful survey of this history, see Elazar, *Community and Polity*, esp. Chaps. 5 and 6.
16. Uriah Z. Engelman, "Educating the Jewish Child," *Jewish Affairs*, 1 Nov. 1946, 3-26.
17. U.S. Bureau of the Census, *Religious Bodies, 1936*. The denominational figures are from annual reports printed by the denominations mentioned.
18. U.S. Bureau of the Census, *Historical Statistics*, 318ff.
19. Eleanor Phillips, "My Church—Yesterday and Today," *Chronicle*, 7 (1944): 39.
20. Figures reported by the Congregational Christian Churches.
21. Walter S. Davison, "The Plight of Rural Protestantism," *Religion in Life* 15 (1946): 377-90.
22. Lenski, *Religious Factor.*
23. U.S. Bureau of the Census, *Historical Statistics*, 140.
24. Sunday School Board of the Southern Baptist Convention, *Southern Baptist Handbook* (Nashville; 1947), 7.
25. Methodist Church, *Minutes of the Annual Conferences* (New York: Methodist Publishing House, 1947), 257.
26. Presbyterian Church in the United States of America, *Minutes of the General Assembly, Part I: Journal and Statistics* (Philadelphia: Office of the General Assembly, 1947), 1058; *Yearbook of the Congregational Christian Churches of the United States of America* (New York: General Council of the Congregational Christian Churches, 1947), 284; United Lutheran Church in America, *Minutes of the Sixteenth Biennial Convention* (Philadelphia: United Lutheran Publication House, 1948), 22.
27. Davison, "The Plight of Rural Protestantism," 378.
28. Fosdick, *Faith for Tough Times*, 114.
29. James Wayland McGlathery, "Don't Live in the Past," *Moody Monthly*, Aug. 1947, 811-12.
30. Ferré, *Return to Christianity*, 10.
31. W. A. Criswell, "Fires of Evangelism," *Moody Monthly*, Sept. 1950, 12.

32. Ecumenical Methodist Conference, *Proceedings* (Nashville: Methodist Publishing House, 1947), 11; address by Bishop Lewis Hartman of Boston.

Chapter 3

1. Anton Chell, "The Church and Postwar Needs," *Religious Digest*, Jan. 1946, 5.
2. *Christian Century*, 9 May 1951, 593.
3. *Bensalem Methodist Church: 150th Anniversary* (Cornwells Heights, Pa., 1960). Pamphlet available at Speer Library, Princeton Theological Seminary.
4. Richard C. Brown, *The Presbyterians*, 52.
5. *Thine is the Power: The Story of the First Baptist Church, Alexandria, Virginia, 1803-1903* n.p., n.d.), 36. Pamphlet available at Speer Library, Princeton Theological Seminary.
6. Montgomery, *Old Stone Presbyterian Church*, 47.
7. Cohelan, "The Organization of the Church," 65 and passim.
8. John LaFarge, "American Catholics in a Changing World," *America*, 16 Aug. 1947, 543.
9. United Lutheran Church in America, *Minutes of the Sixteenth Biennial Convention*, 22.
10. *History of Three Bridges Reformed Church* (Three Bridges, N.J., 1973) Pamphlet available at Speer Library, Princeton Theological Seminary.
11. Leiffer, *Methodist Ministry in 1948*.
12. Letter to the editor, printed in *Christian Century*, 10 Jan. 1945, 53.
13. Oxnam, *Church and Contemporary Change*, 1.
14. See especially Reinhold Niebuhr, *Irony of American History*.
15. Quoted in *The Catholic World*, Dec. 1945, 193.
16. *Ibid.*, 199.
17. "Time for Christian Action," *Christian Century*, 10 Jan. 1951, 38.
18. Francis Cardinal Spellman, "Introduction," pp. xi-xii in Brunini, *What Catholics Believe*, xi.
19. Bennett, *Christian Ethics*, 90.
20. "American Foreign Policy," *Revelation*, Nov. 1946, 497-500.
21. Quoted in Robert C. Tucker, "Keeping Peace Between the Superpowers," *Princeton Alumni Weekly*, 6 Nov. 1985, 21.
22. A letter to Carl F. H. Henry, quoted in "The Vigor of the New Evangelicalism," *Christian Life*, Jan. 1948, 30.
23. George H. Gallup, *Gallup Poll* 2: 680.
24. *Ibid.*, 798.
25. *Ibid.*, 493, 594.
26. "Protestants Must Plan!" *Christian Century*, 5 Sept. 1945, 998.
27. George H. Gallup, *Gallup Poll* 2: 566, 933.
28. Quoted in *Christian Century*, 6 Nov. 1946, 1333.
29. *Ibid.*
30. *Twohey Analysis of Newspaper Opinion*, selected volumes, 1939-1948.
31. Letter to the editor, *Christian Century*, 19 Sept. 1945, 546.

32. For an example, see Luther J. Holcomb, "Christian America's Contribution to World Peace," *Moody Monthly*, Feb. 1947, 98.
33. Commager, *American Mind*, 433.
34. Daniel Day Williams, *God's Grace*, 368.
35. George H. Gallup, *Gallup Poll*, 2: 872.
36. *Twohey Analysis of Newspaper Opinion*, 1 Jan. 1949, 1.
37. Cyril R. Richardson, "Some Thoughts on the Christian Hope," *Religion in Life* 17 (1948): 534.
38. National Catholic Welfare Conference, "The Christian in Action," issued 21 November 1948 in Washington, D.C.
39. For a literary example of this view, see Knowles, *Peace Breaks Out*, which is set in the immediate postwar period.
40. John A. Mackay, "The Endless Journey Starts," *Theology Today* 5 (1948): 317.
41. Quoted in Arthur Hedley, "Rejoicing in Prosperity," *Revelation*, May 1946, 195-96.
42. "The Churches and World Order," reprinted in *Christian Century*, 7 Feb. 1945, 174-77.
43. "Protestants Must Plan!" *Christian Century* 5 Sept. 1945, 998.
44. Doris Coffin Aldrich, "Our Children and the Next War," reprinted in *Religious Digest*, June 1946, 55-58.
45. "Current Events in the Light of the Bible," *Our Hope*, June 1948, 742.
46. Henry, "Vigor of the New Evangelicalism," 32; emphasis in original.
47. Jessup, *Ideas of Henry Luce*, 291.
48. General Convention of the Protestant Episcopal Church, *Minutes* (Philadelphia, 1946), 58-59.
49. C. Stanley Lowell, "The Conversion of America," *Christian Century*, 28 Sept. 1949, 1134.
50. William Culbertson, "1952: A Sequel," *Moody Monthly*, March 1951, 444.
51. Hutchinson, *New Leviathan*, 231.
52. John P. Delany, "The Word," *America*, 2 Feb. 1946, 504.
53. Philip S. Bernstein, "Strength, Not Idealism," *Christian Century*, 20 July 1949, 864.
54. Ben Zion Bokser, "Rabbinic Judaism and the Problem of Egoism," in *Conflicts of Power*, ed. Bryson, Finkelstein, and McIver, 432.
55. Marshall, *Meet the Master*, 95-99.
56. Board of Sponsors, "Toward a Christian Approach to International Issues," *Christianity and Crisis*, 9 Dec. 1946, 1-3.
57. John C. Bennett, "Turn Communists to Christianity," *Christian Century*, 18 April 1951, 495.
58. Fosdick, *Faith for Tough Times*, 124.
59. Edward Skillen, Jr., "A Note on Anti-Communism," *Commonweal*, 28 Feb. 1947, 490.
60. H. Richard Niebuhr, "The Hidden Church and the Churches in Sight," *Religion in Life* 15 (1945-46): 106-16.

61. H. Richard Niebuhr, "The Gift of the Catholic Vision," *Theology Today* 4 (1947): 520.
62. Mackay, *Christianity on the Frontier*, 41.

CHAPTER 4

1. H. Richard Niebuhr, "The Gift of the Catholic Vision," 510.
2. P. B. Fitzwater, "The Church," *Moody Monthly*, June 1947, 671-72.
3. Henry, *Uneasy Conscience*, 88.
4. Ferré, *Return to Christianity*, 36.
5. Criswell, "Fires of Evangelism," 11.
6. Ordway Tead, "The Economic Channeling of Personal Power as Related to Cultural Fulfillment," in *Conflicts of Power*, ed. Bryson, Finkelstein, and McIver, 401.
7. Clyde Kluckhohn and Florence R. Kluckhohn, "American Culture: Generalized Orientations and Class Patterns," in *Conflicts of Power*, 106-28.
8. Kingsley Davis, *Human Society*, 143.
9. Robin M. Williams, *American Society*, 373.
10. See especially his "The Place of Ultimate Values in Sociological Theory," *International Journal of Ethics*, 45 (1935): 295 and passim.
11. National Catholic Welfare Conference, "Statement on Secularism," issued 14 November 1947; reprinted in *Pastoral Letters of the United States Catholic Bishops*, Vol. 2, ed. Hugh J. Nolan (Washington, D.C.: United States Catholic Conference, 1984), 75.
12. O'Brien, *Truths Men Live By*, 196ff.
13. Mumford, *Faith for Living*, 165-70.
14. Hugh L. Lamb, "Sermon," *Bulletin of the National Catholic Educational Association, Proceedings and Addresses, Forty-Sixth Annual Meeting* (Aug. 1949), 50.
15. Macartney, *Strange Texts*, 55.
16. Louis Wirth, "Ideas and Ideals as Sources of Power in the Modern World," in *Conflicts of Power*, ed. Bryson, Finkelstein, and McIver, 502.
17. John Courtney Murray, "How Liberal is Liberalism?" *America*, 6 April 1946, 6-7.
18. John C. Winston, "Christ or Communism," *Christian Life*, Dec. 1947, 25.
19. Arthur Hedley, "Only Christ Can Save," *Moody Monthly*, Nov. 1947, 228-29.
20. Oxnam, *Church and Contemporary Change*, 29-30.
21. Criswell, "Fires of Evangelism," 13-14.
22. Bailey, *Southern White Protestantism*, 132.
23. Handlin, *American People*, 222.
24. Fry, "Changes in Religious Organizations," 1009-60.
25. Bennett, *Christian Ethics*, 105.
26. Culbertson, "1952: A Sequel," 444.
27. Douglass and Brunner, *Protestant Church*, 184.
28. Bailey, *Southern White Protestantism*, 135-36.
29. Warner, *Democracy in Jonesville*, 149.

30. Oscar F. Blackwelder, "The Church and Our Time," *Theology Today*, 5 (1948): 157.
31. F. Ernest Johnson, "The Influence of Religion on Power Relationships," in *Conflicts of Power*, ed. Bryson, Finkelstein, and McIver, 367-75.
32. *Christian Century*, 16 Nov. 1946, 563.
33. Gollagher, *Quotable Eisenhower*, 65ff.
34. Sevareid, *In One Ear*, 227.
35. C. Stanley Lowell, "Summons to Protestants," *Christian Century*, 25 Oct. 1950, 1261.
36. "Priests and Politics," *America*, 30 March 1946, 655.
37. George W. Davis, "In Praise of Liberalism," *Theology Today* 4 (1947): 487.
38. Paul McGuire, "There is a Solution," *Integrity*, Nov. 1946, 4.

Chapter 5

1. Herberg, *Protestant-Catholic-Jew*. Summarizing his main argument, Herberg wrote: "With the religious community as the primary context of self-identification and social location, and with Protestantism, Catholicism, and Judaism as three culturally diverse representations of the same 'spiritual values,' it becomes virtually mandatory for the American to place himself in one or another of these groups. It is not external pressure but inner necessity that compels him. For being a Protestant, a Catholic, or a Jew is understood as the specific way, and increasingly perhaps the only way, of being an American and locating oneself in American society" (p. 39).
2. Lenski, *Religious Factor*, see especially pp. 362-66.
3. Glock and Stark, *Religion and Society*, 122.
4. Greeley, *Denominational Society*. See also Moberg, *Church as Social Institution*, especially Chaps. 11 and 12.
5. Roof and McKinney, "Denominational America," 26. The chapter organization of this volume also largely follows Herberg's tripartite division. Other recent works on American religion that also take this division for granted as an organizational rubric include McNamara, *Religion: North American Style*; and Reichley, *Religion in American Public Life*.
6. "Now Will Protestants Awake?" *Christian Century*, 26 Feb. 1947, 262-64.
7. Reported in *Christian Century*, 10 Jan. 1951, 62.
8. Ware W. Wimberly, "The Mixed Marriage," *Presbyterian Tribune*, Jan. 1946, 9-10.
9. National Association of Evangelicals, *Evangelicals Move Forward for Christ: A Report of the Eighth Annual Convention* (Indianapolis, 1950), 10.
10. Quoted in *Christian Century*, 1 June 1955, 661.
11. Ernest Gordon, "Unity or Separation?" *Sunday School Times*, 2 Feb. 1946, 89-90.
12. Blanshard, *American Freedom*. Blanshard's appeal was explicitly aimed at Catholics as well as Protestants, for he saw the danger as that of a totalitarian hierarchy directed by Rome, rather than a grass-roots movement on the part of Catholic laity.

13. Wilhelm Pauck, "The Roman Catholic Critique of Protestantism," *Theology Today* 5 (1948): 34.
14. *Look*, 18 May 1954.
15. Daniel Day Williams, *God's Grace*, 123. Williams's remarks were first presented as the Rauschenbusch lectures at the Colgate-Rochester Divinity School in 1948.
16. Quoted in *Christian Century*, 12 Nov. 1947, 1370.
17. Daniel Day Williams, *God's Grace*, 325.
18. *Christian Century*, 14 Feb. 1945, 198-200.
19. "They Will Change the Bible, If Need Be!" *Our Hope*, Oct. 1947, 240.
20. J. E. Harris, "Why Evangelize the Jew?" *Sunday School Times*, 2 Feb. 1946, 85-86.
21. Wuthnow, "Anti-Semitism and Stereotyping," 154-55.
22. Glock and Stark, *Christian Beliefs*, see especially pp. 43-80.
23. Douglass and Brunner, *Protestant Church*, 99.
24. Webber, *Evangelicals on the Canterbury Trail*, 13.
25. Lynd and Lynd, *Middletown*, 332-34.
26. T. T. Brumbaugh, "How Protestant Localism Grows," *Christian Century*, 11 Sept. 1946, 1091-93.
27. Glock and Stark, *Christian Beliefs*, 22. There is some ambiguity, of course, in what the phrase "member of your particular faith" might have meant to respondents. That it meant their own denomination rather than the Christian faith more generally seems evident from the fact that the question followed two others that were more oriented to the Christian faith generally, and it drew smaller percentages of affirmative answers than these earlier questions.
28. Stark and Glock, *American Piety*, 166.
29. Findings reported in *Christianity Today*, 7 Jan. 1957, 32.
30. Glock, Ringer, and Babbie, *To Comfort and to Challenge*, 188-89.
31. "Onward Christian Soldiers," stanza two.
32. John D. Rockefeller, Jr., "The Christian Church, What of Its Future?" *Chronicle* 8 (1945): 52.
33. On Rockefeller's role in the Interchurch World Movement, see Harvey, "Religion and Industrial Relations," 199-227.
34. "The Sentiment for Church Union," in *Yearbook of American Churches: 1933*, ed. Herman C. Weber (New York: Roundtable Press, 1933), 308-11.
35. Figures cited in Wilbur M. Smith, "The Steady Movement toward Church Union," *Our Hope*, July 1950, 18.
36. One of the most comprehensive compendiums on American religion, for example, indicates that the number of denominations had climbed to approximately 1,200 by the mid-1970s, up from less than a quarter that number at the start of the century. Calculated from Melton, *Encyclopedia of American Religions*. Some caution is needed in interpreting this figure, however, because a large number of the groups enumerated are not actually denominations. Many are single congregations, communes, ashrams, small clusters of three or four churches, and so on. Indeed, one could argue that the sizable number of such groups that are not denominations represents a shift away from denomination-

alism as a mode of religious organization. If one limits the field to religious organizations that are large enough to actually function as denominations, though, one still sees little evidence of any significant decline.

37. These figures were calculated from statistics reported in the *Yearbook of American Churches* for 1947 (ed. Benson Y. Landis and George F. Ketcham [Lebanon, Pa.: Sowers Printing Company, 1947]) and for 1985 (ed. Constant H. Jacquet, Jr. [Nashville: Abingdon, 1985]).

38. These statistics, of course, provide at best only weak indications of denominationalism. It could be, for instance, that more members concentrated in fewer and larger denominations would actually increase the significance of denominational rivalries.

39. H. Richard Niebuhr, *Sources of Denominationalism.*

40. For a review of studies examining regional differences in American religion, see Sopher, "Geography and Religions," 510-24.

41. This position was clearly evident in studies conducted earlier in the century. A study of the 1932-1933 edition of *Who's Who* showed that Episcopalians were overrepresented by a factor of eight relative to their proportion in the total population. Data collected in 1936 showed that Episcopalians had the most expensive church buildings of any denomination. A study in 1950 of the 500 largest companies in the U.S. showed that a third of their chief executive officers were Episcopalians.

42. For example, data collected in 1976 showed that Episcopalians were still twice as likely on average compared to the rest of the population to hold professional and managerial positions and that their family incomes were still 1.4 times the national average. A study of the 500 largest companies in 1976, however, did reveal that the proportion of chief executives who were Episcopalians had dropped from a third to a fifth. For the material on Episcopalians in *Who's Who*, see Herman C. Weber, "The 1932-33 Edition of *Who's Who* and Organized Religion," in *Yearbook of American Churches: 1933*, ed. Weber, 314-16. On representation in large companies, see Konolige and Konolige, *Power of Their Glory*, 321. Data on value of church buildings are from U.S. Bureau of the Census, Religious Bodies, 1936. Figures on occupational representation were calculated from the 1960 and 1976 National Election Surveys for white male heads of households. In both years Episcopalians were 2.1 times more likely than the national average to be in professional or managerial occupations. Presbyterians were 1.8 times more likely in 1960 but only 1.4 times more likely in 1976. The data on mean family incomes were calculated from the 1960 and 1980 National Election Surveys. Mean family incomes for Episcopalians were 1.45 times the national average in 1960 and 1.40 times the national average in 1980; for Presbyterians, 1.14 in 1960, and 1.35 in 1980; and Baptists, 0.85 in 1960, and 0.86 in 1980. The National Election Surveys are conducted by the Center for Political Studies at the University of Michigan. Major surveys are conducted every four years during presidential elections; minor surveys are conducted midway between the major studies during congressional elections. The data analyzed are on tapes at the Princeton University Computer Center.

These tapes are available through the Inter-University Consortium for Political and Social Research at the University of Michigan.

43. These figures were calculated from the national enumerations of religious memberships conducted by the National Council of Churches for each of these years; see *Churches and Church Membership in the United States: An Enumeration and Analysis by Counties, States and Regions* (New York: National Council of the Churches of Christ in the U.S.A., 1952), and Bernard Quinn, *Churches and Church Membership in the United States, 1980* (Atlanta, Ga.: Glenmary Research Center, 1982).

44. Studies emphasizing the overall continuities in regional distributions of religious bodies have tended to overlook the significance of some of these localized effects. Another way in which the tendency toward greater regional intermixing of Protestants and Catholics can be seen is by examining the composition of persons migrating to different parts of the country. In the northeastern states, for example, the ratio of Protestants to Catholics is only .82 to 1 among residents who grew up in these states. Among residents who grew up elsewhere and moved to the Northeast, however, the ratio of Protestants to Catholics is 4.00 to 1. In other words, the effect of regional migration into the Northeast is to bring a disproportionate share of Protestants to the region, thereby making it less predominately Catholic. In the South, just the opposite trend is occurring. Among those who grew up in the South and still live there, the ratio of Protestants to Catholics is 9.00 to 1. In contrast, this ratio is only 2.85 to 1 among those who were raised elsewhere and moved to the South. The effect of interregional migration here, then, is to bring a disproportionate number of Catholics to the South. These figures were calculated from the General Social Survey Cumulative Data File, a file of national survey data collected annually between 1972 and 1984 by the National Opinion Research Center at the University of Chicago and available through the Inter-University Consortium for Political and Social Research at the University of Michigan.

45. The total variance for all the regions is 24 percentage points for natives, compared with only 7 points for migrants. For Catholics, there also appears to be a homogenizing trend in church attendance patterns associated with regional migration. In the Midwest, for example, natives to the region are 10 percentage points more likely than the national average to attend church regularly. Among newcomers to this region, the difference is only 7 points. And among Catholics in the West, natives are 17 points below the national average on church attendance, compared with a deficit of only 4 points among newcomers to the West. Overall, the regional variance for Catholics adds up to 31 percentage points among natives, compared to only 12 points among migrants.

46. Figures calculated from the studies of churches and church membership cited in n. 43 above, for the respective years.

47. The 1956 data are from the national survey conducted by the Census Bureau in that year, as reported in Bernard Lazerwitz, "Religion and Social Structure," 426-39. The 1980 figures were derived from the National Election Survey data from that year.

48. These figures were obtained by analyzing the General Social Survey Cumula-

tive Data File for the years 1972-1982 and are for white respondents only. These data were used because they give the most sizable, and therefore most stable, numbers of respondents for each of the denominations. The numbers on which the percentages are based range from a low of 102 for Jews and 140 for Episcopalians to a high of 1086 for Baptists and 1292 for Catholics.

49. Reported in *Christian Century*, 6 April 1955, 411.

50. These results are from my analysis of data obtained from the Gallup Organization, Princeton, N.J. The survey was conceived by George Gallup, Jr., and designed in consultation with the author. Field work among a nationally representative sample of the noninstitutional adult population in the continental U.S., following normal Gallup polling procedures, was conducted in June 1984. Support for the survey was provided by the Robert Schuller Ministries, Inc. Further results of the study are presented in Chaps. 7 and 9.

51. These data are from an analysis of the General Social Survey Cumulative Data File, 1972-1982. They are based on nearly 12,000 cases from representative adult samples of the U.S. population.

52. Results from analysis of the 1984 Gallup survey cited in n. 50 above.

53. More detailed results from the same study give an idea of what kinds of cross-denominational attendance are most and least common. Lutherans were quite likely to have attended services at Catholic churches (76 percent of those who were currently Lutherans had done so). It was also common for Methodists to have attended services at Baptist churches (71 percent of those who were currently Methodists had done so). It was fairly common, too, for Baptists to have attended services at Methodist churches (60 percent of the Baptists had done so). Lutheran-Baptist, Methodist-Catholic, and Lutheran-Methodist exchanges were fairly frequent as well. Least common were exchanges between Baptists and Catholics.

54. Specifically, the percentages who had attended six or more different denominations were: grade school, 11 percent; high school, 16 percent; some college, 34 percent; college graduate, 35 percent. For zero to two denominations: grade school, 52 percent; high school, 42 percent; some college, 28 percent; college graduate, 27 percent.

55. For example, 36 percent of all persons who were raised as Lutherans and who have been to college have switched to another denomination, compared to only 26 percent of those raised as Lutherans who have not been to college. Similarly, 45 percent of one-time Methodists in the college educated category have switched, compared to 38 percent of their less educated counterparts. This pattern holds for denominations in which overall levels of education are quite high as well. For example, by a margin of 41 percent to 35 percent college educated Episcopalians are more likely to have switched than non-college educated Episcopalians. Among Presbyterians, the difference is smaller but in the same direction (47 percent versus 44 percent). And among denominations that start out with relatively *low* levels of education, the patterns are again evident. A third of all former Baptists have switched if they have been to college, compared to a quarter of those who have not been to college. Similarly, nearly half of all one-time members of Protestant sects who have been to college have switched

denominations, compared to about a third of those who have not been to college. Just as among Protestants, the differences are also evident among Catholics. Specifically, 23 percent of college educated persons raised as Catholics have switched to another faith, compared with 15 percent of their less educated counterparts. These results are from an analysis of the data in the General Social Survey Cumulative File, 1972-1982. They are based on more than 8,000 persons without college educations and nearly 4,000 persons who had been to college.

56. Results from analysis of the 1984 Gallup survey cited in n. 50 above.

57. The 1965 and 1975 figures are reported in Cohen, *American Modernity and Jewish Identity*, 56; the 1983 figure is from Steven M. Cohen, *The 1984 National Survey of American Jews: Political and Social Outlooks* (New York: American Jewish Committee, 1984), 51.

58. Among Methodists, for instance, only 31 percent of the younger cohort, compared with 43 percent of the older cohort, had married endogamously. The proportions among Presbyterians were 25 percent and 35 percent respectively. And among Lutherans, the difference was 30 percent versus 57 percent. Of the Protestant denominations studied, only Baptists failed to show a strong trend (58 percent versus 62 percent). And for Catholics, the trend was in the same direction, but relatively weak (58 percent versus 66 percent). See Robert Alan Johnson, *Religious Assortative Marriage*, 160.

59. Newport, "The Religious Switcher," 540.

60. Specifically, a comparison of data from the mid-1970s and the mid-1950s shows that the percentage of married people with spouses belonging to the same religion as themselves declined by the following amounts: among Baptists, 4 percentage points; among Lutherans, 9 percentage points; among Methodists, 11 percentage points; among Presbyterians, 25 percentage points; among Catholics, 11 percentage points; and among Jews, 14 percentage points. The data for the 1950s are reported in Greeley, *Denominational Society*, 245. The data for the 1970s are from an analysis of the General Social Survey Cumulative File, 1972-1982.

61. These results are from an analysis of the General Social Survey Cumulative File, 1972-1982. Specific percentages were as follows for respondents and spouses having been raised in the same denomination: Methodists, 36 percent among college educated, 37 percent among non-college educated; Lutherans, 27 percent and 40 percent respectively; Presbyterians, 17 percent and 25 percent respectively; Episcopalians, 24 percent and 10 percent respectively; Catholics, 57 percent and 63 percent respectively; and Jews, 79 percent and 78 percent respectively. The percentage of married respondents who reported that their spouses' denomination was currently the same as their own, for college educated persons and non-college educated persons respectively were: Baptists, 74 and 82; Methodists, 69 and 71; Lutherans, 66 and 76; Presbyterians 69 and 65; Episcopalians, 71 and 48; Catholics, 74 and 78; and Jews, 89 and 76. A log linear analysis of the same data, taking into account the effects of both cohort and educational level, suggests that the effects of education are not significant; it may be, however, that the differences (as these figures suggest) are

significant for some denominations but not for others, thereby canceling out any overall effects; in any case, see the very useful paper by Allan L. McCutcheon, "Denominations and Religious Intermarriage: Marital Cohorts of White Americans in the Twentieth Century," presented at the 1984 annual meeting of the Society for the Scientific Study of Religion at Chicago.

62. The percentages on which these ratios are based are reported in Wuthnow, "Anti-Semitism and Stereotyping," 150.

63. See n. 50 above.

64. Survey conducted by the author in 1979 as part of the "Lutheran Listening Post," a national survey of the members of the Lutheran Church in America. Some results from this survey have been reported in Roger A. Johnson, *Views from the Pews.*

65. These results are from the 1984 survey from which the earlier findings on denominational switching were drawn. See n. 50 above.

66. The Episcopal Church, *The Lambeth Conferences, 1968: Resolutions and Reports* (New York, 1968), 42.

67. These quotations are used by permission from Deborah Melanie Sharpe, "Denominationalism: What the Cynic Sees" (Senior Thesis, Princeton University, 1985), 44-45, 67.

68. Gallup polls conducted in 1967 and in 1978 showed respectively that 89 percent and 91 percent of the public said they would vote for a Catholic for president. The latter figure was higher than the proportion who said they would vote for someone who had been divorced; *Gallup Opinion Index*, Nov. 1978.

69. *Gallup Opinion Index*, Aug. 1979, 29-30.

70. *Gallup Report*, No. 213, June 1983.

71. *Gallup Opinion Index*, Nov. 1972, 13.

72. Memo from the Center for the Study of American Pluralism, National Opinion Research Center, University of Chicago, dated September 5, 1973.

73. See also Greeley, *American Catholic*, 50-68.

74. For example, see Westoff, "Catholic Reproductive Behavior," 231-40.

75. These conclusions are drawn from an analysis of data from the General Social Survey Cumulative File, 1972-1984. These data contained approximately 2,200 Catholics under age 40 and approximately 2,000 Catholics age 40 or over. Specific percentages for younger and older Catholics respectively who had each of the following characteristics were: college degree, 16 and 9; foreign born, 9 and 12; originated from Polish, Irish, or Italian stock, 38 and 46; lived in the South, 18 and 13; identified themselves as Democrats, 43 and 53; and identified themselves as "strong" Catholics, 34 and 50.

76. Sally Cunneen, "Continual Reformation at Last?" *Christian Century*, 14 May 1969, 670-71.

77. "Understanding the Papacy," *Christian Century*, 6 Sept. 1967, 1115-16.

78. John Van Engen, "Catholicism 20 Years After Vatican II," *Christianity Today*, 18 Feb. 1983, 50.

79. Wuthnow, "Anti-Semitism and Stereotyping," 154-56.

80. Selznick and Steinberg, *Tenacity of Prejudice.*

81. Martire and Clark, *Anti-Semitism*; see also Gregory Martire and Ruth Clark,

"Anti-Semitism in America," *Public Opinion* 5 (1982), 56-59. The partial correlation coefficient between an index of Christian fundamentalism and anti-Semitism, controlling for education and race, was an insignificant .01.

82. *Gallup Report*, No. 213, June 1983.

83. Kenneth A. Briggs, "Change Is Found in Jewish Views of Intermarriage," *New York Times*, 24 Jan. 1979. Other questions in national polls also pointed toward relatively low levels of tension between Christians and Jews. For example, in a 1979 survey only 2 percent of Protestants and 2 percent of Catholics said they had ever had an experience that made them dislike Jews. *Gallup Opinion Index*, Aug. 1979, 29-30.

84. "The Vatican's Dilemma," *Christian Century*, 7 July 1965, 859.

85. James Kelly, Department of Sociology, Fordham University, personal correspondence.

86. A. James Rudin, "Catholics, Jews: 20 Good Years," *New York Times*, 23 Feb. 1985.

87. Johnson and Cornell, *Punctured Preconceptions*, 14.

88. These figures were calculated from the reports printed in annual yearbooks of the respective denominations. The particular denominations, as well as the years for which comparisons were made, were chosen because of comparable reporting procedures. The three denominations also vary considerably in the extent to which they are popularly perceived as being run by central bureaucracies. Because of differences in allocating expenses, the percentages are not strictly comparable across the three denominations. Insofar as the number of central boards and committees can be taken as a measure of bureaucratic centralization, there is also little evidence of growth at this level. For example, the Southern Baptist Convention had 12 boards and standing commissions in 1946, 13 in 1968, and 11 in 1977. The Episcopal church actually *reduced* its number of central commissions and committees from 40 in 1945 to 20 in 1967. Data from other denominations, although not quite as comparable, also reveal a lack of growth in fiscal centrality: in the Methodist church, the proportion of total gifts which went to district or conference treasurers declined from 3.1 percent in 1946 to 1.9 percent in 1969 and to 1.2 percent in 1980; American Baptists held their Unified Budget for General Programs and Administration constant between 1946 and 1967, while total giving to the denomination increased fourfold, thereby effecting a reduction in the proportion of funds going to central agencies from 16 percent to 4.1 percent.

Chapter 6

1. Kenneth Scott Latourette, *A History of Christianity*, 934.
2. *American Bible Society Record*, May 1985, 27-29.
3. These figures are from the *Encyclopedia of Associations* (New York: Gale, 1985).
4. The data on denominations on which these comparisons are made are from Melton, *Directory of Religious Bodies* , with corrections made as indicated. These figures include a considerably larger number of denominational bodies than do those cited in many other sources.

5. Bell, *Contradictions of Capitalism*, 194-99.
6. A recent issue of the *Briefcase*, the official newsletter of the Christian Law Association, for example, is filled with stories of the association's activities in court cases involving children's homes and parochial elementary schools.
7. Only about 100 organizations use these terms, or derivatives thereof, in their titles.
8. The figures reported in this section are from a 1984 survey of the adult population in the U.S. conducted by the Gallup Organization and made available to the author for further analysis. See Chap 5, n.50.
9. One source of information on the kinds of programs that attract people to churches is *The Unchurched American* (Princeton: Princeton Religion Research Center, 1978). Some of the other points in this paragraph are based on data from a national survey conducted by the author in 1984 in cooperation with the Gallup Organization as part of the Annenberg/Gallup Study of Religious Television.
10. Michels, *Political Parties*.
11. The two clusters were obtained by factor analyzing the data. The principal component scores on the first factor were: healing ministries, .672; prison ministries, .599; Bible study groups, .576; charismatic groups, .540; and world hunger ministries, .442. On the second factor, the scores were: protest activities, .717; antinuclear coalitions, .603; holistic health groups, .521; positive thinking seminars, .498; and therapy sessions, .453. Default options of the SPSS factor analysis module were used for the analysis. The existence of two distinct factors was confirmed using oblimax and varimax rotations.

Chapter 7

1. See the 1984 Gallup survey cited in Chap. 5, n.50.
2. Peggy L. Shriver, "The Paradox of Inclusiveness-that-Divides," *Christian Century*, 21 Jan. 1984, 194.
3. Barbara Ehrenreich, Elizabeth Hess, and Gloria Jacobs, "Unbuckling the Bible Belt," *Mother Jones*, July/Aug. 1986, 46.
4. Particularly useful sources on this period include Marsden, *Fundamentalism and American Culture*; and Szasz, *Divided Mind*.
5. Having failed to seize theological control of the Northern Baptist Convention in 1922, the fundamentalists in that denomination had formed a separate organization in 1923, called the Baptist Bible Union, and then split off officially in 1932, becoming the General Association of Regular Baptist Churches.
6. Those who continued to regard fundamentalism as an important phenomenon in American religion still tended to view it as the work of extremely small denominations or of independent churches, rather than a movement within the larger denominations; for example, see Harvey McArthur, "Liberal Concessions to Fundamentalism," *Religion in Life* 14 (1944-45): 535-44.
7. Nels F. S. Ferré, "Present Trends in Protestant Thought," *Religion in Life* 17 (1948): 336.
8. Cyril C. Richardson, "Some Thoughts on the Christian Hope," *Religion in Life* 17 (1948): 531-39.

9. F. Ernest Johnson, "The Churches in America during 1945-1946: Achievement and Opportunity," in *Yearbook of American Churches: 1947*, 158-63.
10. *The Presbyterian*, 11 April 1946, 3.
11. *Christian Century*, 19 Oct. 1949, 1222.
12. Mackay, *Christianity on the Frontier*, 46-47.
13. *Christianity Today*, 10 June 1957, 3-6, 25.
14. Henry, *Protestant Theology*, 92.
15. "Twelve Great Churches: Editorial," *Christian Century*, 3 Jan. 1951, 8.
16. Headley, *Christian Heritage*, 162-63.
17. Henry Sloane Coffin, "Be Fair to Liberalism," *Theology Today* 4 (1947): 498-99.
18. Schofield, *Methodist Church*, 122. On moral issues, Methodists also maintained their commitment to traditional positions. As late as 1950, for example, a carefully planned campaign by the denomination resulted in an outpouring of some 200,000 letters to a congressional committee in favor of an antiliquor bill. J. Paul Williams, *What Americans Believe*, 286.
19. Sherwood Eliot Wirt, "Billy Graham in San Francisco," *Christian Century*, 12 Jan. 1955, 47-48.
20. J. Paul Williams, *What Americans Believe*, 110.
21. *Ibid.*, 115.
22. Quinley, *Prophetic Clergy*, 139.
23. Myrdal, *American Dilemma*.
24. Dean R. Hoge, *Division in the Protestant House* (Philadelphia: Westminster, 1976).
25. These and other figures from the San Francisco area are from a representative sample survey of 1,000 residents of the greater San Francisco metropolitan area conducted by the author in 1973. For greater detail, see my *Consciousness Reformation*.
26. George Gallup, Jr., *Religion in America, 1979-80*, 34. *Religion in America* is generally published biennially under the general editorship of George Gallup, Jr., and provides valuable summaries of recent Gallup poll data on religion. Copies can be purchased from the Gallup Organization, 53 Bank Street, Princeton, N.J. 08540. Some libraries also obtain these volumes and catalog them together with the *Gallup Opinion Index* or *Gallup Report*.
27. The question asked specifically about participation in "an encounter group or similar kind of training such as sensory awareness, sensitivity training, a T-group, or growth group."
28. These figures are calculated from relevant editions of the *Statistical Abstract of the United States*, compiled by The Bureau of the Census, and from data reported in *Public Opinion* 5 (1982): 29.
29. Based on numbers of persons age 14 through 24.
30. For specific question wordings and percentages, see Wuthnow, *Consciousness Reformation*, 23-30.
31. Nunn, Crockett, and Williams, *Tolerance for Nonconformity*, 38-41.
32. See Wuthnow, *Consciousness Reformation*, 12-48.
33. Selznick and Steinberg, *Tenacity of Prejudice*, 72.

34. Nunn, Crockett, and Williams, *Tolerance for Nonconformity*, 60.
35. Wuthnow, *Consciousness Reformation*, 164-71.
36. For discussions of the "new class," see Gouldner, "The New Class Project"; Bazelon, *Power in America*, especially Chap. 11; and Bell, "The New Class."
37. Ladd, "Pursuing the New Class," 101-22.
38. Wuthnow and Shrum, "Knowledge Workers," 471-87.
39. Wuthnow, "Cultural Religious Commitment."
40. Calculated from figures reported in *Public Opinion* 5 (1982): 25.
41. Some statistical evidence on these effects is presented in Wuthnow, *Experimentation in American Religion.*
42. Glock, Ringer and Babbie, *To Comfort and to Challenge*, 119-25.
43. Hadden, *Gathering Storm*, 145.
44. A study of California clergy in 1968, for example, showed that only 1 percent of the ministers who scored at the "low" end of a scale of clergy activism felt they received encouragement for social activism from their parishioners, while 34 percent of those at the "high" end of the scale felt they received this kind of support. See Quinley, *Prophetic Clergy*, 182.
45. The first set of figures cited is from annual polls conducted by the Gallup Organization; the second set is from an analysis of national surveys conducted in election years by the Center for Political Studies at the University of Michigan.
46. Calculated from figures reported in George Gallup, Jr., *Religion in America, 1981.*
47. See especially Wuthnow, *Consciousness Reformation.*
48. John P. Dessauer, "Book-Buying Patterns in the '70s Showed Real Gains—Mostly Through Retailers," *Publishers Weekly*, 221 (1981), 37-39.
49. *Gallup Report*, No. 236, May 1985.
50. The figures in this paragraph are based on national surveys conducted by the Gallup Organization and reported in *ibid.*, and in various issues of the Princeton Religion Research Center's newsletter, *Emerging Trends.*
51. Martire and Clark, *Anti-Semitism*, 72.
52. Calculated from *Encyclopedia of American Religions.*
53. *Emerging Trends*, Jan. 1986.
54. Angela Aidala, Rutgers University; personal communication.
55. Popenoe and Popenoe, *Seeds of Tomorrow*, 89-107.
56. Calculated from figures reported in George Gallup, Jr., *Religion in America, 1982.*
57. Data cited in George Gallup, Jr., *Religion in America, 1979-80.*
58. Based on a discriminant analysis of the data.
59. From analysis conducted by the author of data from a 1983 Gallup survey.
60. This result is from an analysis of data collected in 1982 by the Gallup Organization. Given a 7-point scale ranging from "male" to "female," 68 percent of those who had not finished high school and 59 percent of those who had finished high school, compared with only 36 percent of the college graduates, chose the option at the extreme male end of the scale.

61. Analysis of data from national surveys conducted as part of the General Social Survey between 1972 and 1984 (cumulative), whites only.
62. Using a composite measure of liberalism/conservatism to summarize attitudes toward a number of these issues, Simpson found that 87 percent of the grade school educated scored high on conservatism, compared with 70 percent of the high school educated, 53 percent of those with two-year college degrees, 48 percent among graduates from four-year colleges, and 36 percent among persons with postgraduate degrees. See Simpson, "Moral Issues and Status Politics," 195.
63. These figures are calculated from national surveys conducted in 1958 and in 1982 by the Center for Political Studies at the University of Michigan as part of its National Election Surveys. The next most serious decline was in the youngest, non-college educated category: a difference of 11 percentage points. In the category of college educated persons age 45 or older, the difference was only 6 points. And in the two older categories of non-college educated persons: 4 points, and 5 points, respectively. Separate analysis for Protestants and Catholics shows the effects of education for both but also indicates that these effects were much stronger among Catholics. Between 1958 and 1982 there was a decline of 6 percentage points in regular church attendance among college educated Protestants, compared with a 4 point increase among non-college educated Protestants. Among Catholics, the better educated showed a difference of negative 34 points; the less educated, a difference of negative 12 points. Another notable effect of these changes was to make religious participation rates among Protestants and Catholics much more similar among the better educated. By 1982, only 1 percentage point separated Protestants and Catholics on church attendance among those who had been to college; among others, there was a 14 percentage point difference. The fact that college educated Protestants and Catholics had virtually converged in levels of church attendance represented a considerable change since 1958. In that year, Catholics were 29 percentage points more likely than Protestants (both having at least some college education) to attend church regularly.
64. *Gallup Report*, No. 236, May 1985.
65. Results from analysis of the 1984 Gallup survey cited in Chap. 5, n.50.
66. Reported in *Eternity*, Nov. 1983.
67. See for example, Guth, "Southern Baptist Clergy," 122-23.

Chapter 8

1. Henry, *Uneasy Conscience*, 81.
2. Joel Carpenter, "Geared to the Times, but Anchored to the Rock," *Christianity Today*, 8 Nov. 1985, 44-47.
3. James E. Bennet, "The Forward March of Fundamentalism," *Christian Life*, Jan. 1948, 21-23, 70.
4. Pollock, *Billy Graham*.
5. J. Elwin Wright, "Growth of N.A.E. is Modern Evangelical Miracle," *Religious Digest*, June 1946, 32-34.

6. For example, see Harold John Ockenga, "Can Fundamentalism Win America?" *Christian Life*, June 1947, 13-15.
7. Henry, *Uneasy Conscience*, 87.
8. Harold John Ockenga, "We Will Be Free," *Christian Life*, Feb. 1948, 95.
9. W. Richie Hogg, "The Role of American Protestantism in World Missions," in *American Missions in Bicentennial Perspective*, ed. R. Pierce Beaver (South Pasadena, Calif.: William Carey Library, 1977), 354-502. See especially pp. 396-404.
10. Billy James Hargis, *My Great Mistake* (Green Forest, Ark.: New Leaf Press, 1985), 42.
11. Baker, *Southern Baptist Convention*, 360-62.
12. The figures in this paragraph are from Kelley, *Conservative Churches*, 20-32.
13. *The Record of the National Council of Churches*, rev. ed. (Wheaton, Ill.: The Church League of America, 1969), 23-39.
14. These data are from John Stephen Hendricks, "Religious and Political Fundamentalism: The Links between Alienation and Ideology" (Ph.D. diss., University of Michigan, 1977).
15. These results are from the 1968 National Election Survey conducted by the University of Michigan. More specifically, 32 percent of the members of conservative Protestant denominations said they favored desegregation, compared with 35 percent of the members of liberal or moderate Protestant denominations. Within each group, persons who regarded the Bible as God's literal word were also almost as likely to favor desegregation as persons with more liberal views of the Bible: 32 percent versus 40 percent among liberal Protestants; 31 percent versus 38 percent among conservative Protestants. On Vietnam, 55 percent of conservative Protestants and 64 percent of liberal or moderate Protestants said the U.S. should have stayed out. Within each group, biblical conservatives were somewhat more likely to give this response than biblical liberals: 65 percent versus 62 percent among liberal Protestants; 56 percent versus 53 percent among conservative Protestants. Conservative Protestants in this study included all persons coded as "neo-fundamentalists" by the University of Michigan. This group in 1968 was comprised mainly of members of the Church of Christ, the Pentecostal Church, Assemblies of God, the Church of God, and Nazarenes.
16. Pierard, *Unequal Yoke*, 174.
17. Howard Hagerman, "Cancelled Flight," *HIS*, Dec. 1969, 3.
18. Leighton Ford, "Evangelism in a Day of Revolution," *Christianity Today*, 24 Oct. 1969, 6-12.
19. Kilian McDonnell, "A Catholic Looks at Evangelical Protestantism," *Commonweal*, 21 Aug. 1970, 409.
20. Stark and Glock, *American Piety*, 200. The study did not examine the effects of educational levels.
21. Quebedeaux, *Worldly Evangelicals*, 3.
22. Kenneth S. Kantzer, "Documenting the Dramatic Shift in Seminaries from Liberal to Conservative," *Christianity Today*, 4 Feb. 1983, 10-11. In 1956, the leading seminaries by order of size were: Southern (SBC), Southwestern (SBC),

Concordia (LC-MS), Union (in New York), Garrett, Yale, Luther, Princeton, New Orleans (SBC), and Candler. By 1981, the top ten were: Southwestern (SBC), Fuller (independent evangelical), Southern (SBC), New Orleans (SBC), Southeastern (SBC), San Francisco, Trinity (independent evangelical), Princeton, Concordia (LC-MS), and Asbury (evangelical). Seven other evangelical seminaries also had enrollments of 400 or more students.

23. George Gallup, Jr., *Religion in America, 1982*, 34.
24. Kenneth S. Kantzer, "The Charismatics among Us," *Christianity Today*, 22 Feb. 1980, 25-29.
25. Russell T. Hitt, "California God Rush," *Eternity*, March 1978, 31-34.
26. George Gallup, Jr., *Religion in America, 1977-78* (Princeton: Princeton Religion Research Center, 1978); and *Religion in America, 1982*.
27. Editorial Staff, "The Christianity Today-Gallup Poll: An Overview," *Christianity Today*, 21 Dec. 1979, 12-19; David O. Moberg, "Do the Properly Pious Really Care?" *Christianity Today*, 19 Sept. 1980, 25-27. Further analysis of these data, using a different religious classification scheme, is found in Hunter, *American Evangelicalism*.
28. Hunter, *Evangelicalism: The Coming Generation*, 136. These data were collected among nearly 2,000 students at evangelical colleges in spring 1982.
29. *Ibid*., based on analysis of national General Social Survey data, 150-54.
30. Horsfield, *Religious Television*, 9.
31. Steve Chapple, "Whole Lotta Savin' Goin' On," *Mother Jones*, July/Aug. 1986, 37-45.
32. D'Souza, *Falwell Before the Millennium*, 59.
33. Robert Wuthnow, "The Political Rebirth of American Evangelicals," in *The New Christian Right*, ed. Robert C. Liebman and Robert Wuthnow (New York: Aldine, 1983), 173.
34. Richard N. Ostling, "Power, Glory—And Politics," *Time* 17 Feb. 1986, 63.
35. *Religious Television in America* (Sept. 1983), report written by the author for the Gallup Organization as part of the Annenberg/Gallup Study of Religious Television.
36. *Ibid*., 25.
37. George Gallup, Jr., *Religion in America, 1982*.
38. George Gerbner, *Religion and Television* (Philadelphia: Annenberg School of Communications, University of Pennsylvania, 1984), 41-46.
39. Horsfield, *Religious Television*, 148.
40. FitzGerald, *Cities on a Hill*, 154.
41. Glenn Hewitt, "Unity and Disunity among Southern Baptists," *Christian Century*, 13 June 1984, 592.
42. These figures are from the U.S. Bureau of the Census, *Statistical Abstract of the United States: 1981* (Washington, D.C.: U.S. Government Printing Office, 1982, 148.
43. Winter, "Political Activity Among the Clergy," 178-89.
44. Hoge, "Theories of Denominational Growth," 179-97.
45. These studies are reviewed in Wuthnow, "Political Rebirth of American Evangelicals," 169-72.

46. *Ibid.*, 168-71.
47. Only 5.5 percent of the articles in *Christianity Today* during 1969 and 1970 had dealt with political themes; a decade later, this proportion had tripled.
48. On the ritual aspects of Watergate, see Bergesen and Warr, "Crisis in the Moral Order" and Alexander, "Culture and Political Crisis.
49. Content analysis of the *Readers' Guide to Periodical Literature* conducted by the author showed that the number of entries concerning morality and ethics increased from 55 to 87 between 1969 and 1979, the number of category headings increased from 13 to 18, and the number of institutional spheres (e.g., military ethics, journalistic ethics, business ethics, etc.) increased from 6 to 12.
50. Leslie A. Simons, "Technology, Mass Media, and Social Change: The Case of Contraception in the United States" (Senior Thesis, Princeton University, 1980), 79, 146-47.
51. *Washington Post*, 26 Oct. 1980, 16.
52. William J. Bennett and Terry Eastland, "The 'new right' Christians," *Wall Street Journal*, 17 Sept. 1980.
53. Proverbs 14:34 AV.
54. Wirt, *Social Conscience*, 92.
55. Author's analysis of data collected in 1982 by the Princeton Religion Research Center as part of a study of self-esteem.
56. Steve Silverman, "The Religious Majority" (Unpublished paper, Department of Politics, Princeton University, 1981).
57. Jerry Falwell, *Here's How You Can Help Save America* (Lynchburg: The Old-Time Gospel Hour, 1980), 2.
58. Quoted in William Martin, "God's Angry Man," *Texas Monthly*, April 1981, 153.
59. Richard A. Viguerie, *The New Right: We're Ready to Lead* (Falls Church, Va.: The Viguerie Comapny, 1980), 156.
60. Quoted in Strober and Tomczak, *Jerry Falwell*, 179.
61. George Gallup, Jr., *Religion in America, 1982*.
62. *Religious Television in America*. When asked to select which of a list of seven activities should be among the top three goals of the churches, 57 percent of all religious television viewers chose "maintaining high moral standards," 46 percent chose "evangelism and missionary work," 52 percent chose "encouraging fellowship among believers," and 38 percent chose "preaching and celebrating the Sacraments." Only 22 percent chose "working for social justice." The most commonly selected goal was "helping individual members grow spiritually" (chosen by 77 percent).
63. Gerbner, *Religion and Television*, 113-31.
64. Simpson, "Moral Issues and Status Politics."
65. Jerry Falwell, *Christians in Government: What the Bible Says* (Pamphlet distributed by Moral Majority, Lynchburg, Virginia, 1981).
66. A 1979 direct-mail solicitation from Moral Majority.
67. A 1979 pamphlet describing the organization.
68. A 1979 direct-mail solicitation from Jerry Falwell. Emphasis added.
69. A 1979 direct-mail solicitation from Jerry Falwell. Emphasis added.

70. Direct-mail solicitation, 1980.
71. Quoted in Adam Clymer, "Conservative Political Committee Evokes Both Fear and Adoration," *New York Times*, 31 May 1981.
72. LaHaye, *Battle for the Mind*, 199-200.
73. *New York Times*, 23 March 1981.
74. A 1979 direct-mail solicitation from Jerry Falwell.
75. Art Ringer, "New Right Mullahs," *Playboy*, June 1981, 36.
76. Moral Majority leaflet, 1979.
77. A 1980 memo released by People for the American Way.

Chapter 9

1. These and subsequent figures in this section are from the 1984 study conducted by the Gallup Organization cited in Chap. 5, n.50. The specific wording on this question was "How much tension would you say there is at present between people with conservative religious views and people with liberal religious views—quite a lot, a fair amount, or only a little?" Conservatives consisted of respondents who selected "1" or "2" on a 6-point scale ranging from conservative to liberal; liberals included respondents who selected "5" or "6." The question read simply, "Where would you place yourself on this scale in terms of your RELIGIOUS views?" Respondents were then given a hand card showing the 6-point scale.
2. Quoted in Shriver, *Bible Vote*, 145.
3. The exact percentages were: among conservatives, 29 percent of those who said they had had a great deal of contact with liberals scored high on the antiliberal stereotype index (selected at least four of the six negative phrases), as did 20 percent of those who had had a fair amount of contact, 5 percent of those with only a little contact, and 11 percent among those with none. Among liberals, 60 percent of those who said they had had a great deal of contact with conservatives scored high on the anticonservative index (selected at least four of the seven negative phrases), as did 56 percent of those who had had a fair amount of contact, 47 percent of those with only a little contact, and 38 percent of those with none.
4. To provide somewhat more detail, only 8 percent of the conservatives who had had contact with liberals in a prayer fellowship scored high on the antiliberal index, compared with 26 percent whose contact came from family and 20 percent whose contact had been in a former church. Among liberals, 42 percent scored high on anticonservative feeling when their contact had been in a prayer group, compared with 59 percent whose contact had been through relatives and 66 percent whose contact had been in a former church. The high figures for former churches suggest that people may be switching from congregation to congregation with some sense of concern about whether particular churches are too liberal or too conservative for their own taste.
5. The percentages who scored high on the antiliberal index were: college graduates, 21 percent; some college, 17 percent; high school graduates, 12 percent; less than high school, 15 percent.
6. Specifically, among liberals who have participated in humanistic groups, 64

percent scored high on the anticonservative index, compared with 48 percent of the liberals who had not participated. Among conservatives, 19 percent of those who had participated in evangelical special purpose groups scored high on the antiliberal index, compared with 12 percent of the nonparticipants. Looked at differently, the data also lend themselves to the interpretation that negative stereotyping may reinforce participation in each kind of group. Among those who scored high on antiliberalism, 49 percent were participants in evangelical groups, compared with only 19 percent of those who scored low on antiliberalism. Among those who scored high on anticonservatism, 17 percent were involved in humanistic groups, compared with only 7 percent of those who scored low on this index.

7. Cohen, *1984 National Survey of American Jews*, 33.
8. Results based on a discriminant analysis involving seventeen test parameters (variance explained, 89.7 percent; Wilks lambda, .781). Canonical discriminant function coefficients for the nine social issues included as test parameters averaged .181; for the eight religious items included, .108. Average ranking of the two sets of items was: social issues, 6.9; religious items, 11.4.
9. For instance, in the 1968 National Election Survey, a third of those with theologically conservative views of the Bible among liberal and conservative Protestant denominations alike said blacks should be kept out of white neighborhoods; in comparison, only a fifth of those with theologically liberal views in both kinds of denominations said this.
10. *Ibid.*
11. Data from an analysis of the 1980 National Election Survey.
12. For this and subsequent figures, see George Gallup, Jr., *Religion in America, 1982*. Figures not reported there are from the author's analysis of other Gallup surveys of nationally representative samples conducted between 1980 and 1984.
13. These differences between men and women are also evident in most European countries, despite the fact that overall levels of religious commitment are much lower. My own analysis of data collected in 1983 by the *Eurobarometer* survey, for example, showed that the proportion of women who said they were "religious" was 7 points higher than the proportion for men in France; 6 points higher in Belgium; 4 points higher in the Netherlands; 15 points higher in Germany; 10 points higher in Italy; 8 points higher in Luxembourg; 10 points higher in Denmark; 25 points higher in Ireland; 14 points higher in the United Kingdom; and 11 points higher in Greece. Differences of 12 percentage points on the average separated men and women on reporting that God was "very important" in their lives.
14. For an early empirical study concerned with the "comforting" qualities of religion for women, see Glock, Ringer, and Babbie, *To Comfort and to Challenge*.
15. These results are from an analysis conducted by the author of data from the General Social Survey Cumulative File, 1972-1984, which contains information from approximately 10,000 men and women in national surveys conducted during the years indicated. For the entire sample, women were 12 per-

centage points more likely to say they attended religious services almost every week or more often than were men. The differences ranged from 8 points for members of Protestant sects to 13 points among Baptists and Methodists. Controlling for level of education, the differences were 15 percentage points among Protestants with at least some college training, 10 points among Protestants with no college training, 8 points among Catholics with some college training, and 14 points among Catholics with no college training. Among men and women under age 40, there was a 12 point spread for those with some college training, a 9 point spread for those with no college training. And among full-time participants in the labor force, the difference among men and women with some college training was 7 points, and among men and women with no college training, 9 points. Evidence from earlier studies of religious commitment also suggests that gender differences in religiosity have not diminished substantially. A question about belief in life after death asked in a 1944 survey, for example, produced a 6 percentage point gap between men and women; asked again in 1960, the same question generated a 10 point difference; and in 1981, a difference of 11 points. See Hazel Gaudet Erskine, "The Polls: Personal Religion," *Public Opinion Quarterly* 29 (1965): 145-57; and George Gallup, Jr., *Adventures in Immortality*. On church membership rates, some evidence does suggest that gender differences may be smaller now than in the past. But the reason cannot be traced to declining membership rates among women. Instead, membership has actually grown among both men and women. But the growth has been faster among men than among women, resulting in some convergence between the two. Thus, data from the 1926 religious census showed that 63 percent of adult females and 48 percent of adult males were church members, a gap of 15 points; by 1985, the comparable figures were 73 percent and 63 percent, a gap of only 10 points. See Douglass and Brunner, *Protestant Church*; George Gallup, Jr., *Religion in America: Fifty Years, 1935-1985* (Princeton: Princeton Religion Research Center, 1985). Douglass and Brunner attributed the lower rates of religious membership among men to the demands of farming. By implication, the partial convergence of rates among men and women may be a function of urbanization. Other characteristics of urbanization, such as shift-work in industry, however, would seem to militate against this explanation.

16. Wuthnow, *Consciousness Reformation*, see especially p. 261.
17. Penny A. Edgell Becker, "An Analysis of Receptivity to Women in Leadership Roles in Liberal and Conservative Protestant Churches" (Senior Thesis, Department of Sociology, Princeton University, 1986), 57.
18. Charlene Spretnak, "The Politics of Women's Spirituality," in *The Politics of Women's Spirituality: Essays on the Rise of Spiritual Power Within the Feminist Movement*, ed. Charlene Spretnak (Garden City, N.Y.: Anchor, 1982), 396.
19. A Gallup poll conducted in May, 1947, showed that 43 percent of the public thought a woman would make as good a minister as a man, while 47 percent disagreed with this view. On the same survey, 46 percent of the public ex-

pressed approval of having more women serve as governors, senators, doctors, lawyers, and in other professions.

20. Lehman, *Women Clergy*, 6-17.

21. Greeley and Durkin, *Angry Catholic Women.*

22. These results are based on an analysis of data from the General Social Survey Cumulative File, 1972-1984.

23. Quoted in Becker, "Analysis of Receptivity," 48.

24. *Ibid.*, 50-51.

25. To examine the relations between religious involvement and political participation among women, data were analyzed from the National Election Surveys conducted by the Center for Political Studies at the University of Michigan during the 1976, 1980, and 1984 presidential elections. Women who said they attended church or synagogue "almost every week" or more often were compared with women who said they attended "once a month" or less. Political participation was measured by a standard set of items asking about attendance at political meetings, talking about politics, working in the campaign, and making political contributions. Respondents were assigned a value of "high" if they scored two or more on the scale.

26. The percentages who scored high on political participation among frequent and infrequent church attenders, respectively, were 17 percent and 12 percent in 1984, 16 percent and 12 percent in 1980, and 16 percent and 14 percent in 1976; only the 1980 and 1984 results were statistically significant at the .05 level of probability.

27. The percentages who scored high on political participation among frequent and infrequent church attenders, respectively, were 19 percent and 9 percent among women who disapproved of the equal rights amendment, 30 percent and 17 percent among women who were registered as Republicans, 24 percent and 14 percent among women who felt the government had grown too powerful, and 21 and 13 percent among women who felt the government should provide fewer welfare services. All of these relations were significant at or beyond the .05 level. The differences were not significant among women in the contrasting subgroup on each of these items (e.g., those who approved of the amendment, Democrats, etc.). The differences among Carter voters were 9 and 17 percent, respectively; among Reagan voters, 26 and 22 percent. These differences were only marginally significant (at the .15 level).

28. Specific percentages scoring high on political participation in 1984 for women who attended church regularly and women who did not, respectively, were: 23 percent and 16 percent among Republicans, 20 percent and 15 percent among Reagan voters, 17 percent and 21 percent among Mondale voters, 19 and 12 percent among persons who wished to increase defense spending, and 16 and 8 percent among persons who felt women's place was in the home. These differences were significant at or beyond the .05 level; differences among contrasting subgroups were not significant.

29. From literature provided by the movement.

30. Luker, *Politics of Motherhood*, 196-97.

31. These conclusions summarize findings from the author's analysis of national

survey data collected in 1984 as part of the Annenberg/Gallup study of religion and television.

32. Survey of women in 23 evangelical churches conducted in 1985 by Bruno & Ridgway Associates, Inc.

33. Specifically, 20 percent of those who attended church almost every week or more often scored high on political participation in the entire sample, compared with 13 percent of those who attended church less regularly. Among members of liberal Protestant denominations, the proportions, respectively, were 22 percent and 14 percent; among members of conservative Protestant denominations, 12 percent and 9 percent; among Catholics, 17 percent and 8 percent; among persons who felt the Bible was entirely true, 19 percent and 8 percent; and among persons who took a more qualified view of the Bible, 22 percent and 16 percent. These results are from an analysis of the 1968 National Election Survey conducted by the Center for Political Studies at the University of Michigan.

34. These findings clearly run against the grain of popular images of the civil rights movement which portray integrationists in the churches as more politically activist than segregationists. However, the two sets of findings are not contradictory. What is at issue here is the *relationship* between church attendance and political participation, not the absolute level of political participation. The relationships between church attendance and political participation were significant for segregationists but not for integrationists. In absolute terms, though, political participation was still higher overall among integrationists than among segregationists.

Chapter 10

1. Durkheim, *Religious Life*. For a useful discussion of this aspect of Durkheim's work, see the introductory essay in Bellah, *Emile Durkheim*.

2. Richard Neuhaus has noted that "an inescapable fact about America and Americans is the propensity to define and redefine ourselves" and suggests that this tendency is itself "an essential part of the definition of America." See his paper "From Providence to Privacy: Religion and the Redefinition of America," presented at the conference on "Unsecular America," sponsored by the Center on Religion and Society, New York, January 1985, p. 1. Work on other societies suggests that this trait is not uniquely American; see for example, T. Dunbar Moodie, *The Rise of Afrikanerdom* (Berkeley: University of California Press, 1975). Especially valuable on the public theology of America are Sidney E. Mead, *The Nation with the Soul of a Church* (New York: Harper & Row, 1975), and Wilson, *Public Religion*.

3. The distinction drawn here between utterances and broader legitimating assumptions parallels that of Jürgen Habermas, "What is Universal Pragmatics?" in his *Communication and the Evolution of Society* (Boston: Beacon Press, 1979), 1-68. For an attempt to explicate the relevance of Habermas's discussion for the sociology of culture, see Robert Wuthnow, James Davison Hunter, Albert Bergesen, and Edith Kurzweil, *Cultural Analysis: The Work of Peter L.*

Berger, Mary Douglas, Michel Foucault, and Jürgen Habermas (London: Routledge and Kegan Paul, 1984), 179-239.

4. Rousseau, *Social Contract*, 7.
5. Kohn makes this point with specific reference to the American case: "American national consciousness is based upon the conviction of being different from other nations—different not in representing a peculiar and unique development of human history but in realizing, as the first people, with the greatest possible approximation to perfection, the general trend of human development towards a better rational order, greater individual liberty, and basic equality." Kohn, *Idea of Nationalism*, 291.
6. See especially his book *The Broken Covenant.*
7. Useful overviews of the literature on American civil religion are found in Gehrig, *American Civil Religion*; Phillip E. Hammond, "The Sociology of American Civil Religion: A Bibliographic Essay," *Sociological Analysis* 37 (1976): 169-82; and Robert N. Bellah and Phillip E. Hammond, *Varieties of Civil Religion* (New York: Harper & Row, 1980).
8. Francis A. Schaeffer, *A Christian Manifesto*, 33.
9. Historians are, in fact, divided on the question of how much the Founding Fathers may have been guided by religious principles. British historian Paul Johnson, for example, asserts: "No one who studies the key constitutional documents in American history can doubt for a moment the central and organic part played by religion in the origins and development of American republican government" ("The Almost-Chosen People: Why America is Different," Erasmus Lecture, New York, January 1985, 2). A different view which emphasizes the departures from religious principles is presented in Mark A. Noll, Nathan O. Hatch, and George M. Marsden, *The Search for Christian America* (Westchester, Ill.: Crossway Books, 1983).
10. Tuveson, *Redeemer Nation.*
11. Herman Melville, *White-Jacket, or, The World in a Man-of-War* (Boston: Page, 1982 [c. 1850]), 144.
12. From *The Complete Writings of Walt Whitman*, Vol. 9 (New York: G. P. Putnam's Sons, 1902), 186-97.
13. Peale, *One Nation Under God*, 6-7.
14. Walton, *One Nation Under God*, 16, 21.
15. Edward L. R. Elson, "The Source of Our Life," *Decision*, July 1969, 3.
16. Otis, *Solution to Crisis-America*, 53.
17. Rogers, *Let Freedom Ring!* 19-20.
18. Hatfield, *A Hard Place*, 92.
19. Falwell, *Fundamentalist Phenomenon*, 212.
20. Linder and Pierard, *Twilight of the Saints*, 156.
21. Falwell, *Fundamentalist Phenomenon*, 212.
22. LaHaye, *Battle for the Mind*, 35.
23. Bright, *Come Help Change the World*, 172.
24. Kenneth S. Kantzer and Paul Fromer, "When Should Christians Stand against the Law?" *Christianity Today*, 4 March 1983, 11.

25. Interview reported in Rodney Clapp, "Where Capitalism and Christianity Meet," *Christianity Today*, 4 February 1983, 27.
26. George Gilder, "Moral Sources of Capitalism," *Society*, Sept./Oct. 1981, 27.
27. Falwell, *Wisdom for Living*, 131, 102. Falwell also attempts to insure that this doctrine is taught at Liberty Baptist College. According to its catalog, "The college aggressively supports the free enterprise system." Quoted in D'Souza, *Falwell Before the Millennium*, 186.
28. Robertson, *Secret Kingdom*, 151.
29. Ronald H. Nash, "The Christian Choice Between Capitalism and Socialism," in *Liberation Theology*, ed. Ronald H. Nash (Milford, Mich.: Mott Media, 1984), 60.
30. "Bill Armstrong: Senator and Christian," *Christianity Today*, 11 November 1983, 23.
31. Christenson and Wimberley, "Who is Civil Religious?" 77-83; and Wimberley and Christenson, "Civil Religion," 91-100; and as background, see Ronald C. Wimberley, "Testing the Civil Religion Hypothesis," 341-52.
32. Shupe and Stacey, "The Moral Majority Constituency," 104-17.
33. Connecticut Mutual Life Insurance Company, *The Connecticut Mutual Life Report on American Values in the '80s: The Impact of Belief* (Hartford, 1981), 63.
34. George Gallup, Jr., *Religion in America, 1982*, 129ff.
35. Board of Social Ministry, *World Community: Ethical Imperatives in an Age of Interdependence* (New York: Lutheran Church in America, 1970), 1.
36. Richard J. Niebanck, *World Community: Challenge and Opportunity* (New York: Lutheran Church in America, Board of Social Ministry, 1970), 1.
37. Jean Caffey Lyles, "NAE's Focus on the Family," *Christian Century*, 7 April 1982, 398.
38. Research Division of the Support Agency, *Presbyterian Panel* (New York: United Presbyterian Church, U.S.A., 1982).
39. For a useful introduction to this debate, see Judith A. Dwyer, ed. *The Catholic Bishops and Nuclear War* (Washington, D.C.: Georgetown University Press, 1984).
40. Hoge, "Theological Views of America," 127-40.
41. Jim Wallis, "The Churches at the Crossroads," *Progressive*, July 1984, 62-63.
42. John Langan, "The Bishops and the Bottom Line," *Commonweal*, 2-16 Nov. 1984, 586-92.
43. "Excerpts from Draft of Bishops' Letter on the U.S. Economy," *New York Times*, 12 Nov. 1984.
44. *The Harris Survey*, No. 104, 22 Dec. 1983.
45. Donald E. Miller, "The Future of Liberal Christianity," *Christian Century*, 10 March 1982, 266.
46. It is interesting to note that the conservative vision often seems to embody what Weber termed the "priestly" function of religion, while the liberal vision more often seems to express religion's "prophetic" function. Weber's discussion of priests and prophets in the evolution of modern religion is found in Weber, *Sociology of Religion*, especially Chaps. 2 and 4. As priest, the conser-

vative offers divine sanction to America, legitimating its form of government and economy, explaining its privileged place in the world, and justifying a uniquely American standard of luxury and morality. As prophet, the liberal raises questions about the American way of life, subjects political and economic policies to transcendent concerns, and challenges Americans to act on behalf of all humanity rather than their own interests alone.

47. Bellah, *Beyond Belief*, 179, 186. A similar point is argued by Ward, *Nationalism and Ideology*, 118-25.

48. Wallis, "The Churches at the Crossroads," 63.

49. Commenting on the bishops' letter on economic justice, for example, Jerry Falwell suggested to a conference of evangelical clergy that the letter was merely an endorsement of socialism: "While the bishops don't advocate redistributing the nation's wealth, they come close to it, and that's socialism, which isn't any more than shared poverty." Quoted in James R. Dickenson, "President Welcomes Draft of Bishops' Pastoral Letter," *Washington Post*, 14 Nov. 1984. Jim Wallis has been described by conservative writers as a socialist who uses a double standard in criticizing America but failing to point out the evils of other regimes. See, for example, Lloyd Billingsley, "First Church of Christ, Socialist," *National Review*, 28 Oct. 1983; and Franky Schaeffer, *Bad News for Modern Man* (Westchester, Ill.: Crossway Books, 1984), 57-58.

50. This, at least, is the argument that Bellah and others have put forward. Many of the discussions of the Civil War period, however, suggest that it shaped American civil religion in retrospect, as the nation reflected back upon its time of trial, but leave open the question of whether civil religion during the war itself was weakened or strengthened by the religious cleavage that accompanied the fighting. Certainly Lincoln drew on civil religious themes as a rallying cry for the North.

51. Novak, *Democratic Capitalism*.

52. *Ibid.*, 336.

53. Leonard Silk, "Bishops' Letter and U.S. Goals," *New York Times*, 14 Nov. 1984.

54. Robert J. Samuelson, "Bishops' Letter Smacks of Economic Make-Believe," *Washington Post*, 28 Nov. 1984.

55. George F. Will, "The Vanity of the Bishops," *Washington Post*, 15 Nov. 1984.

56. Quoted in *Public Opinion*, June/July 1982. This and subsequent surveys from *Public Opinion* are from the journal's "Opinion Roundup" section, which gives additional information on question wording, response categories, and dates when the poll was conducted.

57. Potter, *People of Plenty*, 37.

58. Tocqueville, *Democracy in America* I:317.

59. George Gallup, Jr., *Religion in America, 1982*. Two national surveys conducted in 1968 and in 1971 which asked respondents to rank a list of 18 "terminal [basic] values" found that "freedom" (defined as "independence" or "free choice") ranked third (after "a world at peace" and "family security"). In comparison, the one religious value included in the list—"salvation"—ranked

eighth and ninth in the two surveys. See Rokeach, *Nature of Human Values*, 133.

60. *New York Times Magazine*, 11 December 1983.

61. *Public Opinion*, Feb./March 1984.

62. Friedman, *Capitalism and Freedom*, 3.

63. Gilder, *Wealth and Poverty*, 29.

64. Many of Friedman's and Gilder's arguments are, in fact, presaged in the writing of eighteenth-century economists; see Hirschman, *Passions and Interests*.

65. *Public Opinion*, April/May 1980.

66. David S. Broder, "Is It 'Growth'—Or Just 'Greed'?" *Washington Post*, 21 Nov. 1984.

67. Leonard Silk, "In Celebration of Creative Capitalism in Society," *New York Times*, 7 Nov. 1984.

68. Will, "The Vanity of the Bishops."

69. Robert J. Samuelson, "The Bishops Are Wrong," *Washington Post*, 28 Nov. 1984.

70. This study also provided some rare comparative evidence on how people in other countries view themselves and how they view the United States. National samples in Canada, the United Kingdom, West Germany, Switzerland, and Brazil were asked the same battery of questions. Two results were striking. First, most of the respondents in these countries agreed with Americans in giving the U.S. very high ratings on freedom. For example, 83 percent of the Canadians said people in the U.S. enjoy a great deal of freedom, as did 73 percent of the British, 85 percent of the West Germans, and 81 percent of the Swiss. In all of these countries the U.S. in fact received the highest percentages, with the occasional exception of Canada. Second, Americans rated the freedoms in all of these other countries lower than did people in their own countries. For example, Canada was rated 7 points lower by Americans than by Canadians themselves; Britain, 13 percent lower than it was by the British; and West Germany, 37 percent lower than by West Germans. In other words, Americans showed some tendency to magnify the importance of their own freedoms by failing to recognize the freedoms in other countries which citizens of those countries themselves perceived. *Gallup Report*, Nos. 220/221, Jan./Feb. 1984.

71. From an interview in *Public Opinion*, Feb./March 1982.

72. James P. Mullins, "The Real Nature of International Power: We Still Have Control of Our Destiny," *Vital Speeches* 49 (15 May 1983): 467-70.

73. Richard Sennett and Jonathan Cobb have noted this tendency in their interviews with working-class Americans. They write: "People whose material freedom or freedom to act in an institutional setting is limited in a threatening way, make freedom for themselves by constructing reality so that the real part of themselves must feel free of performing *in response to* the demands of another." *Injuries of Class*, 200.

74. *Self-Esteem Study* (Princeton: The Gallup Organization, 1982). The study focused specifically on sources of perceived self-worth, not merely valuing work or deriving satisfaction from work. Respondents who indicated that work was an important source of their self-worth scored higher on Rosenberg's Self-Es-

teem Scale, on a scale of leadership qualities, and on a self-report measure of productivity.

75. Connecticut Mutual, *Report*, 166-67.

76. The high degree to which the market encourages belief in the individual's control over his own fate has been emphasized in Robert E. Lane, "Personal Freedom in a Market Society," *Society*, March/April 1981, 63-76.

77. Nixon's fondness for quoting this dictum is cited by Charles Colson in his book *Loving God* (Grand Rapids, Mich.: Zondervan, 1983), 97.

78. Bellah, *Broken Covenant*, 73. Henry Steele Commager writes: "They believed passionately in themselves and their destiny, and . . . did not preclude pride in what they had themselves accomplished. . . . As the rich and spacious continent had dazzled but not confounded their imagination, so their speedy conquest of it induced a sense of limitless power." *American Mind*, 29. On the other hand, Paul Johnson sees no sign of a shift away from religious to secular, pragmatic assumptions during this period. He writes, "The cold, secularising wind which in Europe progressively denuded government of its religious foliage, left America virtually untouched" ("The Almost-Chosen People," 8).

79. Quoted in Rosenberg, *Spreading the American Dream*, 74. Another useful source for this period is Dallek, *American Style of Foreign Policy*.

80. Reinhold Niebuhr, "America's Eminence," *Christianity and Society* 13 (1948): 3-4.

81. Elwyn A. Smith, "Anti-Americanism, French Style," *Christian Century*, 10 March 1965, 300-303.

82. Robert N. Bellah, "Cultural Pluralism and Religious Particularism," in *Freedom of Religion in America: Historical Roots, Philosophical Concepts, and Contemporary Problems*, ed. Henry B. Clark II (New Brunswick, N.J.: Transaction Books, 1982), 51.

83. *Gallup Report*, Nos. 220/221, Jan./Feb. 1984.

Chapter 11

1. Commager suggests: "On the whole the war . . . confirmed Americans in their optimism, their self-confidence, and their sense of superiority, for it ended, after all, in the greatest of victories and one for which they could claim a major part of the credit." *American Mind*, 431.

2. Paul Hutchinson, "America's Greatness," *Christian Century*, 20 Oct. 1948, 1103-05.

3. James N. Rosenau and Ole R. Holsti, "U.S. Leadership in a Shrinking World: The Breakdown of Consensuses and the Emergence of Conflicting Belief Systems," *World Politics* 35 (April 1983): 369. Also see Ole R. Holsti and James R. Rosenau, "Vietnam, Consensus, and the Belief Systems of American Leaders," *World Politics* 32 (Oct. 1979): 1-56; and Holsti and Rosenau, *American Leadership*.

4. Novak, *Democratic Capitalism*, 31.

5. "The Superdollar," *Business Week*, 8 Oct. 1984.

6. Robert S. Walters, "America's Declining Industrial Competitiveness: Protectionism, the Marketplace and the State," *PS* 16 (1983), 30.

7. This is a theme that runs throughout much of Habermas's work, but see especially Habermas, *Legitimation Crisis.*
8. Bellah, "Cultural Pluralism and Religious Particularism," 52.
9. Stanley Hoffman, "Semidetached Politics," *New York Review of Books*, 8 Nov. 1984, 36.
10. *Ibid.*
11. For an especially perceptive account of the effects of the Vietnam War on American policy, see Schurmann, *Logic of World Power.*
12. See Lincoln P. Bloomfield, "United States Foreign Policy for the Mid-'80s: A New Great Debate?" *International Journal* 38 (Winter 1982-83): 1-17.
13. *The Harris Survey*, No. 77, 26 Sept. 1983.
14. U.S. Department of Defense, *Annual Report: Fiscal Year 1982* (Washington, D.C.: U.S. Government Printing Office, 1982), 16.
15. U.S. Bureau of the Census, *Statistical Abstract of the United States: 1983* (Washington, D.C.: U.S. Government Printing Office, 1983), 868.
16. *Ibid.*, 876, 822.
17. Henry A. Kissinger, "Ronald Reagan's Great Opportunity," *Washington Post*, 20 Nov. 1984.
18. *Statistical Abstract: 1983*, 824.
19. Lester C. Thurow, "A Path for America," *Dissent*, Winter 1983, 26-28.
20. Robert Reich, "The Next American Frontier," *Atlantic Monthly*, March 1983, 44.
21. *Ibid.*, pp. 44-54. For a lengthier discussion, see Reich, *Next American Frontier.*
22. *Public Opinion*, April/May, 1982.
23. *Public Opinion*, Feb./March, 1982.
24. *Public Opinion*, Dec./Jan. 1984.
25. *Public Opinion*, April/May, 1983.
26. Included in a 1982 Harris survey was the question: "Many people have said that Japanese laborers are very diligent and dedicated—that is, devoted to hard work. From what you know or have heard, how would you rate the diligence and dedication of Japanese workers compared to workers in the U.S.—more diligent and dedicated, about the same, or less diligent and dedicated than workers in the U.S.?" Seventy-four percent of the U.S. respondents said the Japanese workers were more diligent, 20 percent thought Japanese and American workers were equally diligent, and only 3 percent thought the Japanese were less diligent. Compared with a similar survey in 1971, these figures represented a 13 point increase in the tendency to rate Japanese workers more highly than Americans. *The Harris Survey*, 19 April 1982.
27. Tocqueville, *Democracy in America* 2: 131.
28. Bellah, "Cultural Pluralism and Religious Particularism," 43.
29. From an interview in *Public Opinion*, June/July 1982.
30. Bellah, "Cultural Pluralism and Religious Particularism," 43.
31. Meg Greenfield, "Arguing About the Poor," *Washington Post*, 21 Nov. 1984.
32. These impressions seemed to be supported by other surveys asking about involvement in charitable activities. For example, a 1981 Gallup survey found

that only 29 percent of the public claimed to be "involved in any charity or social service activities, such as helping the poor, the sick or elderly." A survey conducted by the U.S. Bureau of the Census in 1974 supported this figure, showing that 24 percent of the adult population had done some kind of unpaid volunteer work during the past year. But, in comparison, a similar survey in 1965 had shown that almost this many (18 percent), had been involved in such work during the past *week*, suggesting at least indirectly that the annual figure had probably been higher then than a decade later. These figures are all reported in *Public Opinion*, Feb./March 1982.

33. *Public Opinion*, Aug./Sept. 1982. In a 1981 Gallup poll which asked the public to rank twelve occupational groups according to their "contribution to the general good," "business executives" ranked ninth (below "clergy," "medical doctors," "public school teachers," "public school principals," "judges," "funeral directors," "bankers," and "lawyers"; those ranked lower were "local political officeholders," "realtors," and "advertising practitioners"). *Gallup Report*, No. 193, Oct. 1981. Another Roper poll conducted a year earlier demonstrated that the growth of big business has probably contributed to the perception that business leaders act for self-interest rather than the public good. When asked if large business corporations were responsive to people's needs, only 32 percent of the sample said "yes." In comparison, 65 percent of the sample thought small business corporations were responsive to people's needs. *Public Opinion*, Feb./March 1982. Supporting this finding, another survey which probed attitudes toward big business found that only 32 percent of the public thought "most profits are plowed back to improve performance and efficiency," while 48 percent felt that "most profits go to make rich people richer." *Public Opinion*, Oct./Nov. 1982.

34. *The Harris Survey*, 17 March 1983.

35. Prentiss L. Pemberton and Daniel Rush Finn, "Economics and Christian Values," *Commonweal*, 2-16 Nov. 1984, 602. See also their book *Christian Economic Ethic*.

36. Oscar Handlin, "The Idea of Opportunity," *Public Opinion*, June/July 1982, 3.

37. *Public Opinion*, June/July 1982.

38. *Ibid.*

39. *Ibid.*

40. *Ibid.* Americans' uncharitable attitude toward immigrants also tends to be reflected in opinions about illegal aliens. In a 1983 Gallup poll which asked, "Do you think it should or should not be against the law to employ a person who has come into the United States without proper papers?" 79 percent of the public responded "should" and 18 percent responded "should not." *Gallup Report*, No. 218, Nov. 1983.

41. The tendency for freedom to become increasingly redirected toward self-absorption has been suggested in a content analysis of best selling fiction from 1950 through 1979. See Lynn S. Mullins and Richard E. Kopelman, "The Best Seller as an Indicator of Societal Narcissism: Is There a Trend?" *Public Opinion Quarterly* 48 (1984): 720-30.

42. Ronald Goetz, "The Freedom of Necessity," *Christian Century*, 3 March 1982, 230-31.
43. Jeffers, "Shine, Republic," 57-58.
44. Jerry Falwell, "Introduction," in Viguerie, *New Right*, vii.
45. Neuhaus, "From Providence to Privacy," 15.
46. "It is not enough that the individual look upon the key meanings of the social order as useful, desirable, or right. It is much better (better, that is, in terms of social stability) if he looks upon them as inevitable, as part and parcel of the universal 'nature of things.' " Berger, *Sacred Canopy*, 24. See also Peter L. Berger and Thomas Luckmann, *The Social Construction of Reality* (Garden City, N.Y.: Doubleday, 1966), 90, 105.
47. Polanyi, *Livelihood of Man*, 5-17. Polanyi suggests that an "economistic fallacy" was important in legitimating the market system: "a broad, generic phenomenon was somehow taken to be identical with a species with which we happen to be familiar. In such terms, the error was in equating the human economy in general with its market form" (p. 6).
48. N. Bruce Hannay and Robert E. McGinn, "The Anatomy of Modern Technology: Prolegomenon to an Improved Public Policy for the Social Management of Technology," *Daedalus* 109 (Winter 1980): 27.
49. The current ambiguity between technology in a generic sense and technology in its fully developed contemporary sense is evident even in an authoritative work such as Jacques Ellul's *The Technological Society* (New York: Vintage Books, 1964). Ellul defines "technique" in the most general terms as "the totality of methods rationally arrived at and having absolute efficiency . . . in every field of human activity" (p. xxv). Yet later he limits technique to the period since the advent of modern science and suggests that its quantitative increase has resulted in a qualitative change in its social role. For a useful critique of Ellul's work on technology, see Leslie Sklair, "The Sociology of the Opposition to Science and Technology: With Special Reference to the Work of Jacques Ellul," *Comparative Studies in Society and History* 13 (April 1971). Popular works which depict a continuous, evolutionary movement from simple machines to modern technology often confuse the issue as well by paying more attention to the continuities than the discontinuities (e.g., works such as those of Lewis Mumford, Carl Sagan, and Jacob Bronowski). For example, Bronowski's emphasis on evolutionary "ascent" often leads him to emphasize similarities in all types of technology, e.g., "Every machine is a kind of draught animal—even the nuclear reactor." Jacob Bronowski, *The Ascent of Man* (Boston: Little, Brown, 1973), 79.
50. Wesley Shrum, "Scientific Specialties and Technical Systems," *Social Studies of Science* 14 (1984): 63-92.
51. Langdon Winner, "Do Artifacts Have Politics?" *Daedalus* 109 (Winter 1980): 122.
52. Frank Press, "Rethinking Science Policy," *Science*, 1 Oct. 1982, 28-30.
53. Bob Kuttner, "France's Atari Socialism," *New Republic*, 7 March 1983, 19-23; Malcolm G. Scully, "Many Countries Stressing Quality in Universities," *Chronicle of Higher Education*, 7 Nov. 1984; Toshio Shishido, "Japanese In-

dustrial Development and Policies for Science and Technology," *Science* 21 Jan. 1984, 259-64.

54. "Educated men and women today must speak the language not only of science but of technology as well." Henry Petroski, "Technology Is an Essential Component of Today's Liberal Arts Education," *Chronicle of Higher Education*, 14 Nov. 1984.

55. Kenneth Prewitt, "Scientific Illiteracy and Democratic Theory," *Daedalus* 112 (Spring 1983): 49. Another writer suggests that the meaning of science is becoming increasingly utilitarian: "Science is seen as a purely utilitarian enterprise, a 'craft' that is to be valued and justified solely in terms of its material benefits and its contribution to the enlargement of national power and prestige, or as an ideological reinforcement and chief productive force sustaining a repressive society of manipulative rationality." J. W. Grove, "Science as Technology: Aspects of a Potent Myth," *Minerva* 18 (Summer 1980): 293.

56. Memo dated 21 April 1982, accompanying the *Annual Science and Technology Report to the Congress: 1981* (Washington, D.C.: Office of Science and Technology Policy, 1982).

57. "America Rushes to High Tech for Growth," *Business Week*, 28 March 1983, 94.

58. National Science Board, *Science Indicators, 1982* (Washington, D.C.: U.S. Government Printing Office, 1983), 214.

59. Reich, "The Next American Frontier," 47.

60. *Statistical Abstract: 1983*, 596.

61. Cf. Booth Fowler and Saul Brenner, "In Defense of Optimism," *Humanist*, March/April 1982, 12-19.

62. Robert Nisbet, "Utopia's Mores: Has the American Vision Dimmed?" *Public Opinion*, April/May 1983, 9.

63. Sheldon S. Wolin, "Theme Note," *Democracy* 3 (Spring 1983): 6.

64. Daniel Boorstin, "Science as Mythology," *Science Digest*, Dec. 1984, 104. Borgmann adds that part of this mythology is the idea of a linear progression into the future which is dictated by the machines themselves: "Technological progress is seen as a more or less gradual and straightforward succession of lesser by better implements. The wood-burning stove yields to the coal-fired central plant with heat distribution by convection, which in turn gives way to a plant fueled by natural gas and heating through forced air, and so on." Borgmann, *Technology and Contemporary Life*, 41.

65. National Science Board, *Science Indicators, 1980* (Washington, D.C.: U.S. Government Printing Office, 1981), 337.

66. J. D. Miller, Kenneth Prewitt, and R. Pearson, *The Attitudes of the U.S. Public Toward Science and Technology* (Chicago: National Opinion Research Center, 1980), 251-53.

67. Union Carbide Corporation, *An Analysis of Public Attitudes Toward Technology and Investment* (Boston: Cambridge Reports, Inc., 1978), 14.

68. *Public Opinion*, June/July 1983.

69. *Gallup Cross-National Values Surveys* (Princeton: Gallup Organization, 1981). The question read: "In the long run, do you think that scientific ad-

vances we are making will help or harm mankind?" In the U.S., 58 percent said "will help," 16 percent said "will harm," and 22 percent said "some of each." Responses in the other countries ranged from 48 percent in Great Britain who thought science would help to only 23 percent in the Netherlands who gave this response. The figures reported in the text are based on the ratio of respondents in each country who said "will help" as opposed to "will harm." This ratio for each of the European countries was: Spain (2.4), Great Britain (2.2), Italy (1.9), France (1.7), Northern Ireland (1.7), West Germany (1.6), Sweden (1.6), Denmark (1.6), Belgium (1.5), Norway (1.4), Republic of Ireland (1.4), Finland (1.3), and the Netherlands (0.6).

70. *Public Opinion*, Aug./Sept. 1982.
71. *Public Opinion*, April/May 1980.
72. National Science Board, *Science Indicators, 1980*, 347.
73. Union Carbide, *An Analysis of Public Attitudes*, 2.
74. This conviction is, of course, subject to some misgivings in view of technological accomplishments by America's military and economic competitors; e.g., Russian achievements in space exploration and Japanese accomplishments in microelectronics. These accomplishments are often explained away by attributing them to purchases or outright theft of American technology. For example: "By searching through scientific publications, by diligently planting agents and recruiting industrial spies, the Soviet Union is adding ominously to its capacities in applied high technology." Walter Guzzard, Jr., "Cutting Russia's Harvest of U.S. Technology," *Fortune*, 30 May 1983, 102. Or in the case of Japan, the General Accounting Office has estimated that the Japanese have received $10 billion worth of advanced technology from the U.S. since 1950, prompting a Commerce Department official to describe this exchange as "the biggest fire sale in history." "The Dangers of Sharing American Technology," *Business Week*, 14 March 1983, 109-16.
75. *Public Opinion*, June/July 1983.
76. James D. Watkins, "Technology Transfer," *Vital Speeches* 49 (15 March 1983): 322-24.
77. Charles A. Gabriel, "The Leakage of Western Technology," *Vital Speeches* 49 (5 Oct. 1982): 2-4.
78. George Schultz, "U.S. Foreign Policy: Realism and Progress," *Vital Speeches* 49 (1 Dec. 1982): 99.
79. Rocco J. Marano, "Educational Disenfranchisement in a Technological Age," *Vital Speeches* 48 (15 Jan. 1982): 222.
80. "America Rushes to High Tech," *Business Week*, 84.
81. James M. Beggs, "Why the United States Needs a Space Station," *Vital Speeches* 48 (1 Aug. 1982): 617.
82. Walter B. Wriston, "The Information Society," *Vital Speeches* 49 (15 Nov. 1982): 94.
83. David F. Noble, "Present Tense Technology," *Democracy* 3 (Spring 1983): 10.
84. An exceptionally clear application of this distinction for ideological purposes was evident in a speech by the chairman of Allegheny International: "*Scientific*

engineers . . . have the unchanging laws of chemistry, physics, and the other natural sciences to guide your efforts. By means of those laws, you can predict the behavior of the materials and forces of nature. Discovery upon discovery continues. . . . But the *social engineers* who have been running our lives for the last three or four decades either know nothing of nature's immutable laws or choose to ignore them. Instead, they have their man-made and variable laws of compulsions, prohibitions, and other restrictions on the free actions of individuals." Robert J. Buckley, "Can We 'Engineer' Ourselves Out of the Crisis of Costs?" *Vital Speeches* 48 (15 Sept. 1982): 723.

85. The connection between science and technology has in fact been challenged by studies examining the sources of technological innovation. One study of more than 900 inventions, for example, found that many had no identifiable scientific component at all, and the stimulus for these inventions was generally economic rather than scientific. Jacob Schmookler, *Invention and Economic Growth* (Cambridge: Harvard University Press, 1966). Another study concluded that new technology generally grew from pre-existing technology, not from scientific research. John Langrish, *Wealth from Knowledge* (London: Macmillan, 1972). The point is that, even though scientific research is an important part of the technological society, the connection between scientific laws and specific avenues of technological development is by no means conclusive.

86. See especially, Jürgen Habermas, "Technology and Science as 'Ideology,' " in his *Toward a Rational Society* (Boston: Beacon Press, 1970), 81-122. For an extension of this argument to liberal politics, see Thomas A. Spragens, Jr., *The Irony of Liberal Reason* (Chicago: University of Chicago Press, 1981).

87. John P. Mascotte, "Technology and the Environment," *Vital Speeches* 49 (15 Jan. 1983): 220.

88. Jeff Douthwaite, "The Terrible Temptation of the Technological Fix," *Science, Technology, and Human Values*, Winter 1983, 31.

89. According to a national survey conducted in September 1984, 72 percent of the public supported increased spending for medical research and 63 percent supported increased spending for higher education; in contrast, only 35 percent supported more spending for social welfare and an even smaller proportion (28 percent) supported more spending for national defense. Jean Evangelauf, "Poll Finds 63 Pct. Want More Aid for Colleges," *Chronicle of Higher Education*, 24 Oct. 1984.

90. This approach to policy making has been referred to as a case of "reverse adaptation"—where the means available to measure or solve a problem determine how the problem is defined in the first place; or simply, a case of human ends being adjusted to match the character of available means. Langdon Winner, *Autonomous Technology* (Cambridge: MIT Press, 1977), 229.

91. *Public Opinion*, Dec./Jan. 1984.

92. Ellul, *Technological System*, 109.

93. Harvey Brooks, "Some Issues of Technology," *Daedalus* 109 (Winter 1980): 12.

94. Harold S. Mohler, "The Condition of Education in America Today," *Vital Speeches* 48 (15 Aug. 1982): 658. The relationship between technology and

markets is, of course, perceived as being exceedingly close. Technology has a kind of unquestioned superiority in ideological discourse because it is assumed to constitute a necessary condition for maintaining the United States' position in world markets. The following statement by Charles S. Robb, representing the National Governors' Association, in testimony before a congressional subcommittee, is illustrative: "The industrialized world stands on the threshold of a technological revolution that will change the American way of life and the composition of the nation's work force as much as the industrial revolution did a century age. . . . Our ability to lead this technological revolution, as indeed the United States led the industrial revolution a century or so ago, will bear directly on our share of world markets—a share that will continue to erode unless we act promptly and wisely." U.S. House of Representatives, Subcommittee on Science, Research and Technology, Committee on Science and Technology, *Hearings*, 29 April 1982.

95. Ferkiss, *Technological Man*, 207.

96. Hannay and McGinn, "The Anatomy of Modern Technology," 37.

97. W. Fred Graham, "America's Other Religion," *Christian Century*, 17 March 1982, 306-7.

98. *Christian Century*, 6 Oct. 1948, 1048.

99. John McLaughry, "Where Is the Mob? I Am Its Leader," *Vital Speeches* 48 (1 Nov. 1981): 39.

100. David F. Noble, "A Neo-Luddite Plea," *Harper's*, Nov. 1984, 22.

101. Maxine Berg has examined these reactions during the Industrial Revolution in great depth. She concludes that technology was capable of being challenged then because it was not yet taken for granted as something which was inevitable. Workers were convinced they could halt the process of rapid technological change, or at least help direct it. Maxine Berg, *The Machinery Question and the Making of Political Economy, 1815-1848* (Cambridge: Cambridge University Press, 1980).

102. Edward Abbey, *The Monkey-Wrench Gang* (New York: Avon, 1976).

103. Noble, "A Neo-Luddite Plea," 9.

104. Emile Zola, *La Bête Humaine* (London: Penguin, 1977 [1890]), 58.

Chapter 12

1. Many efforts have been made to describe modern religion in broad evolutionary terms. Marx, Weber, and Durkheim all formulated implicit theories of the direction of modern religious evolution, not to mention the more explicit scenarios advanced by Comte, Toennies, Spencer, and others. A more recent generation of social theorists—including Talcott Parsons, Marion Levy, Jr., E. O. Wilson, Peter L. Berger, Thomas Luckmann, and Bryan Wilson, to name a few—has also contributed to this literature. The following discussion draws mainly on the work of Robert N. Bellah, Jürgen Habermas, and Niklas Luhmann. See especially Bellah, *Beyond Belief*, 20-50; Jürgen Habermas, *Communication and the Evolution of Society* (Boston: Beacon Press, 1979), and "History and Evolution," *Telos* 39 (1979): 5-44; and Niklas Luhmann, "Soci-

ety, Religion, and Meaning—Based on Self Reference," *Sociological Analysis* 44 (1985): 1-24.

2. Wolfhart Pannenberg, *Christian Spirituality* (Philadelphia: Westminster Press, 1983), 35.
3. George A. Lindbeck, *The Nature of Doctrine: Religion and Theology in a Postliberal Age* (Philadelphia: Westminster Press, 1984), 33.
4. For example, see Vincent Brummer, *Theology and Philosophical Inquiry* (Philadelphia: Westminster Press, 1982); and Mark C. Taylor, *Erring: A Postmodern A/theology* (Chicago: University of Chicago Press, 1984).
5. See my article, "Religious Beliefs and Experiences: Basic Patterns," in *Views from the Pews*, ed. Roger A. Johnson, 10-32.
6. Thomas Piazza and Charles Y. Glock, "Images of God and Their Social Meanings," in *The Religious Dimension*, ed. Robert Wuthnow (New York: Academic Press, 1979), 69-92.
7. See, for example, Hunter, *American Evangelicalism*, 91-99.
8. Ludwig Wittgenstein, *Tractatus Logico-Philosophicus* (Atlantic Highlands, N.J.: Humanities Press, 1974).
9. The figures cited in this section are from two studies conducted by the Gallup Organization: "Jesus Christ in the Lives of Americans Today" (1983), and "How Can Christian Liberals and Conservatives Be Brought Together?" (1984). Some of the results of the first study have been published in George Gallup, Jr., *Who Do Americans Say That I Am?* (Philadelphia: Westminster Press, 1986).
10. Andrew M. Greeley, "Religious Imagery as a Predictor Variable in the General Social Survey" (Paper presented at a plenary session of the Society for the Scientific Study of Religion, Chicago, Nov. 1984).
11. Pannenberg, *Christian Spirituality*, 47.
12. These results are from an analysis of the 1968 and 1980 National Election Surveys conducted by the University of Michigan. Since the conclusions reported in the text are based on analyses involving the simultaneous relations among four variables and depend on the presence or absence of so-called "interaction effects," full details of the results are too complex to report as percentage tables. Suffice it to say that simple chi-square tests of statistical significance at the .05 level of probability revealed significant relations between church attendance and political participation (using the scale discussed in Chapter 9) for segments of the overall samples in both 1968 and 1980 who felt government was too powerful, but not for those who disagreed that government was too powerful, and this "specification" of the relation held when controls were introduced for the other issues mentioned in the text.
13. These results are presented in a forthcoming article, Robert Wuthnow and Clifford Nass, "Government Activity and Civil Privatism: Evidence from Voluntary Church Membership," *Journal for the Scientific Study of Religion* 27 (1988). The results are for membership in Protestant churches only because membership in Catholic parishes and Jewish congregations tends to be determined by residence rather than voluntary affiliation.

SELECTED BIBLIOGRAPHY

Alexander, Jeffrey. 1986. "Culture and Political Crisis: 'Watergate' and Durkheimian Sociology." Pp. 175-201 in *Neofunctionalism*, ed. by Jeffrey Alexander. Beverly Hills, Calif.: Sage.

Bailey, Kenneth K. 1964. *Southern White Protestantism in the Twentieth Century*. New York: Harper & Row.

Baker, Robert A. 1974. *The Southern Baptist Convention and Its People, 1607-1972*. Nashville: Broadman.

Barnett, Lincoln. 1948. "God and the American People." *Ladies' Home Journal* (November): 37, 230-234.

Bazelon, David T. 1963. *Power in America: The Politics of the New Class*. New York: New American Library.

Bell, Daniel. 1976. *The Cultural Contradictions of Capitalism*. New York: Basic.

———. 1979. "The New Class: A Muddled Concept." *Society* (January/February): 15-30.

Bellah, Robert N. 1970. *Beyond Belief*. New York: Harper & Row.

———. 1975. *The Broken Covenant*. New York: Seabury.

———, ed. 1973. *Emile Durkheim on Morality and Society*. Chicago: University of Chicago Press.

Bennett, John C. 1946. *Christian Ethics and Social Policy*. New York: Scribner.

Berger, Peter L. 1969. *The Sacred Canopy*. Garden City, N.Y.: Doubleday.

Bergesen, Albert and Mark Warr. 1979. "A Crisis in the Moral Order: The Effects of Watergate upon Confidence in Social Institutions." Pp. 277-298 in *The Religious Dimension*, ed. by Robert Wuthnow. New York: Academic Press.

Blanshard, Paul. 1949. *American Freedom and Catholic Power*. Boston: Beacon Press.

Borgmann, Albert. 1984. *Technology and the Character of Contemporary Life*. Chicago: University of Chicago Press.

Bright, Bill. 1970. *Come Help Change the World*. Old Tappan, N.J.: Revell.

Brown, Norman O. 1966. *Love's Body*. New York: Vintage Books.

Brown, Richard C. 1983. *The Presbyterians: Two Hundred Years in Danville, 1784-1984*. Danville, Ky.: Presbyterian Church.

Brunini, John Gilland. 1946. *What Catholics Believe—and Why*. Garden City, N.Y.: Garden City Books.

Bryson, Lyman, Louis Finkelstein, and R. M. McIver, eds. 1947. *Conflicts of Power in Modern Culture*. New York: Harper & Brothers.

Christenson, James A. and Ronald C. Wimberley. 1978. "Who is Civil Religious?" *Sociological Analysis* 39: 77-83.

Cohelan, F. D. 1948. "The Organization of the Church in the United States." Pp. 65-92 in *The Catholic Church, U.S.A.*, ed. by Louis J. Putz. Chicago: Fides.

Cohen, Steven M. 1983. *American Modernity and Jewish Identity.* New York: Tavistock.

Commager, Henry Steele. 1950. *The American Mind: An Interpretation of American Thought and Character Since the 1880s.* New Haven: Yale University Press.

D'Souza, Dinesh. 1984. *Falwell Before the Millennium.* Chicago: Regnery Gateway.

Dallek, Robert. 1983. *The American Style of Foreign Policy: Cultural Politics and Foreign Affairs.* New York: New American Library.

Davis, Kingsley. 1949. *Human Society.* New York: Macmillan.

Dolan, Jay P. 1985. *The American Catholic Experience: A History from Colonial Times to the Present.* Garden City, N.Y.: Doubleday.

Douglas, Mary. 1966. *Purity and Danger.* Baltimore: Penguin.

Douglass, H. Paul and Edmund deS. Brunner. 1935. *The Protestant Church as a Social Institution.* New York: Russell and Russell.

Durkheim, Emile. 1965 [1915]. *The Elementary Forms of the Religious Life.* New York: Free Press.

Elazar, Daniel J. 1976. *Community and Polity: The Organizational Dynamics of American Jewry.* Philadelphia: Jewish Publication Society of America.

Ellul, Jacques. 1980. *The Technological System.* New York: Continuum.

Falwell, Jerry. 1981. *The Fundamentalist Phenomenon: The Resurgence of Conservative Christianity.* Garden City, N.Y.: Doubleday.

———. 1984. *Wisdom for Living.* Wheaton, Ill.: Victor Books.

Ferkiss, Victor C. 1969. *Technological Man: The Myth and the Reality.* New York: New American Library.

Ferré, Nels F. S. 1943. *Return to Christianity.* New York: Harper & Brothers.

FitzGerald, Frances. 1986. *Cities on a Hill.* New York: Simon & Schuster.

Fosdick, Harry Emerson. 1952. *A Faith for Tough Times.* New York: Harper & Brothers.

Friedman, Milton. 1962. *Capitalism and Freedom.* Chicago: University of Chicago Press.

Fry, C. Luther. 1934. "Changes in Religious Organizations." Pp. 1009-1060 in *Recent Social Trends in the United States.* New York: Whittlesey House.

Gallup, George H. 1972. *The Gallup Poll: Public Opinion, 1935-1971,* 3 vols. New York: Random House.

Gallup, George, Jr. 1980. *Religion in America, 1979-80.* Princeton: Princeton Religion Research Center.

———. 1981. *Religion in America, 1981.* Princeton: Princeton Religion Research Center.

———. 1982. *Adventures in Immortality.* New York: McGraw-Hill.

Gehrig, Gail. 1979. *American Civil Religion: An Assessment.* Storrs, Conn.: Society for the Scientific Study of Religion.

Gilder, George. 1981. *Wealth and Poverty.* New York: Bantam.

Glock, Charles Y. and Rodney Stark. 1965. *Religion and Society in Tension.* Chicago: Rand-McNally.

———. 1966. *Christian Beliefs and Anti-Semitism.* New York: Harper & Row.

Glock, Charles Y., Benjamin R. Ringer, and Earl Babbie. 1967. *To Comfort and to Challenge: A Dilemma of the Contemporary Church*. Berkeley and Los Angeles: University of California Press.

Gollagher, Elsie, ed. 1967. *The Quotable Dwight D. Eisenhower*. New York: Grosset and Dunlap.

Gouldner, Alvin W. 1978. "The New Class Project." Parts 1, 2. *Theory and Society* 6: 153-203; 7: 343-387.

Greeley, Andrew M. 1972. *The Denominational Society: A Sociological Approach to Religion in America*. Glenview, Ill.: Scott, Foresman.

———. 1977. *The American Catholic*. New York: Basic.

Greeley, Andrew M. and Mary G. Durkin. 1984. *Angry Catholic Women*. Chicago: Thomas More.

Guth, James L. 1983. "Southern Baptist Clergy: Vanguard of the Christian Right?" Pp. 117-130 in *The New Christian Right*, ed. by Robert C. Liebman and Robert Wuthnow. New York: Aldine.

Habermas, Jürgen. 1975. *Legitimation Crisis*. Boston: Beacon Press.

Hadden, Jeffrey K. 1969. *The Gathering Storm in the Churches*. Garden City, N.Y.: Doubleday.

Handlin, Oscar. 1954. *The American People in the Twentieth Century*. Cambridge: Harvard University Press.

Harvey, Charles E. 1981. "Religion and Industrial Relations: John D. Rockefeller, Jr., and the Interchurch World Movement of 1919-1920." *Research in Political Economy* 4: 199-227.

Hatfield, Mark. 1976. *Between a Rock and a Hard Place*. Waco, Tex.: Word.

Headley, George. 1946. *The Christian Heritage in America*. New York: Macmillan.

Hennesey, James. 1981. *American Catholics: A History of the Roman Catholic Community in the United States*. Oxford: Oxford University Press.

Henry, Carl F. H. 1947. *The Uneasy Conscience of Modern Fundamentalism*. Grand Rapids, Mich.: Eerdmans.

———. 1950. *Fifty Years of Protestant Theology*. Boston: W. A. Wilde.

Herberg, Will. 1955. *Protestant-Catholic-Jew*. Garden City, N.Y.: Anchor.

Hirschman, Albert O. 1977. *The Passions and the Interests*. Princeton: Princeton University Press.

Hoge, Dean R. 1976. "Theological Views of America among Protestants." *Sociological Analysis* 37: 127-140.

———. 1979. "A Test of Theories of Denominational Growth and Decline." Pp. 179-197 in *Understanding Church Growth and Decline, 1950-1978*, ed. by Dean R. Hoge and David Roozen. New York: Pilgrim Press.

Holsti, Ole R. and James R. Rosenau. 1983. *American Leadership in World Affairs: The Breakdown of Consensus*. Boston: Allen and Unwin.

Horsfield, Peter G. 1984. *Religious Television: The American Experience*. New York: Longman.

Hunter, James Davison. 1983. *American Evangelicalism: Conservative Religion and the Quandary of Modernity*. New Brunswick, N.J.: Rutgers University Press.

Hunter, James Davison. 1987. *Evangelicalism: The Coming Generation*. Chicago: University of Chicago Press.

Hutchinson, Paul. 1946. *The New Leviathan*. Chicago: Willett and Clark.

Jeffers, Robinson. 1965. "Shine, Republic." Pp. 57-58 in *Selected Poems*. New York: Vintage Books.

Jessup, John K., ed. 1969. *The Ideas of Henry Luce*. New York: Atheneum.

Johnson, Douglas W. and George W. Cornell. 1972. *Punctured Preconceptions: What North American Christians Think about the Church*. New York: Friendship Press.

Johnson, Robert Alan. 1980. *Religious Assortative Marriage in the United States*. New York: Academic Press.

Johnson, Roger A., ed. 1983. *Views from the Pews*. Philadelphia: Fortress.

Kean, Charles D. 1948. "God, Gods, and Dr. George Gallup." *Christianity and Society* 13: 17-19.

Kelley, Dean M. 1977. *Why Conservative Churches are Growing*. New York: Harper & Row.

Knowles, John. 1983. *Peace Breaks Out*. New York: Bantam.

Kohn, Hans. 1944. *The Idea of Nationalism*. New York: Collier.

Konolige, Kit and Frederica Konolige. 1978. *The Power of Their Glory: America's Ruling Class: The Episcopalians*. New York: Wyden Books.

Ladd, Everett Carll, Jr. 1979. "Pursuing the New Class: Social Theory and Survey Data." Pp. 101-122 in *The New Class?* ed. by B. Bruce-Briggs. New York: McGraw-Hill.

LaHaye, Tim. 1980. *The Battle for the Mind*. Old Tappan, N.J.: Revell.

Laski, Harold. 1948. *The American Democracy*. New York: Viking.

Latourette, Kenneth Scott. 1975. *A History of Christianity*. Vol. 2, *Reformation to the Present*. New York: Harper & Row.

Lazerwitz, Bernard. 1964. "Religion and Social Structure in the United States." Pp. 426-439 in *Religion, Culture and Society: A Reader in the Sociology of Religion*, ed. by Louis Schneider. New York: Wiley.

Lehman, Edward D., Jr. 1985. *Women Clergy: Breaking Through Gender Barriers*. New Brunswick, N.J.: Transaction Books.

Leiffer, Murray H. 1948. *The Methodist Ministry in 1948: Its Composition and Training and the Recruitment Needs of the Church*. Chicago: Methodist Publishing House.

Lenski, Gerhard. 1961. *The Religious Factor: A Sociological Study of Religion's Impact on Politics, Economics, and Family Life*. Garden City, N.Y.: Doubleday.

Linder, Robert D. and Richard V. Pierard. 1978. *Twilight of the Saints: Biblical Christianity and Civil Religion in America*. Downers Grove, Ill.: InterVarsity Press.

Luker, Kristin. 1984. *Abortion and the Politics of Motherhood*. Berkeley and Los Angeles: University of California Press.

Lynd, Robert S. and Helen Merrell Lynd. 1929. *Middletown: A Study in Modern American Culture*. New York: Harvest Books.

Macartney, Clarence E. 1953. *Strange Texts but Grand Truths*. New York: Abingdon-Cokesbury.

Mackay, John A. 1950. *Christianity on the Frontier*. New York: Macmillan.

McNamara, Patrick H. 1984. *Religion: North American Style*, 2nd ed. Belmont, Calif.: Wadsworth.

Marsden, George M. 1980. *Fundamentalism and American Culture: The Shaping of Twentieth-Century Evangelicalism, 1870-1925*. Oxford: Oxford University Press.

Marshall, Peter. 1949. *Mr. Jones, Meet the Master: Sermons and Prayers*. New York: Revell.

Martire, Gregory and Ruth Clark. 1982. *Anti-Semitism in the United States*. New York: Praeger.

Mead, Frank S. 1951. *Handbook of Denominations in the United States*. New York: Abingdon-Cokesbury.

Melton, J. Gordon. 1978. *Encyclopedia of American Religions*, 2 vols. Wilmington, N.C.: McGrath.

———. 1983. *Directory of Religious Bodies in the United States*. Wilmington, N.C.: McGrath.

Michels, Robert. 1962 [1915]. *Political Parties: A Sociological Study of the Oligarchical Tendencies of Modern Democracy*. New York: Free Press.

Moberg, David O. 1962. *The Church as a Social Institution*. Englewood Cliffs, N.J.: Prentice-Hall.

Montgomery, John Fleshman. 1983. *History of the Old Stone Presbyterian Church, 1783-1983*. Parsons, W.Va.: McClain Printing Company.

Mumford, Lewis. 1940. *Faith for Living*. New York: Harcourt Brace.

Myrdal, Gunnar. 1944. *An American Dilemma*. New York: Harper & Brothers.

Newport, Frank. 1979. "The Religious Switcher in the United States." *American Sociological Review* 44: 528-552.

Niebuhr, H. Richard. 1929. *The Social Sources of Denominationalism*. New York: World.

Niebuhr, Reinhold. 1952. *The Irony of American History*. New York: Scribner.

Novak, Michael. 1982. *The Spirit of Democratic Capitalism*. New York: Simon & Schuster.

Nunn, Clyde Z., Harry J. Crockett, Jr., and J. Allen Williams, Jr. 1978. *Tolerance for Nonconformity*. San Francisco: Jossey-Bass.

O'Brien, John A. 1949. *Truths Men Live By: A Philosophy of Religion and Life*. New York: Macmillan.

Otis, George. 1972. *The Solution to Crisis-America*. Old Tappan, N.J.: Revell.

Oxnam, G. Bromley. 1950. *The Church and Contemporary Change*. New York: Macmillan.

Peale, Norman Vincent. 1971. *One Nation Under God*. Pawling, N.Y.: Foundation for Christian Living.

Pemberton, Prentiss L. and Daniel Rush Finn. 1985. *Toward a Christian Economic Ethic*. New York: Winston Press.

Pierard, Richard V. 1970. *The Unequal Yoke*. Philadelphia: Lippincott.

Polanyi, Karl. 1977. *The Livelihood of Man*. New York: Academic Press.

Pollock, John. 1966. *Billy Graham: The Authorized Bibliography*. New York: McGraw-Hill.

Popenoe, Cris and Oliver Popenoe. 1984. *Seeds of Tomorrow: New Age Communities That Work*. San Francisco: Harper & Row.

Potter, David. 1954. *People of Plenty*. Chicago: University of Chicago Press.

Primer, Ben. 1979. *Protestants and American Business Methods*. Ann Arbor: UMI Research Press.

Quebedeaux, Richard. 1978. *The Worldly Evangelicals*. New York: Harper & Row.

Quinley, Harold E. 1974. *The Prophetic Clergy: Social Activism among Protestant Ministers*. New York: Wiley.

Reich, Robert. 1983. *The Next American Frontier*. New York: Penguin.

Reichley, A. James. 1985. *Religion in American Public Life*. Washington, D.C.: Brookings Institution.

Robertson, Pat. 1982. *The Secret Kingdom: A Promise of Hope and Freedom in a World of Turmoil*. Nashville: Thomas Nelson.

Rogers, Dale Evans. 1975. *Let Freedom Ring!* Old Tappan, N.J.: Revell.

Rokeach, Milton. 1973. *The Nature of Human Values*. New York: Free Press.

Roof, Wade Clark and William McKinney. 1985. "Denominational America and the New Religious Pluralism." *Annals of the American Academy of Political and Social Science* 480: 24-38.

Rosenberg, Emily S. 1982. *Spreading the American Dream: American Economic and Cultural Expansion, 1890-1945*. New York: Hill and Wang.

Rousseau, Jean-Jacques. 1967 [1762]. *The Social Contract*, ed. by Lester G. Crocker. New York: Washington Square Books.

Schaeffer, Francis A. 1981. *A Christian Manifesto*. Westchester, Ill.: Crossway Books.

Schofield, Charles Edwin. 1949. *The Methodist Church*. New York: Abingdon-Cokesbury.

Schurmann, Franz. 1974. *The Logic of World Power: An Inquiry into the Origins, Currents, and Contradictions of World Politics*. New York: Pantheon.

Selznick, Gertrude J. and Stephen Steinberg. 1969. *The Tenacity of Prejudice*. New York: Harper & Row.

Sennett, Richard and Jonathan Cobb. 1973. *The Hidden Injuries of Class*. New York: Vintage Books.

Sevareid, Eric. 1952. *In One Ear*. New York: Knopf.

Shriver, Peggy L. 1981. *The Bible Vote: Religion and the New Right*. New York: Pilgrim Press.

Shupe, Anson and William Stacey. 1983. "The Moral Majority Constituency." Pp. 104-117 in *The New Christian Right*, ed. by Robert C. Liebman and Robert Wuthnow. New York: Aldine.

Simpson, John H. 1983. "Moral Issues and Status Politics." Pp. 187-205 in *The New Christian Right*, ed. by Robert C. Liebman and Robert Wuthnow. New York: Aldine.

Sopher, David E. 1981. "Geography and Religions." *Progress in Human Geography* 5: 510-524.

Stark, Rodney and Charles Y. Glock. 1968. *American Piety: The Nature of Religious Commitment.* Berkeley and Los Angeles: University of California Press.

Strober, Gerald and Ruth Tomczak. 1979. *Jerry Falwell: Aflame for God.* Nashville: Thomas Nelson.

Szasz, Ferenc Morton. 1982. *The Divided Mind of Protestant America, 1880-1930.* University, Ala.: University of Alabama Press.

Thomas, John L. 1963. *Religion and the American People.* Westminster, Md.: Newman Press.

Toqueville, Alexis de. 1945 [1835]. *Democracy in America*, 2 vols. New York: Vintage Books.

Tuveson, Ernest Lee. 1968. *Redeemer Nation: The Idea of America's Millennial Role.* Chicago: University of Chicago Press.

U.S. Department of Commerce, Bureau of the Census. 1941. *Religious Bodies, 1936, Vol. 1: Summary and Detailed Tables.* Washington, D.C.: U.S. Government Printing Office.

U.S. Department of Commerce, Bureau of the Census. 1975. *Historical Statistics of the United States: Colonial Times to 1970.* Washington, D.C.: U.S. Government Printing Office.

Walton, Rus. 1975. *One Nation Under God.* Old Tappan, N.J.: Revell.

Ward, Barbara. 1966. *Nationalism and Ideology.* New York: Norton.

Warner, W. Lloyd. 1949. *Democracy in Jonesville.* New York: Harper & Row.

Webber, Robert E. 1985. *Evangelicals on the Canterbury Trail.* Waco, Tex.: Word.

Weber, Max. 1963 [1922]. *The Sociology of Religion.* Boston: Beacon Press.

Westoff, Charles F. 1979. "The Blending of Catholic Reproductive Behavior." Pp. 231-240 in *The Religious Dimension: New Directions in Quantitative Research*, ed. by Robert Wuthnow. New York: Academic Press.

Williams, Daniel Day. 1949. *God's Grace and Man's Hope.* New York: Harper & Brothers.

Williams, J. Paul. 1952. *What Americans Believe and How They Worship.* New York: Harper & Brothers.

Williams, Robin M., Jr. 1947. *American Society.* New York: Macmillan.

Wilson, John F. 1979. *Public Religion in American Culture.* Philadelphia: Temple University Press.

Wimberley, Ronald C. 1976. "Testing the Civil Religion Hypothesis." *Sociological Analysis* 37: 342-352.

Wimberley, Ronald C. and James A. Christenson. 1981. "Civil Religion and Other Religious Identities." *Sociological Analysis* 42: 91-100.

Winter, J. Alan. 1973. "Political Activity among the Clergy: Sources of a Deviant Role." *Review of Religious Research* 14: 178-189.

Wirt, Sherwood Eliot. 1968. *The Social Conscience of the Evangelical.* New York: Harper & Row.

Wuthnow, Robert. 1976. *The Consciousness Reformation*. Berkeley and Los Angeles: University of California Press.

———. 1977. "A Longitudinal, Cross-National Indicator of Cultural Religious Commitment." *Journal for the Scientific Study of Religion* 16: 87-99.

———. 1978. *Experimentation in American Religion*. Berkeley and Los Angeles: University of California Press.

———. 1982. "Anti-Semitism and Stereotyping." Pp. 137-187 in *In the Eye of the Beholder: Contemporary Issues in Stereotyping*, ed. by Arthur G. Miller. New York: Praeger.

Wuthnow, Robert and Wesley Shrum. 1983. "Knowledge Workers as a 'New Class': Structural and Ideological Convergence among Professional-Technical Workers and Managers." *Work and Occupations* 10: 471-487.

Zola, Emile. 1977 [1890]. *La Bête Humaine*. London: Penguin.

Index

Library of Congress Cataloging-in-Publication Data

Wuthnow, Robert.
The restructuring of American religion.

(Studies on church and state)
Bibliography: p. Includes index.
1. United States—Religion—1945- . I. Title.
II. Series.
BL2525.W88 1988 306'.6'0973 87-25903
ISBN 0-691-07328-7 (alk. paper)